DEEP S
TRAVEL

GW00467524

A GUIDE THAT GUIDES

DEEP SOUTH
TRAVEL ✦ SMART®

Second Edition

Carol and Dan Thalimer

John Muir Publications
Santa Fe, New Mexico

John Muir Publications, P.O. Box 613, Santa Fe, New Mexico 87504

Copyright © 2000, 1998 by John Muir Publications
Cover and maps © 2000, 1998 by John Muir Publications
All rights reserved.

Printed in the United States of America.
Second edition. First printing January 2000.

ISSN 1093-4588
ISBN 1-56261-485-1

Editors: Peg Goldstein, Carol Muse Evans, Ginjer Clarke
Graphics Editor: Ann Silvia
Production: Marie J. T. Vigil, Scott Fowler
Design: Marie J. T. Vigil
Cover Design: Janine Lehmann
Typesetting: Melissa Tandysh
Map Style Development: American Custom Maps—Jemez Springs, NM
Map Illustration: Julie Felton, Kathy Sparkes
Printing: Publishers Press
Front Cover: small—Leo de Wys Inc./George Schaub (French Quarter, New Orleans)
                large—© John Elk III (Avery Island, Louisiana)
Back Cover: © John Elk III (Mississippi River, Creole Queen riverboat)

Distributed to the book trade by
Publishers Group West
Berkeley, California

While every effort has been made to provide accurate, up-to-date information, the author and publisher accept no responsibility for loss, injury, or inconvenience sustained by any person using this book.

DEEP SOUTH TRAVEL•SMART: A GUIDE THAT GUIDES

Most guidebooks are primarily directories, providing information but very little help in making choices—you have to guess how to make the most of your time and money. *Deep South Travel•Smart* is different: By highlighting the very best of the region and offering various planning features, it acts like a personal tour guide rather than a directory.

TAKE THE STRESS OUT OF TRAVEL

Sometimes traveling causes more stress than it relieves. Sorting through information, figuring out the best routes, determining what to see and where to eat and stay, scheduling each day—all of this can make a vacation feel daunting rather than fun. Relax. We've done a lot of the legwork for you. This book will help you plan a trip that suits you—whatever your time frame, budget, and interests.

SEE THE BEST OF THE REGION

Authors Carol and Dan Thalimer have lived near Atlanta for more than 20 years. They have hand-picked every listing in this book, and they give you an insider's perspective on what makes each one worthwhile. So while you will find many of the big tourist attractions listed here, you'll also find lots of smaller, lesser known treasures, such as the Civil Rights Institute in Birmingham and Blaine Kern's Mardi Gras World in New Orleans. And each sight is described so you'll know what's most—and sometimes least—interesting about it.

In selecting the restaurants and accommodations for this book, the authors sought out unusual spots with local flavor. While in some areas of the region chains are unavoidable, wherever possible the authors direct you to one-of-a-kind places. We also know that you want a range of options: One day you may crave French Creole cuisine, while the next day you would be just as happy (as would your wallet) with fried chicken. Most of the restaurants and accommodations listed here are moderately priced, but the authors also include budget and splurge options, depending on the destination.

CREATE THE TRIP YOU WANT

We all have different travel styles. Some people like spontaneous weekend jaunts, while others plan longer, more leisurely trips. You may want to cover as much ground as possible, no matter how much time you have. Or maybe you prefer to focus your trip on one part of the region or on some special interest, such as history, nature, or art. We've taken these differences into account.

Though the individual chapters stand on their own, they are organized in a geographically logical sequence, so that you could conceivably fly into Atlanta, drive chapter by chapter to each destination in the book, and end up close to where you started. Of course, you don't have to follow that sequence, but it's there if you want a complete picture of the region.

Each destination chapter offers ways of prioritizing when time is limited: In the Perfect Day section, the authors suggest what to do if you have only one day to spend in the area. Also, every Sightseeing Highlight is rated, from one to four stars: ★★★★—or "must see" sights first, followed by ★★★ sights, then ★★ sights, and finally ★ or "see if you have time" sights. At the end of each sight listing is a time recommendation in parentheses. User-friendly maps help you locate the sights, restaurants, and lodging of your choice.

And if you're in it for the ride, so to speak, you'll want to check out the Scenic Routes described at the end of several chapters. They take you through some of the most scenic parts of the region.

In addition to these special features, the appendix has other useful travel tools:

- The Planning Map and Mileage Chart help you determine your own route and calculate travel time.
- The Special Interest Tours show you how to design your trip around any of five favorite interests.
- The Resource Guide tells you where to go for more information about national and state parks, individual cities and counties, local bed-and-breakfasts, and more.

HAPPY TRAVELS

With this book in hand, you have many reliable recommendations and travel tools at your fingertips. Use it to make the most of your trip. And have a great time!

WHY VISIT
THE DEEP SOUTH?

Begin with that famed southern hospitality, which really does exist in generous quantities. Then add a mild year-round climate, diverse terrain, luxuriant gardens, and historic sites. Finally add the spice of different cultures—Western European, African American, Cajun, and Creole, among others, and you'll see why millions of people vacation in the Deep South (Alabama, Georgia, the Florida panhandle, Louisiana, and Mississippi) each year.

So much more than moonlight and magnolias, hoopskirts and parasols, coquettes and courtly gentlemen, the New South is a delightful blend of old and new. Beautiful antebellum mansions sit in the shadow of towering rockets. Stately public buildings coexist with gaudy new casino boats.

Still, visitors will feel the irresistible pull of history as they travel from big cities such as Atlanta, Birmingham, and New Orleans to dozens of small, one- to two-century-old towns with charming, shady town squares, rustic covered bridges, and imposing historic buildings.

Although it comes as a big disappointment to some visitors that *Gone With the Wind*'s Tara and Twelve Oaks plantations never existed outside Margaret Mitchell's imagination, you can still visit real Greek Revival plantations and townhouses in pockets of the Old South. Many of these fabulous homes operate as bed-and-breakfasts. So you might be able to relax on white wicker furniture on a wide veranda, shaded by creamy magnolia blossoms and waxy green leaves as you sip a mint julep. Southerners have a deep reverence

I

for history and a passion for tradition, whether it be in their architecture, food, music, literature, or art, and they're only too happy to share their past and present with anyone who is interested.

HISTORY

Fossils indicate that mammoths, mastodons, and giant sloths roamed the region 10,000 years ago, but before that the area was under a huge ocean. Later, the territory was subjected to several ice ages, which apparently caused the demise of those prehistoric creatures.

Artifacts indicate that humans lived in what became the Deep South 4,000 years ago. Although these early humans left little trace of their existence, an advanced culture of Mound Builders inhabited the region from A.D. 900–1500, and they left much for us to examine. They lived in villages, hunted, and farmed. They built immense mounds—flat-topped pyramids that held temples and housing for their chiefs. At the chief's death, he was buried in the mound with his possessions.

Spanish explorer Hernando deSoto met these Mound Builders when he scouted the region in 1539 and 1540. But the Mound Builders mysteriously disappeared, leaving only their pyramids to tantalize future historians.

During the 1700s, the French and Spanish struggled over control of southeastern North America, with England joining the fray later. Georgia was one of the original 13 colonies and the fourth state to join the Union. The rest of the Deep South didn't join the United States until the Louisiana Purchase in 1803, and statehood came even later.

The Deep South turned out to be ideal for growing cotton, and the planter aristocracy purchased vast holdings of farmland. Cotton production and processing was labor intensive, and planters began importing slaves from Africa and the Caribbean as early as 1719.

Although planter society created the stereotype of the southern aristocracy, relatively few families actually belonged to this class or enjoyed its benefits. Most white southerners were small landholders or small businesspeople who just got by.

During the 1830s gold was found in the mountainous area of Georgia. This discovery perpetrated one of the most shameful events in American history. Because the gold was on Indian land, the government seized all the property and forced the Native Americans to march to Oklahoma, where they were banished to a reservation. During this "Trail of Tears," half the deportees died.

The agricultural, slave-based economy of the South led to the region's most painful period—the Civil War, which was not only about slavery but also about states' rights and defending one's home when invaded. The Confederacy was born in Montgomery, Alabama, where Jefferson Davis became its president. Four years of war decimated the economy of the South and took the lives of hundreds of thousands of its men. Civilians suffered unimaginable deprivation as well.

It took at least 20 years for the area to begin to recover. Railroading, mining of coal and iron ore, steel manufacturing, machine building, and textile manufacturing led the gradual rejuvenation. By the end of the nineteenth century, hundreds of new towns had grown up around the railroad lines. As affluence returned for some, southerners began to build fanciful Victorian homes with towers, turrets, steeply sloped gables, and gingerbread ornamentation. In the early and mid-twentieth century, wars brought major military bases, military manufacturing, and prosperity to the South.

Ironically, 100 years after Montgomery became the Cradle of the Confederacy, it served as the Cradle of the Civil Rights movement. Protests, marches, sit-ins, voter registration rallies, and other activities brought the South worldwide attention during the 1960s. Amid the turmoil and violence, the back of segregation and Jim Crow was finally broken.

Despite improved race relations, the Civil War still casts a shadow over the South. Visual reminders are widespread, including Confederate monuments in practically every town and controversial state flags that incorporate the Confederate battle flag. As everywhere, more work needs to be done in the area of racial equality.

As the twentieth century draws to a close, airlines and superhighways have replaced the railroads, and high-tech, information, and medical services are dominating the Southern economy. More and more big companies, both American and international, are moving their headquarters to the South—particularly to Atlanta.

Tourism is big business, and every kind of recreation is available—from beaches to ski slopes. Gaming is new to Mississippi and Louisiana, as are horse racing and greyhound racing, which can be found in Alabama and Florida as well.

CULTURES

The Deep South was originally inhabited by Native Americans and then explored by the Spanish and French. Ultimately, British, Scottish, and Irish settlers made the area their own, and wealthy planters imported slaves to work their plantations. Every one of these groups left an indelible imprint on the culture of the Deep South.

The aristocratic antebellum planter class valued education and cultural activities—if only for their own kind. They founded schools, libraries, museums, archives, and performing arts groups, which ultimately improved the cultural life of all white southerners.

Although slaves and, later, free blacks were denied the benefits of these institutions, they preserved and added their own creative traditions to the South's cultural landscape.

Tourists can see what life was like for the extremely wealthy, the middle class, poor farmers, and slaves by visiting living history homes, farmsteads, and forts throughout the South. These sites open a window onto the architecture, furnishings, farm equipment, military accoutrements, and culture of several centuries of southerners.

Numerous fairs, folk festivals, harvest celebrations, storytelling festivals, and other events offer more glimpses into the lives of early residents. Here, southerners celebrate and preserve their traditional arts and crafts, music, stories, dancing, and folklore.

THE ARTS

Native American petroglyphs and pottery are evidence of the earliest human inhabitants of the Deep South. Early European settlers had to make almost everything they needed. Eventually, their weaving, quilting, pottery making, basket making, birdhouse making, willow furniture construction, and other skills took on folk art status. Many authentic examples are found in museums and antiques stores, while modern artisans keep the folk traditions going.

Music is ingrained in southern life. Slaves chanted and sang to ease their burdens and communicate with each other. Many slave songs and musical styles were passed down from generation to generation and incorporated into other musical forms, such as gospel, jazz, and blues. All are distinctly southern inventions.

W. C. Handy, "Father of the Blues," was born in Alabama. Country music pioneer Jimmie Rodgers was born in Mississippi, as was current blues star B. B. King and the King of Rock and Roll himself, Elvis Presley. Jazz is synonymous with Bourbon Street in New Orleans, where greats such as Al Hirt, Pete Fountain, and Harry Connick Sr. play. Bluegrass evolved from Scottish and Irish folk tunes, and zydeco is a lively mix of French, Caribbean, and blues elements.

Classical music isn't forgotten, however. Symphonies, including the world-renowned Atlanta Symphony Orchestra, play throughout the Deep South, as do chamber ensembles and other small groups. Atlanta and most of the larger cities boast opera companies. Several cities offer outdoor summer concerts.

The South has spawned many literary giants such as William Faulkner, Tennessee Williams, Eudora Welty, Flannery O'Connor, Truman Capote, and Harper Lee. Contemporary Southern writers include Shelby Foote, Anne Rice, James Dickey, Pat Conroy, and John Grisham.

Art museums and galleries abound, and they put a great emphasis on folk arts. Museums in both Birmingham and Montgomery have acclaimed permanent collections. The High Museum in Atlanta sponsors several traveling shows each year.

When it comes to live theater, Montgomery is outstanding. The city is home to the Alabama Shakespeare Festival, the only theater in the United States permitted to fly the flag of the Royal Shakespeare Company. Atlanta boasts two dozen theatrical groups. Its Alliance Theater produces an ambitious list of plays each year—some old favorites, but often new works of southern and black playwrights. Atlanta and other large cities are always on the itinerary for major Broadway show road tours.

CUISINE

Southern cooking is founded on western European traditions, brought to North America by early settlers. Once here, settlers supplemented their recipes with foods of Native American, African American, and other cultures. Okra, yams, and greens were staples of African diets. Native Americans introduced corn, dried beans, potatoes, tomatoes, squash, and native fruits and nuts. The growing season in the South is long and, in some cases, permits two or more harvests. So the new ingredients were readily obtainable.

Fried chicken, as well as fried anything, including steak, is a favorite southern meal. Accompaniments such as hush puppies and grits are characteristic of southern cuisine as well. Grits are made from ground corn and are often served swimming in butter or cheese. Most people either love them or hate them. Grits are filling, which was important when other foods were scarce. Hush puppies, which are simply balls of fried dough, are said to have gotten their name during the Civil War. Food was scarce and everyone was hungry. It is said that when babies were crying pitiably and dogs were howling with hunger, mothers fried little balls of dough and gave them to the children and pets saying, "Hush babies, hush puppies."

Vegetables and fruits feature prominently in southern recipes. Fried green tomatoes and various types of stewed greens are typical. Fish and shellfish are caught in quantity from the rivers, lakes, and oceans. Gumbos were a popular way of making meat, seafood, and vegetables stretch further.

Soul food, which originated with southern blacks, was created in poverty.

Those who didn't have enough to eat couldn't waste anything, so gizzards, brains, livers, hearts, and even intestines (chitlins) made their way onto the table.

Barbecue probably originated when southerners spiced and smoked meat to disguise poor quality, spoilage, or bad taste. Of course, today barbecue is the regional dish—whether it be beef, pork, or chicken, with sauce or not. You will find more barbecue restaurants in the South than any other type of eatery.

Other typical southern dishes include country-fried steak with gravy, Brunswick stew, biscuits and gravy, cornbread, fruit cobblers, and pecan pie—all accompanied by unlimited iced tea. In most southern restaurants iced tea already has sugar in it. So if you don't want the sugar, be sure to ask for unsweetened tea.

Today's chefs strive to use the region's many traditional dishes in creative new ways. Many restaurants, particularly upscale ones, have several health-conscious items on the menu. But be forewarned. If you're going to worry about calories or cholesterol, you probably shouldn't order typical southern cuisine.

FLORA AND FAUNA

From seashore to mountains, the plants and animals of the region change subtly with altitude and climate. An abundance of flowering trees and shrubs make the region a springtime wonderland of blooming azaleas, camellias, rhododendron, mountain laurel, dogwood, and redbud to name just a few. These grow wild in the woods and are carefully planted in manicured lawns.

During summer, wildflowers grow abundantly in meadows and woods. Beaches bloom with waving sea oats (it is illegal to pick them), wild beach roses, and morning glories. You might see palm trees in coastal areas, but they probably are not native and instead have been introduced. A network of state and national parks protect thousands of acres in their natural state.

Perhaps the most stereotypical southern plant is Spanish moss. This wispy gray plant, related to the pineapple, hangs in draperies from huge oak trees (the moss is not a fungus and doesn't damage the trees) and drifts slowly with the breeze. Spanish moss is generally found close to the coast in the extreme southern parts of the states.

The southern plant that came to dinner and wouldn't leave is kudzu. This leafy ground cover was imported from Japan to prevent erosion. What no one apparently realized was that the hearty plant grows incredibly quickly (a foot a day) and that it's almost impossible to kill. You'll see it not only covering the ground but also creeping up tree trunks and telephone poles. It has even swallowed up entire buildings. There's a law in Georgia that you can't let your kudzu creep onto your neighbor's property.

Because the majority of the Deep South has a temperate climate, its forests are a mix of deciduous hardwoods and evergreens. In autumn they provide a spectacular display. You can actually follow the fall colors and stretch the trip out over several weeks, as first the trees in the north and at higher elevations, and then those in the south, put on their show.

When it comes to wild animals, you'll see mostly small ones—chipmunks, squirrels, groundhogs, raccoons, rabbits, and beaver—although deer are plentiful, and wild horses live on Cumberland Island off the coast of Georgia. Bears, mountain lions, and foxes are seen only occasionally.

More than 200 species of birds have been identified, from the robin and cardinal you're likely to see in your yard to a resurgence of American eagles. Wild game birds include turkeys, ducks, geese, quail, and pheasants. Waterfowl and wading birds are plentiful along the shore and at some inland lakes.

The ocean yields game fish and shellfish. Marshes, swamps, and bayous produce shellfish, alligators, and turtles. Inland streams, rivers, and lakes yield a wide variety of freshwater fish. Beautiful monarch butterflies make their first landfall on their journey from South America to North America at Dauphin Island, Alabama.

On the down side, shallow lakes and standing water, as well as a lack of freezing temperatures, allow mosquitoes to breed. Other pests include flies, gnats, and no-see-ums. Ticks and chiggers are becoming major problems. Wear insect repellant on your body and clothes. When hiking in deep woods, you should wear long pants and fasten them tightly around your ankles.

Be on the lookout for snakes. Only rattlesnakes, water moccasins, and cottonmouths are poisonous, but you don't want any unpleasant surprises, so watch where you step.

GEOGRAPHY

The landscape of the Deep South is as varied as it is beautiful. Elevations range from sea level to almost 5,000 feet. The advance and retreat of ice age glaciers sculpted and scoured the land. Earthquakes and erosion have further defined the terrain.

Running northeast-southwest in northern Georgia and Alabama, the Appalachian and Blue Ridge Mountains feature dramatic gorges, deep riverbeds, caves, and waterfalls. From the mountains, the terrain drops to foothills and then to the rich farmland of the Piedmont Plateau.

Southern Georgia and Alabama, and nearly all of the Florida panhandle, Mississippi, and Louisiana, are flat coastal plains at or slightly above sea level. Marshes, swamps, and bayous characterize coastal areas.

Each of the five states has access to the ocean: Georgia to the Atlantic, and the remainder of the states to the Gulf of Mexico. Beaches are among the region's most appealing features.

The Mississippi River creates the border between Mississippi and Louisiana. The Chattahoochee divides Alabama and Georgia. The Sabine forms the state line between Louisiana and Texas. Other major rivers include the Savannah and Flint in Georgia; the Tennessee, Tombigbee, and Alabama in Alabama; and the Apalachicola and Chipola in Florida. The rivers provided the only quick mode of transportation in the early days, and today they permit both transportation and recreation.

ACTIVITIES

When visiting an area as large and diverse as the Deep South, it should come as no surprise that you'll find a wide array of recreation opportunities, both indoor and outdoor. From aircraft dogfights to zydeco, something is available to suit every taste.

The Atlantic and Gulf of Mexico provide numerous opportunities for swimming, surfing, sailing, windsurfing, sea kayaking, and deep-sea and surf fishing. Numerous rivers and inland lakes—both natural and artificial—offer water sports as well.

In the northern mountains of Georgia, you can hike portions of the Appalachian, Benton MacKaye, and William Bartram trails. Other challenging trails are found in northern Alabama. The mountains provide ample opportunities for serious rock climbing and white-water rafting. Mountain streams yield trout and other prize catches, which make the region a fishing paradise. The biggest surprise to some may be that skiing is available in the mountains of both Georgia and Alabama, as long as temperatures are low enough to make artificial snow.

Less challenging hiking and biking trails crisscross the remainder of the Deep South. Both sports are particularly popular near beaches. Horseback riding is widely available and ranges from short rides along the beach to week-long riding-camping experiences in the mountains.

As environmental awareness increases, a new word has been coined to describe travel activities that do not harm the environment: ecotourism. In this category are hiking, biking, rock climbing, sailing, rafting, canoeing, kayaking, and the like. Not only are these pursuits kind to the environment but they are also much cheaper than sports such as snowmobiling, motorcycling, and powerboating.

Licenses are generally required for fishing, boating, and hunting, and may, in some cases, be required for camping and campfires as well. Each state's regulations are different, so if you plan to engage in any of these activities, check in advance for the particulars.

PLANNING YOUR TRIP

Before you set out on your trip, you'll need to do some planning. Use this chapter in conjunction with the tools in the appendix to answer some basic questions. First of all, when are you going? You may already have specific dates in mind; if not, various factors will probably influence your timing. Either way, you'll want to know about local events, the weather, and other seasonal considerations. This chapter discusses all of that.

How much should you expect to spend on your trip? This chapter addresses various regional factors you'll want to consider in estimating your travel expenses. How will you get around? Check out the section on local transportation. If you decide to travel by car, the Planning Map and Mileage Chart in the appendix can help you figure out exact routes and driving times, while the Special Interest Tours provide several focused itineraries. The chapter concludes with some reading recommendations, both fiction and nonfiction, to give you various perspectives on the region. If you want specific information about individual cities or counties, use the Resource Guide in the appendix.

HOW MUCH WILL IT COST?
The Deep South is large and extremely varied, so the cost of a typical day will vary, too. In New Orleans, Savannah, and Atlanta, food and a night's stay can

9

cost two to three times as much as in Macon or Lafayette. Of course, personal choices have an impact on cost as well. You could spend $300 per day in rural Alabama if you really worked at it.

However, for between $150 and $200 per day, two people traveling through the Deep South can stay in comfortable and sometimes historic accommodations, enjoy some of the best area cuisine, visit several tourist attractions, and get a good feel for the region. Budget $75 for a night's lodging, $25 for gasoline, $25 for entrance fees to attractions, and the following per-person meal costs: $5 for breakfast, $10 for lunch, and $25 for dinner.

In Atlanta, Savannah, and New Orleans, the average hotel room will be more expensive—easily $130 to $150 per night or more. Rooms in small towns can be as low as $35 per night. Of course, if you stay at a B&B, breakfast is included, and often afternoon tea and desserts, or cocktails and hors d'oeuvres, as well. Many hotels and chains also offer a simple continental breakfast.

True bargain hunters can probably cut daily costs to under $100, and campers can reduce the total by another $20 to $25. Gasoline prices in the Deep South, except Florida, are lower than most of the rest of the country. Currently, regular gas averages about 99 cents per gallon.

Many free attractions are offered throughout the region. State parks are sometimes free, and even those that charge generally do so for parking, rather than per person. Only a few attractions charge more than $10 per person.

Crafts and souvenirs can be expensive. Some of the most interesting items are mountain crafts from North Georgia and Alabama, as well as Cajun crafts from the bayous of Mississippi and Louisiana. If they are authentic handmade items, you'll pay a premium for them. Of course, there is no shortage of souvenir shops that purvey T-shirts and other items in the $5 to $10 range.

One way to save is to avoid "special seasons," such as leaf season in the Alabama and Georgia mountains, Mardi Gras in New Orleans and Mobile, St. Patrick's Day in Savannah, spring break in the Florida panhandle, and spring and fall pilgrimages in Natchez, Vicksburg, Savannah, Mobile, and several other cities. During these times the prices increase right along with the crowds.

CLIMATE

When it comes to the weather, you can always visit the Deep South. Even in the middle of winter, the weather is mild, although the Georgia and Alabama mountains occasionally get snow. The Alabama and Mississippi coasts and the Florida panhandle are particularly popular with "snowbirds" from late December to early April, which is considered high season.

In mid-summer it can be pretty hot and humid in the southern part of the region—especially along the coasts. But North Georgia and Alabama are at their most popular during summer.

WHEN TO GO

St. Patrick's Day in Savannah, leaf season—especially weekends—in North Georgia and Alabama, Mardi Gras and Jazzfest in New Orleans, and spring break in Panama City are all extremely crowded. Some people try to avoid these times. If you do plan to visit during special events, make your reservations well in advance and be prepared to pay as much as 100 percent more. Hotels will likely require a two- to three-night minimum stay and full, nonrefundable payment in advance.

College football in the Deep South is serious business—football weekends can create problems for unsuspecting travelers. For instance, when LSU plays at home, you will be hard-pressed to find a room in Baton Rouge. On Sugar Bowl weekend in New Orleans, even Baton Rouge and Mobile hotels are at capacity.

While the Deep South does not have any true "off seasons," you'll find spring, before schools let out, and fall, right after children are back in school, the least crowded. You'll also find the best weather during these seasons. If you are traveling with school-age children, visit as early in summer as possible. The later you visit in summer, the hotter, more humid, and more crowded it gets.

TRANSPORTATION

Either a major air carrier or at least one commuter airline services almost all of the towns discussed in this book. The only exceptions are the mountain regions of Georgia and Alabama. The primary hub airports in the region are in Atlanta and New Orleans. All major domestic airlines fly to these cities, as do some international carriers.

Rail travel in many parts of the country is very limited at best, and the Deep South is no exception. However, AMTRAK does offer some service. The Crescent runs from Washington, D.C., to New Orleans, with one eastbound and one westbound train per day. Another AMTRAK line runs between Chicago and New Orleans.

The Deep South is well served by the interstate system. I-10 and I-20 cross the region east to west—I-10 running just north of the Gulf Coast and I-20 about 100 miles north of I-10. Obey traffic laws scrupulously on I-10 in Louisiana. Because it is a major route for drug traffickers between Florida and

Texas, the local authorities are very aggressive in making stops and searches. You can have your car and all your possessions confiscated by police for the most minor infraction.

The major north-south interstates are I-95, I-85, I-75, I-65, and I-55. One more major interstate, I-59, cuts across the Deep South on a diagonal. It begins in the northwest corner of Georgia and ends in New Orleans.

Bus travel is considered passé by most, but it is economical and also a great way to meet some interesting people. Most of the towns in the book can be reached via bus, and many tour operators provide luxury coach tours within the region. The large cities and even some of the small towns have local bus service as well.

CAMPING, LODGING, AND DINING

The Deep South abounds with state and national parks that have some excellent campgrounds. One of the most unusual camping spots is in the Okefenokee Swamp. Campsites are located along canoe trails through the swamp. Platforms give campers a firm, dry surface and, most important, keep them safely out of reach of alligators.

The area offers many private campgrounds—ranging from big chains to small, mom-and-pop facilities with only a couple of spots. Among the most popular are those in the mountains of northern Georgia and Alabama, situated along unspoiled streams or on mountaintops. One is only accessible via a three- to four-hour horseback ride through first- and second-growth forest.

While the Deep South has its share of hotels, motels, and cookie-cutter franchises, the region is just beginning to realize the potential of smaller, more personal accommodations. B&Bs in the area have increased by almost 33 percent over the last two years, with a good mix of restored historic homes and a few new facilities built specifically as inns. You might stay in an impressive Victorian-era mansion in Georgia or Alabama or even a spectacular plantation in Louisiana or Mississippi.

Wherever you have gorgeous white sand beaches, broad bays, soaring mountains, majestic rivers, and glitzy casinos, you'll find resort properties. The resorts that dot the Deep South can compete with the best in the world. If your budget can handle the cost, these properties afford guests just about anything they might desire in hotel service, amenities, and sports facilities. Some even offer meal plans. Several resorts have extensive children's programs.

If you're a native of the South, you'll feel at home in the vast array of restaurants that serve familiar regional cuisine. If you aren't a native, you can try southern fried chicken, country fried steak, stewed vegetables, and other home-cookin' specialties. The area is also home to Cajun and Creole cooking, some of the best barbecue in the world, and plenty of freshwater fish and seafood.

We try to give the reader an assortment of places (and prices) to consider. Whenever possible, smaller, family-run, home-style restaurants are described, as well as some truly superior gourmet restaurants presided over by world-renowned chefs such as John Folse in Baton Rouge and Guenter Seeger in Atlanta.

WHAT TO BRING

Obviously, what you bring for a trip to the Deep South depends on the time of year and whether your vacation will be athletic or not. While it seldom gets bitter cold, the area experiences below-freezing temperatures one or more times during the winter months. In the summer it can get pretty hot and sticky. Along the seashore, though, summer evenings can be cool, and in the mountains summer nights can drop into the 40s.

Bring lightweight clothing that can be worn in layers, so that if the temperature goes up or down significantly, you can add or remove a layer or two. Unless you are staying at an expensive resort or plan to eat in a pricey restaurant, you'll have little reason to dress up. The South is mainly casual. Even many business offices have done away with coats and ties in favor of slacks and polo shirts.

Don't forget your umbrella and a light, waterproof jacket. It can and does rain during all seasons of the year. Pack one or more bathing suits, even if you're traveling during winter. Many hotels and resorts have indoor pools, and some smaller properties have indoor hot tubs. Bring plenty of sunscreen, a hat, and insect repellent. Insects, especially if you're exploring swamps or if the sea breeze stops at the beach, can be a nuisance. A short hike will take you to many of the region's best sights, so good walking shoes are a must. If you plan to horseback ride, golf, or play tennis, bring the appropriate attire.

Be sure to bring your camera, a spare set of batteries, and plenty of film or videotape. These items can cost twice as much at a resort or tourist attraction as they do at home. The new, one-use cameras take surprisingly good pictures, and you might want to pick up several.

Finally, as you cross the border into each state, stop at the Welcome Center and pick up a free official state highway map, state travel guide, and brochures about attractions, lodgings, parks, and restaurants. Several of the states publish separate guides to bed-and-breakfasts, state parks, outdoor activities, and the like. Because many of the maps and guides are expensive to produce, they often are kept behind the counter and are only made available to those who specifically ask for them, so don't be shy. In addition, the staff and volunteers who work these Welcome Centers are very knowledgeable and can give you good advice about travel within their state.

RECOMMENDED READING AND VIEWING

Books such as Margaret Mitchell's *Gone With the Wind*, Alex Haley's *Roots*, Mary Chestnut's *Diary*, and Shelby Foote's three-volume *Civil War* give invaluable insight into the antebellum South and the Civil War. Joel Chandler Harris's *Tales of Uncle Remus* give a different viewpoint on the same era and are favorites with children.

Books set in this century include Tennessee Williams's *Cat on a Hot Tin Roof* and *Streetcar Named Desire*, William Faulkner's *Light in August*, *Go Down Moses*, and *Sanctuary*, Eudora Welty's *Robber Bridegroom* and *Delta Wedding*, Harper Lee's *To Kill a Mockingbird*, Truman Capote's *A Christmas Memory*, Flannery O'Connor's *Wise Blood* and *A Good Man Is Hard to Find*, and Alice Walker's *The Color Purple*. Mark Childress' *Crazy in Alabama* is a send-up of the typical southern opus, with an underlying serious theme about Civil Rights. Many of these books have been reenacted numerous times on the stage and screen.

1
ATLANTA

Modern, vibrant Atlanta—not only the capital of Georgia but also the center of the New South—is one of the few great cities in North America that is not on a major seaport, river, or waterway. The city instead owes its creation, existence, and dynamic growth first to the railroads and now to the airlines and interstate highways.

Its central location among the southern states made Atlanta vitally important during the Civil War. When the city fell on September 2, 1864, the South's cause was lost. The Atlanta that literally rose from the ashes is frequently described as a phoenix, and that mythical creature is often used as the city's insignia.

Although regrowth was slow, the city blossomed during the golden years of the railroads, between the 1880s and the turn of the century. Atlanta newspaperman Henry Grady coined the phrase "New South" after Reconstruction, when the region's economy began to depend less on agriculture and more on business.

Today, the city seems to be in a constant frenzy of tearing down the old and building anew. Strenuous preservation efforts have saved some historic sights, but you shouldn't expect to see very many of them. And, by the way, although there's a Tara Boulevard, *Gone With the Wind*'s plantations—Tara and Twelve Oaks—never existed. What you will find in Atlanta are a variety of museums, upscale shopping opportunities, a wealth of theatrical venues, great restaurants and nightspots, and more than enough attractions to satisfy any visitor.

DOWNTOWN ATLANTA

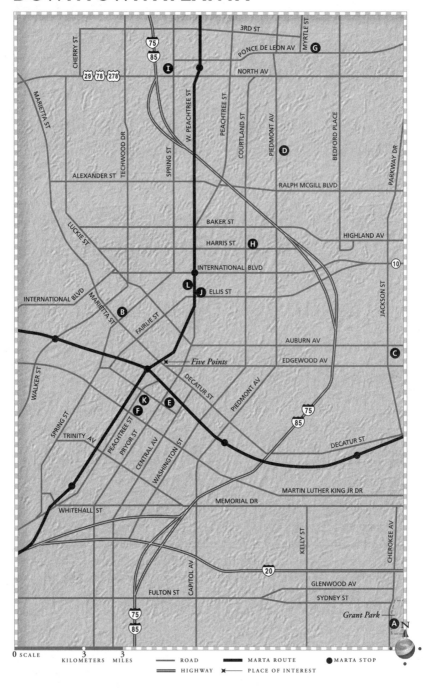

3RD ST
MYRTLE ST
PONCE DE LEON AV
G
CHERRY ST
75
85
29 78 276
I
NORTH AV
MARIETTA ST
TECHWOOD DR
SPRING ST
W. PEACHTREE ST
PEACHTREE ST
COURTLAND ST
PIEDMONT AV
D
BEDFORD PLACE
PARKWAY DR
ALEXANDER ST
RALPH MCGILL BLVD
LUCKIE ST
BAKER ST
HIGHLAND AV
HARRIS ST
H
10
INTERNATIONAL BLVD
L
INTERNATIONAL BLVD
MARIETTA ST
J ELLIS ST
JACKSON ST
B
FAIRLIE ST
AUBURN AV
C
Five Points
EDGEWOOD AV
WALKER ST
DECATUR ST
SPRING ST
K
PIEDMONT AV
F E
75
TRINITY AV
85
PEACHTREE ST
PRYOR ST
CENTRAL AV
WASHINGTON ST
DECATUR ST
MARTIN LUTHER KING JR DR
WHITEHALL ST
MEMORIAL DR
KELLY ST
CHEROKEE AV
CAPITOL AV
20
FULTON ST
GLENWOOD AV
SYDNEY ST
75
Grant Park
85
A
N

0 SCALE
3   3
KILOMETERS   MILES

—— ROAD   —— MARTA ROUTE   ● MARTA STOP
═══ HIGHWAY   ✕—— PLACE OF INTEREST

A PERFECT DAY IN ATLANTA

Begin with a hearty breakfast at Murphy's in the fashionable Virginia-Highland neighborhood. Make your next stop the Atlanta History Center in Buckhead to learn about the city, the South, and the Civil War. You will need a good half-day to do the entire center justice. Have lunch at the museum or at the Swan Coach House next to the facility.

Head downtown to Auburn Avenue to visit the Martin Luther King Jr. National Historic Site. Then it's only a few blocks to Centennial Olympic Park. Another few blocks away is Underground Atlanta, an unusual shopping, dining, and entertainment complex. There, drop in during happy hour at Dante's Down the Hatch for drinks, fondue, and live jazz from the Paul Mitchell Trio.

After all that excitement you may not want any dinner. But if you do, Buckhead is the place to go. After dinner, nightspots and comedy clubs are located nearby, but other excellent entertainment options can be found at Underground, in Little Five Points, or in Virginia-Highland.

End your evening back downtown with a moonlit horse-and-carriage ride from Underground. Then take the elevator to the top of the Peachtree Plaza Hotel for a nightcap and a gorgeous view of the city from the Sun Dial Restaurant.

SIGHTSEEING HIGHLIGHTS: DOWNTOWN ATLANTA

★★★★ **ATLANTA CYCLORAMA**
Georgia and Cherokee Avenues S.E., Grant Park
404/658-7625 www.webguide.com/cyclorama.html

SIGHTS

- Ⓐ Atlanta Cyclorama
- Ⓑ CNN Center
- Ⓒ Martin Luther King Jr. National Historic Site and Center for Nonviolent Social Change
- Ⓓ SciTrek: The Science and Technology Museum of Atlanta
- Ⓔ Underground Atlanta
- Ⓕ World of Coca-Cola
- Ⓐ Zoo Atlanta

FOOD

- Ⓖ The Abbey
- Ⓗ Nickolai's Roof
- Ⓘ The Varsity

LODGING

- Ⓙ Ritz-Carlton (Downtown)
- Ⓚ Suite Hotel at Underground
- Ⓛ Westin Peachtree Plaza

Note: Items with the same letter are located in the same area.

When this gigantic, circular painting of the Battle of Atlanta was completed in 1885, cycloramas were a popular art form, and hundreds of them were displayed in the United States and abroad. Today Atlanta's painting is one of only 20 left in the world. As the comfortable stadium seating revolves around the beautifully restored painting, narration, sound effects, and lighting re-create the feel of the battle. The painting merges imperceptibly into a three-dimensional diorama, further enhancing the "you-are-there" ambience. The building also displays artifacts from the Civil War and the locomotive *Texas,* which earned fame during the war by recapturing a hijacked train. **Zoo Atlanta** is right next door, so if you plan to make it part of your itinerary, see it in conjunction with the Cyclorama.

Details: June–Labor Day daily 9:20–5:30; to 4:30 rest of the year. $5 adults, $4 seniors, $3 children. (1 hour)

★★★★ **MARTIN LUTHER KING JR. NATIONAL HISTORIC SITE AND CENTER FOR NONVIOLENT SOCIAL CHANGE**
449 Auburn Avenue, N.E., 404/524-1956
Located on Auburn Avenue downtown—once the most prosperous street of African American businesses in the country—are several sights significant in the life of Dr. Martin Luther King Jr. Begin at the visitors center, where you can pick up brochures for a self-guided tour or join a guided tour. Among the sights are the two-story Victorian home where King was born, Ebenezer Baptist Church, where both King, his father, and his grandfather preached and which is still an active congregation, a reflecting pool with the Civil Rights leader's tomb in the middle, and the Center for Nonviolent Social Change.

Details: Daily 9–5; to 6 in summer. Free. (2 hours)

★★★ **CNN CENTER**
Marietta Street at Techwood Drive, 404/827-2491
At the headquarters of Turner Broadcasting, CNN, and Headline News, you can take tours daily and join a live studio audience on CNN Talk-Back Live on weekdays. The complex also includes a movie theater, specialty shops, eateries, an athletic club, and the Omni Hotel.

Details: Studio tours daily 9–6. $7 adults, $5 seniors, $4.50 ages 6–12. Under 6 not permitted. (1 hour)

★★★ SCITREK: THE SCIENCE AND TECHNOLOGY MUSEUM OF ATLANTA
395 Piedmont Avenue, 404/522-5500
Ranked as one of the top-ten science centers in the country, SciTrek features more than 100 interactive exhibits, as well as live demonstrations, workshops, lectures, films, and even exciting overnight programs.

Details: Mon–Sat 10–5, Sun noon–5; extended hours in summer. $7.50 adults, $5 seniors, college students, military, and children 3–17. (2 hours)

★★★ UNDERGROUND ATLANTA
55 Upper Alabama Street, 404/523-2311
www.underatl.com
If you're confused by addresses such as Upper and Lower Alabama Streets and Upper and Lower Pryor Streets, don't feel bad. Two sets of these streets are situated one above the other. When Atlanta was in its infancy, businesses began to grow up around the railroad depot, at the same level as the tracks. When train and buggy traffic jams became habitual, elevated roadways were built over the tracks, leaving the storefronts below street level. Enterprising merchants simply created new entrances on the second floors of their buildings and took deliveries at the now underground level. Largely abandoned over the years, the six-block, below-street level has been reincarnated as a spirited urban marketplace of 120 stores, 12 restaurants, and several nightclubs open until the wee hours of the morning. The Atlanta Underground Trolley runs between the complex and five major downtown hotels.

Details: Shops open Mon–Sat 10–9:30, Sun noon–6. Restaurants and nightspot hours vary. (2–3 hours)

★★★ WORLD OF COCA-COLA
55 Martin Luther King Jr. Drive, 404/676-5151
Atlanta is home of the world-famous soft drink, so it's only natural that a museum devoted to Coca-Cola would be found in Atlanta as well. Located between Underground and the State Capitol, the museum presents the story of Coca-Cola past, present, and future. It offers exhibits, the world's largest collection of Coca-Cola memorabilia, a fanciful representation of the bottling process, a futuristic soda fountain that dispenses experimental flavors, and an extensive gift shop. Get there early; there's almost always a line.

Details: Mon–Sat 9–9:30, Sun noon–6; extended hours in summer; last admission one hour before closing. $6 adults, $4 seniors, students 12 and older, and children 6–11; free under 6 accompanied by adult. (1¹/₂ hours)

★★★ **ZOO ATLANTA**
800 Cherokee Avenue S.E., Grant Park, 404/624-5600
www.zooatlanta.org
Although small compared to many major zoos, Atlanta's is still a gem. Despite its squeezed-in location in a turn-of-the-century neighborhood (next door to the Cyclorama), the zoo presents 1,000 animals in naturalistic habitats, including the Ford African Rain Forest and Masai Mara African Plains. Beginning fall of 1999 the Asian Forest Exhibit will feature two giant pandas on long-term loan from China. The zoo is world renowned for its primate collection, and other attractions include a petting zoo and a miniature train ride.

Details: Daily 10–4:30; to 5:30 on summer weekends. $10 adults, $8 seniors, $6 children 3–11; discounted in winter. (2–3 hours)

SIGHTSEEING HIGHLIGHTS: GREATER ATLANTA

★★★★ **ATLANTA HISTORY CENTER**
130 West Paces Ferry Road, 404/814-4000
www.ngcwrt.com/ahcmus.html
This beautiful museum is immensely fortunate to be the recipient of the DuBose collection of Civil War memorabilia—the largest private collection in the country. You can actually pick up a foot soldier's full backpack, haversack, and rifle to get an idea of the common soldier's burden. The current exhibit, "Through These Eyes," is a compilation of photographs by P. H. Polk, the former head of the Photography Committee at Tuskegee University in Alabama and the university's official photographer until his death in 1984.

Also on the property and open for tours are the neoclassical Swan House, built in 1928, the Tullie Smith farmstead from the 1840s, and 33 acres of gardens and nature trails. Each July a Civil War reenactment takes place, and living history demonstrations are held periodically at the farm. The Swan Coach House, adjacent to the complex, contains a gift shop, restaurant, and gallery.

Details: *Mon–Sat 10–5:30, Sun noon–5:30. $7 adults, $4 children. (3–4 hours)*

★★★ ATLANTA BOTANICAL GARDEN/PIEDMONT PARK
Piedmont Avenue at the Prado, 404/876-5859

Bordering Piedmont Park, Atlanta's largest park (designed by Central Park landscape architect Frederick Law Olmstead for the 1895 Cotton States Exposition), the garden contains 33 acres of forest with walking paths, a small Japanese garden, other seasonal gardens, and the modernistic Dorothy Chapman Fuqua Conservatory. The garden sponsors many flower shows and special programs such as workshops, moonlight strolls accompanied by live music, and tours of private gardens around the city.

Details: *Tue–Sun 9–6; to 7 during Daylight Savings Time. $6 adults, $5 seniors, $3 students, free under 6 and garden members. Free Thur from 3 until closing. (1 1/2 hours)*

★★★ CALLANWOLDE FINE ARTS CENTER
980 Briarcliff Road, N.E., 404/872-5338

Completed in 1920, this outstanding, 27,000-square-foot Gothic–Tudor mansion was originally the home of Charles Howard Candler, the oldest son of Coca-Cola founder Asa Candler. The public can wander through the mansion and explore Callanwolde's 12 acres of restored sculptured gardens, lawns, and nature trails. The Callanwolde Gallery, located on the second floor of the mansion, features exhibits of emerging local talent. Special events include poetry readings, jazz and classical concerts on the lawns, and the Stories for a Tuesday Evening storytelling series. Christmas at Callanwolde is a two-week Atlanta tradition as top local interior and floral designers transform the mansion with spectacular displays for the holiday season.

Details: *Mon–Fri 10–8, Sat 10–4. Gallery, mansion, and grounds free. Call for prices for special events. (1–3 hours)*

★★★ FERNBANK SCIENCE CENTER AND MUSEUM OF NATURAL HISTORY
767 Clifton Road, N.E., 404/370-0960 (museum)
404/378-4311 (science center)

Situated in a 150-acre environmental/educational complex near Emory University, Fernbank delves into Georgia's past, present, and future. The science center is home to one of the nation's largest planetariums, an observatory, and an exhibit hall. Among the museum's permanent exhibits are "A Walk Through Time in Georgia," "Cultures of the World," "First Georgians," "Spectrum of the Senses"—an interactive gallery dealing with light and sound—an IMAX theater, and Children's Discovery Rooms.

Details: *Mon–Sat 10–5, Sun noon–5; call for IMAX theater hours. Museum $8.95 adults, $7.95 seniors and college students, $6.95 ages 3–12. Members and children 2 and under free. IMAX and planetarium admissions extra; combination tickets are available. For ticket information, call 404/370-0730. (2–3 hours)*

★★★ **GEORGIA'S STONE MOUNTAIN PARK**
U.S. 78, Stone Mountain, 770/498-5600
www.stonemountainpark.org
Originally created as a Civil War memorial, the park venerates Confederate leaders Jefferson Davis, Robert E. Lee, and Stonewall Jackson in a Mt. Rushmore-like carving on the face of the world's largest exposed mass of granite. Now much more than simply a memorial, the 3,200-acre park offers swimming, fishing, tennis, golf, a

CONFEDERATE MEMORIAL, STONE MOUNTAIN, GEORGIA

© Carol Thalimer

cable car to the mountaintop, a museum of Civil War memorabilia, an antique car museum, a petting zoo, a ride around the base of the mountain on an old-fashioned train, a nightly laser show in summer, a southern plantation home and outbuildings, a paddle wheeler, two hotels, several restaurants, and a campground. Numerous festivals are held at the park as well.

Details: June–Aug 10–9, Sept–May 10–5. Parking $6 per car; attractions cost extra. (Full day)

★★★ **HIGH MUSEUM OF ART**
1280 Peachtree Street, N.E., 404/733-4400 or
404/733-HIGH www.high.org
Among the permanent exhibits in the stunningly modern building next to the Woodruff Arts Center in Midtown are European and American paintings, an extensive collection of African art, decorative and twentieth-century art, and photography. In addition, the museum hosts numerous traveling exhibits such as one highlighting the works of Matisse and another showcasing Picasso.

Details: Tue–Sat 10–5, Sun noon–5. $6 adults, $4 seniors and college students, $2 children 6–17. Costs vary for special exhibits. (2 hours)

★★★ **JIMMY CARTER LIBRARY AND MUSEUM**
1 Copenhill, 404/331-0296 or 404/331-3942
At the official library of Georgia's only native-born president, visitors learn about the life and administration of Jimmy Carter as well as the office of the presidency. Displays include an interactive video where you can ask the former president scripted questions. Other exhibits include gifts the Carters received during their tenure in Washington and a life-size model of part of the Oval Office. Tours are self-guided; groups of 25 or more should call ahead to schedule tours. In addition to a café and gift shop, a pleasant outdoor patio overlooks the tranquil Japanese gardens and the Atlanta skyline.

Details: Mon–Sat 9–4:45, Sun noon–4:45. $5 adults, $4 seniors, free 16 and under. (2 hours)

★★★ **KENNESAW MOUNTAIN NATIONAL**
BATTLEFIELD PARK
Old U.S. 41 and Stilesboro Road, Kennesaw, 770/427-4686
Here, outnumbered and outprovisioned Confederate soldiers held off the Union assault on Atlanta for several weeks in the summer of

1864. Eventually they were outflanked and ultimately defeated by William Tecumseh Sherman's troops, and Atlanta's last safeguard was gone. The city fell a few weeks later. Today the 2,882-acre park includes numerous hiking trails. On the occasional clear day, the view from the mountaintop is spectacular. The small museum at the base of the mountain offers a 10-minute slide presentation about the battle. Bring a lunch and enjoy one of several picnic sites throughout the park.

Details: Daily 7:30–dusk. Free. (2 hours)

★★ **CENTER FOR PUPPETRY ARTS**
1404 Spring Street at Eighteenth Street N.W.
404/873-3391
With one of the nation's most extensive and impressive collections of puppets, the center is appealing to both adults and children. It also offers an ambitious variety of performances and workshops for all ages.

Details: Mon–Sat 9–5. Call for a schedule of performances and events. Museum $5 adults, $4 children; performances extra. (1 hour)

FITNESS AND RECREATION

Flowing desultorily through the metropolitan area, the Chattahoochee River provides innumerable opportunities for the outdoor devotee. Forty-eight miles of riverfront are designated as a national recreation area, with 14 separate parks. Heavily wooded banks along the river offer hiking trails—several with fitness stations—and biking trails, as well as boat launches, picnic areas, and excellent fishing. A favorite pastime from late spring through early fall is to put on your bathing suit and lots of sunscreen, load up a cooler with cold drinks, and float lazily down the river in a raft or inner tube. The Chattahoochee Outdoor Center, either the Johnson Ferry or Powers Island center, offers two- to five-hour float trips by raft or canoe with rentals and return shuttle service. For more information about the recreation area, contact the park headquarters at 1990 Island Ford Parkway, Atlanta; 770/395-6851.

Jogging is a popular activity everywhere in the metropolitan area, from sidewalks along main thoroughfares to wooded paths through public parks and office campuses. The Peachtree Road Race, held each Fourth of July, attracts almost as many participants as the Boston Marathon. In-line skating is gaining in popularity as well, and you can rent skates adjacent to Piedmont Park. Many opportunities for tennis and golf are available nearby—ask your concierge.

After food and drink, Atlantans as a group love sports above all other forms of entertainment. The city is the home of several professional teams: the World Series–winning Braves, who play at a new stadium constructed for the Olympics, modified for baseball, and now known as Turner Field (404/522-7630); the Falcons football team, which plays at the Georgia Dome (404/223-8000); the Hawks basketball team, which plays at Philips Arena (404/827-3800); and the Atlanta Thrashers ice hockey team, which also plays at Philips Arena (404/584-7825). In addition, with Georgia Tech, Georgia State, and Atlanta University located in town, college sports are popular.

Several amusement parks offer all-day fun for the entire family: Six Flags Over Georgia (off I-20, Atlanta; 770/948-9290), American Adventures and the Foam Factory, and White Water (next door to each other on Cobb Parkway off I-75 at exit 113, Marietta; 770/424-9283).

FOOD

Sometimes Atlanta seems like a city obsessed with food. Restaurants of every stripe and price range open with much fanfare almost weekly, but they often close quite suddenly and quietly within months. We've tried here, therefore, to recommend only eateries that have been around for a long time. But, in order not to miss someplace spectacular, check with your concierge to see what new restaurants are currently in vogue. Prices run the gamut from pocket change to the national debt, and menus focus on everything from hot dogs to sushi.

In the inexpensive category, **The Varsity** (61 North Avenue, N.W., 404/881-1706) in Midtown, which claims to be the world's largest drive-in restaurant, has been an Atlanta institution for more than 60 years. Everyone should eat there at least once. Most famous for its chili dogs and onion rings, it also offers hamburgers, French fries, and other fast food items. This may not be New Orleans, but you can get piping hot and crispy beignets at **Huey's**, 1816 Peachtree Road, N.W., 404/873-2037, which is something folks often do in lieu of dessert after the theater or other late-night activity. The small, casual restaurant offers Cajun and Creole cuisine and serves a variety of salads and sandwiches.

The city has a plethora of casual, mid-priced restaurants. A simple, neighborhood restaurant, **Murphy's** (997 Virginia Avenue, N.E., 404/872-0904), in Virginia-Highland, attracts diners for lunch, dinner, and Saturday and Sunday brunch. The portions are gigantic, and there's a bakery for take-out breads and desserts. They do not take reservations but "call aheads" for dinner are a very good idea—long lines frequently snake around the corner no matter what the weather. For a casual ambience and moderately priced southwestern cuisine,

GREATER ATLANTA

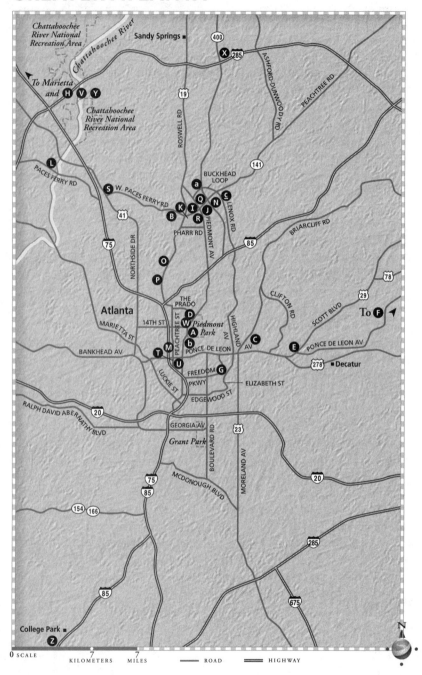

Chattahoochee
River National
Recreation Area

Chattahoochee River

Sandy Springs ■

400

X 285

ASHFORD-DUNWOODY RD

PEACHTREE RD

To Marietta
and H V Y

Chattahoochee
River National
Recreation Area

ROSWELL RD

19

141

PACES FERRY RD

L

S W. PACES FERRY RD

BUCKHEAD
LOOP

a

K I Q N c

41

B R J

LENOX RD

PHARR RD

PIEDMONT AV

75

NORTHSIDE DR

85

BRIARCLIFF RD

78

O

P

THE
PRADO

CLIFTON RD

29

SCOTT BLVD

To F

Atlanta

MARIETTA ST

14TH ST

PEACHTREE ST

D

W Piedmont
Park

A

HIGHLAND AV

C

E PONCE DE LEON AV

BANKHEAD AV

M

b PONCE DE LEON

278 ■ Decatur

T

U

FREEDOM G

LUCKIE ST

PKWY

ELIZABETH ST

RALPH DAVID ABERNATHY BLVD

EDGEWOOD ST

20

GEORGIA AV

BOULEVARD RD

23

Grant Park

MORELAND AV

75

85

MCDONOUGH BLVD

20

154 166

285

85

College Park ■

675

Z

0 SCALE   7   7
        KILOMETERS   MILES   ROAD   HIGHWAY

N

try the **Georgia Grill**, 2290 Peachtree Road, 404/352-3517, which is tucked into the back corner of a small strip center in Buckhead. During good weather, outdoor dining is available on the deck. **Canoe**, 4199 Paces Ferry Road, 770/432-2663, in a wooded setting in Vinings, is the only place along the Chattahoochee River with open-air dining at the river's edge. New American cuisine is served in a casual atmosphere. Sunday brunch is very popular.

Visitors to Atlanta will probably want to eat at least one meal in an Old South setting. Located in a beautifully furnished and decorated 1797 plantation house tucked away from the hustle and bustle of Buckhead, **Anthony's**, 3100 Piedmont Road, N.E., 404/262-7379, is considered one of the top-ten continental restaurants in the country.

If you want something really upscale (read pricey), you can choose from dozens of elegant Atlanta restaurants. One of the most unusual is **Kamogawa**, 3300 Peachtree Road, 404/841-0314, located on the lobby level of the Grand Hyatt Hotel in Buckhead. Not only does the restaurant serve authentic Japanese cuisine and the best sushi in town, but the entire restaurant was also constructed by artisans in Japan, dismantled, shipped to Atlanta, and reassembled. If you haven't tried it before, have a traditional meal served while sitting on the floor in a tatami room. (Don't worry, wells for your feet will

SIGHTS

- Ⓐ Atlanta Botanical Gardens/Piedmont Park
- Ⓑ Atlanta History Center
- Ⓒ Callanwolde Fine Arts Center
- Ⓓ Center for Puppetry Arts
- Ⓔ Fernbank Science Center and Museum of Natural History
- Ⓕ Georgia's Stone Mountain Park
- Ⓓ High Museum of Art
- Ⓖ Jimmy Carter Library and Museum
- Ⓗ Kennesaw Mountain National Battlefield Park

FOOD

- Ⓘ 103 West
- Ⓙ Anthony's
- Ⓚ Atlanta Fish Market
- Ⓙ Buckhead Diner
- Ⓛ Canoe
- Ⓜ Country Place
- Ⓝ The Dining Room
- Ⓞ Georgia Grille
- Ⓟ Huey's
- Ⓠ Kamogawa
- Ⓖ Murphy's
- Ⓡ NAVA
- Ⓢ Pano's and Paul's
- Ⓣ Peasant
- Ⓤ Pleasant Peasant
- Ⓥ Public House
- Ⓦ Veni, Vidi, Vici

LODGING

- Ⓓ Ansley Inn
- Ⓧ Holiday Inn Crowne Plaza-Ravinia
- Ⓖ King-Keith House Bed and Breakfast
- Ⓨ Marietta Conference Center and Resort
- Ⓩ Renaissance Concourse Hotel
- ⓐ Ritz-Carlton (Buckhead)
- ⓑ Shellmont Bed and Breakfast
- Ⓢ Sheraton Buckhead
- Ⓖ Sugar Magnolia Bed and Breakfast

Note: Items with the same letter are located in the same area.

help you sit comfortably.) Chair seating is also available. **The Dining Room** in the Ritz-Carlton Hotel in Buckhead (3434 Peachtree Road, 404/237-2700) serves unsurpassed dinners. It is Atlanta's only five-diamond (AAA rating) restaurant, presided over by Chef Xavier Salomon. You can find a creative menu, energetic ambience, excellent service, and great people-watching of the rich and famous at the **Buckhead Diner**, 3073 Piedmont Road, 404/262-3336, Atlanta's favorite casual (but expensive) restaurant.

Atlanta boasts two premier restaurant groups that have about a half-dozen to a dozen restaurants each. We highly recommend any of the Peasant restaurants, which include the **Peasant**, 3402 Piedmont Road N.E., 404/231-8740, the **Pleasant Peasant**, 555 Peachtree Street N.E., 404/874-3223, the **Public House**, 605 S. Atlanta Street, Roswell, 770/992-4646, the **Country Place**, 1197 Peachtree Street, 404/881-0144, **Veni, Vidi, Vici**, 41 14th Street, 404/875-8424, and others. We also recommend any of the Buckhead Life restaurants, including **103 West**, 103 W. Paces Ferry Road, 404/233-5993, **Pano's and Paul's**, 1236 W. Paces Ferry Road, 404/261-3362, **NAVA**, 3060 Peachtree Road, 404/240-1984, and the **Atlanta Fish Market,** 265 Pharr Road, 404/262-3165. You'll be guaranteed excellent food and superb service at any of these restaurants.

Among some other suggestions are **The Abbey** (163 Ponce de Leon Avenue, 404/876-8532), where continental cuisine is served by waiters dressed as monks in an old church with 60-foot vaulted ceilings and massive stained-glass windows, and **Nickolai's Roof** (Courtland and Harris Street N.E. at the top of the Atlanta Hilton and Towers, 404/221-6362), which specializes in classic French and authentic Russian cuisine and where the service is the best we've ever had—no contest.

LODGING

You could hardly find a more convenient location than the **Suite Hotel at Underground**, 54 Peachtree Street, S.W., 404/223-5555. Located downtown adjacent to Underground, the hotel is only steps away from the Five Points MARTA (rapid transit) station. There, you can board north-south and east-west lines, as well as trains to the Capitol, government offices, downtown shopping, and several sports venues. The historic 17-story building has been modified to provide European-style accommodations in a variety of large and small suites.

If you're looking for the sublime, either of the two **Ritz-Carltons** (downtown: 181 Peachtree Street, N.E., 404/659-0400, or Buckhead: 3434 Peachtree Road, N.E., 404/237-2700) are consistently rated by *Condé Nast Traveler* as among the top ten hotels in the country. Also downtown is the

HELPFUL HINTS

- **Getting Around:** The Metropolitan Atlanta Rapid Transit Authority (MARTA) operates an extensive network of rapid rail lines with 33 stations, as well as 700 buses on 150 routes to downtown, the suburbs in Fulton and DeKalb counties, and the airport. The fare is $1.50 one way. For more information, route maps, and schedules, call 404/848-4711.
- **Peachtree Streets:** All the jokes about every Atlanta street being named Peachtree are close to true, so be sure to check addresses and directions very carefully. Thirty-four streets in the metro area contain Peachtree in their names, so make sure you are heading for the right one.
- **Safety Downtown:** Atlanta, like many other major cities, has a vibrant, safe downtown during the business day. But the city empties out at night except for patrons of hotels and restaurants. Exercise prudence when going out at night: keep to well-lit, busy areas; don't walk alone; and take a taxi if you are going more than a block or two.

Westin Peachtree Plaza, 210 Peachtree Street, N.W., 404/659-1400, a 73-story glass cylinder with several restaurants and bars, including the Sun Dial, which is the best vantage point for panoramas of the city.

In addition to the expensive choices in Buckhead, a moderately priced and conveniently located hotel is the **Sheraton Buckhead**, 3405 Lenox Road, 404/261-9250, just across the street from Lenox Square Mall and a MARTA station and only a block from Phipps Plaza. Recently refurbished, the comfortable, low-key hotel offers a restaurant and a pool.

Surrounding Atlanta, along the I-285 perimeter highway, are just about every chain hotel and motel you can think of. Near Atlanta-Hartsfield International Airport, you might choose the upscale **Renaissance Concourse Hotel**, 1 Hartsfield Centre Parkway, S.W., College Park; 404/209-9999. In historic Marietta is a grand new luxury hotel, the **Marietta Conference Center and Resort** (55 Club Drive off Powder Springs Road, 770/427-2500), which resembles the world-famous Greenbrier Resort in West Virginia. On the north side of town, on I-285 near GA 400, is the

Holiday Inn Crowne Plaza-Ravinia, 4355 Ashford-Dunwoody Road, N.E. (I-285 perimeter in Dunwoody), 770/395-7700.

On a completely different scale are several glamorous yet homey bed-and-breakfasts. Among the standouts are **Shellmont** (821 Piedmont Avenue, N.E., 404/872-9290) and the **Ansley Inn** (253 15th Street, 404/872-9000). Inman Park, with its multitude of Victorian houses, is a perfect setting for B&Bs, about a dozen of which are present here. Our favorite is **Sugar Magnolia** (804 Edgewood Avenue, N.E., 404/222-0226), located in an imposing Queen Anne mansion. Another is the **King-Keith House** (889 Edgewood Avenue, 404/688-7330), a striking Second Empire Victorian filled with antiques.

CAMPING

Since Atlanta spreads out so far from its center, you have to go a good way out to find a campground. To the east, more than 400 sites are available at Georgia's Stone Mountain Park (U.S. 78, Stone Mountain, 770/498-5710). North of the city, you'll find the Lake Lanier Islands Campground, 6950 Holiday Road, Lake Lanier Islands, 770/932-7270. Two KOA campgrounds are situated around the metro area: 2000 Old Highway 41, N.W., Kennesaw, 770/427-2406, and 281 Mount Olive Road, McDonough, 770/957-2610. The Atlanta West Campground is located at 2420 Old Alabama Road, Austell, 770/941-7485, only three miles from the Six Flags Over Georgia amusement park.

NIGHTLIFE

Whether you want jazz, blues, golden oldies, country, or classical music, dancing, comedy, or something else, Atlanta is noted for its energetic nightlife. Probably the hottest concentration of nightspots is in Buckhead, where LuLu's Bait Shack (3057 Peachtree Road, N.E., 404/262-5220) and Tongue and Groove (3055 Peachtree Road, N.E., 404/261-2325) are the current favorites. But this neighborhood on and just off Peachtree Road around Paces Ferry and Roswell Roads is jammed with pubs and comedy clubs—most within easy walking distance of each other.

Downtown, a perennial favorite is the Hard Rock Cafe (215 Peachtree Street, N.E., 404/688-7625), an institution of rock-and-roll where 300 pieces of memorabilia are displayed, and you might see Atlanta and Hollywood stars. Just across the street is the equally popular Planet Hollywood (218 Peachtree Street, N.W., 404/523-7300), owned by Arnold Schwarzenegger, Sylvester Stallone, Bruce Willis, and Demi Moore, who make an appearance from time to time.

For a change of pace, try an original, audience-participation murder mystery served along with your dinner at Agatha's—a Taste of Mystery (693 Peachtree Street, N.E., 404/875-1610). You might even be the murderer. Dave and Buster's, (2215 Dave and Buster's Drive, I-75 at Delk Road, Marietta; 770/951-5554), a restaurant and entertainment extravaganza in suburban Cobb County, boasts four bars, Million Dollar Midway, pocket billiards, and a mystery dinner theater. The middle-aged crowd hangs out to boogie, jitterbug, shag, and twist, primarily to the tunes of the '50s to the '80s, but also to those of the '40s at Johnny's Hideaway (3771 Roswell Road, N.E., 404/233-8026), a small, crowded, smoky bar and dance hall in Buckhead, which is open until four in the morning.

Those who are more interested in culture may want to check the schedule of the Atlanta Symphony Orchestra (1293 Peachtree Street, N.E., 404/733-5000), which plays an impressive fall through spring series at Symphony Hall in the Woodruff Arts Center in Midtown. In summer, the orchestra gives a series of pops concerts with well-known guest performers at the Chastain Park amphitheater (4469 Stella Drive, N.W.) on Wednesday, Friday, and Saturday. Patrons take a small table, elegant table linens, a gourmet picnic supper, flower arrangements, and even silver candelabra to create a romantic evening. Call the symphony box office (above) for more information. On the other evenings a series sponsored by Coca-Cola and Michelob is held at the same amphitheater. Call Ticketmaster at 404/249-6400 for more information.

Any night of the week, as many as 30 theatrical performances may be given around Atlanta in a variety of large and small theaters. Traveling Broadway shows often appear at the opulent Fox Theater. Other "in" places are the entertainment emporiums in Underground Atlanta, the Virginia-Highland neighborhood, and the Little Five Points neighborhood.

2
NORTH GEORGIA MOUNTAINS

As you travel south to north in Georgia, you pass out of the level coastal plain, through the rolling Piedmont, and finally into a mountainous area that rivals those of Tennessee, Kentucky, North Carolina, the mid-Atlantic states, and New England. These picture-postcard mountains of North Georgia are the southern foothills of the Appalachian and Blue Ridge Mountains.

Here you'll find tall peaks, deep valleys, rushing streams, crashing waterfalls, heavy forests, and twisting mountain roads. No cities and only a few large towns are located in the mountainous area of North Georgia. Instead, dozens of small towns are filled with friendly folks, shops that sell antiques, crafts, and folk art, restaurants that feature Southern home cookin', and a variety of lodging options that range from primitive campsites to large resorts. Rand McNally's *Places Rated* consistently names several North Georgia communities among the best retirement spots in the country. Life here definitely operates at a slower pace than it does at lower elevations.

Some surprises you'll encounter in the mountains are an alpine village, a ski resort, several wineries, and dozens of carpet mills. The area is rich in Native American and Civil War history and was the site of the first gold rush in the United States. Three different kinds of people come to the mountains: those who seek physical activities in the outdoors, those who are interested in sightseeing and shopping, and those who want to do everything.

NORTH GEORGIA MOUNTAINS

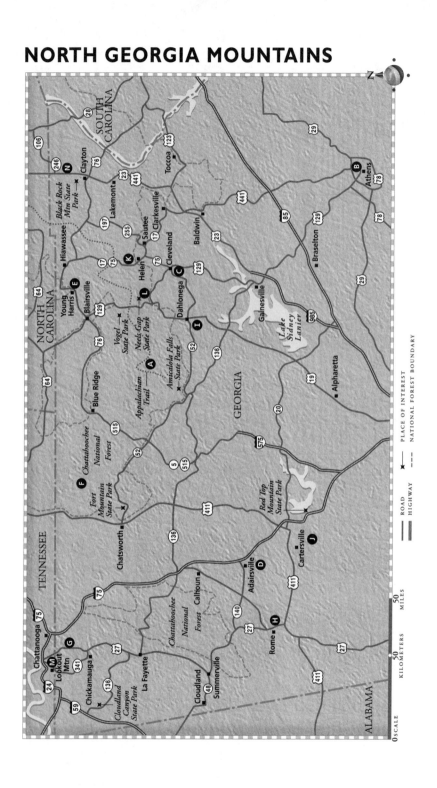

A PERFECT DAY IN THE NORTH GEORGIA MOUNTAINS

Begin in Dahlonega, the site in 1828 of the first gold rush in the United States. The quaint mountain village has a town square containing in its center an old courthouse and the Dahlonega Courthouse Gold Museum and surrounded by numerous shops and boutiques—all circa the late 1800s. If you're having a sweet attack, stop for a pick-me-up at the ice cream parlor or fudge store on the square. Take GA 52 east and you'll pass through a small town called Cleveland, home of the original Cabbage Patch dolls. You can stop by BabyLand General Hospital to see them being "born" and perhaps adopt one. Turn north on GA 75 and you'll arrive in the Bavarian-like village of Helen. Have lunch outside on the deck of the International Café, which juts out over the Chattahoochee River. Then visit the Museum of the Hills to learn more about the history of Helen and the surrounding area. Have dinner at one of the town's German restaurants, then go to the Fest Hall for entertainment by German oompah bands, singing, and dancing.

SIGHTSEEING HIGHLIGHTS

★★★★ HELEN
GA 75, Helen, 706/878-2180 or 706/878-1619
Sometimes referred to as Alpine Helen, the village is situated amidst the natural beauty of the mountains at the headwaters of the Chattahoochee River and re-creates one you might find in Switzerland, Germany, or Austria. This illusion is created with jaunty facades, as well as red tile roofs, flower-filled window boxes, colorful

---

SIGHTS

- **A** Appalachian Trail
- **B** Athens
- **C** Babyland General Hospital
- **D** Barnsley Inn and Golf Resort and Barnsley Gardens
- **E** Brasstown Bald
- **F** Chattahoochee National Forest
- **G** Chickamauga and Chattanooga National Military Park
- **H** Chieftains Museum
- **C** Cleveland
- **I** Dahlonega
- **J** Etowah Indian Mounds State Historic Site
- **K** Helen
- **L** Neel's Gap
- **M** Rock City Gardens
- **N** Sky Valley

Note: Items with the same letter are located in the same area.

---

balconies, and murals on the sides of buildings. In addition, narrow, winding, cobblestone-paved alleys are filled with shops.

How did this picturesque village come to exist in the Georgia mountains? Helen was incorporated in 1913 as a logging village and was named for a town official's daughter. About 25 years ago, the small town was dying because of a severe decline in the timber business. Enterprising citizens banded together to bring tourism to town, re-creating Helen as a replica of a Bavarian village. The plan worked beyond the residents' wildest imagination. The town is booming and holds numerous festivals during the year. Helen's biggest drawback is that it has only one two-lane through street, and traffic often moves at a snail's pace. Parking can be a problem as well.

Shops, staffed by costumed shopkeepers, sell European goods such as sweaters, porcelain, and cuckoo clocks. Most restaurants offer wursts, strudels, and German beer and wine. Entertainment runs to oompah bands and German folk dancing.

Helen celebrates the South's largest Oktoberfest, running through both September and October. Another lively event is Fasching, which is similar to Mardi Gras or Carnival. Alpenlights is a winter light festival that lasts from mid-November through early February.

In addition to shopping, eating, drinking, and dancing, you can take a horse-and-carriage or trolley ride around town or visit the **Museum of the Hills**, where wax figures depict southern mountain people.

Details: Apr–Nov 15 daily 10–9; to 6 rest of the year. $5 adults, $4 seniors 62 and older, $3 students 13 and older, $2 children, free 4 and under with adult (2 hours)

★★★★ **CHICKAMAUGA AND CHATTANOOGA NATIONAL MILITARY PARK**
U.S. 27, Fort Mountain, Oglethorpe, 706/866-9241
This park, created on the site of two bloody Civil War battles, extends into both Georgia and Tennessee. The battles, fought by the Confederates under General Braxton Bragg and by the Union under generals George H. Thomas, William Rosecrans, and Ulysses S. Grant, resulted in a Confederate victory at Chickamauga, but an ultimate Union victory at Chattanooga. Combined, the two armies suffered 34,000 dead and wounded in the battles. Designated as the country's first military park in 1890, this park is the nation's most visited battlefield.

This description is limited to the Georgia portion of the park. Begin at the ultra-modern visitors center to see the impressive Fuller Gun Collection and a multimedia presentation about the battles. Afterward, take a self-guided walking or driving tour along the seven-mile route through the park and see monuments, plaques, artillery, and two log cabins. Hiking, biking, and horseback riding trails are available as well. Civil War reenactments are held periodically.

Details: Memorial Day–Labor Day 8–5:45; to 4:45 rest of the year. Park is free; movie $3 adults, $1.50 children. (1–2 hours)

★★★★ DAHLONEGA
U.S. 19, 706/864-2257

The town's name is the Cherokee word for "precious yellow metal," which was discovered here. The phrase "There's gold in them thar hills" originated in Dahlonega. Unfortunately, the gold rush led directly to the expulsion of the Cherokee from Georgia in 1838 via the infamous Trail of Tears. Prospectors almost immediately abandoned the area when richer veins of gold were discovered in California. Visit the **Dahlonega Courthouse Gold Museum**, where you can view a film called *Gold Fever*, as well as mining tools and other memorabilia.

Details: Museum open Mon–Sat 9–5, Sun 10–5. $2.50 adults, $1.50 children. (1 hour)

★★★★ ETOWAH INDIAN MOUNDS STATE HISTORIC SITE
813 Indian Mounds Road, Cartersville, 770/387-3747

Between A.D. 1000 and 1500, Native Americans of the Mississippian culture lived in the Etowah Valley and built several gigantic temple and funeral mounds. Three of these mounds remain, and one of them has been excavated. Artifacts discovered on the site are displayed in the visitors center, where an interpretive film is also shown. The biggest adventure is climbing the steep stairways to the tops of the mounds (the tallest is 63 feet).

Details: Tue–Sat 9–5, Sun 2–5:30. $3 adults, $2 children 6–18, free under 6. (1–2 hours)

★★★ ATHENS
280 East Dougherty Street, 706/353-1820 (Welcome Center)

This pleasant antebellum town on the bluffs of the Oconee River is the home of the **University of Georgia**, www.uga.edu, which in

WINE COUNTRY

Despite cold winters, the North Georgia mountain climate is very hospitable to the production of grapes, and several small wineries have opened. **Chateau Elan**, 7000 Old Winder Highway at exit 48 off I-85, Braselton, 770/932-0900, is the most ambitious. Housed in an imposing replica of a French chateau, the winery offers guided and self-guided tours, all of which end with a wine tasting. The complex also includes a European-style inn, several restaurants, a gift shop, spa, golf course, and equestrian center.

Three other small wineries are also open for tours and tastings: **Chestnut Mountain Winery** in Braselton (706/867-6914), **Habersham Winery** in Baldwin (706/778-9463), and **Georgia Winery** near Chattanooga (706/937-2177).

1785 became the first chartered state university in the United States. Since then, the heart of the town has been the university. Athens was spared by Union General William Tecumseh Sherman during his march across Georgia, so several historic homes survived, such as the **Church-Waddell-Brumby House**, which serves as the City of Athens Welcome Center (280 East Dougherty Street, 706/353-1820), and the **Taylor-Grady House** (634 Prince Avenue, 706/549-8688), as well as commercial buildings open for tours. In addition, visit the **Georgia Museum of Art** (90 Carlton Street, University of Georgia, 706/542-4662), the **State Botanical Garden of Georgia** (2450 S. Milledge Avenue, 706/542-1244), and, if you're interested in sports, the **Butts-Mehre Heritage Hall** (Lumpkin and Pinecrest Streets, 706/542-9094). Learn about the development and growth of the U.S. Navy Supply Corps at the **U.S. Supply Corps Museum** (Prince and Oglethorpe Avenues, 706/354-7349).

Details: (half–full day)

★★★ **BARNSLEY INN AND GOLF RESORT AND BARNSLEY GARDENS**
597 Barnsley Gardens Road, Adairsville, 770/773-7480
barnsley@mindspring.com

After the Cherokee were removed from the area in 1838, Geoffrey Barnsley took advantage of the land lottery to acquire acreage for a vast estate—on which he built an Italianate mansion and a formal, 30-acre garden. The estate survived a brief skirmish and Union occupation during the Civil War, but was nearly destroyed in a 1906 tornado. Eventually, the estate was abandoned. Today the gardens have been restored and opened to the public, and the surviving section of the house serves as a museum. Closed in 1998 for major construction, it has reopened as a full-service luxury boutique resort with 70 guest suites and 5,000 square feet of meeting space. The resort also offers a gourmet restaurant, German beer garden, and 18-hole championship golf course with a country club, full spa, pool, tennis courts, and much more.

Details: Call for prices and hours. (2 hours)

★★★ BRASSTOWN BALD
GA Spur 180, Blairsville, 706/745-6928
The highest point in Georgia at 4,784 feet, the mountaintop offers a 360-degree panorama of Georgia, Tennessee, North Carolina, and South Carolina. To get to the summit, drive about three-quarters of the way up the mountain and park at the welcome center. From there, you can either walk or take a shuttle to the top, where a visitors center has interpretive displays and a slide presentation about the area and its flora and fauna. The temperature atop the mountain is often 20 degrees cooler than in Atlanta, so dress accordingly.

Details: Welcome and visitors centers daily 9–5. Free admission, $1 parking, $2 shuttle fee. Closed Nov–Mar; Apr–Memorial Day weekends; after Memorial Day daily. (1–2 hours)

★★★ ROCK CITY GARDENS
1400 Patten Road, Lookout Mountain, 706/820-2531
www.seerockcity.com
Although many people associate this attraction with Chattanooga, it is actually located in Georgia. The 14-acre site is a geological marvel featuring gigantic rock formations created millions of years ago by erosion. In the 1920s Garnet and Frieda Carter bought the site and created a series of landscaped gardens for their own pleasure. Eventually they opened the gardens to the public, and over time **Fairyland Caverns** and **Mother Goose Village** were added.

Among the sights are 400 species of wildflowers, a stunning waterfall, several overlooks including the famous view of seven states from **Lover's Leap**, and **Deer Park**, where unusual white fallow deer roam.

Details: Daily 9–5. $9.95 adults, $5.50 children 3–12, free under 3. (2 hours–half day)

★★ APPALACHIAN TRAIL

Seventy-nine miles of the 2,000-mile Appalachian Trail are in Georgia. The southern end of the trail begins at **Springer Mountain** in **Amicalola Falls State Park** near Dahlonega. Eight other access points to the trail can be reached within Georgia including **Neels Gap**, where it crosses the highway.

Details: For information contact the Georgia Appalachian Trail Club, Inc., P.O. Box 654, Atlanta, GA 30301. (half–full day)

★★ BABYLAND GENERAL HOSPITAL
73 West Underwood Street, Cleveland, 706/865-2171

If you're traveling with children or have a special child in your life, stop at BabyLand General Hospital, a turn-of-the-century house that once operated as a medical clinic. Cute, cuddly, one-of-a-kind Cabbage Patch dolls are "delivered" from cabbages here, then placed for adoption. Also for sale are clothing and accessories for the dolls. While you're in town, stop by the old courthouse, which contains a museum. Cleveland is also noted for its gargantuan Easter egg hunt.

Details: Mon–Sat 9–5, Sun 10–5. Free. (1 hour)

★★ CHATTAHOOCHEE NATIONAL FOREST

National forest occupies an enormous part of North Georgia—more than a half-million acres. Various areas of the forest have roads, parking areas, and recreational facilities; other parts are wilderness and archaeological areas, accessible only on foot. The forest provides innumerable recreational activities.

Details: For maps and other information, contact Forest Supervisor, U.S. Forest Service, 508 Oak Street, N.W., Gainesville, GA 30501; 770/536-0541. (half–full day)

★★ CHIEFTANS MUSEUM
501 Riverside Parkway, Rome, 706/291-9494

In the early 1800s, Major Ridge, a Cherokee chief who fought in the War of 1812 with Andrew Jackson and was awarded the rank of major for his service, moved his family into a cabin in what is now Rome. Over the next several years, Ridge converted the cabin into a splendid plantation house—an impressive example of both Moravian and Cherokee craftsmanship. Now a history museum, the home holds exhibits on the Cherokee, Rome's history, and Major Ridge. The original cabin can still be seen in a cutaway section upstairs.

Details: Tue–Sat 10–4. $3 adults, $2 seniors, $1.50 students. (1 hour)

★★ NEEL'S GAP
U.S. 19, Dahlonega, 706/745-6095

This remote area of the mountains, which Native Americans called Land of the Dancing Rabbits, was a region of moonshine stills, pioneer cabins, and logging camps. Today residential developments are starting to encroach on the pristine forests, but so far they are tucked away out of sight. The Appalachian Trail crosses U.S. 19 at Neel's Gap. Stop here for a fabulous view of the mountains

When traveling in the mountains, allow extra driving time. Roads are tortuous. Be especially cautious in winter—the mountains get frequent snow and ice storms.

and valleys from the overlook. At the rustic fieldstone information center, built in 1937, you can buy hiking gear, maps, picnic supplies, and crafts.

Details: Welcome center daily 9–5. Free. ($^1/_2$–1 hour)

★★ SKY VALLEY
1 Sky Valley Way, 706/746-5301 or 800/437-2416

No, you haven't been transported to some northern state. This is, indeed, Georgia, and, yes, this is a ski resort. Sky Valley and a similar resort in northern Alabama are the southernmost ski resorts in the East. Although the area gets several snowstorms each winter, natural snow isn't even necessary. Cold temperatures are all that's required to make artificial snow. Four slopes and a bunny hill range in length from 400 to 2,000 feet. A double chairlift and a rope tow propel skiers up the hills. The resort also has a golf course (when there's no natural snow, it's often possible to ski for several hours and play golf on the same day), as well as tennis courts, a swimming pool, and a wide variety of accommodations.

Details: *Call for skiing conditions and hours of operation. Resort is free, prices vary for recreational activities. (half–full day)*

FITNESS AND RECREATION

With their lakes, forests, and streams, the mountains of Georgia offer almost any outdoor sport you can think of—hiking, white-water rafting, camping, fishing, rock climbing, horseback riding, mountain biking, canoeing, and skiing. Hayrides are another popular activity. Something you can do here, but not many other places, is pan for gold and gems.

Outfitters abound in the area. They know the rivers and forests and can provide you with guides. Because the North Georgia rivers have some Class IV and V sections, never go white-water rafting without an experienced guide. Hiking is less dangerous, but some trails can be treacherous, especially near the waterfalls, so be sure to check with the forest service before going too far into a national or state forest.

FOOD

The North Georgia mountains are dotted with a variety of restaurants, which range from barbecue stands to elegant dining rooms. Only a few are described here.

Chateau Elan in Braselton (7000 Old Winder Highway at exit 48 off I-85, Braselton, 770/932-0900) houses several restaurants. **Café Elan** is a casual French bistro. Light meals include sandwiches, salads, and continental entrees. **Le Clos** features fine dining in a formal atmosphere. Jackets are required for men. The five-course prix fixe dinner is accompanied by wine. Reservations are a must. Other restaurants are located at the hotel, golf clubhouse, Irish pub, and spa.

The restaurant in the delightful, 100-year-old **Glen-Ella Springs Inn** (Bear Gap Road, Clarkesville, 706/754-7295 or 888/455-8786) serves breakfast to overnight guests only and dinner to the public. Many locals go here for a special night out. The menu is classically continental with a southern flair. Reservations are strongly recommended. The **Trolley Restaurant**, 1460 Washington Street, on the square in Clarkesville, 706/754-5566, is housed in a 1907 drugstore, which retains its soda fountain. The comprehensive menu runs the spectrum from fountain treats to gourmet dining. Dinner is offered Tue–Sat at 5 p.m. and later. Reservations are recommended.

Green Shutters Restaurant in Clayton has two locations: Main Street (706/782-3342) and U.S. 441 (800/535-5971). The restaurant is noted for its food cooked over a woodstove. The original restaurant is located in an old building that overlooks a farmyard filled with small animals. In good weather, you can dine on the screened-in porch. A gift shop carries the restaurant's specialty food items, cookbooks, and other gifts. The new restaurant is located in a contemporary building that lacks the ambience of the original. Make Thanksgiving reservations well in advance. Closed from after Thanksgiving to March.

Harry Bissett's New Orleans Café, 279 East Broad Street, Athens, 706/548-0803, is a favorite upscale Athens hangout. Diners sit in the brick-walled atrium of a historic, late-nineteenth–century commercial building, located downtown near the University of Georgia's quadrangle and famous arch. Menu items, which have a Cajun/Creole tang, include pastas, veal, chicken, beef, and seafood.

In good weather, the ambience of the casual **Café International** (GA 75, Helen, 706/878-3102) is only one reason for eating here—but it's a good one. A large covered deck hangs right over the burbling Chattahoochee River, which sings to you while you dine on sandwiches, salads, and light entrees from various European countries, with an emphasis on German dishes. If the weather is less than ideal, you can sit in the indoor dining room.

Located on the shores of Lake Burton, **LaPrade's** (GA 197N, Clarkesville, 706/947-3312) is a rustic fishing camp with primitive cabins, boat rentals, and fishing gear. The complex has a restaurant that draws folks from miles around to eat the gargantuan portions of fish and chicken (mostly fried) and lots of vegetables—all served family style. Open April 1 through December 1.

Poised almost on the state line between Georgia and Alabama, the rustic **Lookout Restaurant**, GA 48 at Lookout Mountain Parkway (GA 157), Cloudland, 706/862-2515, is well known for its steaks and generous portions of potatoes, vegetables, and desserts. No alcoholic beverages are served.

Bernie's at the Nacoochee Valley Guest House in Sautee near Helen (GA 17, Sautee, 706/878-3830) is located in an extremely modest 1920s house, which contains several surprises: the restaurant, a bakery, and a bed-and-breakfast—all overlooking the scenic Sautee Valley. They serve lunch and dinner only and are closed Tuesdays. Reservations are a good idea but not required. From the wraparound porches of the 1837 **Stovall House** (GA 25, Sautee, 706/878-3355), you can get a 360-degree view of the pastoral Nacoochee Valley backed by mountains. Dinner entrees include such specialties as citrus trout.

NORTH GEORGIA MOUNTAINS

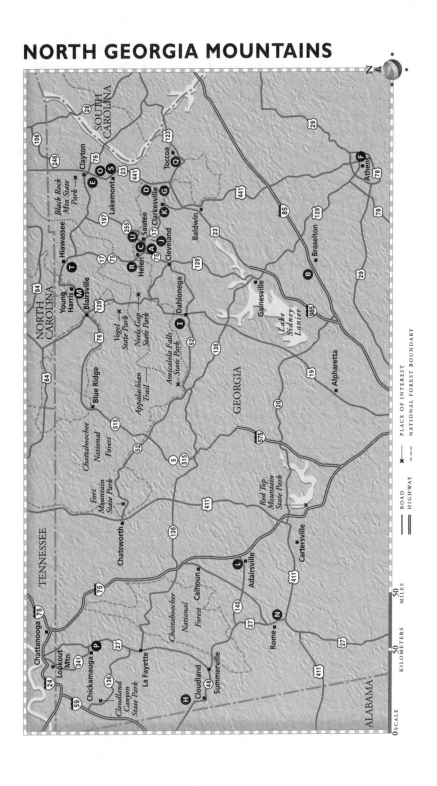

N

SOUTH CAROLINA

NORTH CAROLINA

TENNESSEE

GEORGIA

ALABAMA

Chattanooga
Lookout Mtn
Chickamauga
Cloudland Canyon State Park
La Fayette
Cloudland
Summerville
Chatsworth
Fort Mountain State Park
Blue Ridge
Chattahoochee National Forest
Calhoun
Adairsville
Cartersville
Rome
Red Top Mountain State Park
Chattahoochee National Forest
Vogel State Park
Neels Gap State Park
Appalachian Trail
Amicalola Falls State Park
Dahlonega
Young Harris
Blairsville
Hiawassee
Black Rock Mtn State Park
Clayton
Lakemont
Sautee
Helen
Cleveland
Clarkesville
Baldwin
Toccoa
Gainesville
Lake Sidney Lanier
Alpharetta
Braselton
Athens

28
106
246
76
23
441
123
29
679
76
S
O
E
D
G
K
197
255
U
C
A
17
75
R
T
17
75
129
52
136
64
76
515
52
5
515
411
136
75
27
341
136
48
59
140
27
N
411
27
27
19
20
575
985
85
441
78
78
129
B
M
I
52
H
L
P
Q
F

PLACE OF INTEREST
NATIONAL FOREST BOUNDARY
ROAD
HIGHWAY

0 SCALE
50 MILES
50 KILOMETERS

A famous family-style restaurant, the **Smith House Restaurant** (202 South Chestatee Street, Dahlonega, 706/867-7000 or 800/852-9577), was built in 1884 over a gold seam. The same family has operated it since 1946. Diners will enjoy an immense southern meal, usually including at least three meats, dozens of vegetables, biscuits, sweet rolls, and dessert. Reservations are not accepted except in groups, and lines are often long, but you can while away the time by rocking on the veranda or even panning for gold. Bed-and-breakfast accommodations are also offered at the Smith House Country Inn.

LODGING

More bed-and-breakfasts are situated in this area than any other in Georgia, with the exception of the coast. They run the gamut from rustic cabins to antebellum mansions. The **Claremont House** (906 East Second Avenue, Rome, 706/291-0900 or 800/254-4797) is a Second Empire Victorian mansion, perched on a wooded hillside. Special features include heavily carved woodwork, inlaid floors, floor-to-ceiling windows, elaborate mantelpieces, and an antique sterling silver urinal (no longer in use). Luxurious accommodations are offered in five rooms and two suites.

English Manor Inns (GA 76, Clayton, 706/782-5789 or 800/782-5780) started modestly enough in a 1912 house with an engaging full-length veranda.

FOOD

- Ⓐ Bernie's
- Ⓑ Café Elan
- Ⓒ Café International
- Ⓓ Glen-Ella Springs Inn
- Ⓔ Green Shutters Restaurant
- Ⓕ Harry Bissett's New Orleans Café
- Ⓖ LaPrade's
- Ⓑ Le Clos
- Ⓗ Lookout Restaurant
- Ⓘ Smith House Restaurant
- Ⓙ Stovall House
- Ⓚ Trolley Restaurant

LODGING

- Ⓛ Barnsley Inn and Golf Resort at Barnsley Gardens
- Ⓜ Brasstown Valley Resort
- Ⓝ Claremont House
- Ⓞ English Manor Inns
- Ⓒ Georgia Mountain Madness Adult Resort Cabins
- Ⓓ Glen-Ella Springs Inn
- Ⓟ Gordon-Lee Mansion
- Ⓠ Habersham Manor House
- Ⓑ Inn at Chateau Elan
- Ⓡ Innsbruck Resort and Golf Club
- Ⓢ Lake Rabun Hotel
- Ⓣ Mountain Memories Inn
- Ⓤ Royal Windsor

Note: Items with the same letter are located in the same area.

COVERED BRIDGES

Georgia has only a few surviving covered bridges, two of which are found in this region:

- **Elder Mill Bridge**, GA 15, Watkinsville
  Located in Watkinsville near Athens, Elder Mill Bridge was built around 1800 over Rose Creek and is still in use. Drive through it and enjoy the sound of the clattering floorboards.
- **Stovall Covered Bridge**, GA 255, Sautee
  This bridge, located in the Sautee Valley near Helen, was built in 1895. Only 33-feet long, it is Georgia's smallest covered bridge. The road, GA 255, has been routed around the one-span-wide, Kingpost-design bridge to help preserve it. You can pull off and park, then walk through the bridge.

The current owners added on to the house several times, then built more houses on the property. In all, the estate now encompasses seven buildings with 39 rooms and 10 suites, as well as kitchen facilities, a swimming pool, and a hot tub. Some rooms have fireplaces and Jacuzzis. A full country breakfast is served.

Located on 16 rural acres, the renovated, 100-year-old **Glen-Ella Springs Inn** (Bear Gap Road, Clarkesville, 706/754-7295 or 888/455-8786) is distinguished by its wraparound porches and the rustic simplicity of its 16 rooms and suites. No TV is included except the one in the lounge, but some guest rooms boast fireplaces and whirlpools. In addition, the inn has a restaurant, a swimming pool, gardens, and hiking trails.

A beautiful antebellum Greek Revival home with the requisite white columns, the **Gordon-Lee Mansion** (217 Cove Road, Chickamauga, 706/375-4728 or 800/487-4728) was commandeered by Union General William Rosecrans during the nearby Civil War battle. It's hard to imagine that the lovely library was once used as an operating room. Lovingly restored and exquisitely furnished, the inn features three rooms and one suite and a small Civil War museum. Another gorgeous Greek Revival home, the **Habersham Manor House** (326 West Doyle Street, Toccoa, 706/886-6496) offers elegantly furnished guest rooms with gas log fireplaces.

An entirely different kind of hostelry, the **Lake Rabun Hotel** (Lake Rabun Road, Lakemont, 706/782-4946) is a rustic mountain inn built in 1922.

The walls are paneled, the floors are bare, and the guest rooms are exceedingly spartan. Most rooms share a bath. Swimming, fishing, and boating are available across the street.

Perched atop the highest point in Hiawassee, the contemporary **Mountain Memories Inn** (385 Chancey Drive, Hiawassee, 706/896-VIEW or 800/335-VIEW) affords a 360-degree view of sparkling Lake Chatuge, Brasstown Bald Mountain, and the surrounding mountains of Georgia, Tennessee, and South Carolina. Each spacious, romantically decorated guest room features a king- or queen-size bed, private outside entrance, private bath, cable TV, and a VCR. The *piece de resistance* in each room, however, is a two-person Jacuzzi. The breakfast buffet—the most generous we've ever had at a B&B—is served in a large dining room, where you can admire spectacular views from three sides. Dessert is served in the evening, and complimentary cruises on Lake Chatuge are available.

You'll find a little touch of England in the mountains at the **Royal Windsor** (GA 356, Sautee, 706/878-1322). Host Don Dixon has created a homey but elegant bed-and-breakfast with impeccable service, named for the royal family in his native England. Featured in *Southern Living*, each of its four guest accommodations is decorated in floral prints and includes a private bath, queen-size bed, and private porch, deck, or balcony. Guests enjoy English tea and biscuits (cookies) and partake of a full English breakfast, which includes scones, clotted cream, crumpets, and smoked bacon. The heavily wooded property surrounding the contemporary house provides stunning mountain views and several hiking trails.

Among North Georgia's many state parks, several feature lodges or cabins. Amicalola Falls, Red Top Mountain, and Unicoi boast both; Black Rock Mountain, Cloudland Canyon, Fort Mountain, and Vogel offer cabins. Rental agencies and realtors are another good source for private rental cabins. **Georgia Mountain Madness Adult Resort Cabins** (Chimney Mountain Road, Helen, 706/878-2851) are rustic one- and two-bedroom cabins situated in heavily wooded grounds to guarantee privacy. Most feature fireplaces and whirlpools.

An exciting resort near Young Harris is the **Brasstown Valley Resort** (U.S. 76, Young Harris, 706/379-9900 or 800/201-3205). The main lodge has a lobby reminiscent of those built in the national parks at the turn of the century. Guest rooms include two wings of modern rooms and several cabins with four suites each. The resort boasts a championship golf course, tennis center, health spa, indoor/outdoor pool, and hiking trails.

The **Inn at Chateau Elan** (7000 Old Winder Highway at exit 48 off I-85, Braselton, 770/932-0900) was constructed in French Country style to complement the architecture of the winery. The guest rooms and suites are furnished in the same fashion. In addition to a European spa that offers health

FALLING WATERS

The mountains of North Georgia boast dozens of waterfalls that range from tiny cascades to thundering cataracts. Some are easily accessible, whereas others require a strenuous hike. Only a few are listed here.

Named for the Cherokee word for "tumbling waters," **Amicalola Falls**, GA 52, Dahlonega, 706/265-2885, is located in the state park of the same name and is considered one of the Seven Wonders of Georgia. At 729 feet, it is the tallest waterfall in the state and one of the highest in the East.

Anna Ruby Falls, GA 356, Sautee, 706/878-3574, www. rubyfalls.com, is actually a double falls created by Curtis and York Creeks, which flow parallel to each other and drop in side-by-side cascades. Curtis Falls plunges 150 feet; York Falls drops 50 feet.

Dukes Creek Falls, GA 348, 706/754-6221, is accessed via a one-mile hike downhill (which means an uphill return), it's but well worth the exertion to see the falls, which plummets 300 feet into a rocky gorge.

and beauty treatments, guests can enjoy several restaurants, as well as the golf course, tennis courts, and equestrian center.

An ideal place for families, the **Innsbruck Resort and Golf Club** (666 Bahn Innsbruck, Helen, 800/204-3536) is an all-suite property with accommodations running up to four bedrooms. Most suites feature kitchen facilities, a fireplace, and a whirlpool. The resort boasts a golf course, tennis courts, and swimming pools.

The premier resort in the North Georgia mountains is the **Barnsley Inn and Golf Resort and Barnsley Gardens** (597 Barnsley Gardens Road, Adairsville, 770/773-7480, barnsley@mindspring.com), located on a historic estate. Seventy exquisite guest suites are located in superbly furnished duplex cottages created to resemble English country cottages. Each cottage features a living room with a complete entertainment center and fireplace, a luxurious bedroom with a four-poster bed, and two comfortable porches. The resort also boasts an 18-hole golf course, a gourmet restaurant, a casual German beer garden, full spa facilities, a pool, and tennis courts.

CAMPING

The Chattahoochee National Forest offers more than 500 developed campsites. Primitive camping is allowed in much of the forest. For more information, contact the U.S. Forest Service, 508 Oak Street, N.W., Gainesville, GA 30501; 770/536-0541.

Georgia Power Company, the state's electric utility, maintains several lakes for hydroelectric generation. The company has developed several recreational areas around these lakes, some of which offer camping facilities. For information, contact Georgia Power Company at 404/506-3978. The U.S. Army Corps of Engineers also maintains several lakes and camping sites. To find out more, contact the U.S. Army Corps of Engineers, 30 Pryor Street, S.W., Atlanta, GA 30335; 404/562-5000.

For a complete list of parks and facilities, contact Georgia State Parks and Historic Sites, 1352 Floyd Tower East, 205 Butler Street, N.E., Atlanta, GA 30334; 800/3GA-PARK in Georgia or 800/864-7275 outside Georgia.

NIGHTLIFE

Most visitors to the crisp, clean air of the North Georgia mountains exert themselves all day in vigorous physical pursuits or exhaust themselves sight-seeing and shopping. So they're usually more than ready to turn in early.

For the rare traveler who yearns for even more to do, however, some nightlife options can be found. In Helen, some restaurants have live entertainment in the evenings. During September and October, Oktoberfest activities are held at the Fest Hall, with bands, dancing, and sing-alongs. Fasching is a Mardi Gras-like celebration in February or March.

Several counties prohibit the sale of liquor, so some small towns have no bars or evening entertainment. In fact, it's a good idea to bring your own alcoholic beverages when you visit the mountains.

Scenic Route: Blue Ridge Lake to Lake Burton

The town of Blue Ridge is a small, historic mountain community with numerous an-
tique and crafts shops, specialty stores, and restaurants. Stop at the Chamber
Welcome Center (off U.S. 76, Blue Ridge, 706/745-5789) and pick up the brochure
Backroads Driving Tours.

Blue Ridge is surrounded by campgrounds, rustic and deluxe cabins, and some
bed-and-breakfasts. **Blue Ridge Lake**, one of the lakes in the vast Tennessee
Valley Authority system, offers boating, fishing, swimming, and other watersports, as
well as camping and picnicking. The sprawlingChattahoochee National Forest surrounds the lake.

From Blue Ridge, take GA 60 southeast. South of Morganton, watch for the
signs to the **Chattahoochee National Fish Hatcher**y (706/838-4723), an interesting stop. Continue south to Suches, where you will turn north on GA 180. You will
be driving parallel to the Appalachian Trail, in case you want to stop and hike. Pass the
GA 348 intersection and look for signs to **Brasstown Bald** (706/745-6928) on the
GA 180 Spur. At 4,784 feet, this peak is the tallest in Georgia. From the summit you
can see four states: Georgia, North Carolina, Tennessee, and on a very clear day South

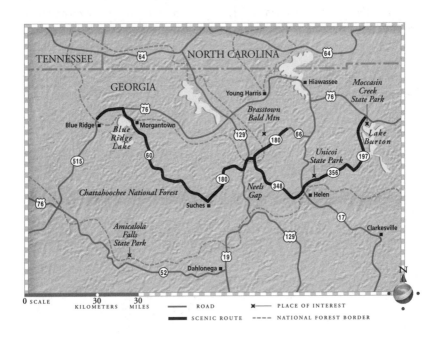

Carolina. You can drive most of the way to the top, then walk or take a shuttle van to the summit.

Retrace GA 180 Spur and GA 180 to GA 348 and turn south. GA 348, called the **Russell-Brasstown Scenic Highway**, offers some of Georgia's most spectacular scenery as it twists and turns, drops and climbs over mountainous terrain. Be on the lookout for wild animals—particularly deer—that come out of the woods and may cross the highway at dawn and dusk. Look for the signs to **Dukes Creek Falls** (706/754-6221). A steep, unpaved trail drops 300 feet to the base of the picturesque falls. But once you've seen and photographed the falls, it's all uphill on the way back.

Continue south on GA 348, and when the highway dead-ends into GA 75, turn north to **Helen**, the Bavarian village described in the North Georgia Mountains chapter. You can easily spend a day in Helen browsing through the specialty shops, visiting the **Museum of the Hills**, taking a carriage or trolley ride, sampling the German food, beer, and wine, and even panning for gold and gemstones. A short but rough side trip off GA 356 on unpaved Forest Service Road 44, and then a short hike, will take you to the base of **Horse Trough Falls** (706/754-6221). If you care to spend the night in Helen, the town offers dozens of pseudo-Bavarian motels, rustic cabins, the lodge at **Unicoi State Park** (706/878-2201), Innsbruck Resort, and several nearby bed-and-breakfasts.

Leave Helen via GA 356 to the northeast, which will take you past Unicoi State Park. Stop to see twin waterfalls at **Anna Ruby Falls** (706/878-3574, www.rubyfalls.com). The state park features a lodge, cabins, camping, swimming, fishing, tennis, hiking, and boating. Canoes and paddleboats are available to rent. Continue northeast on GA 356 to GA 197 and turn north. You will be skirting the western shores of **Lake Burton**, which offers close to 3,000 acres of water surface and 62 miles of shoreline. At the northern end of the lake is **Moccasin Creek State Park** (706/947-3194). The park, whose slogan is "where spring spends the summer," offers shady campsites, a boat dock and ramp, a fishing pier, and hiking trails.

3
AUGUSTA

One of Georgia's best-kept secrets, Augusta is a delightful town to visit over and over again. Most people know the small city as the home of the Master's Golf Tournament, but they may not know that Augusta bills itself as the Water Sports Capital of the South and sponsors several major boating competitions each year.

In the early days of Georgia, Augusta was the second most important settlement after Savannah and served as an outpost for the British. The settlement functioned as the capital of Georgia from 1783 to 1795. The canal and locks, built so that settlers in the interior could ship goods down the river to Savannah and get goods in return, still play an important part in community life.

Augusta enjoyed a long period around the turn of the century as a popular resort. Both coastal lowlanders and wealthy northerners discovered the city and made it a year-round haven. At that time, before vacationers discovered Florida, north-south railroad lines ended in Augusta. Remnants of that golden age of tourism can still be enjoyed today.

A PERFECT DAY IN AUGUSTA

Begin at the Old Cotton Exchange, once the center of business life in Augusta, which now serves as the welcome center. Stroll up the brick courtyard, past the fountains to Riverwalk, a bricked path along the top of the canal levee. Have lunch at the King George Pub in the courtyard for an authentic English

AUGUSTA

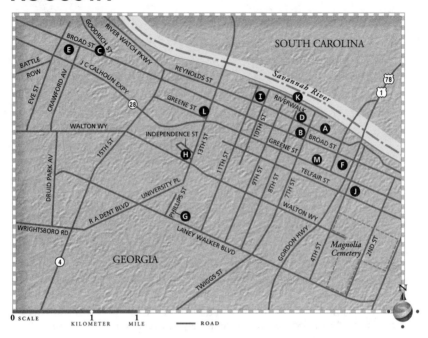

SIGHTS

- **A** Augusta-Richmond County Museum
- **B** Civil War Memorial
- **C** Confederate Powder Works
- **D** Cotton Exchange/Welcome Center
- **E** Ezekiel Harris House
- **F** Haunted Pillar
- **G** Lucy Craft Laney Museum and Conference Center
- **H** Meadow Garden
- **I** Morris Museum of Art
- **J** Olde Town Pinch Gut Historic District/Olde Town
- **K** Riverwalk/Takarazuka
- **L** Sacred Heart Cultural Center
- **M** Signer's Monument

meal. Browse through the shops of Cotton Row, then visit the Morris Museum of Art. Just a few blocks away is the new Augusta-Richmond County Museum, a repository of local historical artifacts. Drive to Meadow Garden, which was the home of one of Georgia's signers of the Declaration of Independence. In the evening, have an elegant Continental dinner at Michael's, then relax and listen to music or dance in the adjacent lounge.

SIGHTSEEING HIGHLIGHTS

★★★★ AUGUSTA-RICHMOND COUNTY MUSEUM
560 Reynolds Street, 706/722-8454
The city/county museum contains 23 major exhibits, including historical artifacts, an impressive collection of Civil War memorabilia, and a very popular train display.

Details: Tue–Sat 10–5, Sun 1–5. Tue–Sat $4 adults, $3 seniors and students, $2 children, free under 3; Sun half price. (1 hour)

★★★★ COTTON EXCHANGE/WELCOME CENTER
Eighth Street at Riverwalk, 706/724-4067
Augusta was once the second-largest inland cotton market in the world. Prices were tracked and deals made at the Cotton Exchange, an imposing building constructed in 1886. It is reported that the area between the building and the river was packed with so many cotton bales stacked on one another that a child could jump from bale to bale for more than a mile without ever stepping on the ground.

The rates you see posted on a chalkboard are the very ones that were left there on the last day of trading in the early 1900s. Also displayed are the original adding machines and other trading paraphernalia, as well as cotton planting, picking, weighing, and shipping equipment. You can take a horse-and-carriage tour of Augusta with Garden City Carriage Tours, 706/541-0811.

Details: Mon–Sat 9–5, Sun 1–5. Free. (1 hour)

★★★★ RIVERWALK/TAKARAZUKA
Main Eighth Street, 706/722-1071
Riverwalk is actually a gigantic canal-side park on a flood-prevention levee. The top of the levee is paved, and the sloping sides are lushly landscaped. An archway from the courtyard leads through the levee to a lower level of paths. Granite blocks in this archway record the levels of various floods that Augusta suffered before the levee was built. Along the upper walkway, placards tell the story of Augusta and the canal. Part of the complex is a Japanese garden called Takarazuka, an amphitheater, a children's playground, and numerous overlooks, benches, and picnic tables.

Details: Apr–Sept daily 8–8; Oct–Mar weekdays 11–3, weekends 10–4. (1 hour)

COTTON EXCHANGE/WELCOME CENTER

© Carol Thalimer

★★★ EZEKIEL HARRIS HOUSE
1822 Broad Street, 706/724-0436

Built in 1797 for a tobacco planter and merchant, the late-Georgian-era house with its gambrel roof and exterior stairs is furnished with eighteenth-century antiques.

Details: Tue–Fri 1–4, Sat 10–1. $2 adults, $1 seniors, 50 cents children. (1 hour)

★★★ MEADOW GARDEN
1320 Independence Drive, 706/724-4174

The home of one of Georgia's three signers of the Declaration of Independence, Meadow Garden was begun in 1794. Built in two stages, the simple, Colonial-style structure is furnished in modest pieces. You'll learn more about George Walton, the youngest signer of the famous document, who eventually became governor. Meadow Garden is not only the oldest documented house in Augusta, but it was also the first structure in the state to be preserved for historic reasons.

Details: Weekdays 10–4. $3 adults, $2 students ninth–twelfth grade, $1 kindergarten–eighth grade. (1 hour)

★★★ MORRIS MUSEUM OF ART
1 Tenth Street, 706/724-7501
Conveniently located along the Riverwalk, the Morris is the only museum in the country devoted exclusively to southern arts and artists. The museum has galleries devoted to antebellum portraiture, Civil War art, African American art, southern impressionism, and folk art.

Details: Tue–Sat 10–5:30, Sun 12:30–5:30. $3 adults, $2 seniors and students, free under 6 with an adult. (1 hour)

★★ CIVIL WAR MEMORIAL
Broad and Seventh Streets
It seems that every southern town has a Civil War memorial, and most of them look as if they were carved using the same model. Augusta is no exception to the tradition, but this city's monument is unique. It honors the common foot soldier, placing him at the top of a column and situating officers around the bottom.

Details: (15 minutes)

★★ CONFEDERATE POWDER WORKS
Augusta Canal at Goodrich Street
Although it was not built as a monument, a gigantic, 176-foot chimney serves as the only reminder left of a structure commissioned by the Confederacy. During only three years of operation, the munitions factory produced 2.3 million pounds of gunpowder. A plaque identifies the chimney "as a fitting monument to the dead heroes who sleep on the unnumbered battlefields of the South."

Details: (15 minutes)

★★ HAUNTED PILLAR
Fifth and Broad Streets
The site was once a market, and a preacher was denied permission to preach there. He cursed the market, and later it was destroyed by a tornado except for this one column.

Details: (15 minutes)

★★ LUCY CRAFT LANEY MUSEUM AND CONFERENCE CENTER
1116 Phillips Street, 706/724-3576
Laney, who was born a slave, later graduated from Atlanta University

and became an educator. She started the first kindergarten for blacks and the first nurse training class for blacks and established her own school, the Haines Institute, where she educated thousands.

Details: Weekdays 9–1, weekends by appointment only. $2 adults, 75 cents children. (1 hour)

★★ OLDE TOWN PINCH GUT HISTORIC DISTRICT/ OLDE TOWN

This historic residential neighborhood exhibits many of the architectural styles that were popular at the turn of the century. Take special notice of the unusually shaped rooflines and the intricate gingerbread trim on the porches. This area got its unusual name from the corsets women wore when the neighborhood was new.

Details: (1 hour)

★★ SACRED HEART CULTURAL CENTER
1301 Greene Street, 706/826-4700

Once a Catholic church that was deconsecrated as citizens left downtown for the suburbs, the structure was threatened with demolition but was saved and restored by concerned citizens. Today it houses offices of the ballet, symphony, theater, and other cultural groups, and is used for special events. Walk around the outside to admire the twin, tin-roofed spires and challenge yourself to find the 15 ornate patterns in the brickwork. Inside, stained-glass windows cast colorful shadows on the carved white Italian marble.

Details: Weekdays 9–5. Donations requested. (1/2 hour)

★★ SIGNER'S MONUMENT
Greene and Gwinnett Streets

Georgia's three signers of the Declaration of Independence are honored here.

Details: (15 minutes)

FITNESS AND RECREATION

Just as it has done for more than 100 years, the towpath along the nine-mile Augusta Canal provides opportunities for biking, hiking, fishing, bird-watching, and nature studies. Canoeing is popular on the canal, and a canoe portage is located between the Savannah River and the canal, which is designated as a National Historic Landmark. The Savannah Rapids Park, located on the river adjacent to the canal, offers a breathtaking view of the rapids from an 80-foot bluff that overlooks the Augusta River and the canal. Take advantage of a new improved children's park and ample opportunities for canoeing, fishing, walking, and bicycling. The canal's head gates are pre–Civil War. The old pavilion and other sites along the canal are to be restored as part of the National Heritage Corridor. Details: 3300 Evans-to-Lock Road, Augusta; 706/868-3349.

A very few will be lucky enough to get tickets to see the Master's Golf Tournament. If you are one of the lucky ones, make hotel reservations far in advance by contacting the Master's Housing Bureau, P.O. Box 211416, Augusta; 800/626-8258.

For the rest of us, plenty of other spectator sports are available. One of the most popular annual activities is the Augusta Futurity, the largest cutting horse tournament east of the Mississippi and one of the 10 largest in the world. For more information, call 706/724-0851. March brings the Augusta Invitational Rowing Regatta, where top rowing teams from around the world compete in light- and heavyweight classes. RegattaFest activities occur simultaneously. In June, the city gears up for River Race Augusta, the premier event of the Outboard Grand Prix Series. The Augusta Southern Nationals Dragboat Race follows this race in July. Call the Port Authority at 706/724-4148 for more information about these races. It's a good idea to make lodging reservations far in advance for these events as well. As if all this activity isn't enough, Augusta also has a minor-league baseball team, the Augusta Green Jackets, who play at Lake Olmstead Stadium. Call 706/736-7889 for information.

FOOD

Located in the historic Partridge Inn, the **Dining Room** (2110 Walton Way, 706/737-8888) offers a romantic, gracious, southern-plantation ambience to accompany its excellent dishes of beef, fish, and fowl. A fireplace and wide verandas add to the appeal. Live jazz is performed on weekend evenings.

Michael's (2860 Washington Road, 706/733-2860) is a popular meet-and-greet restaurant in Augusta. Its unpretentious exterior and its location along a commercial strip belie its coolly elegant interior and fine French and continental cuisine. Rack of lamb is the signature dish.

Voted the best restaurant in Augusta for four straight years, the **French Market Grill** (425 Highland Avenue, 706/737-4865) specializes in Louisiana cuisine. Among its other offerings are American wines, imported beers, and an oyster bar. Dress is casual and the atmosphere is lively.

AUGUSTA

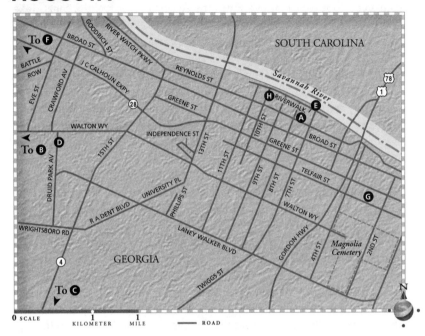

FOOD

- Ⓐ Cotton Row Café
- Ⓑ Dining Room
- Ⓒ Fort Gordon Dinner Theater
- Ⓓ French Market Grill
- Ⓔ King George Pub
- Ⓕ Michael's

LODGING

- Ⓖ Azalea Inn
- Ⓑ Partridge Inn
- Ⓗ Radisson Riverfront Hotel

Note: Items with the same letter are located in the same area.

All the details you'd expect to encounter at an English pub, right down to the red telephone booth, are found at the **King George Pub** (2 Eighth Street, 706/724-4755) located between the Cotton Exchange and the Riverwalk along Cotton Row. As you'd also expect, you can dine on shepherd's pie, bangers and mash, a ploughman's lunch, and a variety of ales. Another casual eatery nearby is the **Cotton Row Café**

(2 Riverwalk/Eighth Street, 706/828-2100), where you can get a variety of sandwiches, burgers, and appetizers. When the weather's nice, you can eat outside and watch the children (and some adults) play in the Riverwalk fountain. In the evenings, sporting events are shown on the restaurant's big-screen TV, and entertainment is provided on weekends. Reservations are not accepted.

Fort Gordon Dinner Theater (Fort Gordon Performing Arts Center) offers five to six productions throughout the year. For a good meal and entertainment all wrapped into one, this venue is the place to go. Call 706/793-8552 for reservations and show times.

LODGING

Listed on the National Register of Historic Places and one of only five Georgia properties in the National Trust for Historic Preservation's *Historic Hotels of America*, the sprawling, Victorian-style **Partridge Inn** (2110 Walton Way, 706/737-8888 or 800/476-6888) began life in 1879 as a private home. It grew over the next 100 years to become one of the country's first all-suite hotels. Today, painstakingly restored and beautifully furnished with period reproductions, it operates as a bed-and-breakfast with both suites and guest rooms. Among its many attractions, the hotel offers a quarter mile of wicker-filled verandas and private balconies, as well as a swimming pool and a fine restaurant.

Located in the Old Town Historic District, the **Azalea Inn** (312 Greene Street, 706/724-3454, www.theazaleainn.com) is made up of a group of Victorian houses. Some of the 21 guest rooms offer whirlpool baths and fireplaces, and they all have king- or queen-size beds. The inn is within walking distance of Riverwalk and many downtown attractions. If you'd rather stay in a modern hotel, you couldn't do better than to choose the **Radisson Riverfront Hotel** (2 Tenth Street, 706/722-8900), located on Riverwalk, across from the Morris Museum of Art and within walking distance of all the downtown attractions. The hotel has a pool, restaurant, and lounge.

CAMPING

A. H. Stephens State Park in nearby Crawfordville (706/456-2602) offers not only campsites but also two lakes, several picnic pavilions, hiking trails including the six-mile Beaver Lodge Trail, the Liberty Hall mansion, and a Civil War museum.

NIGHTLIFE

Augusta is a quiet town with a moderate amount of live entertainment during the week. Downtown, the place to go for dinner or a drink accompanied by jazz is the Word of Mouth Café, 724 Broad Street, 706/722-3477, voted the Best Late-Night Spot by, of all things, the Augusta Symphony. Joe's Underground Café (Eighth and Broad Streets, 706/724-9457) offers music nightly, and its kitchen is always open. Voted the Best Dance Club in Augusta, the Baha Club (Washington Road, 706/738-1079) is a perpetual party.

The Augusta Symphony (706/826-4705) performs 22 concerts a year at Bell Auditorium and Augusta State University Performing Arts Theater. Other performing arts groups include the Garden City Chorus. Check with your concierge for more information.

4
SAVANNAH

Savannah was the birthplace of Georgia. With a land grant, General James Oglethorpe founded the settlement on the Yamacraw Bluff of the Savannah River in 1733. It was the first planned community in America, laid out by Oglethorpe in a grid pattern with 24 parks.

Twenty-two of those original parks, now shrouded by gigantic, moss-draped live oaks and surrounded by stately homes and businesses, make up the core of Savannah's 2.2-square-mile National Historic Landmark District, one of the largest in the country. Although Savannah has enjoyed significant volumes of tourism for years, John Berendt's book *Midnight in the Garden of Good and Evil* has given the city almost cultlike status. Adding to the appeal, the city hosts the second-largest St. Patrick's Day celebration in the country. (Book reservations far ahead if you want to stay anywhere near Savannah for St. Patrick's Day.)

Known variously as the Queen City of the South and the Hostess City of the South, Savannah is a significant port that serves as a gateway to the Golden Isles—Georgia's dozen jewel-like barrier islands. The name Golden Isles derives from the color of the sandy beaches. Each island has a completely different personality. Some are major resort destinations, whereas others are undeveloped wildlife refuges with limited access by ferry and strict regulations on tourism. Several were or are privately owned and offer limited accommodations.

SAVANNAH

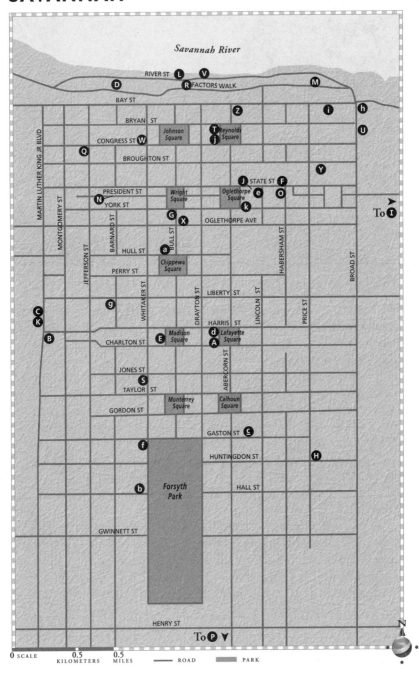

Savannah River

RIVER ST · L · V

D · R · FACTORS WALK · M · i · h

BAY ST · U

MARTIN LUTHER KING JR BLVD

BRYAN ST · Z

CONGRESS ST · W · Johnson Square · T · Reynolds Square · j

Q

BROUGHTON ST

Y

MONTGOMERY ST · PRESIDENT ST · J · STATE ST · F

N · YORK ST · Wright Square · Oglethorpe Square · e · O

BARNARD ST · k

G · X · OGLETHORPE AVE

JEFFERSON ST · BULL ST · HABERSHAM ST · BROAD ST

HULL ST · a

PERRY ST · Chippewa Square

WHITAKER ST · DRAYTON ST · LIBERTY ST · LINCOLN ST · PRICE ST

g

HARRIS ST

C · K

B · E · Madison Square · d · Lafayette Square

CHARLTON ST · A · ABERCORN ST

JONES ST

S

TAYLOR ST

GORDON ST · Monterrey Square · Calhoun Square

GASTON ST · c

f · HUNTINGDON ST · H

Forsyth Park

b · HALL ST

GWINNETT ST

HENRY ST

To P

0 SCALE · 0.5 KILOMETERS · 0.5 MILES · ROAD · PARK

To I

N

A PERFECT DAY IN SAVANNAH AND THE GOLDEN ISLES

Begin at the Central of Georgia Railroad Station, an 1860 depot, which now houses the Georgia Visitors Center and Savannah History Museum. Then go next door to the Central of Georgia Railroad Roundhouse, an antebellum repair shop that is still in use.

You can leave your car at the visitors center and depart from there on numerous guided tours—by van, trolley, or horse and carriage. As an alternative, for a top-quality self-guided tour, rent a tape from Tours on Tape, available at 313 Abercorn Street, 912/232-0582. If you're hungry, make a beeline for Mrs. Wilkes' Boarding House on Jones Street for a hearty southern lunch served family-style.

After lunch, spend some time visiting several of Savannah's historic houses. Finish the afternoon by strolling along River Street, Riverwalk Plaza, and Factors Walk, where you'll find dozens of shops, boutiques, restaurants, and bars.

Dine at award-winning Elizabeth on 37th Street, then wind down the evening by relaxing with a nightcap and entertainment at Hard-hearted

SIGHTS

- **A** Andrew Low House
- **B** Central of Georgia Railroad Roundhouse Complex
- **C** Central of Georgia Railroad Station/Georgia Visitors Center
- **D** Factors Walk/River Street
- **E** Green-Meldrim Mansion
- **F** Isaiah Davenport House Museum
- **G** Juliette Gordon Low Girl Scout National Center
- **H** King-Tisdell Cottage
- **I** Old Fort Jackson
- **J** Owens-Thomas House and Museum

SIGHTS *(continued)*

- **K** Savannah History Museum
- **L** *Savannah River Queen*
- **M** Ships of the Sea Maritime Museum
- **N** Telfair Academy of Arts and Sciences

FOOD

- **O** 17 Hundred 90 Inn
- **P** Elizabeth on 37th
- **Q** Garibaldi's
- **R** Huey's
- **S** Mrs. Wilkes Boarding House
- **T** Olde Pink House
- **U** Pirates' House
- **V** River House
- **W** Sapphire Grill

LODGING

- **X** Ballastone Inn
- **Y** Broughton Street Inn
- **Z** East Bay Inn
- **a** Foley House Inn
- **b** Forsyth Park Inn
- **c** The Gastonian
- **d** Hamilton-Turner Inn
- **e** Kehoe House
- **f** Magnolia Place
- **g** Manor House
- **h** Mulberry Inn
- **i** Olde Harbour Inn
- **j** Planters Inn
- **k** Presidents' Quarters
- **l** River Street Inn

Note: Items with the same letter are located in the same area.

Hannah's, where the famous Emma Kelly, "the lady of six thousand songs," often plays and sings.

SIGHTSEEING HIGHLIGHTS: SAVANNAH

★★★★ CENTRAL OF GEORGIA RAILROAD ROUNDHOUSE COMPLEX
601 West Harris Street, 912/651-6823
Railroad buffs will love this attraction. It was built before the Civil War and is still in use, which makes it the oldest and most complete antebellum locomotive repair shop in America. Thirteen structures include the roundhouse and turntable and a 125-foot smokestack. Among the exhibits are two of the oldest surviving steam engines in the country, antique repair machinery, and various pieces of antique rolling stock.
Details: Daily 10–4. $2.50 adults, $2 children. (1 hour)

★★★★ CENTRAL OF GEORGIA RAILROAD STATION/GEORGIA VISITORS CENTER
301 Martin Luther King Boulevard, 912/944-0455
Located in an old railroad depot on the site of the 1779 siege of Savannah, the visitors center offers an audiovisual presentation, brochures, and advice about attractions, lodgings, and restaurants. Tour companies pick up passengers from the visitors center as well.
Details: Weekdays 8:30–5, weekends 9–5. Free. (1 hour)

★★★★ FACTORS WALK/RIVER STREET
Along the Savannah River are large, late-nineteenth–century commercial buildings that served as warehouses and offices for the cotton brokers, called factors. On the land side of the buildings, the steep cobblestone street is called Factors Walk. On the river side, the street is appropriately called River Street.

Along River Street, a brick esplanade dotted with benches, plantings, and fountains creates **Riverwalk Plaza**, where many festivals are held throughout the year. At the far end of the plaza is the **Waving Girl Statue**, which memorializes Florence Martus, who lost her lover at sea and waved to every ship that came in and out of the harbor for more than 40 years hoping he would return. The buildings along River Street and Factors Walk have been refurbished to house shops, galleries, restaurants, nightspots, museums, and two bed-and-breakfasts. From River Street, you can also embark on a sightseeing cruise.

Details: (2–3 hours)

★★★★ SAVANNAH HISTORY MUSEUM
303 Martin Luther King Boulevard, 912/238-1779
Located in the same building as the visitors center, the museum traces Savannah's past with exhibits such as an 1890 steam locomotive, a cotton gin (invented by Eli Whitney in Savannah), and artifacts from Savannah's wars. An audiovisual presentation describes the Siege of Savannah.

Details: Daily, including holidays, 8:30–5. $2.98 adults, $2.55 seniors, $2.13 children. Includes movie and museum. (2 hours)

★★★ ANDREW LOW HOUSE
329 Abercorn Street, 912/233-6854
When Juliette Gordon, who later founded the Girl Scouts of America, married, she came here to live in the home of her father-in-law, Andrew Low. Built in 1848, the house shows West Indian influences, with stucco-over-brick construction, elaborate ironwork, and jalousied porches. It was from this house that Juliette Gordon Low founded the girl's organization in 1912.

Details: Mon–Sat 10:30–4 (last tour begins 3:30), Sun noon–4, closed Thu. $7 adults, $4.50 children. (1 hour)

★★★ ISAIAH DAVENPORT HOUSE MUSEUM
324 East State Street, 912/236-8097
Restoration of this Federal-style house, which was built by master builder Isaiah Davenport somewhere between 1815 and 1820, was the first preservation project of the Historic Savannah Foundation. Among architectural details to admire are delicate plasterwork, Ionic Tuscan columns, and a gorgeous, elliptical, spiraling, open-well, cantilevered staircase. Among the period furnishings are genuine Chippendale pieces. A hit with visitors of all ages is a collection of nineteenth-century dolls.

Details: Daily 10–4, Sun 1–4. $5. (1 hour)

★★★ JULIETTE GORDON LOW GIRL SCOUT NATIONAL CENTER
142 Bull Street, 912/233-4501

Built in 1820, this beautiful, Regency-style home was the birthplace of Girl Scout founder Juliette Gordon Low. The house, which has been restored to the period of her childhood (1860 to 1886), boasts Egyptian Revival and classic detailing. Many of the furnishings are original to the family, as are Low's art collection and personal memorabilia.

Details: Mon–Sat 10–4, Sun 12:30–4:30, closed Wed. $6 adults, $5 students. (1 hour)

★★★ KING-TISDELL COTTAGE
514 East Huntingdon Street, 912/234-8000

Noted for intricate gingerbread ornamentation on the porch and dormers, the charming cottage was built in 1896. Today it is used as a museum where African American art and historical objects are displayed. Pick up the brochure Negro Heritage Trail, which describes three walking or driving tours.

Details: By appointment only. $3.50. (1 hour)

★★★ *SAVANNAH RIVER QUEEN*
9 East River Street, 912/232-6404

A jaunty replica of a paddle wheeler, the ship makes sightseeing cruises along the river during the day and evening as well as dinner cruises.

Details: Departure times and sightseeing prices vary seasonally. Dinner cruises $13.95 adults, $8.50 children. (1–2 hours)

★★★ TELFAIR ACADEMY OF ARTS AND SCIENCES
121 Barnard Street, 912/232-1177

The stunning structure was designed by architect William Jay. The Octagon Room and the Rotunda Gallery are most impressive. The building is now a museum, displaying art from the eighteenth and nineteenth centuries.

Details: Tue–Sat 10–5, Sun 1–5. $6 adults, $5 seniors and AAA members, $2 college students with I.D., $1 children, free under 6. (2 hours)

★★ GREEN-MELDRIM MANSION
14 West Macon Street, 912/233-3845

This house, Savannah's finest example of Gothic Revival architecture, features a wraparound covered porch and ornate ironwork on the exterior. The interior displays black walnut woodwork, stucco-duro crown moldings, silver-plated doorknobs and hardware, marble mantels, and oriel windows. William Tecumseh Sherman commandeered the house when he occupied Savannah at the end of his march from Atlanta. At his orders, Savannah was not destroyed. Today the house is the Parish House of St. John's Church.

Details: Tue, Thu, Fri, Sat 10–4. $5 adults, $2 children. (1 hour)

★★ OLD FORT JACKSON
1 Fort Jackson Road, 2 miles east of Savannah off President Street Extension, 912/232-3945

The remnants of the original fort, located at a strategic point on the Savannah River, has 13 exhibit areas. The arched rooms were designed to bear the weight of heavy cannons mounted above them. On special occasions, a massive, 32-pound cannon is discharged.

Details: Daily 9–5. $2.50 adults; $2 seniors, students, military, and children; free 6 and under. (1 hour)

★★ OWENS–THOMAS HOUSE AND MUSEUM
124 Abercorn Street, 912/233-9743

Start your tour with a short film in the carriage house, which used to be part of this historic home's slave quarters, then move on to view the house and gardens. Completed in 1819, the house was built for cotton merchant Richard Richardson and is filled with period antiques and furnishings. The lovely estate is part of the Telfair Museum.

Details: Tue–Sat 10–5. $8 adults, $2 children 6–12. (^{1}/$_2$–1 hour)

★★ SHIPS OF THE SEA MARITIME MUSEUM
41 Martin Luther King Jr. Blvd., 912/232-1511

An immense collection of models and memorabilia—from Viking ships to nuclear-powered vessels—traces Savannah and worldwide maritime history. The museum is located in a beautiful historic mansion with formal gardens in the rear.

Details: Tue–Sun 10–5. $5 adults, $4 students and children. (1 hour)

SIGHTSEEING HIGHLIGHTS: GOLDEN ISLES REGION

★★★★ CUMBERLAND ISLAND NATIONAL SEASHORE
912/882-4335

The most precious gem among the barrier islands, Cumberland was designated a national seashore in 1971. The island is a haven for wild horses, deer, armadillos, birds, and other wildlife. Access is only by ferry, and visitors, whether they be day-trippers or campers, are limited to 300 per day and must have reservations.

No vehicles are allowed on the island with the exception of a few owned by the National Park Service. So be prepared to walk everywhere—to the remaining mansions, the pristine, 18-mile-long beach, or a distant campsite. No stores are permitted either, so bring everything you need with you.

One Carnegie family home has been transformed into the Greyfield Inn, 904/261-6408, an exclusive hotel where all meals and activities are included in the price. It gained national attention several years ago when John F. Kennedy Jr.'s party stayed here for his secret wedding. You can reach the inn by a private ferry. Another home, Plum Orchard, is open the first Sunday of the month for tours.

Details: *For ferry reservations and information about Plum Orchard, call Georgia National Park Service at 912/882-4335. Round-trip ferry $10 adults, $8 seniors, $6 children 12 and under; additional $6 for Plum Orchard tour. $4 per person usage fee. (full day)*

★★★★ JEKYLL ISLAND CLUB HISTORIC LANDMARK DISTRICT
Stable Road, Jekyll Island, 912/635-2762

Between 1886 and 1942, the island was owned by 100 millionaires and restricted to their exclusive use as a winter hunting retreat. An opulent, rambling Victorian clubhouse was built and used for communal dining and social activities. Most of the millionaires built their own "cottages"—actually large mansions of up to 8,000-square feet—but a few simply took rooms in the clubhouse. Many of the cottages, which ranged in style from informal shingle to Italian Renaissance, had no kitchens because everyone ate at the club. The millionaires added golf courses, tennis courts, a swimming pool, and other recreational facilities.

They eventually sold the entire island to the state of Georgia, rather than selling it piecemeal to developers, thereby saving the historic buildings from destruction. The restoration of what is known as the Millionaires District—240 acres and 25 buildings—has become one of the biggest preservation and restoration projects in the country. Guided tram tours are given daily with admission to several of the houses. The clubhouse is an operating hotel.

Details: *Tours daily 9–5 except Christmas and New Years Day. Guided tours $10 adults, $6 students 6–18. (2 hours)*

★★★ THE CLOISTER
100 First Street, Sea Island, 912/638-3611 or 800/732-4752
Practically the entire Sea Island is occupied by one fabulous resort, The Cloister, Georgia's only five-star, five-diamond (AAA rating) property. The rest of the island contains upscale residential neighborhoods. Built in 1946, the resort sits on 10,000 acres of beautifully landscaped, park-like grounds and offers five miles of private shoreline.

Details: *(1 hour–full day)*

★★★ FORT PULASKI NATIONAL MONUMENT
U.S. 80, 912/786-5787
Named for Revolutionary War General Casimir Pulaski, the fort was constructed between 1829 and the mid-1840s and was used to guard the Savannah coast and city. Although Confederates thought the fort impregnable, the Union's new rifled artillery forced them to surrender the fort in less than 30 hours. Well preserved, the fort features towering walls, a drawbridge, and two moats.

Details: *Daily 8:30–5:15. $2 adults, free 16 and under. (1 hour)*

★★★ ST. SIMONS ISLAND
The largest of the Golden Isles, it is also the most developed. St. Simons does have some historical attractions, however. Most popular is the **Lighthouse and Museum of Coastal History** at 101 12th Street (912/638-4666). Hardy souls can climb 129 steps to the top of the light for a spectacular view. The museum, located in the old keeper's cottage, contains a gallery with information about the coastal area. Rooms replicate a keeper's dwelling.

Also on the island, the **Fort Frederica National Monument** (Frederica Road, 912/638-3639) is the remnants of an eighteenth-century fort. Guided trolley tours of the island are available and include a stop at Christ Church. Contact 649 Dellwood Avenue, 912/638-8954.

Details: *(3 hours)*

★★ LITTLE ST. SIMONS ISLAND
If you want to get away from it all, this island is the place to do it—no

radios, TVs, or newspapers are available and only a few resort vehicles are allowed. The unspoiled, privately owned, 10,000-acre island offers 6 miles of undeveloped beach and a wide variety of wildlife. The historic main lodge and four newer guest houses accommodate 30 overnight guests, who are transported to the island by private boat. Activities for these guests include horseback riding, fishing, swimming, boccie ball, horseshoes, and canoeing. A limited number of day-trippers are allowed on the island as well in the summer.

Details: *For information write to P.O. Box 21078, St. Simons, or call 912/638-7472. (1 or more days)*

★★ MIGHTY EIGHTH AIR FORCE MUSEUM
175 Bourne Avenue, Pooler, 912/748-8888
The mighty Eighth Air Force was created in Savannah in 1942, and this museum honors the more than one million men and women who have served in the unit.

Details: *Daily 10–6. $7.50 adults, $5.50 children 6–12, free 5 and under. (2 hours)*

★★ TYBEE ISLAND
Off U.S. 80
Located close to Savannah, this family-oriented island has a 1950s ambience with cottages and low-rise motels. The island also offers shops, mom-and-pop restaurants, nightspots, an amusement park, and a water slide. Guided tours are available of the 154-foot **Tybee Lighthouse** (912/786-5801, www.savannahgeorgia.com/tybeelight/), built in 1887. An adjacent museum (912/786-4077) displays lighthouse artifacts.

Adjacent to the lighthouse is **Fort Screven** (912/786-5917), built in 1875 and manned during the Spanish-American War and World Wars I and II. Relics from pre-colonial times through World War II are displayed in the bastioned vaults. Other exhibits contain memorabilia from the island's resort era in the 1920s and 1930s and a collection of dolls.

Details: *(2 hours)*

FITNESS AND RECREATION
Savannah's historic district is so compact that you can walk to all the attractions and eateries. If you want more strenuous exercise, the Savannah Striders

Club has mapped out 5-, 8-, and 10-kilometer routes around the city. Maps are available at the visitors center.

The Golden Isles and their beaches provide many opportunities for walking, bicycling, horseback riding, and nature studies. You can play tennis and golf at the big resorts and on public courts and courses as well. Surf and deep-sea fishing, sailing, windsurfing, sea kayaking, and other water sports are very popular. A fine trap-and-skeet range is located on Sea Island. Horseback riding is available on St. Simons and Little St. Simons. Skidaway Island State Park (Diamond Causeway, Savannah; 912/598-2301) offers a swimming pool, fishing, picnicking, a boat ramp, water-skiing, and nature trails. One trail and campgrounds and picnic sites have ADA (wheelchair) access. For information on the parks and resorts call 912/598-2300 or fax to 912/598-2365.

If you're interested in organized activity, Wilderness Southeast (746 Wheaten Street, 912/897-5108) is an outdoor school that provides guided tours. Several companies offer kayaking and nature tours.

FOOD

Renowned chef Elizabeth Terry researched both eighteenth- and nineteenth-century Savannah cuisine to create the menus for **Elizabeth on 37th** (105 East 37th Street, 912/236-5547) and came up with dishes such as southern-fried grits with country ham, Georgia goat-cheese salad, and barbecued quail with Savannah red rice. Desserts such as Savannah cream cake are to die for. The restaurant, named one of the top 25 in the country by *Food & Wine,* is located in a sumptuous turn-of-the-century mansion.

The stone floors, exposed brick walls, walk-in brick fireplaces, and low-beamed ceilings of the original kitchens create intimate dining rooms on the lower level of the **17 Hundred 90 Inn** (301 East President Street, 912/236-7122 or 800/487-1790). The award-winning restaurant serves continental cuisine.

You'll find an Old South ambience at the **Olde Pink House** (23 Abercorn Street, 912/232-4286), in addition to southern specialties such as crispy scored flounder, black grouper stuffed with blue crab sauce, Vidalia onion cream sauce, and crispy roast duck with wild berry sauce. Built in 1771, the gracious old house looks pink because the red brick bleeds through the white plaster walls. Dine in the lovely, colonial-style main room or several smaller rooms. Reservations are recommended. Before dinner enjoy a drink in the cozy Planter's Tavern downstairs, one of the most popular places in the city for gathering and listening to music. Entire menu is also served in the tavern.

GOLDEN ISLES REGION

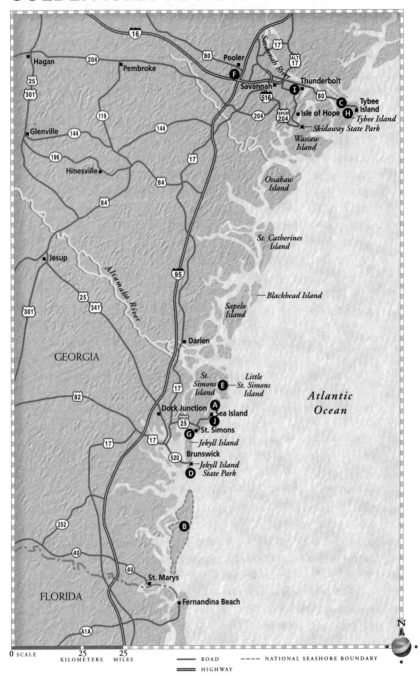

Hagan

Pembroke

Pooler

Savannah River

Thunderbolt

Savannah

Isle of Hope

Tybee Island

Tybee Island

Skidaway State Park

Wassaw Island

Glenville

Ossabaw Island

Hinesville

St. Catherines Island

Jesup

Altamaha River

Blackhead Island

Sapelo Island

GEORGIA

Darien

St. Simons Island

Little St. Simons Island

Dock Junction

Sea Island

St. Simons

Jekyll Island

Brunswick

Jekyll Island State Park

Atlantic Ocean

St. Marys

FLORIDA

Fernandina Beach

N

0 SCALE   25   25
KILOMETERS   MILES

———— ROAD   − − − NATIONAL SEASHORE BOUNDARY

═══ HIGHWAY

Located in the old 1871 Germania firehouse, **Garibaldi's** (315 West Congress Street, 912/232-7118) features pressed-tin ceilings, gilt mirrors, and lots of candlelight. Seafood and veal have an Italian emphasis. Among the standout menu items are a seafood-and-veal combination plate and duck Garibaldi.

The **Pirates' House** (20 East Broad Street, 912/233-5757) is located in one of the oldest buildings in Savannah, constructed in 1734. It even has tunnels—said to have been used by pirates. The rambling structure contains 23 small dining rooms where patrons enjoy seafood specialties.

For a simple down-home breakfast or lunch served family-style, you can't beat **Mrs. Wilkes Boarding House** (107 West Jones Street, 912/232-5997), where Sema Wilkes has been serving locals and visitors since the 1940s. Portions are gigantic, and the food is strictly southern: stewed greens, black-eyed peas, fried chicken, barbecue, and so forth for lunch; eggs, sausage, grits, and biscuits for breakfast. Reservations and credit cards are not accepted, and the house is closed the first two weeks in July. For a casual breakfast or light meal with a Cajun/Creole flair, drop in at **Huey's** (115 River Street, 912/234-7385). The breakfast beignets (square donuts covered with powdered sugar) are just as good as those found in New Orleans. Other Louisiana specialties include po' boys and red beans and rice.

Enjoy the elegant and innovative seasonal cuisine of Chef Chris Nason at the **Sapphire Grill,** located near the City Market, 110 W. Congress St., 912/443-9962. An extensive wine list complements the wide variety of fresh seafood, veal, lamb, and beef dishes. This instant hit was voted Georgia's best new restaurant by *Georgia Magazine*.

SIGHTS
Ⓐ The Cloister
Ⓑ Cumberland Island National Seashore
Ⓒ Fort Pulaski National Monument
Ⓓ Jekyll Island Club Historic Landmark District
Ⓔ Little St. Simons Island
Ⓕ Mighty Eighth Air Force Museum
Ⓖ St. Simons Island
Ⓗ Tybee Island

FOOD
Ⓖ Blanche's Courtyard
Ⓗ Breakfast Club
Ⓐ The Cloister
Ⓓ Jekyll Island Club
Ⓘ River's End

LODGING
Ⓐ The Cloister
Ⓑ Greyfield Inn
Ⓓ Jekyll Island Club
Ⓙ King and Prince

Note: Items with the same letter are located in the same area.

If you're near the river, try the **River House** (125 West River Street, 912/234-1900), which occupies a converted warehouse. The decor is dark wood and brick, and menu items range from seafood and steak to chicken and pasta. The on-site bakery provides freshly baked bread and desserts to eat with meals or take home. You can get even closer to the river at **River's End** (3122 River Drive, Thunderbolt, 912/354-2973), an elegant restaurant in Thunderbolt on Wilmington Island. Located next to the marina, the restaurant is a perfect place from which to watch shrimp- and pleasure-boat traffic while savoring fresh fish and shellfish as well as veal, lamb, and duck.

Savannah doesn't have all the good restaurants, however. One of the most glorious meals to which you can ever treat yourself is at **The Cloister** on Sea Island (100 First Street, Sea Island, 912/638-3611 or 800/732-4752). One of the last bastions of formality, the resort requires that men and boys wear a jacket and tie in the dining room. Outstanding continental cuisine is served in the striking Grand Dining Room at the **Jekyll Island Club** (371 Riverview Drive, Jekyll Island, 912/635-2600).

For Cajun-flavored seafood and steak served in the atmosphere of Victorian New Orleans, dine at **Blanche's Courtyard** on St. Simons Island (440 Kings Way, St. Simons, 912/638-3030). Big-band entertainment pleases patrons on weekends. Down-home and casual, the **Breakfast Club** on Tybee Island (1500 Butler Avenue, Tybee Island, 912/786-5984) has been a fixture for years. Watch breakfast or lunch being prepared from the observation kitchen.

LODGING

Savannah boasts so many exquisite places to stay that it's hard to narrow them down to only a few recommendations. The city has more than 25 elegant bed-and-breakfasts—the most in any one city in Georgia—and several intimate inns. The **Ballastone Inn** (14 East Oglethorpe Avenue, 912/236-1484 or 800/822-4553), one of the city's most sumptuous B&Bs, occupies a four-story Regency mansion built in 1838. It was named for the stones used to construct streets and foundations in early Savannah. Twenty-two rooms and suites are elegantly furnished with different themes, and some boast fireplaces and hot tubs. Another elegant bed-and-breakfast, **The Gastonian** (220 East Gaston Street, 912/232-2869 or 800/322-6603) occupies two connected Regency-Italianate townhouses built around 1868 and a separate carriage house. The 13 rooms and suites are furnished with high-quality Georgian and Regency antiques. Every room has a canopy bed or an elaborately carved four-poster rice bed. All units feature fireplaces and some also offer terraces and hot tubs. Built in 1892, the

Kehoe House (123 Habersham Street, 912/232-1020 or 800/820-1020) is a stately brick B&B on Columbia Square. The 15 rooms and suites are luxuriantly decorated and furnished with antiques. A full-time concierge and on-site chef elevate this B&B to the level of a fine European inn.

The **Hamilton-Turner Inn** (330 Abercorn Street on Lafayette Square, 912/233-1833, www.hamilton-turnerinn.com) is a showplace B&B and a superb example of Second Empire style. The house was built for Samuel Pugh Hamilton in 1873 and is reputed to have a ghost. Museum-quality furnishings on the first floor are original to the house.

A sister property to the Ballastone Inn, the **Manor House** (201 West Liberty Street, 912/233-9597 or 800/462-3595) offers all-suite accommodations in a historic single house. Most suites feature a large sitting room in addition to a bedroom, fireplace, whirlpool bath, and steam shower. Two suites include kitchen facilities. **Broughton Street Inn** (511 East Broughton Street, 912/232-6633) is an exquisite little gem of an inn with three suites and four guest rooms as well as formal and informal parlors. The suites feature a fireplace and a sophisticated bathroom with a Jacuzzi tub/shower.

Other outstanding B&Bs are **Presidents' Quarters,** 225 E. President Street, 912/233-1600, **Foley House Inn**, 14 W. Hull Street, 912/232-6622, **Forsyth Park Inn**, 102 W. Hall Street, 912/233-6800, and **Magnolia Place,** 503 Whitaker Street, 912/236-7674.

Bigger properties that serve breakfast but that are really more like inns are the **East Bay Inn**, 225 E. Bay Street, 912/238-1225, the **Olde Harbour Inn**, 508 E. Factors Walk, 912/234-4100, **Planters Inn**, 29 Abercorn Street, 912/232-5678, and **River Street Inn,** 115 E. River Street, 912/234-6400. For more information about bed-and-breakfasts contact one of several reservation services: Savannah Historic Inns and Guesthouses, 800/262-4667; R.S.V.P. Savannah Reservation Service, 800/729-7787; and Historic Reservations, 800/791-9393.

Not a B&B, the **Mulberry Inn** (601 East Bay Street, 912/238-1200) is located in a cleverly remodeled Coca-Cola bottling plant. Guest rooms surround a beautifully landscaped courtyard with a fountain. Rooms are spacious and nicely decorated with period reproductions. Some suites feature a small refrigerator and a wet bar. Amenities include a restaurant, lounge, swimming pool, and outdoor hot tub.

One of the premier resorts in the country, **The Cloister** on Sea Island (100 First Street, 912/638-3611 or 800/732-4752) has hosted a steady stream of presidents, potentates, and even ordinary people over the last 70 years. Complementing the original hotel building, small wings and guest houses are scattered throughout the magnificent grounds. The resort offers an extensive children's program during the summer and long holidays. Almost any amenity, sport, or activity you can think of is provided—often included in the standard price—as are three meals a day. The resort features a full-service spa as well. You will have no reason on earth to leave the grounds unless you really want to. Nightly rates run from $238 to $552 per couple. Children under 19 stay free except for a meal charge based on age.

Once the private residence of the Carnegie family, the **Greyfield Inn** on Cumberland Island is still owned and operated by family members. The inn is furnished and decorated as it was in 1901, and many rooms share a bath. Three gourmet meals a day are included in the nightly rate. Access to the inn is only by private ferry with advance reservations. The inn is closed in August. Mailing address: 8 North Second Street, Fernandina Beach, Florida 32035-0900; 904/261-6408.

Restored to its former grandeur and furnished with reproductions in a style befitting the 100 millionaires who built it, the **Jekyll Island Club** (371 Riverview Drive, Jekyll Island, 912/635-2600) features two restaurants including the Grand Dining Room. Many guest rooms and suites boast fireplaces or Jacuzzis. A summer program for children is offered, and shuttle buses transport guests to the beach.

Another elegant beachfront resort that caters to families is the palatial, Mediterranean-style **King and Prince** on St. Simons (201 Arnold Road at Downing Street, 912/638-3631 or 800/342-0212). Guests can stay in the original hotel building or in villas scattered around the grounds. Numerous sporting activities are available.

CAMPING

Camping on Cumberland Island (912/882-4335) is not a frivolous undertaking. Access to the island is strictly limited and only by ferry with advance reservations. No stores are permitted on the island, so you must take everything you will need and pack out your trash. Your campsite might be a 10-mile walk from the ferry dock. A developed campsite near the dock offers rest rooms, cold showers, safe drinking water, picnic tables, food cages (to foil raccoons), and a boardwalk to the beach. All other sites are primitive. Campfires are not permitted, so you must bring a camp stove.

Jekyll Island Campground (North Beachview Drive, Jekyll Island, 912/635-3021) is an 18-acre facility with beach access, 200 campsites, a bathhouse, laundry facilities, and a store. Tent and trailer sites are offered at Skidaway Island State Park (Diamond Causeway, Savannah, 912/598-2300). The park has a swimming pool and hiking trails.

NIGHTLIFE

Savannah is a party town that offers dozens of trendy nightspots. They tend to come and go and wax and wane in popularity, so when you get here, be sure to ask what's hot at the moment. Try Hard-hearted Hannah's at the Pirates House (20 East Broad Street, 912/233-5757), Wet Willie's (101 East River Street, 912/233-5650), the Cotton Exchange (201 East River Street, 912/232-7088), Spanky's (317 East River, 912/236-3009), Olympic Café (5 East River Street, 912/233-3131), and Huey's (115 East River Street, 912/234-7385). Live theater is an integral part of life on both St. Simons and Jekyll Islands. During summer the Jekyll Island Musical Theater Festival offers a series of lively, Broadway-type musicals outdoors nightly except Sundays. Call 912/635-3636 or 800/841-6586 for a schedule.

5
TALLAHASSEE

The Florida panhandle is often advertised as "The Other Florida." Its rolling terrain, heavy forests, and other flora and fauna are more like that of New England than the rest of the state. Folks often wonder why Florida's capital is on the panhandle, rather than more centrally located on the peninsula. This is how it happened:

When Florida became a territory in 1822, the governor had one man set out on horseback from St. Augustine and another by boat from Pensacola. Wherever they met would be the capital. Where they met was near a waterfall the Indians called Tallahassee.

But the area had a rich history long before that momentous occasion. Native Americans had lived there for thousands of years. The Spanish landed there in 1539 and celebrated the first Christmas in North America. Control of the region alternated between the Spanish, French, and English for many years. Settlers established small farms and then large plantations in the region. In fact, many plantations still exist, and the Tallahassee-to-Thomasville (Georgia) area has the greatest concentration of working plantations in the United States.

Today Tallahassee is a lovely city with the new and old capitols, several historic districts, Florida State University, four area lakes, and many cultural events. Tallahassee's access to the Gulf of Mexico is through the town of Apalachicola, popular for its seafood and beaches. In fact, the offshore waters contain one of the best oyster beds in the state.

TALLAHASSEE

N

To Jacksonville

To Lake City

To Perry, US 19

SHAMROCK ST

KILLARNEY WAY

RAYMOND DIEHL RD

151

319

27

CAPITAL CIRCLE SE

MACLAY RD

CAPITAL CIRCLE NE

CENTERVILLE RD

61

THOMASVILLE RD

90

APALACHEE PKWY

MAGNOLIA DR

D

SEMINOLE DR

C

BREVARD S

TENNESSEE ST

LAFAYETTE ST

CALHOUN ST

MONROE ST

L

MERIDIAN RD

JOHN KNOX RD

SCOTTY'S LN

N

B

H

ADAMS ST

BRONOUGH ST

A

10

MONROE ST

K

7TH AV

4TH AV

MACOMB ST

GAINES ST

G

J

M

CALLOWAY RD

PULLEN RD

E

WOODWARD ST

PARK AV

LAKE BRADFORD RD

I

To

Lake Jackson

LAKESHORE DR

INDIAN MOUND RD

F

CROWDER RD

27

GRAVES RD

THARPE ST

PENSACOLA ST

366

OLD BAINBRIDGE RD

MISSION RD

90

CAPITAL CIRCLE SW

FRED GEORGE RD

263

CAPITAL CIRCLE NW

SCALE

0   KILOMETERS   2

0   MILES   2

ROAD

PLACE OF INTEREST

HIGHWAY

A PERFECT DAY IN TALLAHASSEE

Start at the Old and New Capitols, which are adjacent to each other. You can learn about the history of the area at the restored Old Capitol. Then ride the elevator to the top of the New Capitol for a sweeping view of the city's historic and modern sections. Next go to the Knott House Museum, a restored historic house furnished with family antiques. From there, drive out of town to the Tallahassee Museum, a living history farmstead and village. Then drive to Wakulla Springs State Park and have lunch in the lodge. Take a narrated boat tour of the springs or go for a swim in the chilly crystal-clear waters. Return to Tallahassee and have dinner at the Silver Slipper.

SIGHTSEEING HIGHLIGHTS: DOWNTOWN TALLAHASSEE

★★★★ MUSEUM OF FLORIDA HISTORY

R.A. Gray Building, Bronough and Pensacola Streets, 850/488-1484, www.dhr.dos.state.fl.us/museum/

Among the exhibits is the skeleton of a mastodon found at Wakulla Springs, 12,000-year-old Native American artifacts, Spanish relics, Civil War remains, and a reconstructed steamboat.

Details: Mon–Fri 9–4:30, Sat 10–4:30, Sun and holidays noon–4:30. Closed Christmas and Thanksgiving. Free. (1 1/2 hours)

SIGHTS

Ⓐ Black Archives Research Center and Museum
Ⓑ The Columns
Ⓒ DeSoto State Archaeological Site
Ⓓ Goodwood Museum and Gardens
Ⓔ Knott House Museum
Ⓕ Lake Jackson Mounds State Archaeological Site
Ⓖ Museum of Florida History
Ⓗ Old and New Capitols
Ⓘ Tallahassee Museum of History and Natural Science

FOOD

Ⓙ Andrew's Second Act
Ⓚ Barnacle Bills
Ⓛ Chez Pierre
Ⓜ Silver Slipper

LODGING

Ⓝ Calhoun Street Inn Bed and Breakfast
Ⓑ Doubletree Hotel
Ⓑ Governors Inn

Note: Items with the same letter are located in the same area.

SIDE TRIP: THOMASVILLE, GEORGIA

Just 28 miles from Tallahassee, Thomasville, Georgia, is known as the Rose City because of the thousands of rose bushes planted in parks, medians, yards, and elsewhere. Each year the city celebrates with a Rose Festival.

In the days when the railroads came south only as far as Thomasville, northern tourists made winter homes there in droves. Many of the glorious mansions in Thomasville's seven historic districts were "cottages" built by these visitors. A few of these homes are open for tours, and several operate as bed-and-breakfasts. You'll also want to visit the Thomas County Historical Museum and take a picture of the Big Oak.

★★★★ **OLD AND NEW CAPITOLS**
Monroe Street and Apalachee Parkway,
850/487-1902 (Old Capitol), 850/413-9200 (New Capitol)
Tallahassee was only 12 years old when the impressive Old Capitol building was constructed. Reminiscent of the U.S. Capitol in Washington, D.C., the building is Greek Revival in style and boasts a large dome with stained-glass windows. Changes were made over time, and eventually the building was no longer adequate to serve as the seat of government. A new high-rise capitol was built next door in 1977. The old building was retained, however, and restored to its 1902 appearance. Today, although it houses some government offices, it serves primarily as a museum. In the New Capitol, you can visit the legislative chambers and ride the elevator to the top floor, where windows on all four sides provide excellent views of Tallahassee.

Details: *New Capitol Mon–Fri 8–5, weekends and holidays 9–3; Old Capitol Mon–Fri 9–4:30, Sat 10–4:30, Sun noon–4:30. Closed Christmas and Thanksgiving. Free. (1 hour each)*

★★★★ **TALLAHASSEE MUSEUM OF HISTORY
AND NATURAL SCIENCE**
3945 Museum Drive, 850/576-1636
The large outdoor site includes a turn-of-the-century farm, plantation house, log cabin, blacksmith shop, farm equipment, and church.

Nature trails meander through the deep woods past streams and lakes, providing visitors with peeks at Florida wildlife.

Details: Mon–Sat 9–5, Sun 12:30–5. $6 adults, $4 children 4–15, free under 4 with adult. (2–3 hours)

★★★ DESOTO STATE ARCHAEOLOGICAL SITE
1022 DeSoto Park Drive, 850/922-6007

Known as the First Christmas site, this place is where Spanish explorer Hernando DeSoto and his men camped in 1539 and celebrated the first Christmas in the Americas. Artifacts are displayed and a reenactment is held annually.

Details: Daily 8:00–sundown. Free. ($^1/_2$ hour)

★★★ KNOTT HOUSE MUSEUM
301 East Park Avenue, 850/922-2459

Affectionately known as the "house that rhymes," this 1840 house was the home of the socially prominent Knott family. Restored to its early appearance, it contains many original pieces. What makes the furnishings so interesting is that Mrs. Knott wrote poems about many pieces and attached them to the items for the amusement of her guests. Amazingly these small, brittle notes have survived for our entertainment.

Details: Wed–Fri, tours at 1, 2, and 3, Sat tours from 10–3 on the hour. Donations appreciated. (1 hour)

★★ BLACK ARCHIVES RESEARCH CENTER AND MUSEUM
Jefferson and Adams Streets, 850/599-3020

Gallie's Hall, an old opera house, was for many years the center of Tallahassee culture. In the early 1980s it was restored to house the archives, which chronicle the history of blacks in Florida. Among the items displayed are more than 500 pieces of Ethiopian art, books predating 1700, and a hands-on Underground Railroad exhibit.

Details: Mon–Fri 9–4, weekends by appointment. Free. (1 hour)

★★ THE COLUMNS
100 North Duval Street, 850/224-8116

Although this house is the oldest remaining residence in Tallahassee, it was not always in this location. The white-columned brick home was built in the 1830s and moved to this spot in 1971, when it was purchased and restored by the chamber of commerce for its head-quarters. It is rumored that a nickel is inlaid in every brick.

Details: Mon–Thu 8–5:30, Fri 8–5. Free. (¹/₂ hour)

★★ GOODWOOD MUSEUM AND GARDENS
1600 Miccosukee Road, 850/877-4202

This estate, one of Tallahassee's most significant antebellum planta-tions, is a work in progress. The house and grounds had fallen into serious disrepair and are currently being restored. The gardens are open to visitors.

Details: Mon–Fri 8–5, Sat 9–noon. Free. (¹/₂ hour)

★★ LAKE JACKSON MOUNDS STATE ARCHAEOLOGICAL SITE
1313 Crowder Road, 850/562-0042

Native American mound-building tribes inhabited the shores of Lake Jackson in about a.d. 1200. The site features six ceremonial mounds and one thought to be a burial mound.

Details: Daily 8–sunset. $2 per vehicle, $1 bicycles and on foot. (1 hour)

SIGHTSEEING HIGHLIGHTS: TALLAHASSEE REGION

★★★★ FLORIDA CAVERNS STATE PARK
2701 Caverns Road, Marianna, 850/482-9598
www.magnet.fsu.edu/visitorinfo/attractions/caverns

This park near Marianna, northwest of Tallahassee, contains the only publicly accessible limestone caverns in Florida. They were described by the Spanish, and artifacts prove that Native Americans used them more than 1,000 years ago. Andrew Jackson and his troops used a natural bridge in the park during his 1818 foray into Spanish Florida to subdue the Indians. Another attraction at the park is the **Blue Hole Spring**, a favorite swimming spot despite the water's constant chilly temperature—71.6 degrees year-round. Other attractions in the park are nature trails, camping, hiking, canoeing, and picnicking.

Details: Daily 8–sunset. For camping information call 850/482-1228. $3.25 per vehicle; cave tours 9:30–4, $4 adults 13 and older, $2 children 3–12. (2–3 hours)

★★★★ PEBBLE HILL PLANTATION
U.S. 319, Thomasville, Georgia, 912/226-2344

Although actually located in Georgia, the plantation is very near Tallahassee and well worth a visit. It was established for growing cotton in the 1820s. The original home, built in 1827, was replaced in 1850 and expanded several times. A 90-foot loggia was added in 1901. In 1934 fire destroyed the house with the exception of the loggia. Miraculously, most of the contents were saved.

The present house was built in 1936. It contains antiques, porcelains, silver, crystal, fine art including 33 original John James Audubon paintings, and an extensive collection of Native American artifacts. Plantation buildings include garages, stables, kennels, a dispensary, veterinary hospital, fire station, and family schoolhouse. In addition, facilities include a swimming pool, tennis courts, and even a cemetery. Two special annual events are the Candlelight Christmas Tour and the Plantation Ball during Thomasville's Rose Festival.

Details: Gates open Tue–Sat 10–5, Sun 1–5. Last house tour before 4. Grounds $3 adults, $1.50 children; house tour $7 adults, $3.50 children. Under 6 not admitted to main house. (2–3 hours)

★★★★ WAKULLA SPRINGS STATE PARK AND LODGE
1 Springs Drive, Wakulla, 850/224-5950

This sinkhole was formed from the eroded bed of ancient limestone and filled by natural springs. A mastodon skeleton was found here. If you're a fan of very old movies, you might recognize the lake—the original Tarzan movies were made at Wakulla Springs. You can take a narrated tour aboard a pontoon boat to learn about the history of the area, as well as the flora and fauna. Swimming in the clear waters is another popular activity. The lodge has a restaurant.

Details: Daily 8–sunset. Park $3.25 per vehicle, boat tours $4.50 adults, $2.25 children 12 and under. (2–3 hours)

★★★ HAVANA/QUINCY
850/627-9231 (Gadsden County Chamber of Commerce)

Havana and Quincy are delightful, picture-perfect little towns northwest of Tallahassee. Their charming, Victorian-era commercial districts are filled with antique shops, art galleries, and restaurants. Surrounding the business districts are neighborhoods of historic homes on tree-lined streets. The towns are stops on the North Florida Art Trail.

Details: 12 miles north of Tallahassee on U.S. 27. (2 hours)

SIDE TRIP: PANAMA CITY BEACH

For a completely different kind of side trip, go west to Panama City Beach—affectionately known as the "Redneck Riviera." Family oriented and inexpensive when compared to resort destinations such as Destin, Panama City Beach can hardly be described as anything but tacky, but you'll never run out of things to do. That's why so many college-age Spring Breakers head there. Dozens of amusement parks, water parks, miniature golf courses, T-shirt and souvenir shops, inexpensive restaurants, and bars will keep the whole family entertained. Accommodations run from tiny motels to the Marriott Bay Point Resort.

★★★ **NATURAL BRIDGE BATTLEFIELD STATE HISTORIC SITE**
Natural Bridge Road off FL 363, Woodville, 850/922-6007
Located south of the city near Woodville, the park commemorates a Civil War battle in which a small Confederate battalion of old men and boys held off Union troops in 1865. Their heroics allowed Tallahassee to be the only state capital east of the Mississippi to remain in Confederate hands. A reenactment is held each March.
Details: Daily 8–sunset. Free. (2 hours)

★★★ **TORREYA STATE PARK**
Off FL 12, Bristol, 850/643-2674
Rare vegetation that isn't known anywhere else in the South is found in this park. In fact, the vegetation is typical of northern states. It was pushed south during the last Ice Age, but didn't retreat when the glaciers receded. As a result, in autumn these plants put on the most colorful show in the South. In addition, the park has a restored antebellum mansion, the Gregory House, open for tours.
Details: Daily 8–sunset. Camping available on first-come first-served basis. $8 non-electric and $10 electric hookups. Park $2 per vehicle, house tours $3 adults, $2 children 17 and under. (2–3 hours)

★★ **BRADLEY'S COUNTRY STORE**
Centerville Road, 850/893-1647

Located at a country crossroads and shaded by live oaks festooned with Spanish moss, sits a real country store. The requisite front porch with rocking chairs makes it a gathering place where locals catch up on the current gossip and swap lies. Inside, the store is packed to the rafters with anything you might need, from groceries to hardware to farm equipment. Gift items and novelties are also found here. What Bradley's is known far and wide for, however, is its sausage, made in a smokehouse in back of the store.

Details: *Mon–Fri 8–6, Sat 8–5. Free. ($^1/_2$ hour)*

FITNESS AND RECREATION

The Tallahassee/Apalachicola area is blessed with ways to stay fit painlessly. The beaches of St. George Island off Apalachicola are flat and firm and provide opportunities for walking, running, and bicycling. The ocean and inland waters afford plentiful chances for swimming, fishing, boating, and other water sports. The rivers of the panhandle provide excellent canoeing, and the state has designated 15 canoe trails, ranging from 4 to 56 miles. Outfitters offer canoe rentals and return transportation.

Although the terrain in and around the capital city is rolling, hiking and biking are not strenuous there. In addition, six golf courses are located near Tallahassee.

In addition to the five state parks described in the Sightseeing Highlights section, several others are particularly suited for outdoor workouts. The Apalachicola National Forest and St. Marks Wildlife Refuge provide miles of trails. In fact, both parks can be reached from Tallahassee by way of the Historic Railroad State Trail or the St. Marks Bike Trail, built on the roadbeds of abandoned railroad tracks. The St. Marks Trail ends at a majestic lighthouse. To reach the parks, follow signs from FL 363, 25 minutes south of Tallahassee. For more information about Apalachicola National Forest and Historic Railroad State Trail call the park service at 850/922-6007. For information on St. Marks call 850/925-6121. Open sunrise–sunset.

Lake Talquin State Recreation Area is known for the state record crappie. Access to the fishing area is at Whippoorwill Sportsmans Lodge (850/875-2605). From Quincy, follow FL 267 to Cook's Landing Road.

FOOD

Andrew's Second Act (228 South Adams Street, 850/222-3444), one of Tallahassee's best restaurants, has been open since 1979. Its continental menu

---

TALLAHASSEE REGION

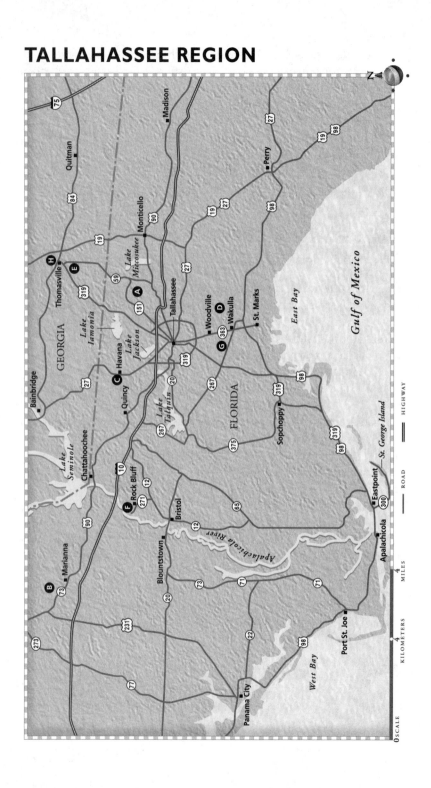

features beef, veal, and seafood, and the restaurant boasts the largest wine cellar in North Florida. Reservations are suggested. **Chez Pierre** (1215 Thomasville Road, 850/222-0936) is the area's premier French restaurant. Located in a grand historic house, it serves outstanding lamb and duck. Reservations are strongly encouraged. The **Silver Slipper** (531 Scotty's Lane, 850/386-9366) is the oldest family-owned restaurant in the state. It has been a favorite of legislators for years. The restaurant is best known for steak, Greek specialties, and fresh seafood. Reservations are suggested.

Casual **Barnacle Bill's** (1830 North Monroe Street, 850/385-8734) serves an average of 3,000 pounds of oysters every week (that's 750 dozen), in addition to house specials such as smoked dolphin and cobia. Reservations are not required but are recommended on weekends.

Nicholson's Farmhouse (15 miles north of Tallahassee off FL 12, Havana, 850/539-5931) advertises "good ole Southern home cooking," which includes superb farm-raised beef, freshly baked breads, crisp vegetables, and delicious desserts. The restaurant is located in a rambling plantation home built in 1820 and filled with all kinds of antique farm implements. Note: BYOB.

LODGING
Of the modern downtown hotels, we suggest the newly renovated **Doubletree Hotel** (101 South Adams Street, 850/224-5000 or Doubletree Central Reservations at 800/222-8733) and the **Governors Inn** (209 South Adams Street, 800/342-7717). Both are upscale.

Live oak trees draped with Spanish moss surround the **Calhoun Street Inn Bed and Breakfast**, 525 N. Calhoun St., 850/425-5095. Guests can soak in one of three clawfoot tubs, snuggle under a handmade quilt in front of one of the inn's six fireplaces, and enjoy a hearty breakfast in the morning.

SIGHTS
- Ⓐ Bradley's Country Store
- Ⓑ Florida Caverns State Park
- Ⓒ Havana/Quincy
- Ⓓ Natural Bridge Battlefield State Historic Site
- Ⓔ Pebble Hill Plantation
- Ⓕ Torreya State Park
- Ⓖ Wakulla Springs State Park and Lodge

FOOD
- Ⓒ Nicholson's Farmhouse

LODGING
- Ⓗ Thomasville B&Bs
- Ⓖ Wakulla Springs Lodge

Note: Items with the same letter are located in the same area.

The inn is the only B&B in downtown Tallahassee, and it's within walking distance of Florida State University, the capitol, and many fine restaurants.

Some of the more interesting hotels are found outside of town. The 27-room **Wakulla Springs Lodge** (550 Wakulla Park Drive, Wakulla, 850/224-5950) was built on the shores of the spring-fed lake in 1937. The building is an unusual mix of formal and rustic styles, featuring wrought iron, hand painted cypress beams, arched windows, marble, and handmade tiles throughout. This comfortable lodge is a great place to get away and relax.

Located at the Florida–Georgia border north of Tallahassee, **Susina Plantation Inn** (Meridian Road, Thomasville, Georgia, 912/377-9644) is the stereotypical antebellum plantation. The gorgeous, white-columned Greek Revival home was built in 1841 and showcases intricate carvings and ornate plasterwork. Antiques fill the public and guest rooms, many of which boast a fireplace, private porch, or balcony. The hostess, a professional chef, serves breakfast and a five-course dinner, both included in the nightly rate. In addition, the live oak–shaded inn offers a swimming pool, lighted tennis courts, and nature trails.

Thomasville also has several other bed-and-breakfasts in magnificent turn-of-the-century mansions: **1884 Paxton House** (445 Remington Avenue, 912/226-5197) now with an indoor heated lap pool, **Evans House Bed and Breakfast** (725 South Hansell Street, 912/226-1343), and **Serendipity Cottage** (339 East Jefferson Street, 912/226-8111 or 800/383-7377).

CAMPING

Florida Caverns State Park (see Sightseeing Highlights) and St. George Island State Park (U.S. 98, Apalachicola, 850/927-2111) offer tent sites, RV camping sites with full hookups, and recreational facilities. Private campgrounds include Red and Sam's Fish Camp (5563 North Monroe Street, Lake Jackson, 850/562-3083); Seminole Reservation (3226 Flastacowo Road, Tallahassee, 850/644-6083); Tallahassee RV Center and Campground (6401 West Tennessee Street, Tallahassee, 850/575-0145); and Tallahassee RV Park (6504 Mahan Drive, Tallahassee, 850/878-7641). Call for information about the facilities at each.

NIGHTLIFE

Buckhead Brewery (1900 Capitol Circle, N.E., 850/942-4947) is Tallahassee's only microbrewery. It offers two Happy Hours daily—from 2 to 6:30 p.m. and 10 p.m. to close. At Dooley's Down Under/Comedy Zone at Dooley's

(Ramada Inn, 2900 North Monroe Street, 850/386-1027), the outback atmosphere is only part of the fun. Professional comedians perform two shows on Friday and Saturday nights. The restaurant/bar features interactive games. The Moon (1105 East Lafayette Street, 850/222-666) is an upscale, high-energy dance club for the young and fit. Country night is on Friday and Saturday's theme is "Dancing on the Moon." For a more sedate crowd, the Sparta 220 Club and Grill (220 Monroe Street, 850/224-9711) features dinner and dancing with live music.

6
THE EMERALD COAST

Among Florida's best-kept secrets, Fort Walton, Destin, and nearby Seaside offer 24 miles of golden, sun-kissed beaches lapped by the blue-green waters of the Gulf of Mexico. The 100 Fathom Curve comes closer to land at Destin than any other place in Florida, creating speedy deepwater access, some of the best fishing in the United States, and some of the best shelling in the world. In this area, 60 percent of the beaches are protected by law and will remain in their pristine state forever.

The sands here, rated among the best beaches anywhere, are sculpted from 100 percent quartz ground into such minute particles that they squeak when you walk on them. Because the powdery sand is crushed so fine, it doesn't get hot despite the heat of the day, so you can walk on the beach without scorching your bare feet.

If you're looking for privacy, you won't have to go far to find a quiet, deserted stretch of beach along the coast. The area draws an older, more upscale clientele than the spring-break destinations not far away. The region is also popular with families who are more interested in nature than amusement parks. The few residential beach communities you'll find here are unpretentious and low key.

The region is rapidly being discovered by peninsular Floridians and out-of-staters, so visit this classy alternative to funky Panama City Beach before it becomes crowded.

EMERALD COAST

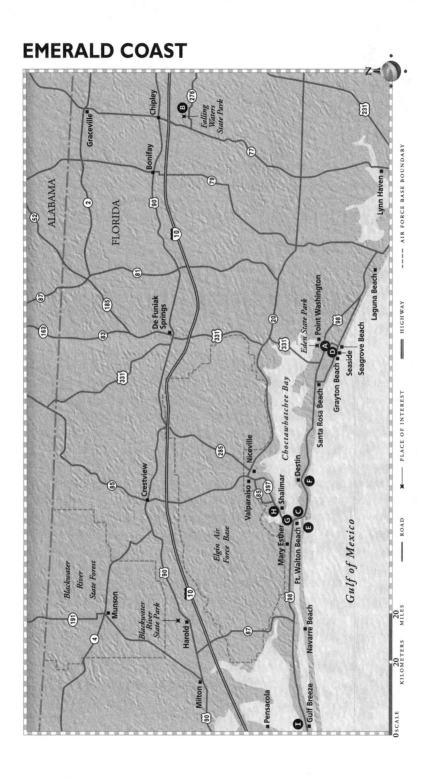

A PERFECT DAY ON THE EMERALD COAST

A perfect day in this glorious region of Florida shouldn't be at all strenuous. In fact, it's a perfect place to do nothing but lie on the beach and maybe read a good book.

When it starts to get hot, throw on some casual clothes and head to Fudpucker's Beachside Bar and Grill for lunch. The name alone should tip you off that this is a fun-loving place. After a leisurely lunch, go into Fort Walton to visit the Indian Temple Mound and Museum. Nearby is the Gulfarium, a forerunner to Sea World–type attractions.

If the idea of getting a little dressed up isn't too unappealing, have a gourmet dinner at the elegant Marina Café overlooking the bay. End the evening by going for a long walk on the beach, then go to bed early so you'll be rested up for another laid-back day in paradise.

SIGHTSEEING HIGHLIGHTS

★★★★ **GRAYTON BEACH STATE RECREATION AREA**
357 Main Park Road, Grayton Beach, 850/231-4210
Condé Nast Traveler and others have named Grayton Beach the most beautiful beach in America. Recreational activities in this 356-acre park include camping, swimming, surf fishing, and hiking on the nature trails.
> **Details:** *Daily 8–sundown. $3.25 per vehicle, $1 per person walking or biking. (half–full day).*

★★★★ **HENDERSON BEACH STATE PARK**
17000 Emerald Coast Parkway, Destin, 850/837-7550
Located just east of Destin on U.S. 98, the 208-acre park is primarily

---

SIGHTS
- Ⓐ Eden State Gardens and the Wesley Mansion
- Ⓑ Falling Waters State Park
- Ⓒ Focus Center
- Ⓓ Grayton Beach State Recreation Area
- Ⓔ Gulfarium
- Ⓕ Henderson Beach State Park
- Ⓖ Indian Temple Mound and Museum
- Ⓗ U.S. Air Force Armament Museum
- Ⓘ The Zoo

CHAUTAUQUA SOUTH

Those familiar with the educational and cultural movement of the 1890s and early 1900s in Chautauqua, New York, will understand the background of DeFuniak Springs, Florida. People gathered near Lake Chautauqua in the summer for concerts, symposia, plays, elocution lessons, and Bible study. The movement became known as Chautauqua and eventually opened a Florida Chautauqua, which met in winter on the shores of Lake DeFuniak. The Chautauqua Hall of Brotherhood still stands and now houses the Walton County Chamber of Commerce. Activities begin in February and culminate in the Chautauqua Day Festival in late May. For information about the Chautauqua Assembly or the Chautauqua Festival, call 850/892-9494.

used for swimming, sunning, and surf fishing. Picnic shelters and rest room facilities are available.

Details: Daily 8–sundown. $2 per vehicle, $1 for walkers and bicyclers. (half-day)

★★★★ **INDIAN TEMPLE MOUND AND MUSEUM**
139 Miracle Strip Parkway, Fort Walton Beach
850/833-9595
The 600-year-old temple mound created by Native Americans of the Mississippian culture is the largest mound near saltwater. The museum traces 10,000 years of habitation by four prehistoric tribes.

Details: Mon–Fri 11–4, Sat 9–4. $2.01 adults, $1.01 children 6–17, free under 6. (1 hour)

★★★★ **U.S. AIR FORCE ARMAMENT MUSEUM**
100 Museum Drive, Eglin Air Force Base, Shalimar
850/882-4189
Located at Eglin Air Force Base, this attraction displays air force weaponry and planes from four wars: World War II, Korean, Vietnam, and the Persian Gulf. Twenty-five reconnaissance, fighter, and bomber planes are on display.

Details: Daily 9:30–4:30. Free. (1–2 hours)

★★★ EDEN STATE GARDENS AND THE WESLEY MANSION
CR 395 off U.S. 98, Point Washington, 850/231-4214

The park incorporates a post–Civil War plantation, including a stately, 1895 Greek Revival mansion. A porch wraps completely around the restored house, which has seven soaring columns on one side. The house is open for tours. The park also includes azalea and camellia gardens and overlooks Choctawhatchee Bay.

Details: Park open 8–sundown, house open Thu–Mon 9–4 with tours on the hour. Park $2 per vehicle, house tour $1.50 per person. (1–2 hours)

★★★ FALLING WATERS STATE PARK
1130 State Park Road, Chipley, 850/638-6130

Florida is relatively flat so you don't generally see waterfalls here, but unusual conditions created this 63-foot waterfall that empties into a 100-foot sinkhole. The water exits the hole by way of an underground river that flows through several caverns. Recreational facilities include swimming and picnic areas.

Details: Daily 8–sunset. $3.25 per vehicle. (2–3 hours)

★★★ FOCUS CENTER
139 Brooks Street, Fort Walton Beach, 850/664-1261

A children's museum of fantasy and science, the Focus Center is full of interactive fun. Kids love the Castle of Mirrors, gigantic bubble makers, the "hair-raising" Vandergraph generator, and the electrifying Illuma Storm.

Details: Daily June–Aug 1–5; Sept–May Sat 10:30–4, Sun 11:30–4. $2.50, free children under 3. (1–2 hours)

★★★ GULFARIUM
1010 Miracle Strip Parkway, S.E., Fort Walton Beach
850/244-5169

Built in 1955, the Gulfarium was the nation's first facility to combine marine research with entertainment. Although its 40 plus years of age show, it's just as informative and entertaining as any of the newer marine amusement parks. Popular bottle-nosed dolphin and California sea lion shows are given several times daily. Exhibits include an exotic bird aviary, Peruvian penguins, otters, geese, and swans. In addition, the staff at the facility care for injured and stranded birds and marine turtles.

Details: Daily May 15–Sept 15 10–6; to 4 rest of the year; shows every two hours. $14 adults, $12 seniors, $10 children. (1–2 hours)

★★★ THE ZOO
5801 Gulf Breeze Parkway, Gulf Breeze, 850/932-2229

Colossus, one of the world's largest gorillas, rules the zoo animals, ranging from giraffes to Bengal tigers, who roam in natural habitats such as the African veldt. Other attractions include a petting zoo, elephant rides, and reptile demonstrations. One of the most popular activities is mounting a 40-foot platform to hand-feed the giraffes.

Details: Daily 9–4; summer extended hours. $9.25 adults, $5.75 children. (2–3 hours)

FITNESS AND RECREATION

Fishing may very well be the number one recreational activity off the beaches of South Walton and the Emerald Coast. It's no wonder—Destin's East Pass is only 10 miles from 100-foot depths, where more than 30 varieties of fish are caught. Whether you're a novice or a seasoned fisherman, you can find a deep-sea fishing experience for as little as $25 for a half-day trip. Fishing is also available from the beach and piers, as well as in the bays and rivers.

You can snorkel and dive directly from the beach because deep water is so close off shore, or you can join a chartered dive. Timber Hole is a submerged petrified forest to which old ships, railroad cars, airplanes, and other refuse have deliberately been added to create an immense artificial reef. It attracts a variety of marine life as well as snorkelers and divers. Other water sports include jet skiing, water-skiing, sailing, and windsurfing. Blackwater State Park and Eglin Reservation offer tubing and canoeing trips.

The area's beaches and flat roads make walking, jogging, bicycling, and in-line skating popular. The area also has 10 golf courses and many tennis courts. Among other favorite pursuits are parasailing and horseback riding.

Shelling is also popular. You probably won't find many shells right on the beaches. You'll have to wade into the water to find the treasures—a sensitive set of toes is your best asset. Sand Dollar City, actually a sand bar, is rich with layers of "sea money."

FOOD

Naturally enough, a vast majority of the restaurants in the region serve seafood and most of them are very casual. Among these is **AJ's Seafood and Oyster House** (one-quarter mile east of the Destin Bridge, Destin, 850/837-1913), located next to a marina where deep-sea fishing charters depart. When lucky fishermen return, they can take their catch right next door to tiki-topped AJ's to be cooked and served. If you haven't gone fishing yourself, AJ's has an extensive menu that ranges from blue crab claws to shrimp.

Fudpucker's Beachside Bar and Grill has two locations: 20001 Emerald Coast Parkway, Destin, 850/654-4200, and 108 Santa Rosa Boulevard, Fort Walton Beach, 850/243-3833. Family oriented, the restaurants offer a wide range of soups, salads, burgers, and sandwiches. The **Back Porch** (Old U.S. 98, Destin, 850/837-2022) is a cedar-shingled seafood shack with a sweeping beach view. It is the originator of char-grilled amberjack, a local delicacy. Another popular family restaurant is **Captain Kidd's Seafood Buffet** (20100 Highway 98 E., Destin, 850/650-1666).

Life at the beach is so casual that few elegant restaurants can be found in the area. However, two are perfect for any special occasion. At the **Marina Café** (404 U.S. 98E, Destin, 850/837-7960), you'll find candlelight and soft piano music. Begin dinner with escargot or Norwegian salmon, followed by entrees with Italian or Cajun influences. The menu changes weekly. At the **Flamingo Café** (414 U.S. 98E, 850/837-0961), the ambience includes crisp table linens and candlelight.

This food court is not your typical mall fare. **Morgan's**, at the Silver Sands Factory Stores, 10406 Emerald Coast Pkwy. W., 850/654-3320, has nine dining venues ranging from a 1950s-style diner to the Harbor Docks, where you can enjoy a microbrew with seafood. You'll also find homemade pasta, sushi, and even a classic bakery. Two large gaming areas let you and the kids play on more than 160 attractions.

LODGING

Named one of America's Top Ten Family Resorts by *Family Circle*, **Bluewater Bay Resort** (1950 Bluewater Road, Niceville, 850/897-3616) boasts 36 holes of championship golf, four pools, 21 tennis courts with three types of surfaces, a beach, rental boats, a 120-slip marina, and a renowned children's activity program. Accommodations are offered in tastefully appointed villas. Another upscale resort, **Sandestin** (9300 U.S. 98W, Destin, 850/267-8000) features 550 luxury hotel rooms and one- to three-bedroom condos, cottages, and villas. Guests can enjoy 63 holes of golf, 16 tennis courts with three types of surfaces, a fitness center, and a full-service marina.

In the mid-price range, both The **Radisson Beach Resort** (U.S. 98 at Santa Rosa Boulevard, Fort Walton Beach, 850/243-9181 or 800/333-3333) and the **Ramada Beach Resort** (U.S. 98E, Fort Walton Beach, 850/243-9161 or 800/874-8962) offer upscale accommodations and the amenities of a full-service hotel.

EMERALD COAST

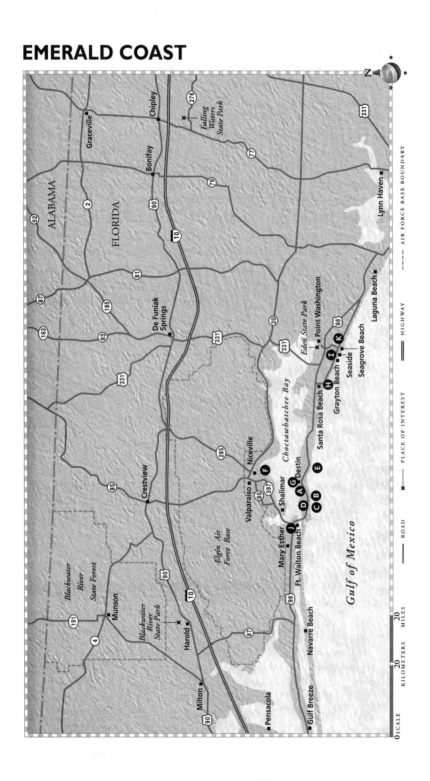

Perfect for a romantic retreat, the rambling, cedar-shingled **Henderson Park Inn** (2700 U.S. 98E, Destin, 850/837-4853 or 800/336-GULF, www.abbottresorts.com) was built as a bed-and-breakfast. Nineteen designer-decorated rooms and suites feature king- or queen-size beds, TVs, small refrigerators, microwave ovens, coffee makers, and in-room safes. Many rooms feature whirlpool baths. The inn offers a heated swimming pool and old-fashioned swings. Breakfast is included for guests, and a restaurant serves lunch and dinner. **Highlands House Bed and Breakfast** (4193 W. 30-A, Santa Rosa Beach, 850/267-0110) is a charming, antebellum-style southern plantation house with direct access to the beach. **Josephine's French Country Inn** (101 Seaside Avenue, Seaside, 800/848-1840) is located in the beachfront village of Seaside. Voted one of the Top Twelve Inns in America by *Country Inns* magazine, the white-columned inn features 11 elegantly furnished rooms and suites. **Sugar Beach Inn Bed and Breakfast** (3501 East Scenic 30A, Seagrove Beach, 850/231-1577) is a romantic, plantation-style inn overlooking the Gulf of Mexico. It offers elegant antique and wicker furniture, fireplaces, and broad verandas.

CAMPING

Camping facilities are available at Blackwater State Park (7720 Deaton Bridge Road, Holt, 850/983-5363), which offers 30 sites for tent and RV camping—some of which have electric hookups. Facilities include a bathhouse, grills, nature trails, and swimming. Among private campgrounds, Crystal Beach Campground (2825 U.S. 98E, Destin, 850/837-6447) has RV sites but no tent sites; Destin Campgrounds (209 Beach Drive, Destin, 850/837-6511) offers tent sites; Destin RV Resort (3175 Cobia Street, Destin, 850/837-6215) is only a five-minute walk to the beach; and Gulf Holiday

FOOD
- Ⓐ AJ's Seafood and Oyster House
- Ⓑ Back Porch
- Ⓐ Captain Kidd's Seafood Buffet
- Ⓒ Flamingo Café
- Ⓓ Fudpucker's Beachside Bar and Grill
- Ⓒ Marina Café
- Ⓔ Morgan's

LODGING
- Ⓕ Bluewater Bay Resort
- Ⓖ Henderson Park Inn
- Ⓗ Highlands House Bed and Breakfast
- Ⓘ Josephine's French Country Inn
- Ⓙ Radisson Beach Resort-Ft. Walton
- Ⓙ Ramada Beach Resort
- Ⓖ Sandestin
- Ⓚ Sugar Beach Inn Bed and Breakfast

Note: Items with the same letter are located in the same area.

Travel Park (10005 West Emerald Coast Parkway, Destin, 850/837-6334) offers the only beach camping on the Emerald Coast. The campground has tent sites as well as RV sites.

NIGHTLIFE

Several nightspots are famous for their specialty drinks. AJ's Club Bimini (116 U.S. 98E, Destin, 850/837-1913) is well known for its Bimini Bash, an almost-lethal mix of cranberry, orange, and pineapple juices with five types of rum. Fudpucker's Beachside Bar & Grill, (20001 Emerald Coast Parkway, Destin, 850/654-4200; 108 Santa Rosa Boulevard, Fort Walton Beach, 850/243-3833) is family oriented during the day and evening, but when late night comes, fun-lovers hit the dance floor. Nightown (140 Palmetto Street, Destin, 850/837-6448), is three different bars under one roof—a pulsating dance club, a rowdy saloon, and a reggae bar. Four neighboring taverns—Hog's Breath Saloon, Hoser's, Timbers, and Thunderbirds—make up Shanty Town. Fun goes on there until 4 a.m. Another popular spot is Press Box Pub (480 Mary Esther Cut-off, Fort Walton, 850/244-7744).

Those in search of culture should check the schedules of the Okaloosa Symphony Orchestra, 850/244-3308, or the OWCC Stage Crafters Community Theater, 850/243-1101, which gives productions at the Civic Auditorium in Fort Walton Beach.

7
PENSACOLA

The farthest west of any city in Florida, Pensacola is a fascinating small metropolis with easy access to beaches, barrier islands, bays, natural harbors, and the Gulf Islands National Seashore. The city is surrounded on three sides by water: Escambia Bay, Pensacola Bay, and Perdido Bay. Sun and pleasant weather make the area popular with sun worshipers, anglers, boaters, and bird-watchers.

During the first 200 years of the city's history, control changed hands 13 times between France, Spain, England, and the Confederacy before the area became a permanent part of the United States. In fact, although St. Augustine claims the crown as the oldest continuously occupied city in North America, a settlement existed near present-day Pensacola six years earlier. It was abandoned, however, and 139 years elapsed before resettlement.

Not surprisingly, the area is dotted with forts and historical sights and showcases a multitude of architectural styles. Home to the Pensacola Naval Air Station, which has been turning out navy pilots since 1914, the city has earned the title Cradle of Naval Aviation. These and other factors make Pensacola a popular and economical family vacation destination. And, adding icing to the cake, an astounding number of attractions can be visited free of charge.

High season, which means crowds and higher prices, is relatively short—only May to September. Fall and spring have delightful weather and

PENSACOLA

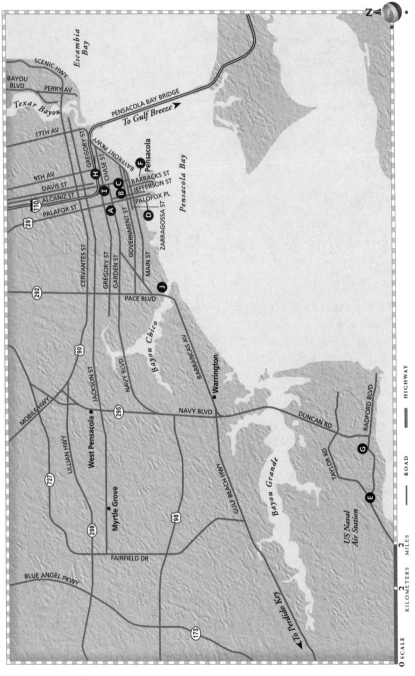

are excellent times to visit, with the added incentive that prices are lower and crowds are fewer.

A PERFECT DAY IN PENSACOLA

Historic Pensacola Village is an excellent place to learn about Pensacola's past and present. It will take you most or all of the morning to see these sights. If you have a little extra time, walk around three more nearby historic districts, all of which are contiguous. Then drive out toward Santa Rosa Island. Stop on the causeway at Boy on a Dolphin restaurant for lunch with a view of the bay. Continue to the island—most of which is protected as the Gulf Islands National Seashore. Take a tour of historic Fort Pickens, then spend a relaxing afternoon at one of the beaches. Have a casual dinner at the Beachside Café or a more formal dinner at the Jubilee Restaurant. Stick around for live entertainment at Capt'n Fun. A long walk on the beach is a great way to work off a big dinner and end the day.

SIGHTSEEING HIGHLIGHTS: DOWNTOWN PENSACOLA

★★★★ **HISTORIC PENSACOLA VILLAGE**
205 East Zaragoza Street, 850/595-5985
Two square blocks of houses and several museums make up this re-created village, where wealthy merchants once built fashionable

SIGHTS

- **Ⓐ** Civil War Soldier's Museum
- **Ⓑ** Colonial Archaeological Trail
- **Ⓑ** Historic Pensacola Village
- **Ⓑ** Museum of Commerce
- **Ⓑ** Museum of Industry
- **Ⓒ** Pensacola Historical Museum
- **Ⓓ** Pensacola Museum of Art
- **Ⓔ** Pensacola Naval Air Station/National Museum of Naval Aviation Building
- **Ⓑ** T. T. Wentworth Jr. Florida State Museum

FOOD

- **Ⓕ** Fish House Restaurant
- **Ⓖ** Lighthouse Point
- **Ⓗ** McGuire's Irish Pub and Brewery
- **Ⓒ** Mr. P's Sandwich Shop

LODGING

- **Ⓘ** Pensacola Grand
- **Ⓙ** Yacht House Bed and Breakfast

Note: Items with the same letter are located in the same area.

homes. Restaurants and shops occupy several of the houses. Most sights are included in one ticket price, but a few have an extra admission cost.

Details: Self-guided tours Tue–Sat 10–4, guided tours 11:30 and 1:30. Two-day passes $6 adults, $2.50 children 4–16, $2 seniors and active military, free under 4. One-week passes are available. (2 hours–full day)

★★★★ MUSEUM OF COMMERCE
201 East Zaragoza Street, 850/595-5985

Once you step into this warehouse in Historic Pensacola Village, you are transported to an 1890s streetscape. You can explore a turn-of-the-century toy store, leather worker's shop, hardware store, music store, pharmacy, and printer's shop, which contains one of the most complete collections of antique presses and type in the Southeast. You'll also enjoy a collection of horse-drawn buggies and a complete, early-twentieth–century gas station.

Details: Daily 10–4. Admission included in Historic Pensacola Village fee. (1 hour)

★★★★ MUSEUM OF INDUSTRY
200 East Zaragoza Street, 850/595-5985

Artifacts from early Pensacola businesses (fishing, brick making, railroading, naval supply, and lumbering) are displayed in two connected warehouses in Historic Pensacola Village.

Details: Daily 10–4. Admission included in Historic Pensacola Village fee. (1 hour)

★★★★ T.T. WENTWORTH JR. FLORIDA STATE MUSEUM
Plaza Ferdinand, 330 South Jefferson Street, 850/595-5985

Built in 1907 as the city hall, this structure is in the elaborate Renaissance Revival style. The private collection of T. T. Wentworth, the largest collection ever given to the state of Florida, is on display. Rotating exhibits depict the area's history, architecture, and archaeology. Among the most-talked-about items are a size 37 shoe, a petrified cat, and a shrunken head. One floor is devoted to the Discovery Gallery, a hands-on exhibit for children. Pick up a questionnaire for a scavenger hunt through the museum.

Details: Daily 10–4. Admission included in Historic Pensacola Village fee. (1 hour)

★★★ CIVIL WAR SOLDIER'S MUSEUM
108 South Palafox Place, 850/469-1900

Exhibits include life-size dioramas of a Union camp and a Confederate field hospital, along with artifacts and relics. The museum was created and assembled by a doctor who amassed surgical and medical implements of the period to chronicle the inadequacies of medical care during the war.

Details: Tue–Sat 10–4:30. $5 adults, $2.50 children 6–12, free under 6. (1 hour)

★★★ PENSACOLA HISTORICAL MUSEUM
405 South Adams Street, 850/433-1559

Built in 1832, the structure was an Episcopal church until 1903. It operated as a library from 1938 to 1957. Since 1960 it has been a museum portraying the story of Pensacola through exhibits about geology, Native American culture, colonial days, and the Civil War.

Details: Mon–Sat 10–4:30. $3 adults, $1 children, includes admittance to the research library on Government Street. $1 museum alone. (1/2 hour)

★★★ PENSACOLA MUSEUM OF ART
407 South Jefferson Street, 850/432-6247

The two-story Mission revival–style building was once the Pensacola city jail and court. In addition to the permanent collections, the museum sponsors traveling exhibits, concerts, and lectures.

Details: Tue–Fri 10–5, to 4 on Sat. $2 adults, $1 seniors and students, free under 5. (1 hour)

★★★ PENSACOLA NAVAL AIR STATION/ NATIONAL MUSEUM OF NAVAL AVIATION
3465 Redford Boulevard, 850/452-3604

The naval air station has 120 historic airplanes, including those used by World War II marine Major Greg "Pappy" Boyington, Lieutenant Junior Grade George Bush, and the legendary Blue Angels Demonstration Team. The museum, one of the three largest air-and-space museums in the world, presents exhibits and films and displays marine and Coast Guard memorabilia. Among the displays are a wood-and-fabric biplane, a Skylab command module, a cockpit simulator, and re-creations of an aircraft carrier deck and a World War II landing strip. The new IMAX Theater (850/453-2024) features movies with themes involving achievement in adversity. If you're lucky, the Blue Angels may be practicing. Also on the base are the remains of the Civil War battery, Fort Barrancas.

Details: *Museum open daily 9–5, IMAX showings each hour 10–4. Museum free; IMAX $5 adults, $4.50 children, military, and seniors. The Naval Air Station (850/455-5167 or 850/452-2311) is open daily 9:30–5, but hours vary seasonally. Self-guided and guided tours Sat and Sun at 2. Free. (1–2 hours)*

★ **COLONIAL ARCHAEOLOGICAL TRAIL**
Plaza Ferdinand to Seville Square, 850/595-5985
A series of archaeological digs and finds are part of Historic Pensacola Village. Among the excavated sites are a British well, a kitchen foundation from the 1771–1821 era, and the foundation of a British government house. Pick up a brochure from the visitors center.

Details: *Free. ($^1/_2$ hour)*

SIGHTSEEING HIGHLIGHTS: PENSACOLA REGION

★★★★ **FORT PICKENS**
Fort Pickens Road, Pensacola Beach, 850/934-2635
The fort was constructed on Santa Rosa Island between 1829 and 1834. Although it began the Civil War in Confederate hands, it was captured by Federal troops. In the mid-1880s Geronimo and other Apaches were held prisoner here. The museum has excellent dioramas portraying wildlife and military history. Two short nature trails provide a glimpse of Santa Rosa's diverse ecosystem, and a longer trail goes around the western tip of the island. Candlelight tours and campfire talks are held periodically.

Details: *Daily Apr–Oct 9:30–5; 8:30–dusk rest of the year; times vary for guided tours. $6 per car for seven-day permit, $20 for yearly permit. (2 hours)*

★★★★ **GULF ISLANDS NATIONAL SEASHORE**
850/934-2600
The park comprises 11 sections in two states and 150 miles of shoreline. Six sections are in Florida around Pensacola and provide beaches, scuba diving, nature trails, fishing, picnicking, and camping.

PENSACOLA REGION

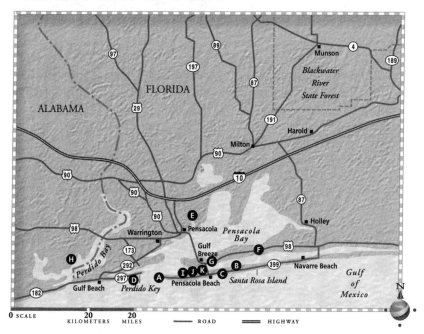

SIGHTS

A Fort Pickens
B Gulf Islands National Seashore
C Pensacola Beach/Santa Rosa Island
D Perdido Key State Recreation Area
E Science and Space Theater
F The Zoo

FOOD

G Boy on a Dolphin
G Chan's Market Café
G Jubilee Restaurant and Entertainment Complex
H Original Point Restaurant
I Peg Leg Pete's Oyster Bar and Restaurant

LODGING

C Best Western Pensacola Beach
C Clarion Suites Resort
J The Dunes
K Holiday Inn Express Pensacola Beach

Note: Items with the same letter are located in the same area.

Among the sights you'll want to see are the Naval Live Oaks Visitor Center near Gulf Breeze, Fort Pickens on Santa Rosa Island, and Fort Barrancas at the Pensacola Naval Air Station. You can get a map from the Naval Live Oaks Visitor Center.

Details: *Visitor center Apr–Oct daily 9–5; 8:30–4:30 rest of the year. Free except at Fort Pickens and Perdido Key, where permits cost $6 per car for seven days or $20 per car for a year. (half day–several days)*

★★★★ **PENSACOLA BEACH/SANTA ROSA ISLAND**

Pensacola Beach on Santa Rosa Island is a bustling upscale resort town with a boardwalk, several mid-rise hotels, restaurants, nightspots, other commercial establishments, and private and rental homes. East of the beach is a long stretch of national seashore, undeveloped except for the Santa Rosa Day Use Facility. Heavily damaged by Hurricane Opal, the facility was reopened in spring 1999. Farther east, Navarre Beach is a smaller version of Pensacola Beach. At the extreme eastern end of the island is the Okaloosa area of the Gulf Islands National Seashore. The entire western end of the island is the Fort Pickens area.

Details: *(full day)*

★★★★ **PERDIDO KEY STATE RECREATION AREA**
850/492-1595

This area adjacent to the national seashore will feel like your own private beach. Sea oats, dunes, and native wildlife dominate the area, which also offers swimming, fishing, rest rooms, and picnic facilities.

Details: *8–sundown. $2 per vehicle. (2 hours–half day)*

★★★ **THE ZOO**
U.S 98, Gulf Breeze, 850/932-2229

More than 700 animals wander freely in natural habitats surrounded by botanical gardens. The zoo is well known for its lowland gorillas in a multilevel complex. At the Farm, children can pet and feed animals, including giraffes from a tall platform. The Safari Line is a miniature train that chugs through the 30-acre grounds. Keep an eye out for wildlife native to western Florida. A restaurant and a snack bar are available if you get hungry.

Details: *Daily 9–4; to 5 in summer. $9.75 adults, $8.75 seniors, $5.75 children. (1 hour)*

★ **SCIENCE AND SPACE THEATER**
1000 College Boulevard, 850/484-1150
Located in the Baroco Center for Science and Advanced Technology
on the main campus of Pensacola Junior College, the facility is more
than a planetarium. Moving, three-dimensional DIGISTAR computer
graphics are projected onto the 40-foot, full-dome, all-sky screen.
Full-range surround sound enhances the experience.
    *Details: Call for schedule. $3 adults, $2 children and students with
I.D. (1 hour)*

FITNESS AND RECREATION

Flat terrain makes exercise here a breeze. Walking, jogging, bicycling, and in-
line skating are all popular. Pensacola Beach has a 5.5-mile paved trail that's
perfect for any of those pastimes. In addition to state and national parks, good
places to hike include the Edward Ball Nature Preserve on the University of
West Florida campus and Bay Bluffs Park, where several elevated boardwalks
provide a bird's-eye view of Florida's only scenic bluffs.

    The Gulf of Mexico and inland waterways provide opportunities for ca-
noeing, tubing, sailing, windsurfing, motor boating, water-skiing, scuba diving,
and snorkeling. Numerous places rent equipment. Several marinas along
Pensacola Bay rent and charter boats. Although you can access all sections of
the national seashore by private boat, you can't launch boats from the park.
Anglers can choose surf fishing, deep-sea fishing, pier fishing, or freshwater
fishing. Among the area's six fishing piers, four have an entrance fee. Some
require a fishing license.

    Big Lagoon State Recreation Area, Black Water River State Park and
Forest, Gulf Islands National Seashore, and Gulf State Park all offer opportunities for recreation. Fort Pickens offers hiking trails, scuba diving, fishing, and
a bike trail. You can rent bikes at the camp store, and snorkeling programs
take place in June and July.

    The wide-open beaches here are perfect for kite flying. In addition, 11 golf
courses and 30 tennis courts can be found in the immediate area. Miniature golf,
go-carts, bowling alleys, batting cages, and other amusements provide family fun.
If you'd rather watch than play, greyhound racing is a popular spectator sport.

FOOD

A great place to spend part of a day or evening is the **Jubilee Restaurant
and Entertainment Complex** (400 Quietwater Beach Road, Pensacola

PENSACOLA'S HISTORIC DISTRICTS

Three historic districts are all adjacent to each other, so you can easily walk the entire area. Historic Pensacola Village takes up most of the primarily residential **Seville District**. Adjacent to it is the primarily commercial **Palafox District**, which was the heart of Old Pensacola. Many buildings have been restored to their original beauty and feature New Orleans–style ironwork balconies. Included in this district are the T. T. Wentworth Jr. Florida State Museum, the Pensacola Museum of Art, Plaza Ferdinand VII, and the Saenger Theater. The **North Hill District**, which occupies 50 blocks, is one of the most intact residential historic districts in Florida. From 1870 to the 1930s, most of the homes were custom designed for their wealthy owners. You'll see styles such as Queen Anne, neoclassical, Tudor revival, craftsman bungalow, art moderne, and Mediterranean revival.

Beach, 850/934-3108 or 800/582-3028). The complex, located at the Quietwater Beach Boardwalk on the Santa Rosa Sound side of the island in Pensacola Beach, sports a special events facility, bar, and coffee and dessert shop. The complex also has two restaurants: The **BeachSide Café** offers casual waterfront dining for all three meals and has an open-air deck. Menu items include soups, salads, sandwiches, and some simple dinner entrees. Live entertainment is offered nightly. Located upstairs from the cafe, **TopSide Dining** is an elegant, formal restaurant with two walls of windows overlooking the sound. Crisp linens, antiques, and contemporary art set the stage for a menu described as Florida-style. Many entrees have a Cajun flavor. Seafood tops the menu, but steak is represented as well. The restaurant serves a Sunday champagne brunch and often provides live entertainment. Reservations are recommended.

   Boy on a Dolphin (400 Pensacola Beach Boulevard, Pensacola Beach, 850/932-7954) has been attracting diners for more than 30 years. The cuisine, dominated by seafood, has a definite Greek flair. Located on the causeway between Gulf Breeze and Pensacola Beach, the restaurant offers sweeping views of Santa Rosa Sound and has outdoor dining in good weather. Whether char-grilled or baked in a traditional Greek marinade, the catch of the day is always excellent. Steak, prime rib, and pasta are also on the menu. Try the traditional desserts: baklava and kadaif.

Chan's Market Café in Pensacola Beach (16½ Via de Luna, 850/932-8454) is open from early morning to late night. The casual, family-oriented restaurant serves hearty breakfasts such as steak and eggs, pancakes, waffles, omelettes, and breakfast sandwiches. Lunches include soups, salads, and sandwiches. Dinner entrees are dominated by chicken and pasta dishes, but also include some beef and fish choices. A bakery is also on site, so you can take home delicious breads and pastries.

The cuisine at casual **Peg Leg Pete's Oyster Bar and Restaurant** (1010 Fort Pickens Road, Pensacola Beach, 850/932-4139) leans heavily on Cajun spices. In addition to oysters served several different ways, you can choose from red beans and rice, jambalaya, and gumbos. In the summer, live entertainment plays every night.

Several restaurants are located in or near Historic Pensacola Village. **Mr. P's Sandwich Shop** (Moreno Cottage, 221 East Zaragosa Street, 850/433-0294) is located in a tiny shotgun house in the village and offers salads, quiche, soup, sandwiches, and daily specials for lunch only.

Lighthouse Point (Pensacola Naval Air Station, 850/452-3251) used to be the Pensacola Air Station Chief's Club but is now open to the public. A wall of picture windows allows diners to gaze over Pensacola Bay to Fort Pickens and Perdido Key. The all-you-can-eat buffet changes daily, but you can count on Tex-Mex dishes, soups, and sandwich fixings, or you can order sandwiches and hot entrees a la carte.

The casual, family-oriented **Original Point Restaurant** (14340 Innerarity Point Road, Perdido Key, 850/492-3577) is known for its seafood and steaks. Most dishes are available fried, broiled, charbroiled, blackened, or steamed. Appetizers include oysters, shrimp, crab claws, gumbos, and bisques. Fresh local seafood is the house specialty. This restaurant is not the place to go if you're worried about your waistline. Accompaniments to the meals include fries, hush puppies, onion rings, and baked beans. A bluegrass band plays on weekends.

Treat yourself to a cool and refreshing red ale at **McGuire's Irish Pub and Brewery**, 600 E. Gregory St., 850/433-6789, winner of Florida's Golden Spoon award for the last five years. In addition to its wide variety of ales, McGuire's is famous for its steaks and award-winning wine cellar. Ask for a tour of the brewery. If you're a home brewer, they'll let you take home some of their yeast to try a batch for yourself.

The **Fish House Restaurant**, 600 Barracks St., 850/470-0003, overlooks the Seville Harbor and marina. Check the chalkboard for daily specials but order quickly—the catch of the day, just off the boat, can sell out quickly. Top off your cashew-crusted softshell crab or ginger fish of the day with authentic Florida key lime pie (none of that fake green stuff here), or try the bread pudding with whiskey sauce. Weekends feature blues musicians, and you might even see Joe Scarborough, a local congressman, jamming with the band.

LODGING

Clarion Suites Resort (20 Via de Luna, Pensacola Beach, 850/932-4300 or 800/874-5303) is a new waterfront property with buildings designed to look like Cape Cod bungalows. Suites, which have a living/dining room in addition to the bedroom, are decorated in airy Florida style. Each suite boasts a queen-size bed, queen-size sofa bed, microwave oven, refrigerator, toaster oven, coffee maker, and two TVs. Units are ideal for a family or two couples traveling together. A continental breakfast is included in the price, and there's a pool.

Best Western Pensacola Beach (16 Via de Luna, Pensacola Beach, 850/934-3300 or 800/528-1234) is a beachside motel where brightly deco-rated guest rooms overlook either the ocean or Pensacola Bay. Rooms have a king-size bed or two queen-size beds, a microwave oven, refrigerator, coffee maker, and wet bar. Continental breakfast is included. Amenities include a restaurant, two pools, and a beach bar. **The Dunes** (333 Fort Pickens Road, Pensacola Beach, 850/932-3536 or 800/833-8637), said to resemble a sand castle, is also a beachfront property. Facilities include a café, bar, and pool.

Rooms at the beachfront **Holiday Inn Express Pensacola Beach** (165 Fort Pickens Road, Pensacola Beach, 850/932-5361 or 800/465-4329) provide views of the island, ocean, and bays. Facilities include tennis courts, racquetball courts, and heated pool. Free continental breakfast.

In downtown Pensacola, the **Pensacola Grand** (200 East Gregory Street, 850/433-3336 or 800/348-3336), a large, modern hotel, is cleverly attached to an old railroad depot that is used for its lobby. The hotel has restaurants, lounges, and a swimming pool.

For an alternative type of lodging, the **Yacht House Bed and Breakfast**, 1820 Cypress Street, Pensacola, 850/433-3634, offers six rooms, three with private decks and hot tubs. Located near the entrance to the Pensacola Yacht Club, it is the oldest and largest B&B in Pensacola.

CAMPING

The national seashore and several state parks offer camping facilities. Fort Pickens/Gulf Islands National Seashore offers 180 sites with and without electric hookups. In addition to easy access to the beach, a camp store, picnic areas, rest room and shower facilities, and nature and bike trails are available. For information call 850/934-2623, 934-2624, or 934-2621 for a 24-hour recorded message. Call 800/365-2267 for reservations.

Big Lagoon State Recreation Area on Perdido Key (FL 292-A, Perdido Key, 850/492-1595) offers 70 campsites with and without electric hookups as well as rest rooms, access to the beach, a boat launch, picnic facilities, nature trails, and a 40-foot-tall observation tower. Blackwater River State Park (7720 Deaton Bridge Road, Holt, 850/983-5363) offers 30 sites for tent and RV camping. Sites have electric hookups. Facilities include a bathhouse, grills, nature trails, and swimming.

Just across the state line in Alabama, Gulf State Park (22050 Campground Road, Gulf Shores, 334/948-6353) is a 468-site campground with beach access, comfort stations, a store, and a restaurant. Twenty-one family cabins round out the facility. Campers can use all the facilities of the resort: beach pavilions, an 825-foot pier, 18-hole golf course, tennis courts, and marina.

Among private campgrounds, Mayfair RV Park (4540 Mobile Highway, Milton, 850/455-8561) has 18 RV sites with and without electric hookups. Navarre Beach Family Campground is on the Santa Rosa Sound side of the island (9201 Navarre Parkway, Navarre, 850/939-2188). Timberlake (2600 West Michigan Avenue, Pensacola, 850/944-5487) has 14 RV sites but no tent camping. The park has a pool, clubhouse, tennis, basketball, and volleyball courts, and a fishing lake. The campground is adjacent to a golf course. Adventures Unlimited Landing (off Tomahawk Landing Road, 850/623-6197) has 22 hookup campsites, 8 primitive sites, a bed-and-breakfast, and 15 cabins, as well as showers, paddleboats, canoes, tubes, and kayaks.

NIGHTLIFE

Most people who spend the day in the sunshine and fresh air, possibly participating in one or more sports, are perfectly content to eat dinner and spend the rest of the evening watching the sun set. However, night people won't be disappointed in Pensacola. During summer, campfires and candlelight tours are offered at Fort Pickens. Amphitheaters at Pensacola Beach and Quietwater Beach offer entertainment.

At the Jubilee Restaurant and Entertainment Complex (400 Quietwater Beach Road, Pensacola Beach, 850/934-3108 or 800/582-3028), the Beachside Café has nightly entertainment. Capt'n Fun, part of the same complex, is a casual beach bar. Other restaurants with entertainment are the Original Point Restaurant (14340 Innerarity Point Road, Pensacola, 850/492-3577), where you can hear bluegrass music on the weekends, and Peg Leg Pete's (1010 Fort Pickens Road, Pensacola Beach, 850/932-4139), where you can hear jazz in summer.

Rusty's in Pensacola (10000 Sinton Drive off Old Gulf Beach Highway, 850/492-1657) is famous for its Bushwhacker cocktail. You can relax with a drink while you look out at Big Lagoon. In addition, they serve a full menu. Drop in at Flora-bama, a popular dive, also at the state border: 17401 Perdido Key Drive, Pensacola, 850/492-0611.

The opulent, restored Saenger Theater (118 South Palafox Place) is a venue for many plays, concerts, and Broadway shows in Pensacola. For a schedule, contact 850/444-7686.

Catch the thrill of high-speed, action-packed dog racing at the Pensacola Greyhound Track (U.S. 98 at Dog Track Road, Pensacola, 850/455-8598 or 800/345-3997). You can watch from the enclosed, climate-controlled Kennel Club, the lounge, the grandstand, or even enjoy rail-side seating outdoors. The Kennel Club offers fine steak and seafood dinners. Races are run nightly, Tuesday, Wednesday, Friday, and Saturday, and matinee races are run on Saturday and Sunday. Closed Tuesday after Labor Day. Simulcast horse racing is broadcast during matinee only. Admission is $2, and $2 for the Kennel Club and Restaurant. Up to four people are admitted free with a hotel or condo key.

Scenic Route: Florida Panhandle via U.S. 98

You can travel the entire Florida panhandle from Cedar Key in the east to Pensacola in the west and, if you use U.S. 98, never be more than a stone's throw from the Gulf of Mexico or the Intracoastal Waterway. Begin your panhandle tour in Apalachicola. One of the Confederacy's most important ports, the city has seen a major preservation and restoration movement in recent years. Places to stay in **Apalachicola** include the Coombs House Inn (80 Sixth Street, 850/653-9199), a stately, three-story, 1905 Victorian home, and the 30-room Gibson Inn (51 Avenue C, just off U.S. 98, 850/653-2191), which overlooks the bay.

From Apalachicola, take CR 300 off the mainland to **St. George Island**. Dr. Julian G. Bruce St. George Island State Park (850/927-2111), at the very tip of the peninsula, offers 9 miles of beach, grassy flats, and abundant wildlife. Activities include swimming, fishing, camping, and hiking.

Return to the mainland and take U.S. 98 west to **Port St. Joe**, the site of Florida's first state convention. The Constitution Convention State Museum (200 Allen Memorial Way off U.S. 98, 850/229-8029) commemorates the event.

Continue west on U.S. 98 through Mexico Beach and you'll come to **Panama**

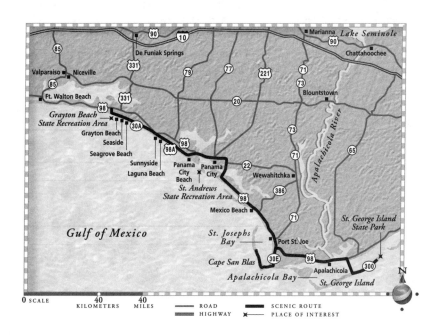

City and **Panama City Beach**. Although local organizations prefer the name "Miracle Strip" for the beaches off Panama City, most Southerners still cling to the affectionate "Redneck Riviera" nickname. This area is the most touristy on the entire panhandle—perhaps in all of Florida. The area's best feature is its beaches—both on the mainland and the barrier islands. You'll also find amusement parks, miniature golf courses, water parks, a giant maze, and seemingly endless T-shirt and souvenir shops here.

Near Panama City, you can camp on the waterfront at St. Andrews Recreation Area (850/233-5140). If you prefer more upscale lodging, we suggest the Marriott Bay Point Resort (100 Delwood Beach Road, 800/874-7105).

Continue west on U.S. 98 to **Seaside**, a planned community of approximately 300 residences, ranging from bungalows to six-bedroom mansions. The town center is a village green, used for special events such as wine tastings, sports, and musical concerts. For information on rental properties here, contact the Seaside Cottage Rental Agency (800/277-8696).

Next stop at Grayton Beach State Recreation Area (FL 30-A south of U.S. 98, 850/231-4210), named the nation's top beach in 1995 by Dr. Stephen Leatherman ("Dr. Beach"), director of the University of Maryland's Laboratory for Coastal Research. Visitors will find camping, swimming, surf fishing, boating, and nature trails in this 356-acre park.

Past Grayton Beach to the west on U.S. 98 you'll find Destin, Fort Walton Beach, Navarre Beach, Woodlawn Beach, Oriole Beach, Pensacola Beach, and the Florida units of the Gulf Islands National Seashore.

8

ALABAMA GULF COAST

The Gulf Coast of Alabama has to be one of the best-kept secrets in America. Tucked as it is between the famous beaches of the Florida panhandle and the gambling casinos of the Mississippi Gulf Coast, the Alabama coast consists of only four towns: Bayou La Batre, Gulf Shores, Orange Beach, and Perdido Key, as well as Dauphin Island. The area has had a varied history because it was at one time or another under six flags: Native American, Spanish, French, English, and Confederate, and finally that of the United States of America.

Fishing and tourism are the only important industries on the coast. Long and flat, the sugar-white beaches provide many opportunities for recreation. The area used to be characterized by year-round homes; rental cottages; small, low-rise, and mid-rise motels; and only one high-rise hotel, but Hurricane Frederic forever changed the Alabama coast from sleepy beach town to resort community. It is still considered a "secret" to Alabamians, though.

A PERFECT DAY ON THE ALABAMA GULF COAST

Begin at the small town of Bayou La Batre, a tiny shrimping port that gained national recognition when it appeared as the home of the Bubba Gump Shrimp Company in the movie *Forrest Gump*. Ride around and admire the stunning antebellum and Victorian houses, photograph the shrimp fleet, stop by a

ALABAMA GULF COAST

net-making company, and drop in at St. Margaret's Catholic Church to admire the stained-glass windows.

Then drive over the three-mile bridge to Dauphin Island and visit Fort Gaines, a Civil War fortification. Have a relaxing lunch at the Seafood Galley, the Isle Dauphine Club, or Barnacle Bill's.

Instead of driving all the way around Mobile Bay, take the auto ferry to Fort Morgan, another Civil War fort. Spend the afternoon at a beach in Gulf Shores, Orange Beach, or Perdido Key, or go surf or deep-sea fishing. Have an elegant dinner at The View. Finally, end the evening with drinks and entertainment at the very informal Flora-bama, a club that sits at the Florida-Alabama state line.

SIGHTSEEING HIGHLIGHTS

★★★★ DAUPHIN ISLAND
334/861-5524, www.gulfinfo.com

Still relatively undiscovered, Dauphin Island boasts white-quartz beaches with dunes up to 35 feet high. The island has little commercial development. In fact, it has only one traffic light, and roads cover only half the island. The fishing here is among the best in the United States. You can buy fish right off boats, and many excellent seafood

---

SIGHTS
- Ⓐ Audubon Bird Sanctuary
- Ⓑ Bayou La Batre
- Ⓒ Dauphin Island
- Ⓓ Fort Gaines
- Ⓔ Fort Morgan
- Ⓕ Gulf Shores
- Ⓖ Gulf State Park
- Ⓗ Orange Beach
- Ⓘ Perdido Key

FOOD
- Ⓕ The Buccaneer
- Ⓓ The Lighthouse
- Ⓓ Live Bait Food and Spirits
- Ⓚ Mary's Place
- Ⓓ Original Oyster House
- Ⓕ Pompano's Restaurant
- Ⓖ Sea 'n Suds Restaurant and Oyster Bar
- Ⓗ Tacky Jack's Tavern
- Ⓔ The View
- Ⓗ Voyagers
- Ⓗ Zeke's Landing Restaurant and Oyster Bar

LODGING
- Ⓕ Beach House Bed and Breakfast
- Ⓖ Gulf State Park
- Ⓗ Perdido Beach Resort

Note: Items with the same letter are located in the same area.

---

restaurants are located here. A major new attraction is Dauphin Island Sealab. Other places to visit include Fort Gaines, the Audubon Bird Sanctuary, the Dauphin Island Fishing Pier, and Shell Mound Park.
Details: (half–full day)

★★★★ FORT GAINES
Bienville Boulevard, Dauphin Island, 334/861-6992
www.dauphine.net/fortgaines/
The five-sided fort contains surviving buildings, original artillery, and a museum that displays artifacts from the Native American period through the 1930s. Costumed guides are on hand and periodically give living history demonstrations. Visitors look forward to various special events: reenactments of the Battle of Mobile Bay, A Taste of the Colony, Fury on the Gulf, Thunder on the Bay, and Christmas at the Fort.
Details: Daily 9–5; to 6 in summer. $3 adults 13 and over, $1 children 5–12, free 4 and under. (1–2 hours)

★★★★ FORT MORGAN
Mobile Point, Gulf Shores, 334/540-7125
Built between 1819 and 1834, the fort helped guard the main shipping channel into Mobile Bay. Although it suffered from a four-day siege and a 24-hour bombardment during the Battle of Mobile Bay, it was able to hold out longer than Fort Gaines during the Civil War—but was eventually forced to surrender as well. The fort was used again during the Spanish-American War, World War I, and World War II. Since then, it has been an historical park. A museum chronicles the fort's history, and displays an exhibit about hurricanes.
Details: Mon–Fri 8–5, weekends 9–5. $3 adults, $1 children. (1–2 hours)

★★★★ GULF SHORES
334/968-7511, www.gulfshores.com
The area encompassing Gulf Shores is actually a 30,000-acre, 32-mile-long island, bounded by the Gulf of Mexico, the Intracoastal Waterway, Perdido Bay, and Mobile Bay. Freshwater rivers, bayous, coves, and lakes add 400,000 acres of water. Gulf Shores boasts a state park and a fishing pier and is also the site of the Gulf Coast Mardi Gras Parade. **Orange Beach** claims to have the largest deep-sea fishing fleet on the Gulf of Mexico and is noted

for the plentiful red snapper caught nearby. **Perdido Key** is known for its back bays, gulf views, and riverfront dockage. Condominiums make up the majority of the accommodations, but one major resort is available.

Details: (half–full day)

★★★ BAYOU LA BATRE
334/824-4088

The Spanish, French, British, and even pirates have occupied the area. In 1699 it was claimed for France, and a small defensive battery was built on the west bank of the bayou. The name of the town is taken from that battery, remains of which can still be seen. Most of the town's citizens claim French ancestry, and French names, cuisine, customs, and celebrations are very much in evidence. Now a tiny shrimping hamlet, the town was the home of *Forrest Gump*'s Bubba Gump Shrimp Company and is recognized as the Seafood Capital of Alabama. A popular and colorful event is the yearly Blessing of the Fleet the first weekend in May. The area has stunning historic homes, and **St. Margaret's Church** has magnificent stained-glass windows.

Details: (1–4 hours)

★★★ GULF STATE PARK
20115 FL 135, Gulf Shores, 334/948-4853 or 800/544-4853

The park offers more than two miles of beachfront, as well as recreational facilities, a hotel, rustic cabins, a campground, and 6,000 acres of wilderness. Hiking trails and two large lakes provide additional recreation opportunities.

Details: 8–dusk. Park is free; fees vary for sports and recreational activities, the fishing pier, and picnic pavilions. (half–full day)

★★ AUDUBON BIRD SANCTUARY
Bienville Boulevard, Dauphin Island, 334/861-2120

Dauphin Island is on a major bird migration flyway between Canada and South America. The 160-acre preserve is frequented by 340 species of birds and is an important bird-watching spot. In spring, the island is the first landfall of millions of monarch butterflies as they migrate north from South America. Trails and boardwalks wind through the oak forests, swamps, and beaches of the preserve.

Details: Daily during daylight hours. Free. (1–4 hours)

FITNESS AND RECREATION

The area's towns, flat roads, and beaches provide many opportunities for walking and bicycling. The Gulf of Mexico, the Intracoastal Waterway, Mobile Bay, Perdido Bay, and inland rivers and lakes provide opportunities for boating, water sports, and fishing.

In addition to the beach, the recreational facilities at family-friendly Gulf State Park (20115 FL 135, Gulf Shores, 334/948-4853 or 800/544-4853) include an 18-hole golf course, lighted tennis courts, volleyball courts, lawn games, water sports at two lakes, and hiking trails. Three other golf courses and 14 public tennis courts are located in the area. This park is one of the few areas in the United States where you can go horseback riding on the beach.

FOOD

Eating establishments on the Alabama Gulf Coast range from funky to sublime. Near Bayou La Batre, **The Lighthouse** (11295 Padgett Switch Road, 334/824-2500) is known for seafood and steaks. **Mary's Place** (5875 AL 188, West Coden, 334/873-4514) is recognized for seafood.

In Orange Beach, **Live Bait Food and Spirits** (24281 Perdido Beach Boulevard, 334/974-1612), a funky and colorful place, serves regional American cuisine with an emphasis on seafood—a lot of it fried. Families enjoy the restaurant and its swamp views for lunch and dinner. Party animals take over for drinks and live entertainment later in the evening. Reservations are not accepted. **Tacky Jack's Tavern** (Cotton Bayou Marina, Orange Beach, 334/981-4144) is located on a bayou off Perdido Bay. It has a tiny indoor eating area and a larger rooftop deck. Be prepared to stand in line for the hearty breakfast. Seafood heads the menu at **Zeke's Landing Restaurant and Oyster Bar** (26619 Perdido Beach Boulevard, Orange Beach, 334/981-4001). The large, airy dining room overlooks Zeke's Landing Marina.

If you really want to splurge, **Voyagers** in the Perdido Beach Resort (27200 Perdido Beach Boulevard, Orange Beach, 334/981-9811) is the only four-diamond (AAA rating) restaurant in Alabama. The ocean is an elegant backdrop for the superior gourmet continental cuisine. Fish and seafood are specialties. Reservations are recommended.

In Gulf Shores the **Original Oyster House** (701 Gulf Shores Parkway, 334/948-2445), located in a simple storefront, is reputed to have the best oysters on the half shell on the Gulf Coast. Other specialties include seafood gumbo and fried and broiled seafood entrees. Reservations are not accepted. **Pompano's Restaurant** (921 West Beach Boulevard, Gulf Shores, 334/948-6874) is a family-oriented seafood eatery with stunning views of the

Gulf of Mexico. Reservations are accepted. Open for breakfast and dinner. The casual **Sea 'n Suds Restaurant and Oyster Bar** (405 East Beach Boulevard, Gulf Shores, 334/948-7894) is located on the pier and affords diners a pleasant view of the ocean. **The Buccaneer** (25125 Perdido Beach Boulevard, Gulf Shores, 334/981-4818) is popular with retirees (and younger people) for dinner and dancing. Located on the top floor of the Gulf Shores Surf and Racquet Club, the elegant **View** (1832 West Beach Boulevard, Gulf Shores, 334/948-8888) is dark, cozy, and romantic. Enjoy the vistas of the ocean while savoring the exceptional cuisine.

LODGING
Perdido Beach Resort (27200 Perdido Beach Boulevard, Orange Beach, 334/981-9811), a shell-pink, Mediterranean-style high-rise on the Gulf of Mexico, has been awarded four diamonds by AAA. All the 345 rooms, furnished in Mediterranean style, have terraces or balconies and ocean views. Other amenities include a children's program, two restaurants, three bars, live entertainment, a spa, sauna, steam room, swimming pool, and whirlpool.

   Gulf State Park boasts a modern resort hotel (21250 East Beach Boulevard, Gulf Shores, 334/948-4853 or 800/544-4853) with 144 rooms, a restaurant, and conference facilities. The exterior resembles a bunker, but you'll find attractive surroundings and every comfort inside. In addition, the park offers rustic cabins.

   One of the only beachfront bed-and-breakfasts along the Alabama coast is the imposing **Beach House Bed and Breakfast** (9218 Dacus Lane, Gulf Shores, 334/540-7039 or 800/659-6004). Perched on a high dune, the contemporary three-story house permits ocean and beach views from just about any room. One bedroom is relatively small, but four others are immense, and two boast whirlpool tubs. Quiet little reading nooks on each floor are brimming with books. Screened porches are furnished with wicker, deck chairs, and hammocks. Gourmet breakfasts begin each lazy day, and wine and cheese are served in the late afternoon.

CAMPING
Fort Gaines Campground (Bienville Boulevard, Dauphin Island, 334/861-2742), next door to the fort, is right on the beach and offers 150 sites, boat launches, a lighted boardwalk, and walking trails that connect to the Audubon Bird Sanctuary. Gulf State Park (22050 Campground Road, Gulf Shores, 334/948-6353 or 800/544-4853) offers a 468-site campground with beach

access, comfort stations, a store, and a restaurant. Twenty-one family cabins round out the facility. Campers can use all of the resort facilities: beach pavilions, an 825-foot pier, 18-hole golf course, tennis courts, a marina, water sports, and restaurant.

NIGHTLIFE

Flora-bama (16296 Perdido Key Drive, Pensacola, FL, 334/980-5119), situated on the Florida/Alabama border, is a casual bar where activities include such highbrow events as the Interstate Mullet Toss. Live bands perform each weekend.

Several amusement parks provide fun for the family. Waterville, USA (AL 59, Foley, 334/948-2106) offers water slides, miniature NASCAR racing, miniature golf, a roller coaster, and arcade games. The waterpark is open Memorial Day through Labor Day, and the rest of the park is open year-round. The Track (AL 59, Foley, 334/968-8111) has go-carts, a sky coaster, bungee jumping, bumper boats, and arcade games. Pirates Island (AL 59, Foley, 334/968-GOLF) is another place to test your skills at miniature golf. Zooland (AL 59, Foley, 334/968-5731) has 250 animals, as well as miniature golf.

9
MOBILE

Often called New Orleans in miniature, Mobile has a French flair, and many structures feature the delicate iron tracery so famous in the Big Easy. The city—Alabama's second largest—has its own personality, however, and doesn't deserve to live in New Orleans's shadow.

Mobile was founded in 1710 and served as the capital of French Louisiana until 1719. Periods of British and Spanish occupation followed before the city became part of the United States in 1814.

With its position at the head of Mobile Bay, the town was a vitally important safe haven for blockade runners during the Civil War. Mobile was one of the last Confederate ports to hold out, and its fall led to the demise of the Confederacy. Shipbuilding became Mobile's road to recovery after the war.

Today Mobile is an active port and shipbuilding center. It is dedicated to historic preservation, and 4,000 of its buildings—many from the antebellum period—are on the National Register of Historic Places. Brochures on walking and driving tours of historic neighborhoods are available at Fort Conde and City Hall.

Although New Orleans is now practically synonymous with Mardi Gras, the first Mardi Gras celebration in North America was held in 1703 near what became Mobile. The city continues the tradition. At the same time as Mardi Gras, Mobile holds the Azalea Trail Festival. The azalea-lined route stretches more than 35 miles. "Azalea Maids," outfitted with hoopskirts, big picture hats,

MOBILE

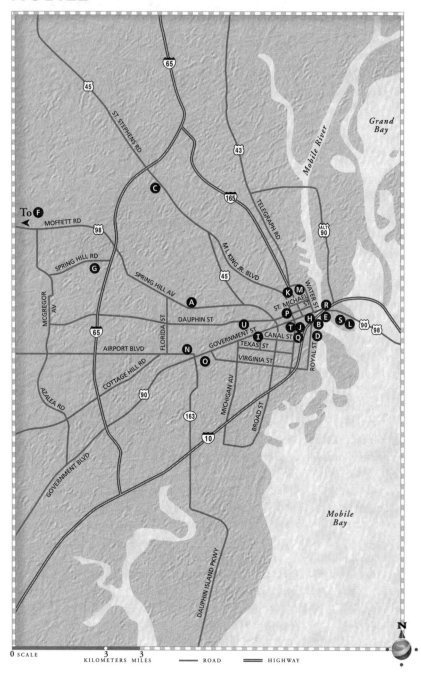

and ruffled parasols, are the ambassadors of the festival. Make reservations far in advance.

A PERFECT DAY IN MOBILE

Begin with a stop at Fort Conde, which also serves as the city's welcome center. You can learn more about the city at the Museum of the City of Mobile. If you don't linger too long at the fort or museum, you might have time before lunch to visit one of Mobile's house museums. An alternative would be a guided tour of the city, which normally includes admission to one or more of these sights. Then have a casual lunch at Port City Brewery. After lunch leave Mobile and head southwest to Bellingrath Gardens and Home—one of the finest gardens in the Southeast. The drive and visit will take up the afternoon. Return to Mobile and have an elegant dinner at La Louisiana. Enjoy a performance at the Saenger Theatre and finish the evening with drinks at Hayley's.

SIGHTSEEING HIGHLIGHTS: MOBILE

★★★★ FORT CONDE
150 South Royal Street, 334/434-7304

Nearly 100 years old, the fort has been occupied by the French,

SIGHTS

- **A** Bragg-Mitchell Mansion
- **B** Conde-Charlotte Museum House
- **C** Eichold-Heustis Medical Museum of the South
- **D** Fort Conde
- **E** Gulf Coast Exploreum Museum of Science and J. L. Bedsole IMAX Dome Theater
- **F** Mobile Botanical Gardens
- **G** Mobile Museum of Art
- **H** Museum of the City of Mobile
- **I** Oakleigh Period House Museum and Historic Complex
- **J** Phoenix Fire Museum
- **K** Richards DAR House
- **L** USS Alabama Battleship Memorial Park

FOOD

- **M** Justine's Courtyard and Carriageway
- **N** La Louisiana Seafood and Pasta Restaurant
- **O** The Pillars
- **P** Port City Brewery
- **Q** Rousso's Restaurant

LODGING

- **R** Adam's Mark Riverview Plaza Hotel
- **S** Best Western Battleship Inn
- **T** Malaga Inn
- **T** Radisson Admiral Semmes Hotel
- **U** Towle House Bed and Breakfast

Note: Items with the same letter are located in the same area.

British, and Spanish. Restored to its eighteenth-century appearance, it contains a museum with furniture, costumes, artillery, and other artifacts from that period. Costumed guides demonstrate eighteenth-century flintlock rifles and describe the fort's history.

Details: *Daily 8–5. Free. (1 hour)*

★★★★ **MUSEUM OF THE CITY OF MOBILE**
35 Government Street, 334/434-7569
The museum is housed in a restored 1872 townhouse enhanced by ornate iron balconies. Inside, the rooms spill over with more than 50,000 artifacts from every period of Mobile's history, including documents, antiques, Mardi Gras coronation costumes, and riverboat and Civil War memorabilia. In an adjacent building, you'll find a superb collection of horse-drawn carriages.

Details: *Tue–Sat 10–5, Sun 1–5. Free. (1–2 hours)*

★★★★ **USS ALABAMA BATTLESHIP MEMORIAL PARK**
2703 Battleship Parkway, Spanish Fort, 334/433-2703
During three years of service in World War II, this ship was known as the Lucky Lady because she survived many battles without any loss of life and little significant damage. Self-guided tours include visits to the ship's operating room, sick bay, blacksmith and metal shops, darkroom, print shop, cobbler shop, tailor shop, barbershop, soda fountain, movie theater, and brig. Make sure to see the movie about the ship's history. Also in the park are the submarine USS *Drum*, historic aircraft, and a Redstone rocket.

Details: *Daily 8–sunset. $8 adults, $4 children; $3 extra for flight simulator. (2–3 hours)*

★★★ **BRAGG-MITCHELL MANSION**
1906 Springhill Avenue, 334/471-6364
Built in 1855 by Judge John Bragg, whose brother was Confederate General Braxton Bragg, the house is the grandest antebellum mansion in Mobile. Set in a grove of stately oaks, the house was constructed in Greek Revival style with Italianate modifications added later. During the battle of Mobile Bay, Judge Bragg sent all his furniture upriver to his plantation for safekeeping. In an ironic twist of fate, the plantation house and its contents were destroyed and Bragg's townhome wasn't damaged at all. Therefore, the current furnishings are typical of the period, but few are original family pieces.

Details: Mon–Fri 10–4, Sun 1–4. $5 adults, $3 children, discounts seniors and groups. (1 hour).

★★★ CONDE-CHARLOTTE MUSEUM HOUSE
104 Theatre Street, 334/432-4722

From Fort Conde, you can go next door to this house museum, which is operated by the Colonial Dames of America. Built in 1822, the house served as the city's first jail as well as the jailer's residence. Furnishings are appropriate to the period. Memorabilia consists of French, British, Spanish, Confederate, and American pieces.

Details: Tue–Sat 10–4. $4 adults, $2 children. (1 hour)

★★★ GULF COAST EXPLOREUM MUSEUM OF SCIENCE AND J. L. BEDSOLE IMAX DOME THEATER
I-10, 334/208-6883 or 877/625-4FUN, www.exploreum.com

This museum allows visitors to experience science and technology firsthand, and offers visiting guest speakers, lectures, classes, and programs. In addition to many fine permanent exhibits, traveling exhibits are often scheduled. Carpe Diem offers coffee and sandwiches. Visitors may purchase science-related items at the gift shop. An IMAX theater was added in 1997 when the new facility was completed. The movies change quarterly.

Details: Mon–Thu 9–5, Fri–Sat 9–9, Sun 10–5; June–Aug Mon–Thu 9–8. Call for prices. (1 hour)

★★★ MOBILE MUSEUM OF ART
4850 Museum Drive, 334/343-2667

The permanent collection encompasses almost 5,000 works displayed in 11 galleries. Among the outstanding collections are nineteenth-century American landscapes, American art of the 1930s and 1940s, and contemporary crafts. Traveling exhibitions are part of the yearly calendar of events. A branch of the museum is located downtown on Dauphin Street.

Details: Mon–Sat 10–5, Sun 1–5. Free, donations welcome. (1 hour)

★★★ OAKLEIGH PERIOD HOUSE MUSEUM AND HISTORIC COMPLEX
350 Oakleigh Place, 334/432-1281

Headquarters of the Historic Mobile Preservation Society, the

For a literary side trip, drive inland to Monroeville. Author Harper Lee, who wrote To Kill a Mockingbird, *is a Monroeville native who still lives there, though reclusively, and Truman Capote spent holidays there with his aunts. The old courthouse, described in Lee's book, is now a museum and gallery.*

complex includes Oakleigh, the Cox-Deasey House, the Minnie Mitchell Archives, and some sunken gardens. An impressive, two-story, T-shaped Greek Revival home, the Cox-Deasey House was built in 1833 and named for the oak grove on the property. Restored to its 1850 appearance, it is furnished with Victorian, Regency, and Empire antiques.

Details: *Mon–Sat 10–4. $5 adults, $4.50 seniors and AAA members, $3 children 12–18, $2 6–11. (1 hour)*

★★★ RICHARDS DAR HOUSE
256 North Joachim Street, 334/434-7320
Located on DeTonti Square, this Italianate townhouse was built in the mid-1800s. Its most notable exterior feature is its lavish ironwork. Irreplaceable panels of Bohemian glass surround the front door. From the outside these panes don't look remarkable, but from the inside they glow blood red. Among the notable interior architectural details are Carrara marble mantels and a curved suspended staircase. The Confederacy and the Union both used the house as a naval headquarters.

Details: *Tue–Sat 10–4, Sun 1–4. $4 adults, $1 children. (1 hour)*

★★ EICHOLD-HEUSTIS MEDICAL MUSEUM OF THE SOUTH
1504 Springhill Avenue, 334/434-5055
For something a little different, visit this museum of medical science, which covers more than two centuries of development in the healing arts. In addition to the main building, the museum has a satellite location at 500 St. Anthony Street.

Details: *Mon–Fri 9–4. Free. (1 hour)*

★★ MOBILE BOTANICAL GARDENS
Pat Ryan Drive, 334/342-0555
These 64 acres of natural southern woodlands are located within the heart of Mobile. The gardens offer seasonal displays of azaleas, camellias, hollies, rhododendrons, and magnolias, and guests can wander to their hearts' content through cultivated areas and nature trails. Guided tours explain the local ecology and flora.
Details: Off Museum Dr. Mon–Fri 8–5. Free. (1–3 hours)

★★ PHOENIX FIRE MUSEUM
203 South Claiborne Street, 334/434-7554
Housed in the old Phoenix Volunteer Fire Company No. 6 firehouse, the museum contains turn-of-the-century firefighting equipment including steam engines, fire alarms, helmets, and other memorabilia.
Details: Tue–Sat 10–5, Sun 1–5. Free. (1 hour)

SIGHTSEEING HIGHLIGHTS: MOBILE REGION

★★★★ BELLINGRATH GARDENS AND HOME
12401 Bellingrath Gardens Road, Theodore, 334/973-2217
Magnificent in any season, this 900-acre estate features 65 land-scaped acres and a mansion. With more than 250,000 plants, some originally brought from France in 1754, the garden contains one of the largest collections of azaleas in the country. Other gardens are devoted to roses, bridal themes, and Asian themes. You'll see cascading mums in fall and poinsettias in December. The house contains antique furnishings, American and European crystal, silver collections, and special pieces including a chess set that was a gift to Paul Morphy, the first American international chess champion. A studio on the property houses the largest display of Boehm porcelain in the world. A riverboat, the *Southern Belle*, leaves from the estate's dock for cruises along the River of Birds.
Details: Daily 8–sunset. Boat tours on the hour. $7.50 for gardens, $13.95 for gardens and home or cruise, $18.95 for gardens, home, and cruise. (2–4 hours)

★★ HISTORIC BLAKELY STATE PARK
33707 State Highway 225, Spanish Fort, 334/580-0005

MOBILE REGION

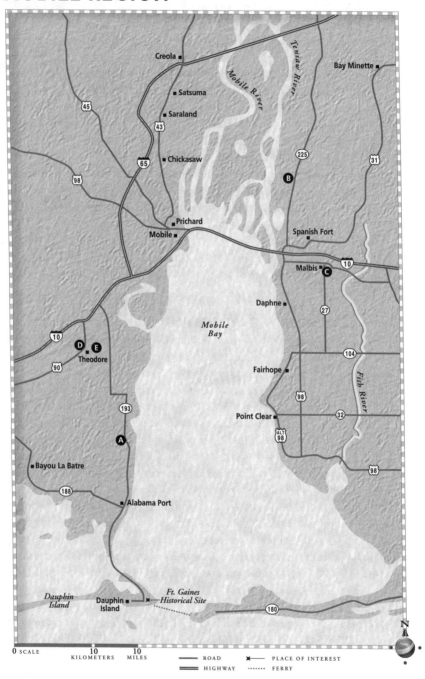

This park was the site of a major Civil War battle, which ironically was fought on April 9, 1865, the very day that Lee surrendered at Appomattox Courthouse. More than five miles of breastworks, the best preserved in the country, stretch through the 3,800-acre park. Earthen forts, redoubts, rifle pits, and battery sites have also survived. Recreational facilities include nature trails, a boardwalk along the Tensaw River, bicycling and bridle trails, fishing ponds, and campsites. A reenactment of the battle and a music festival are held each year.
Details: *Daily 9–5. $2 adults, $1 children 6–12, free under 6. (1–4 hours)*

★★ MALBIS GREEK ORTHODOX CATHEDRAL
29300 County Road 27, Malbis, 334/626-3050
Considered the finest example of neo-Byzantine style in the United States, the church is an exact replica of one in Athens, Greece. The marble was quarried in Greece, and Greek craftsmen and artists spent months creating the murals and mosaics. Look for the stained-glass rose window illuminating the transept and the faux-finished red columns in the nave. This church was the dream of one immigrant, and its $1 million cost was paid for by only 50 families.
Details: *Daily 9–noon 2–5. Free. (1 hour)*

★★ WILDLAND EXPEDITIONS
7536 Tung Avenue North, Theodore, 334/460-8206
The tour company promises participants "the adventure of a life-time." A swamp tour aboard the 25-foot *Gator Bait* allows passengers to examine vegetation and wildlife (much of it endangered) in the Alabama Delta. The boat leaves from Chickasaw Marina in Chickasaw, north of Mobile Bay.
Details: *Tours Tue–Sat 8, 10, and 2. $20 adults, $10 children. (2 hours)*

SIGHTS
Ⓐ Bellingrath Garden and Home
Ⓑ Historic Blakely State Park
Ⓒ Malbis Greek Orthodox Cathedral
Ⓓ Wildland Expeditions

LODGING
Ⓔ Riverhouse Bed and Breakfast

Note: Items with the same letter are located in the same area.

FITNESS AND RECREATION

Historic Blakely State Park (see Sightseeing Highlights) is an ideal place for hiking, bicycling, and horseback riding (bring your own horse). The Azalea Trail Run and Festival, held each March, consists of a two-mile walk/run and a 10K race.

Roller-skating is available at the Dreamland Skate Center (4618 Three Notch-Kroner Road, 334/661-6997). Two miniature golf courses and a game room are found at Mountasia Family Fun Center (5103 Girby Road, 334/661-2777). Tennis is available at the Cottage Hill Tennis Center (1711 Hillcrest Road, 334/666-9539) and the Mobile Tennis Center (851 Gaillard Drive, 334/342-7462).

Mobile Greyhound Park (I-10 West, 334/653-5000) offers live racing nightly except Sunday, with pari-mutuel wagering on horse racing via closed circuit simulcast. The facility also includes a restaurant and a food court. Auto racing provides entertainment at the Mobile International Speedway (7800 Park Boulevard, 334/957-2026).

Professional sports include the Mobile Bay Bears baseball team, which plays at Hank Aaron Stadium (334/479-BEAR), and the Mobile Mysticks hockey team, which plays at the Civic Center, 334/208-PUCK.

FOOD

La Louisiana Seafood and Pasta Restaurant (2400 Airport Road, 334/476-8130) is an elegant, romantic place to go for a special occasion. Subdued lighting from Tiffany lamps and many pictures and wall hangings create a warm, intimate atmosphere. The restaurant is known for its seafood and pastas cooked with either a touch of Italian or Cajun spices. Reservations are recommended. Closed in July.

The Pillars (1757 Government Street, 334/478-6341), housed in a restored mansion with big verandas, is another romantic place for a special occasion. The interior is furnished with antiques. Seafood, lamb, veal, and beef entrees dominate the menu. Reservations are recommended.

Port City Brewery (225 Dauphin Street, 334/438-2739) is one of Alabama's original brewpubs. The beer is brewed on site, and the pizzas are cooked in brick-ovens. Reservations are not accepted.

Justine's Courtyard and Carriageway, 80 St. Michael, 334/438-4535, offers both inside and outside dining in an historic, antebellum setting. The atmosphere is relaxed and casual, although the menu offers sumptuous cut-to-order steaks, gulf seafood, and pastas.

Autographed menus from celebrities, such as Elvis Presley and Martin

Luther King, and historic artifacts from sports and political figures have made **Roussos Seafood Restaurant,** 166 S. Royal St., 334/433-3322, a true Fort Conde Village attraction. Tour the large modern kitchen, then enjoy delightful seafood specialties such as sautéed crab and West Indian salad. The restaurant is housed in a 1870s carriage factory in the historic district near Fort Conde.

LODGING

Adam's Mark Riverview Plaza Hotel (64 South Water Street, 334/438-4000) is a luxurious high-rise that overlooks the Port of Mobile and Fort Conde. Amenities include a swimming pool, restaurant, two bars (one with live entertainment), health club, sauna, and whirlpool. The **Radisson Admiral Semmes Hotel** (251 Government Street, 334/432-8000, www.rdadmsemmes.com), named for the only Confederate commander of the CSS *Alabama*, was built in 1940. Mobile's only hotel in the National Trust for Historic Preservation's *Historic Hotels of America*, it has been restored to its former grandeur. While it retains its original architectural features such as a marble rotunda, modern and luxurious amenities have been added: hair dryers, keyless entry, coffee makers, irons and ironing boards, dataports, VCRs, and in-room safes. Large and comfortable guest rooms are furnished with Queen Anne and Chippendale reproductions. The hotel features a restaurant, bar, pool, and whirlpool as well.

Another historic but much more intimate property, the **Malaga Inn** (359 Church Street, 334/438-4701 or 800/235-1586) occupies two restored, Spanish-style townhouses built in the 1860s. Decorative moldings, fireplaces, and opulent chandeliers enhance high ceilings and hardwood floors. Guest rooms and public spaces are filled with elegant antiques and reproductions. In nice weather guests can relax in the European Courtyard, which holds a pool, fountain, and lush gardens. The restaurant serves breakfast and dinner daily and lunch Wednesday through Friday.

Towle House Bed and Breakfast (1104 Montauk Avenue, 334/432-6440 or 800/938-6953) is a bed-and-breakfast located in a restored Italianate home. It dates from 1874 and was used by the original owner as both his residence and a boys' school. Located in the heart of the historic district, the recently remodeled, antique-filled home offers three guest rooms—all with a private bath and Jacuzzi.

If you want to stay east of Mobile where you have easy access to the USS *Alabama*, harbor cruises, and small towns such as Daphne, Fairhope, and Point Clear, the moderately priced **Best Western Battleship Inn** (2701 Battleship Parkway, 334/432-2703) is a good choice. The hotel has a restaurant and bar. In addition, Mobile offers a wide range of chain hotels and motels.

Quiet and peace surround the colorfully modern **Riverhouse Bed and Breakfast**, near Bellingrath Gardens on the banks of the Fowl River, 13285 Rebel Rd., Theodore, 800/552-9791 or 334/973-2233. All three rooms feature TVs and VCRs, and the innkeeper, Mike Sullivan, has plenty of movies to loan. A 20-minute drive from Mobile, the inn includes a large deck and an in-ground hot tub.

CAMPING

The heavily shaded grounds of Historic Blakely State Park (33707 AL Hwy. 225, Spanish Fort, 334/580-0005) are ideal for camping. The facilities include 16 modern campsites, primitive sites, and a comfort station. Chickasabogue Park Campground (760 Aldcock Road, 334/452-8496) is a 2,100-acre recreation facility and wildlife sanctuary. Facilities include full RV hookups, tent sites, a laundry room, bathhouse, and store. Guests can enjoy canoeing, swimming, mountain biking, disc golf, playgrounds, and ball fields. The I-10 Kampground (6430 Theodore-Dawes Road, 334/653-9816) offers 160 spaces, bathrooms, electricity hookups, and a pool. The I-65 RV Campground (730 Jackson Road, 334/675-6347) offers 76 RV sites, 10 tent sites, a bathhouse, laundry, playground, fishing pond, and store. Aces RV Park (3815 Moffet Road, 334/460-4633) provides electricity hookups, a bathhouse, and laundry. If you want to drive as far as Dauphin Island, the Dauphin Island Campground (Bienville Boulevard, Dauphin Island, 334/861-2742) offers 150 full-service campsites, as well as rest rooms, laundry facilities, a playground, secluded beach, and walking trails into the adjacent Audubon Bird Sanctuary.

NIGHTLIFE

Dauphin Street is the "in" place to go when the sun goes down, whether for an elegant meal, drinks and entertainment, or a quick bite after a show. Port City Brewery (see Food) is a popular spot. Hayley's (278 Dauphin Street, 334/433-4970) is consistently voted "the best bar to hang out in." Grand Central Bar and Grill (256 Dauphin Street, 334/432-6999) is another fashionable meet-and-greet place with superb entertainment. Boo Radley's (276 Dauphin Street, 334/432-1996) is another late-late nightspot and features an "open mike" on Tuesday.

The glorious old USA Saenger Theatre (6 South Joachim Street, 334/438-5686) has been restored to its Renaissance appearance. It is used as the theater of the University of South Alabama and for traveling Broadway shows.

10
MISSISSIPPI
GULF COAST

Although 26 miles of wide sandy beaches edge the Mississippi Gulf Coast, it wasn't always so. The beaches you see today are human-made. In fact, they make up the largest stretch of human-made beach in the world. The area is also rich in natural wonders—islands, bayous, rivers, marshes, and forests—and all the accompanying wildlife.

The coast is also abundant in Native American, Spanish, French, British, Confederate, and U.S. history. Numerous historic sights can be explored. A modern air force base and a NASA space center bring the area firmly into the dawning of the twenty-first century, however.

Biloxi and Gulfport are the largest towns along the coast. They are bordered by several charming small communities: Bay St. Louis, Long Beach, Pascagoula, Pass Christian, and Ocean Springs, each with its own distinct personality. You may also see the name Mississippi Beach and wonder where that is. In actuality, it is the collective name for Biloxi, Gulfport, Long Beach, and Pass Christian.

The area is best known as a vacation destination. In addition to more traditional recreational activities—fishing, swimming, boating, and hiking—a dozen new casinos have turned the area into a mini–Las Vegas—for better or worse. When you're thinking about where to stay along the coast, look beyond the big casino hotels for delightful bed-and-breakfasts—most of them in historic homes.

BILOXI

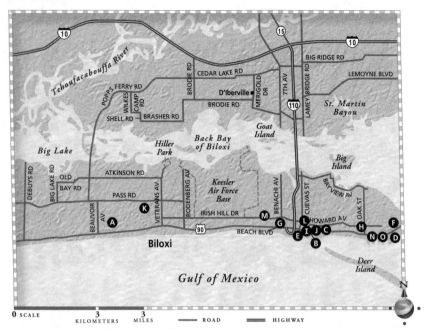

SIGHTS

Ⓐ Beauvoir
Ⓑ Biloxi Shrimping Trip
Ⓒ George E. Ohr Arts and Cultural Center
Ⓓ J. L. Scott Marine Education Center
Ⓔ Magnolia Hotel/Mardi Gras Museum
Ⓕ Maritime and Seafood Industry Museum
Ⓖ Ole Biloxi Tour Train
Ⓗ Tullis-Toledano Manor

FOOD

Ⓘ Beau Rivage
Ⓙ Fountain Restaurant
Ⓚ French Connection
Ⓛ Mary Mahoney's Old French House Restaurant and Complex

LODGING

Ⓘ Beau Rivage
Ⓜ Father Ryan House
Ⓝ Grand Casino Biloxi
Ⓞ Isle of Capri

Note: Items with the same letter are located in the same area.

A PERFECT DAY ON THE MISSISSIPPI GULF COAST

Begin at the historic Brielmaier House/Welcome Center in the center of Biloxi, across the street from the harbor. From there, go to Beauvoir, the gracious antebellum home where Confederate president Jefferson Davis retired. For a complete change of pace, take the Shrimping Tour aboard the *Sailfish*. This excursion will probably whet your appetite, so after returning to land, have lunch at the Fountain, a pleasant indoor/outdoor restaurant in the historic district.

Spend the entire afternoon at the Gulf Islands National Seashore. Take the trip by boat to Ship Island, where you can tour Fort Massachusetts, hike, and swim. Return to the mainland and clean up for a nice dinner at the Chimneys, a casual beachfront restaurant.

Spend the evening gambling or see a floor show at one of the casinos. They are open 24 hours a day, so only you will know when the time has come to turn in.

SIGHTSEEING HIGHLIGHTS: BILOXI

★★★★ **BEAUVOIR**
2244 Beach Boulevard, Biloxi, 228/388-1313
Beauvoir, which means "beautiful view" in French, is a Greek Revival, Louisiana-style raised cottage. It sits on a small rise on a 57-acre estate overlooking the Gulf of Mexico. Despite several years of imprisonment for his part in the Civil War, Jefferson Davis was able to live out the remainder of his life in relative luxury at Beauvoir. After his death, Mrs. Davis opened the estate as a hospital and nursing home for aging Confederate soldiers. Today the hospital serves as a museum. After touring the museum, visit the house, which contains many original Davis family pieces. Then move on to the outbuildings and the cemetery, where you can see the Tomb of the Unknown Confederate Soldier.

Details: Daily 9–4. $7.50 adults; $6.75 seniors, active military, and AAA members; $4.75 children 6–16. (2 hours)

★★★★ **J. L. SCOTT MARINE EDUCATION CENTER**
115 Beach Boulevard, Biloxi, 228/374-5550
The largest aquarium in the state displays coastal-zone marine life. Forty smaller tanks are home to land-based animals and reptiles. In

addition, a touch tank, seashell collections, video presentations, and a whale skeleton will fascinate kids and adults alike.

Details: *Mon–Sat 9–4. $4 adults, $3.50 seniors, $2.50 children 3–17, free 2 and under. (1–2 hours)*

★★★★ **MARITIME AND SEAFOOD INDUSTRY MUSEUM**
Point Cadet Plaza, 115 First Street, Biloxi, 228/435-6320
Packed into a small space in a former Coast Guard station, the museum overflows with exhibits and artifacts. Among the memorabilia are photographs, old boat engines, a lighthouse lens, boat building apparatus, and much more. One exhibit portrays the destruction wrought by several catastrophic hurricanes. In addition, the museum owns two schooners, the *Glenn L. Swetman* and the *Mike Sekul,* which are used in a summer camp program and for other excursions.

Details: *Mon–Sat 9–4:30. $2.50 adults, $1.50 seniors and children. (1–2 hours for museum, 2½ hours for cruise)*

★★★ **BILOXI SHRIMPING TRIP**
Biloxi Small Craft Harbor, U.S. 90, Biloxi, 228/385-1182
The hour-long trip around the harbor aboard the *Sailfish* is short but informative. In addition to explaining shrimping boats and shrimping, the captain nets some marine life and brings it on board for identification before releasing it.

Details: *Tours daily, weather permitting. $10 adults, $6 children, special rates for 15 or more with two-week advance reservations. (1 hour)*

★★ **GEORGE E. OHR ARTS AND CULTURAL CENTER**
136 G. E. Ohr Street, Biloxi, 228/374-5547
Often called the Mad Potter of Biloxi, George E. Ohr created fantastic and magical works of pottery at the turn of the century. An eccentric with an 18–inch mustache, Ohr toured Biloxi on his bicycle and buried a cache of his pottery for a more enlightened generation. Ohr is renowned for his mastery of glazes and the unique shape of his works. Visitors will see hundreds of examples of Ohr's work, as well as traveling exhibits and the works of other local artists.

Details: *Mon–Sat 9–5. $2 adults, free to members, students, and children under 12. (30 minutes–1 hour)*

★★★ **MAGNOLIA HOTEL/MARDI GRAS MUSEUM**
119 Rue Magnolia, Slip 104, Biloxi, 228/432-8806

This white-frame hotel is one of only two resort hotels left on the Mississippi Coast from the antebellum period. (The other is a bed-and-breakfast.) Today it serves as headquarters of the Gulf Coast Carnival Association and houses the organization's Mardi Gras collection. Among the exhibits are costumes and other memorabilia that chronicle the history of the festival on the coast.

Details: Weekdays 11–3. Free, but donations are appreciated. (1 hour)

★★★ OLE BILOXI TOUR TRAIN
228/374-8687

Actually a bus, the tour meanders through Biloxi while a guide narrates the history of the seafood industry and points out 75 significant sights and 20 locations. Bus stops at Tullis-Toledano Manor.

Details: Leaves from Biloxi Lighthouse on Porter Avenue and Beach Boulevard; tours begin at 9 a.m. and run hourly. Closed Dec–Mar. $8 adults, $7 seniors, $3 children 5–12. (1 hour)

★★★ TULLIS-TOLEDANO MANOR
360 Beach Boulevard, Biloxi, 228/435-6293

Built right on the coast in 1856 by a wealthy New Orleans cotton broker, the imposing house has some unusual architectural features: double galleries, elegant exterior staircases, ornate dormers, and accordion and multiple-X railings. The sweeping lawns contain some of Biloxi's oldest live oaks.

Details: Mon–Sat 11–4. $2 adults, $1 seniors and children. (1 hour)

SIGHTSEEING HIGHLIGHTS: MISSISSIPPI GULF COAST

★★★★ GULF ISLANDS NATIONAL SEASHORE
3500 Park Road, Ocean Springs, 228/875-9057 (Visitors Center)

This national park, which stretches for 150 miles, has sections in both Florida and Mississippi. In Mississippi a mainland section is at Davis Bayou in Ocean Springs and several others are on offshore islands (East and West Ship, Horn, and Petit Bois), which can be reached only by boat.

MISSISSIPPI GULF COAST

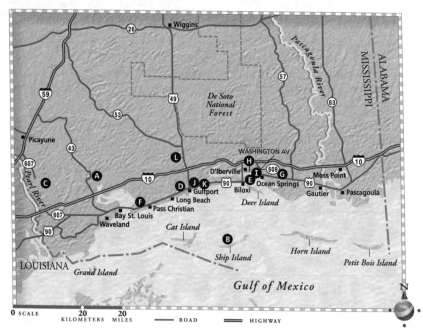

SIGHTS

- **A** Cookie's Bayou Tour
- **B** Gulf Islands National Seashore
- **C** John C. Stennis Space Center
- **D** Marine Life Oceanarium
- **E** Ocean Springs
- **F** Pass Christian
- **G** Walter Anderson Museum of Art

FOOD

- **H** Anthony's Under the Oaks
- **I** Aunt Jenny's Catfish Restaurant
- **J** The Chimneys
- **D** Vrazel's

LODGING

- **K** Grand Casino Gulfport
- **F** Harbor Oaks Inn Bed and Breakfast
- **L** Magnolia Plantation Hotel

Note: Items with the same letter are located in the same area.

The **William M. Colmer Visitors Center** at Davis Bayou serves as the mainland headquarters for the Mississippi segments of the park. It offers a film presentation and exhibits about the park. Other facilities include a fishing pier, boat ramp, campground, nature trails, and picnic areas. Sometimes interpretive programs are offered, including guided hikes, cast net demonstrations, and slide presentations. A Junior Ranger Program is held for children ages 5 through 11.

You can reach **Ship Island** only by ferry (make reservations), which leaves from a marina in Gulfport, or by private boat. It's preferable to set a whole day aside for the excursion. On the island, you can enjoy the beach, hike, or take a guided tour of **Fort Massachusetts**, a fortress with Civil War significance. Rest room and snack facilities are available on the island, but that's all. So don't forget anything you'll need for the day.

Details: Visitors center open daily 8:30–5, park open sunrise–sunset. Free. Ferry: U.S. 90 at Biloxi Point Cadet Marina (228/432-2197), daily Mar–Oct. Call Ship Island Excursions for schedule (228/864-1014 and 800/388-3290, www.gcww.com/shipisland). Round-trip ferry ride $14 adults, $7 children; guided tours of fort Memorial Day–Labor Day. Island and fort free. (full day)

★★★★ **JOHN C. STENNIS SPACE CENTER**
228/688-2370 or 800/237-1821
www.ssc.nasa.gov/public/visitors
NASA's second-largest space research center, large-propulsion space-vehicle engines are tested and flight certified here. Among the attractions at the visitors center are a 90-foot Space Tower, Solid Rocket Booster, Laserjet, rockets, rocket engines, a submersible, films, lectures, and demonstrations. Bus tours of the facility are available. Also located at the complex are the U.S. Navy's Meteorology Oceanography Command and Naval Research Laboratory, the Environmental Protection Agency, the National Data Buoy Center, the National Marine Fisheries Service, and the U.S. Geological Survey, all of which have exhibits in the visitors center.

Details: North of Bay St. Louis between I-10 and I-59 on the Louisiana border. Mon–Sat 9–4, Sun noon–4. Free. (2–3 hours)

★★★★ **OCEAN SPRINGS**
228/875-4424
The town was founded in 1699 and served as the capital of the

Louisiana Territory for several years. Then steamboats and railroads brought prosperity to the village, and it became a resort. Today ancient live oaks tower over turn-of-the-century houses, and picturesque shrimp boats fill the small harbor. Many shops and galleries feature the work of local artists, as does the Walter Anderson Museum of Art. Begin a tour by stopping at the Ocean Springs Chamber of Commerce, located, along with several shops, in the restored Old Louisville and Nashville Railroad Depot. Pick up a Shopping and Dining Guide, which also describes a walking tour.
Details: (1–2 hours)

★★★★ MARINE LIFE OCEANARIUM
Jones Memorial Park, Gulfport, 228/864-2511
www.dolphinsareus.com
In addition to dolphins, sea lions, and loggerhead sea turtles, the complex features a giant reef tank, a simulated South American rain forest, the Listening Post, where you can hear dolphins communicating with each other, and a touch pool where you can learn more about sea life. Macaws perform, a Harbor Tour Train is narrated, and you can explore the *SS Gravity*, which investigates the force of gravity.
Details: Daily 9–3. $12.75 adults, $7.50 children 3–11. (1–2 hours)

★★★ PASS CHRISTIAN
228/452-2252
As early as 1810, the small beachfront community began to attract wealthy businessmen from New Orleans who built impressive summer homes here. At first schooners and then steamboats brought vacationers, but soon trains shortened the journey, and Pass Christian became a bona fide resort town. It is the second oldest non-industrial harbor in the U.S., and it does not have any casinos. Stop at the Chamber of Commerce to pick up a shopping/dining/walking tour brochure.
Details: (1–2 hours)

★★★ WALTER ANDERSON MUSEUM OF ART
510 Washington Avenue, Ocean Springs, 228/872-3164
Anderson (1903–1965), a naturalist, mystic, wood-carver, and critically acclaimed painter from Ocean Springs, created brilliantly colored murals that depicted the flora and fauna of the coastal area.

Among the 150 works displayed are his W.P.A. wall paintings. The illustrations in the Little Room, which was dismantled from his home and reassembled here, cover all the walls, the ceiling, and part of the floor. In addition, the museum shows other permanent and changing exhibitions. A video gives art lovers a glimpse into Anderson's private life.

Details: Mon–Sat 10–5, Sun 1–5. $5 adults, $4 AAA members and military, $3 seniors and college students with I.D., $2 children, free under 6. Free to all first Monday of each month. (1 hour)

★★ **COOKIE'S BAYOU TOURS**
MS 603, Bay St. Louis, 228/466-4824
Although the area's primary aquatic attraction is the Gulf of Mexico, the next most interesting natural spectacle is bayou country. A U.S. Coast Guard–licensed captain narrates this boat tour.

Details: Daily 9–5, weather permitting. Tours 9 and 11 a.m. and 1, 3, and 5 p.m. Daylight Savings Time. $15 adults, $14 seniors, $7 children under 12. (1 1/2 hours)

FITNESS AND RECREATION

With all the coastal and inland waterways, water sports are plentiful here. Guided canoe trips of 4.6 to 35 miles, which include equipment and return shuttle, are provided by Wolf River Canoes (21652 Tucker Road, Long Beach, 228/452-7666); most tours are self-guided.

Gulf Islands National Seashore provides innumerable opportunities for outdoor activities. Davis Bayou offers the short Nature's Way Hiking Trail as well as the Live Oak Bicycle Trail. Its fishing pier is a hot spot for catching mullet and blue crabs. On West Ship Island you can fish from the beach or dock. The trail system on West Ship is 7 miles long, and bird-watching is a popular activity.

Buccaneer State Park (1150 South Beach Boulevard, Waveland, 228/467-3822) is less than one mile from the gulf and offers canoeing, tubing, fishing, sailing, swimming, a nature trail, tennis courts, basketball courts, and a seasonal wave pool and water slide. Shepard State Park (1034 Graveline Road, Gauthier, 228/497-2244) has a nature trail and opportunities for fishing in a small bayou.

The flat terrain on the mainland is perfect for walking, jogging, bicycling, and in-line skating. You can rent bikes by the day at Bikes Ahoy! (702 Beach Drive, Gulfport, 228/896-3469). In addition, 18 area golf courses offer variety and challenge. Horseback riding is available at Lonesome Duck Stables

(2070 Road 534 off Fenton and Dedeaux Road, Kiln/Delisle exit off I-10, 228/255-5043).

FOOD

Immense, 400-year-old live oaks create a giant canopy over **Anthony's Under the Oaks** (1217 North Washington Avenue, Ocean Springs, 228/872-4564), a popular restaurant on the banks of Fort Bayou. Although the building is rustic, linens add a touch of elegance. Enjoy the scenery and passing boats during lunch or brunch or watch the sunset during dinner. Specialties include seafood, veal, and steak. Next door, **Aunt Jenny's Catfish Restaurant** (1217 North Washington Avenue, Ocean Springs, 228/875-9201) is located in a historic house overlooking the same bayou. All-you-can-eat entrees include catfish, fried chicken, and fried shrimp. The Cellar Lounge downstairs is a pleasant place for a drink, but even more delightful is taking it outside so you can enjoy the picturesque and tranquil setting.

The town of Long Beach used to be called the Chimneys because the long line of chimneys on its beautiful houses served as a landmark for passing ships. Named in honor of the old town, **The Chimneys** restaurant (1640 East Beach, Hwy. 90 on the beach in Gulfport, 228/868-7020), located directly west of Gulfport Beachfront Holiday Inn, is in a 100-year-old renovated, two-story antebellum home surrounded by large oak trees. Diners here enjoy the sights and sounds of the ocean while they savor a meal of seafood, beef, chicken, or veal.

A favorite of locals, the **Fountain Restaurant** (111 Magnolia Mall, Biloxi, 228/435-1106) is hidden in a courtyard between Croesus and G. E. Ohr Streets just off U.S. 90. Dine in the glass-enclosed patio—which is luxuriant with tropical plants and, of course, a fountain—or in the clubby inside dining room. The cuisine blends Gulf Coast and French Creole influences and includes many seafood entrees as well as beef. For a very romantic evening, have dinner at the **French Connection** (1891 Pass Road, Biloxi, 228/388-6367), a "casual elegant" restaurant. Located in one of the oldest buildings along the coast—built in 1737—**Mary Mahoney's Old French House Restaurant and Complex** (138 Rue Magnolia, Biloxi, 228/374-0163) is well known for seafood, especially snapper, lobster, and oyster stew. Furnished with antiques, it has an Old South ambience. More informal, the adjacent cafe serves po' boys and other sandwiches. The outbuildings and New Orleans–style courtyard serve as dining areas as well. Next to the French House, an ancient live oak, called the Patriarch, is estimated to be two thousand years old.

HINTS FOR TRAVELERS

The **Beachcomber Trolley Line** runs from Point Cadet Plaza at the eastern edge of Biloxi to Pass Christian in the west. Trolleys operate daily every 35 to 40 minutes from 9 a.m. to 12:20 a.m. You can catch a ride from hotels, restaurants, casinos, and attractions, at designated stops, or by hailing the driver. In addition, numerous bus routes will take you to areas not served by the trolley. Buy a **COAST Tour Pass**, good for a day of unlimited travel on either the trolleys or the buses. For a schedule and fare information, call 228/896-8080 or 228/875-8070.

Vrazel's (3206 West Beach Boulevard, Gulfport, 228/863-2229) has been a longtime favorite with locals. Although Hurricane Camille destroyed the original restaurant in 1969, it was soon back in business in a new location. Favored dining spots include nooks overlooking the beach. Seafood tops the menu, but veal is popular as well. Save room for flaming desserts and coffees prepared at your table.

Beau Rivage, 875 Beach Blvd., Biloxi, 228/386-7111 or 888/750-7111, is the perfect solution when you can't decide exactly what your mood demands. With venues from casual to elegant, this luxurious resort casino offers a medley of choices in its 12 restaurants and cafés. You might choose Coral, the most elaborate of dining options, for elegantly prepared gulf seafood, prime beef, or game. You can watch the staff create your pizza or Tuscany-inspired entrées at La Cucina. Try Take Maku for Japanese offerings such as sushi, fish, and beef or Noodles for American-Chinese, Thai, and Vietnamese dishes. An on-site coffee roaster (both the man and his machine) provides all the restaurants and hotel guests with the freshest of gourmet coffees.

LODGING

The only nineteenth-century operational resort hotel remaining on the coast (the other houses the Mardi Gras Museum), **Harbor Oaks Inn Bed and Breakfast** (126 West Scenic Drive, Pass Christian, 228/452-9399 or 800/452-9399) is a pleasant, two-and-a-half story white-columned house with full-length verandas on the first two stories. Located across the street from the Pass Christian Yacht Harbor, the house is comfortably furnished with a mixture of antiques and more family pieces. Other amenities include a billiard room and guest kitchen; one guest accommodation sports a whirlpool bath.

One of the most gorgeous historic homes on the coast, the **Father Ryan House** (1196 Beach Boulevard, Biloxi, 228/435-1189 or 800/295-1189), named for the poet laureate of the Confederacy, was built in 1841. In addition to the full-length first-floor veranda, several of the antique-filled guest rooms feature private verandas from which visitors can survey the beaches and the Gulf. **Magnolia Plantation Hotel** (16391 Robinson Road, Gulfport, 228/832-8400) is a unique property. Accommodations are available in the formal, plantation-style main house and in rustic cabins that skirt Lake Magnolia. Located north of I-10, the country-estate resort offers quiet seclusion. Rooms and suites are furnished with period reproductions. Breakfast and afternoon tea are served, and the hotel features a pool and Jacuzzi.

Just a few of the large new casino hotels are **Isle of Capri** (151 Beach Boulevard, Biloxi, 800/THE-ISLE), **Grand Casino Gulfport** (U.S. 90, Gulfport, 800/WIN-7777), **Grand Casino Biloxi** (U.S. 90, Biloxi, 800/WIN-2-WIN), and **Beau Rivage** (875 Beach Boulevard, Biloxi, 228/386-7111 or 888/750-7111).

CAMPING

Live oak–shaded Davis Bayou Campground in Gulf Islands National Seashore (3500 Park Road, Ocean Springs, 228/875-9057) has a bathhouse and 51 sites with electricity and water hookups. Primitive camping is allowed in all sections of the park, with the exception of West Ship Island. Horn Island has a ranger station, but no structures are allowed on Petit Bois and East Ship Islands, so you must pack in everything you need and pack out your trash. Fires are not permitted above the high-tide line.

Ocean Springs has improved and tent camping sites at KOA Ocean Springs on Fort Bayou (7501 MS 57, 228/875-2100), which offers a large pool, boat ramp, canoe rental, playground, rec room for teens, tennis, and cable TV. Cajun RV Park in Biloxi (1860 Beach Boulevard, 228/388-5590) attracts long-term campers with its RV area, wooded tenting area, country store, laundry, tile bathrooms, swimming pool, playground, horseshoe pit, pavilions, par-three golf course, and limited cable TV. Southern Comfort Camping Resort (1766 Beach Boulevard, Biloxi, 228/432-1700) offers 114 sites on seven acres. Facilities include grills, picnic tables, patios, a hot tub, pool, kiddy pool, store, bathhouse, laundry room, game room, dog walk, and cable TV. Casino Magic in Bay St. Louis (711 Casino Magic Drive, 800/5-MAGIC-5) has its own RV park with 100 sites, full hookups, cable TV, bathhouse, laundry, and complimentary shuttles to the casino. Buccaneer State Park near Bay St. Louis (1150 South Beach Boulevard, Waveland, 228/467-3822) provides an activity area, bathhouse, developed and primitive camping, and a seasonal wave pool and water slide. Shepard State Park (1034 Graveline Road, Gauthier, 228/497-2244) has tent camping.

Big Biloxi Recreation Area, part of the Desoto National Forest, 601/928-4422, offers 25 wooded campsites, 17 with electricity and water. Primitive campsites with water only are sited on the riverbank. The park is located five miles north of Gulfport. Take Highway 49 to Desoto Park Road in Saucier.

Located right on the beach in Gulfport, San Beach Campground, 1020 Beach Dr., 228/896-7551, offers 102 sites with water, electricity, and sewer hookups. Sixty-one sites have cable TV. Facilities include a swimming pool, laundry room, and clubhouse.

NIGHTLIFE

The casinos are open 24 hours a day but are most active at night. They offer gambling, of course, but they also offer various types of entertainment including major floor shows. For more information contact Casino Info-line: 800/237-9493.

Live theater is another major pastime along the coast. Among the active groups are the Bay St. Louis Little Theater, Biloxi Little Theater Center Stage, Gulfport Little Theater, and the Ocean Springs Community Theater/Walter Anderson Players. Some productions are held at the beautifully restored old Saenger Theater in Biloxi, which serves as a performing arts center.

Drag races are run every Wednesday night at Gulfport Dragway (Canal Road, Gulfport, 228/863-4408). Stock-car races take place on Saturdays from March–October at Sun Coast Speedway (Menge Avenue, Gulfport, 228/255-4110).

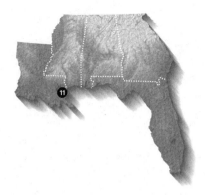

11
NEW ORLEANS

Located in a major bend of the Mississippi River, New Orleans is also known as the Crescent City. Its anything-goes attitude makes "N'awlins" one of the most exciting cities in the United States, if not the world, and has earned the city another nickname, the Big Easy. Surrounded by the Mississippi and Lake Pontchartrain, New Orleans owes much of its history and current appeal to these waterways.

Over several hundred years, New Orleans has successfully blended Native American, Spanish, French, English, African, and Caribbean cultures, which are distinctly evident in the city's architecture, activities, music, and cuisine. Among the most attractive sections of the city are the eighteenth-century French Quarter and the late-nineteenth–century Garden District.

New Orleans is practically synonymous with certain foods and drinks: cafe au lait, beignets, gumbo, jambalaya, Hurricanes, and Sazeracs to name just a few. Don't expect to visit New Orleans without gaining weight, so diet either before or after you come.

Cool blues and hot jazz permeate life in and around New Orleans. Mardi Gras, of course, is the city's biggest drawing card. You don't have to be in town on Fat Tuesday to enjoy the festivities and parades, though, because they begin two weeks prior. The celebration is not for everyone, however. Many consider the (often inebriated) crowds to be too big and the prices too high. If you do plan to come for Mardi Gras, make your

NEW ORLEANS

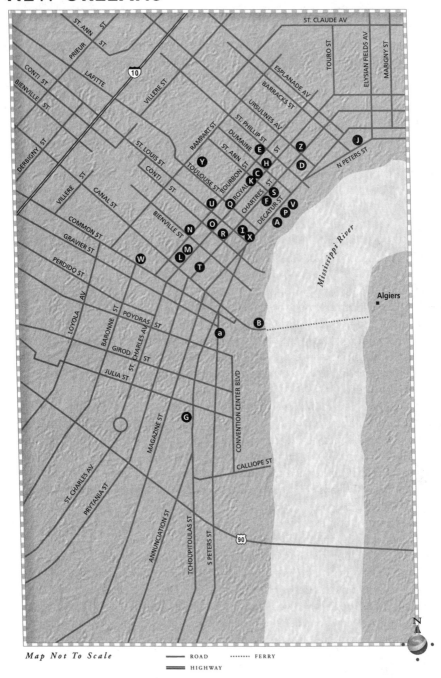

━━━━ ROAD   ········ FERRY

━━━━ HIGHWAY

reservations far, far in advance. And don't overlook the city's other celebrations, such as the Jazz and Heritage Festivals.

A PERFECT DAY IN NEW ORLEANS

The best way to get an overview of the city is to take a guided tour. Many tours are available, ranging in emphasis from architecture to haunted attractions. Spend the rest of the morning at the Louisiana State Museum buildings on Jackson Square: the Cabildo, 1850 House, and Presbytere. Near Jackson Square you'll find a pleasant place to have lunch—Tujague's Restaurant. Afterward, stroll along Woldenberg Riverfront Park to the Aquarium of the Americas. Then, either take a sightseeing cruise aboard a paddle wheeler or take the Canal Street Ferry to the west bank and Blaine Kern's Mardi Gras World, where most Mardi Gras parade floats are made. Dine at upscale Arnaud's Restaurant in the French Quarter, then wander around the quarter and stop in at some famous nightspots such as Pat O'Brien's or Pete Fountain's.

SIGHTSEEING HIGHLIGHTS: NEW ORLEANS

★★★★ **AQUARIUM OF THE AMERICAS**
1 Canal Street, 504/861-2537, ext. 340
Located along the esplanade in Woldenberg Riverfront Park, the aquarium adds a stunning contemporary silhouette to the New

SIGHTS

- Ⓐ 1850 House
- Ⓑ Aquarium of the Americas
- Ⓒ Cabildo
- Ⓓ French Market
- Ⓔ French Quarter
- Ⓕ Jackson Square
- Ⓖ Louisiana Children's Museum
- Ⓗ New Orleans Historic Voodoo Museum
- Ⓘ New Orleans Pharmacy Museum
- Ⓙ Old U.S. Mint
- Ⓚ Presbytere

FOOD

- Ⓛ Alex Patout's Louisiana Restaurant
- Ⓜ Antoine's Restaurant
- Ⓝ Arnaud's Restaurant
- Ⓞ Brennan's Restaurant
- Ⓟ Café du Monde
- Ⓠ Court of Two Sisters Restaurant
- Ⓡ K-Paul's Louisiana Kitchen
- Ⓢ La Madeleine French Bakery and Café
- Ⓣ Mr. B's Bistro
- Ⓤ Petunia's
- Ⓥ Tujague's Restaurant

LODGING

- Ⓦ Fairmont Hotel
- Ⓧ Historic French Market Inn
- Ⓨ Maison Dupuy Hotel
- Ⓩ Soniat House
- ⓐ Windsor Court

HELPFUL HINTS

New Orleans is extremely user-friendly. One example is **Information A la Carte**. This small, golf cart–like vehicle run by the city provides brochures describing many attractions. A knowledgeable and friendly driver dispenses the brochures and answers your questions.

You can view the spectacular architecture along St. Charles Avenue in the Garden District from a seat on the historic **St. Charles Streetcar** or ride between riverfront attractions aboard the **Riverfront Streetcar**. The St. Charles Streetcar operates 24 hours a day, seven days a week. The Riverfront Streetcar operates Monday through Friday from 6 a.m. to 11 p.m. and weekends from 8 a.m. to 11 p.m. With a one- or three-day **VisiTour Pass**, you can get on and off the streetcar as many times as you wish. Passes are available at many hotels and some shops. For information, call 504/248-3900.

Since 1827, the **Canal Street Ferry** has been the easiest way to get to Algiers Point on the west bank of the Mississippi River across from Jackson Square. The ferry is free to autos and pedestrians. During commuter hours, two ferries operate every 15 minutes; the remainder of the time, one ferry departs every half hour.

Orleans skyline. Inside, four major habitats, including a Caribbean reef, have been re-created. In excess of 7,500 specimens, including the world's largest collection of sharks, swim in more than one million gallons of salt and freshwater. In addition, an IMAX theater hosts exciting and informative movies. From the aquarium, many visitors take a one-hour (each way) cruise to the Audubon Zoo aboard the riverboat *John James Audubon*.

Details: Hours vary seasonally. $12 adults, $6 children, extra for IMAX films and riverboat. For IMAX, call 504/581-IMAX (4629). (1 1/2 hours)

★★★★ FRENCH QUARTER

Old World charm permeates the French Quarter, an easily walkable area 11 blocks wide and 7 blocks deep. Get a map at the Visitor

Information Center of Greater New Orleans, located in the Pontalba Building on Jackson Square. Thirty-eight significant buildings, many of which are open for tours, are described on the map. The French Quarter also contains many restaurants, bars, and shops.

Details: *Bounded by the Mississippi River, North Rampart Street, Barracks Street, and Bienville Street. (3–4 hours)*

★★★★ JACKSON SQUARE
Decatur Street between St. Peter and St. Ann Streets

Originally the French called it Place d'Armes because the land was set aside in 1721 as a drill field. The Spanish used the square for the same purpose. In 1848 it was renamed Jackson Square in honor of Andrew Jackson. The park today is a landscaped oasis where you'll often find jazz bands, street performers, and artists. Horse-and-carriage rides leave from here as well. On two sides of the park are the Pontalba buildings, one of which is the 1850 House. At the head of the square are St. Louis Cathedral, the Presbytere, and the Cabildo.

Details: *(3–4 hours)*

★★★★ JEAN LAFITTE NATIONAL HISTORICAL PARK AND PRESERVE
French Market, 504/589-2636

Centered at the French Market, the park interprets the history and cultural variety of the Mississippi Delta region. Walking tours of the French Quarter and the Garden District leave from the French Quarter Visitor Center.

Details: *Daily 8:30–5. Free. (1–2 hours)*

★★★★ LOUISIANA STATE MUSEUM
504/568-6968

One of America's largest museum complexes and one of New Orleans's top-ten attractions, this facility includes four significant buildings. During Spanish rule, the governing body of the colony was known as the **Cabildo**, and the building in which it met (701 St. Ann Street, Jackson Square) was given the same name. The governments of Spain, France, the Confederacy, and the United States used the structure, which was built in the 1790s. France ceded the Louisiana Territory to the United States at this site. Today the building displays historical artifacts from the time of the explorers through the Civil War. Its ornate, wrought-iron balcony is considered to be the finest piece of ironwork in the city. Although the **Presbytere** (751 Chartres Street, Jackson Square) was begun in 1791 to serve as a residence for the clergy of St. Louis Cathedral, it was not finished until 1913, and it never served its original purpose. Today it contains cultural and maritime memorabilia, as well as decorative arts and costumes. Located in a three-story section of the Pontalba Buildings, **1850 House** (525 St. Ann Street, Jackson Square) has been restored to represent a mid-eighteenth–century New Orleans residence. Furnishings include antiques created in New Orleans by master furniture makers such as Francois Seignouret and Prudent Mallard. The **Old U.S. Mint** (400 Esplanade Avenue) produced coins for both the Confederacy and the Union at different times. A small exhibit in the 1835 building describes the mint operations. However, its most popular exhibits are about New Orleans jazz and Mardi Gras costumes and memorabilia.

Details: Tue–Sun 9–5. Each building $5 adults; $4 seniors, children, and active military; free under 3; tickets can also be purchased for a combination of buildings. (1 hour each)

★★★ LOUISIANA CHILDREN'S MUSEUM
420 Julia Street, 504/523-1357

You don't have to be a child to be fascinated by the colorful and fascinating hands-on exhibits at this fun-filled museum. The official rules are "Please Touch!" Children can captain a tugboat, read the news in a miniature TV studio, shop in a mini-supermarket, learn how facilities can be adapted for the disabled, and much, much more.

Details: Tue–Sat 9:30–4:30, Sun noon–4:30. $5, free children under 1. (2 hours)

★★ FRENCH MARKET
Decatur Street and St. Ann to Esplanade Street

For more than 165 years, the French Market has been a vital part of New Orleans. At the area farthest from Jackson Square is a bustling farmers market where you can buy fruits, vegetables, and other foods. Dozens and dozens of craftspeople and shopkeepers sell clothing, arts and crafts, and flea market–type items. The area closest to Jackson Square has several permanent buildings that house shops and cafés with indoor and outdoor seating. You can usually count on hearing at least one live jazz band during the day and more than one at night.

Details: (1–2 hours)

★★ NEW ORLEANS HISTORIC VOODOO MUSEUM
724 Dumaine Street, 504/523-7685

In this fascinating museum you'll see artifacts and memorabilia that explain the origin and uses of voodoo in Africa, the Caribbean, and the United States—particularly Louisiana. The museum also operates swamp, plantation, and voodoo tours.

Details: *Daily 10–8. $5.25 adults, $3.15 students. (1 hour)*

★★ NEW ORLEANS PHARMACY MUSEUM
514 Chartres Street, 504/565-8027

An old apothecary shop built in 1823 by Louis J. Dufho Jr., the country's first licensed pharmacist, is the home of this museum. Visitors can see antique pharmacy equipment and hand-blown apothecary bottles arrayed in beautiful, hand-carved rosewood cabinets.

Details: *Tue–Sun 10–5. $2. ($^1/_2$ hour)*

SIGHTSEEING HIGHLIGHTS: NEW ORLEANS REGION

★★★★ AUDUBON ZOOLOGICAL GARDENS
6500 Magazine Street, 504/861-2537, ext. 340

Rated as one of the top five zoos in the United States, the complex occupies 58 acres of beautifully landscaped grounds in Audubon Park, named for the famous naturalist and painter John James Audubon. More than 1,500 animals roam freely in natural-looking habitats, and the zoo also boasts 10,000 fish, birds, and reptiles. Among the most popular displays is the Louisiana Swamp Exhibit, which includes white alligators. The park contains a golf course, tennis courts, a miniature train ride, and rental horses and bicycles. You can take a one-hour sightseeing cruise from the zoo to the aquarium or vice versa aboard the John James Audubon, which makes four round trips a day.

Details: *Hours vary seasonally. $8.75 adults, $4.50 children, extra for riverboat shuttle. Combo rate is offered for cruise, zoo, and aquarium: $26.50 adults, $13.25 children 2–12. (1$^1/_2$ hours for the zoo, 2 hours for cruise)*

★★★★ BLAINE KERN'S MARDI GRAS WORLD
233 Newton Street, 504/362-8211

NEW ORLEANS REGION

Without this facility, Mardi Gras might be a far different festival. This gigantic warehouse/workshop is where most of the outlandish floats are made, and you can see them in various stages of development. A short video is shown and costumes and props are on display. Be sure to take your camera and have your picture taken beside some of the fantastic, giant characters, or the folks at home won't believe what you're telling them. Take the free Canal Street Ferry to Algiers Point, where a free shuttle bus picks up visitors. Guided tours on hour and half-hour.

Details: *Daily 9:30–4:30. $9.50 adults, $7.50 seniors, $3.75 children 3–12. (1 hour)*

★★★ LONGUE VUE HOUSE AND GARDENS
7 Bamboo Road, 504/488-5488, www.longuevue.com

An outstanding example of a private city estate, Longue Vue consists of a neoclassical Greek Revival raised mansion with Palladian details. Built between 1939 and 1942, it is furnished with fabulous eighteenth- and nineteenth-century French and English antiques original to the Stern family, who built the estate. An eight-acre Spanish and English garden surrounds a formal Spanish courtyard. House tours are guided, whereas gardens tour are self-guided.

Details: *Mon–Sat 10–4:30, Sun 1–5. House and gardens $7 adults, $6 seniors, $3 children, free under 5. (1 1/2 hours)*

★★★ NEW ORLEANS MUSEUM OF ART
1 Collins Diboll Circle, City Park, 504/488-2631

Follow the oak alley in City Park to this stately museum, where special collections include Impressionist paintings, contemporary art, pre-Columbian art, sculpture, photographs, and decorative arts. Among the collections is an outstanding group of Fabergé eggs.

Details: *Tue–Sun 10–5. $6 adults, $3 children. (1 1/2 hours)*

SIGHTS
- Ⓐ Audubon Zoological Gardens
- Ⓑ Blaine Kern's Mardi Gras World
- Ⓒ Jean Lafitte National Historical Park and Preserve
- Ⓓ Longue Vue House and Gardens
- Ⓔ New Orleans Botanical Garden
- Ⓕ New Orleans Museum of Art
- Ⓖ Rivertown Museums

LODGING
- Ⓗ Le Pavillon Hotel
- Ⓘ Pontchartrain Hotel

★★ NEW ORLEANS BOTANICAL GARDEN
Victory Avenue, 504/483-9386
Depending on the season, the gardens bloom with a profusion of azaleas, camellias, or roses, as well as annuals and perennials interspersed with art deco fountains, ponds, and sculptures. The Pavilion of the Two Sisters is a horticultural education center.
Details: Tue–Sun 10–4:30. $3 adults, $1 children 5–12. (1 hour)

★★ RIVERTOWN MUSEUMS
405 Williams Boulevard, Kenner, 504/468-7231 or 800/473-6789
In nearby Kenner, Rivertown U.S.A. features six museums including the Jefferson Parish Mardi Gras Museum and the Saints Hall of Fame. Other attractions include LaSalle's Landing and quaint shops in a Victorian setting.
Details: Tue–Sat 9–5. $3 adults, $2 children. (2 hours)

FITNESS AND RECREATION
New Orleans is extremely user-friendly when it comes to fitness and recreation. Not only does the flat terrain generally invite walking, jogging, bicycling, and in-line skating, but the area is also dotted with parks and other recreational areas. You could walk for three hours just to cover all the streets in the French Quarter. Walkways and parks along the river make pleasant promenades. Audubon Park is the home of the zoo, where you can exercise painlessly.

With 1,500 acres, City Park (1 Palm Drive, 504/482-4888) is a huge complex with many attractions. Among them are the New Orleans Botanical Gardens, a historic, hand-carved wooden carousel, a mini-train, kiddie rides, horseback riding, and Storyland—a fairy-tale theme park with exhibits and puppet shows. The Tennis Center provides 36 lighted, hard and soft courts, racquet rentals, and lessons. The park also has an 18-hole golf course with electric cart and club rentals, instruction, and a lighted driving range.

For more information on golfing, contact Golf Outings of Louisiana (436 Turquoise Street, 504/593-9199). Two organizations sponsor almost 100 running and walking events each year: New Orleans Track Club (4245 Arkansas Avenue, Kenner, 504/482-6682) and Southern Runner Productions (6112 Magazine Street, New Orleans, 504/899-3333). Cyclists can rent bikes and accessories at Olympic Bike Rental and Tours (1618 Prytania Street, 504/522-6797).

NEW ORLEANS PADDLE WHEELERS

Paddle wheelers have always evoked a romantic, Old South ambience, and in New Orleans you can find several that offer sightseeing tours of the Mississippi River as well as dinner and entertainment. The **Natchez** is an authentic steam-powered boat, and the **Creole Queen** and **Cajun Queen** are replicas. In general they offer a morning tour, one or two afternoon tours, and an evening cruise, but call for schedules.

The *Natchez* departs from the Toulouse Street Wharf at JAX Brewery. Call 504/586-8777 or 800/233-2628 for information. The *Creole Queen* and *Cajun Queen* depart from the Canal Street/ Aquarium Dock, 27 Poydras Street Wharf. Call **504/529-4567** or 800/445-4109 for more information. Sightseeing cruises cost $12 to $14.75 for adults, $6 to $7.25 for children. Dinner cruises cost considerably more.

For a day at the races, go to the Fair Grounds Race Course (1751 Gentilly Boulevard, 504/944-5515 or 800/262-7983), which offers competition from mid-November to March. Simulcast wagering on races from other courses is offered year-round.

New Orleans offers many other spectator sports as well. The New Orleans Saints football team plays at the Superdome. Tickets are available at Ticketmaster or through the team's administrative offices (6928 Saints Drive, Metairie, 504/733-0255). The New Orleans Zephyrs is a minor-league, AAA-class farm team of the Milwaukee Brewers. They play 72 home games at the University of New Orleans's Privateer Park. Contact their administrative offices at 504/734-5155.

FOOD

Dining in New Orleans is a production that is often partaken in the European style—late, leisurely, and often outdoors. As an added reason to linger over your meal, live jazz or blues frequently accompany repasts. New Orleans–style cuisine is an art form that blends two others: Cajun (heavy on the spices) and Creole (heavy on the sauces). It will take you hardly any time at all to learn the meaning of andouille, beignet, boudin, cafe broulet, crawfish, dirty rice, dressed, etouffee, grillades, muffuletta, and po' boy.

New Orleans has so many wonderful restaurants that picking just a few to describe is extremely difficult. We've chosen the ones we're most often asked about, with a pair of other suggestions added.

Alex Patout's Louisiana Restaurant (211 Royal Street, 504/525-7788) gets constant glowing reviews from several prestigious food and wine magazines. The authentic southern Louisiana cuisine changes seasonally but generally features fish, shellfish, duck, rabbit, and other unusual entrees. The ambience at the formal restaurant is classy and subdued. **Antoine's Restaurant** (221 Royal Street, 504/581-4422) in the French Quarter guarantees a memorable gourmet meal just as it has since 1840. The renowned eatery is run by the fifth generation of the same family. Classical French and Creole cuisine is prepared from original recipes, and the extensive wine cellar is renowned. **Arnaud's Restaurant** (813 Bienville Street, 504/523-0611) in the French Quarter features unsurpassed French Creole cuisine and outstanding service. Dining rooms are decorated in turn-of-the-century Victorian decor, which perfectly complements the formality of the restaurant. Jazz musicians perform in the Richelieu Room. Be sure to go upstairs to visit the Mardi Gras Museum, which has a spectacular collection of historical Mardi Gras royalty costumes and accessories. **Brennan's Restaurant** (417 Royal Street, 504/525-9711), located in an historic building in the French Quarter and opulently decorated and furnished, is operated by a father and three sons. In addition to 12 formal dining rooms, the restaurant also offers dining in a tropical courtyard. Although a dinner of French Creole cuisine is a superb experience, the restaurant is also world-renowned for its sumptuous breakfast, including its signature Bananas Foster. The **Court of Two Sisters Restaurant** (613 Royal Street, 504/522-7261) has several claims to fame: It has the largest courtyard dining area in the French Quarter as well as an enclosed dining room overlooking the patio. Jazz is an integral part of every meal, and a strolling trio of musicians performs during the jazz buffet. Dinner is served by gaslight on the patio or by candlelight indoors. Famous New Orleans drinks such as the Sazerac and the Hurricane are served in the Carriageway Bar.

You simply can't go to New Orleans without stopping at least once at the **Café du Monde** (800 Decatur Street, 504/581-2914 or 800/772-2927). Located in the heart of the French Quarter, the original coffee stand has served café au lait and beignets (square donuts with no hole, covered with powdered sugar) since 1862. Servings consist of three of the sinful delicacies. If you don't drink coffee, the cafe also serves milk, juice, and hot chocolate. Open 24 hours a day, seven days a week. No charge cards accepted.

Although it's a chain restaurant and found in other cities besides New Orleans, **La Madeleine French Bakery and Café** (547 St. Ann Street on Jackson Square, 504/568-9950) is an authentic French café with moderate prices. Items such as soups, salads, sandwiches, pastas, hot entrees, and pastries are served cafeteria style, so you don't have to wait to eat (as long as tables are available). This cafeteria is upscale. The interior is cozy-casual and features a double-sided fireplace. In addition, you can take away many items.

Tujague's Restaurant in the heart of the French Quarter (823 Decatur Street, 504/525-8676) has been an old standby in New Orleans since 1856. Although ceramic tile floors, dark paneled walls, high ceilings, crisp table linens, and fresh flowers give the restaurant formality, a coat and tie are not required. Lunch is a la carte, but dinner is a six-course table d'hote with several entree choices. **K-Paul's Louisiana Kitchen** (416 Chartres Street, 504/524-7394) and **Petunia's** (817 St. Louis Street, 504/522-6440) are also highly recommended.

Helping redefine Creole cooking with homemade sausages, smoked meats, chutneys, and organically grown produce, **Mr. B's Bistro**, 201 Royal St., 504/523-2078, has been a renowned French Quarter tradition for 20 years. The barbecued shrimp is famous, and desserts are sinfully rich. You can enjoy live piano music during dinner or a festive jazz brunch at this upscale casual bistro. Reservations are suggested.

LODGING

New Orleans boasts dozens and dozens of bed-and-breakfasts and intimate inns. For your clarification, a B&B is owner occupied. A guest house or inn has fewer than 15 rooms, but is not occupied by the owner. Anything bigger is defined as a hotel. The array of choices among B&Bs is dizzying —some advertise, some don't (and are hard to find because of it). Unless you know of a B&B by reputation, you should consult a travel agent or reservation service to find one. Some of these agencies are Bed and Breakfast and Beyond (3225 Napoleon Avenue, 504/822-8525), Bed and Breakfast, Inc. (1021 Moss Street, 504/896-9977), New Orleans Accommodations Bed and Breakfast Service (671 Rosa Avenue, Suite 201, Metairie, 504/838-0071), and Accommodations in the French Quarter Extraordinaire (1000 Conti Street, 504/524-2075 or 800/272-2075).

Among the small hotels, you couldn't do better than the **Soniat House** (1133 Chartres Street, 504/522-0570), a planter's townhouse built in 1830. Its graceful exterior is embellished with lacy iron balconies. It was named one of the 10 best small hotels in America and the hotel that best reflects the spirit of

New Orleans by *Condé Nast Traveler*. Furnished with fine English and French antiques, the romantic hotel also features spiral staircases and a hidden courtyard. You have to pay for this luxury, however; rates run from $165 to $590 per night.

Located at the edge of the Quarter across from Armstrong Park (named after Louis Armstrong), the **Maison Dupuy Hotel** (1001 Toulouse Street, 504/586-8000 or 800/535-9177) occupies several historic buildings. These buildings surround a lush courtyard with a pool, fountain, and outside dining. Accommodations are roomy and beautifully furnished. Some feature iron balconies overlooking the French Quarter or Armstrong Park. The **Historic French Market Inn** (501 Decatur Street, 504/561-5621 or 800/548-5148) overlooks the river in the heart of the French Quarter. Accommodations, which are more moderately priced than those of the Maison Dupuy, are in historic buildings with modern amenities. Continental breakfast and an evening cocktail served in the romantic courtyard are included in the nightly rate. The inn also boasts a swimming pool.

Located just one block outside the French Quarter, the **Fairmont Hotel** (123 Baronne Street at University Place, 504/529-7111 or 800/527-4727) is a grand historic hotel built in 1893. It features ornate public spaces and spacious guest rooms with high ceilings and all the modern amenities. The Sazerac cocktail was invented here, and one of the restaurants is named in its honor. Classic Creole cuisine heads the menu. Facilities include three lounges, a pool, and rooftop tennis. In the same vein as the Fairmont, only smaller, **Le Pavillon Hotel** (833 Poydras Street, 504/581-3111 or 800/535-9095) has been the belle of New Orleans since 1907. The graceful hostelry features ornate public spaces and large, high-ceilinged guest rooms furnished with American and European antiques and original artwork. Amenities include a restaurant, lobby lounge, rooftop pool, health club, and spa. Although located in the business district close to the federal courts and City Hall, it is just a short walk to the French Quarter. The deluxe, European-style hotel belongs to both Preferred Hotels and Historic Hotels of America.

Unquestionably the most luxurious hotel in New Orleans, the **Windsor Court**, located in the business district (300 Gravier Street, 504/523-6000), is the city's only AAA five-diamond hotel. It offers unsurpassed service in addition to luxury accommodations—most of which are suites—and a five-diamond restaurant. Located in the Garden District, the venerable **Pontchartrain Hotel** (2031 St. Charles Avenue, 504/524-0581 or 800/777-6193) has a reputation for impeccable service. Although the building is not architecturally significant, the rooms are spacious and well decorated. Renowned gourmet seafood is served in the Cafe Pontchartrain. As an added attraction, the hotel is on the St. Charles streetcar line and easily accessible to the French Quarter.

New Orleans has just about every chain hotel and motel you can think of. But remember that this is New Orleans, so even the chains are not cheap here. The average nightly rate is well over $100, and many rooms are over $125.

CAMPING

Jude Travel Park of New Orleans (7400 Chef Menteur Highway, 504/241-0632 or 800/523-2196) offers 43 campsites with full hookups, as well as cable TV, rest rooms, pool, hot tub, and laundry facilities. What's even better is that you can leave your car and take the shuttle or city bus to the French Quarter. Guided tour companies also pick up at the campground four times a day. The New Orleans West KOA Kampground (11129 Jefferson Highway, River Ridge, 504/467-1792) is the city's largest campground and offers shaded RV sites, landscaped common areas, rest rooms, a pool, lounge, and laundry facilities. Internet access is also available. Tour companies pick up from the campground, and you can take a city bus to the French Quarter. The New Orleans Riverboat Travel Park (6232 Chef Menteur Highway, 504/246-2628 or 800/726-0985) offers 68 RV sites with full hookups, TV, a pool, and a convenience store. The park is located on a bus line that you can take to the French Quarter.

NIGHTLIFE

New Orleans has rightly earned its reputation as a party town and a city that never sleeps. The French Quarter and Bourbon Street alone have dozens and dozens of nightclubs, jazz clubs, blues clubs, and bars. Among the jazz clubs, three are known worldwide. Pat O'Brien's Bar (718 St. Peter Street, 504/561-1200), home of the famous Hurricane cocktail, has entertainment in the main bar, the patio bar, and the piano lounge. Pete Fountain's Night Club in the New Orleans Hilton Hotel (2 Poydras Street, 504/524-6255 or 800/256-9979) features the living legend on clarinet as well as other jazz musicians. Fountain performs with his six-piece jazz band Tuesday, Wednesday, Friday, and Saturday at 10 p.m. Reservations are strongly recommended. The revolving Top of the Mart (2925 World Trade Center, 2 Canal Street, 504/522-9795) is also a popular spot with its panoramic views of New Orleans and the Mississippi River. And it seems that no American city is complete these days without a Hard Rock Cafe (418 North Peter, 504/529-7211) and a Planet Hollywood (Jackson Brewery, 504/529-5617).

In addition, many shops in the French Quarter are open very, very late to cater to tourists out wandering around at all hours.

In recent years, several casinos with a full range of wagering games have been added to this mix. They tend to come and go, however. Currently operating is Bally's Casino Lakeshore Resort (South Shore Harbor, 1 Stars and Stripes Boulevard, 504/248-3200 or 800/57-BALLY). The three paddle wheelers, *Natchez, Cajun Queen,* and *Creole Queen* (see Sightseeing Highlights), have dinner and entertainment cruises—most often with Dixieland jazz bands. As if all of these activities aren't enough, New Orleans has a very active cultural arts scene. The Louisiana Philharmonic Orchestra plays at the Orpheum Theater on University Place. Contact the symphony's administrative offices for a schedule and ticket prices (305 Baronne Street, 504/523-6530). Traveling Broadway shows, concerts, and other events are performed at the historic Saenger Theater (143 North Rampart Street, 504/525-1052). Other venues offer repertory theater, children's theater, and much more.

12
BATON ROUGE

Laissez les bon temps rouler—"Let the good times roll." New Orleans perhaps best exemplifies this southern Louisiana attitude, but Baton Rouge runs a close second.

Baton Rouge, which offers everything from alligators to zydeco, is a blend of Cajun, Creole, Old South, and New South. Located at a deepwater harbor on the Mississippi River, it is not only the state capital but also the home of Louisiana State University and Southern University. The city prospers from oil refineries and shipping. Although these industries can be unsightly, the refineries look like fairylands when they are lit up at night.

Baton Rouge is a delightful destination for tourists, offering neighborhoods of imposing antebellum and Victorian homes. Its riverfront has been transformed into a tasteful park. Tourists can visit the World War II destroyer USS *Kidd,* as well as gaudy casinos along the riverfront. Those who are interested in folklore will want to ask a native about politician Huey Long's story.

Baton Rouge celebrates Mardi Gras in almost as big a fashion as New Orleans does. In fact, some folks stay in Baton Rouge to enjoy its Mardi Gras and then travel to New Orleans for more festivities.

Once you get out of the city, you'll find beautiful plantation country and mysterious bayous and swamps. The Mississippi River Road between Baton Rouge and New Orleans offers one gorgeous plantation after another. Several small towns in the vicinity are worthy of a visit.

BATON ROUGE

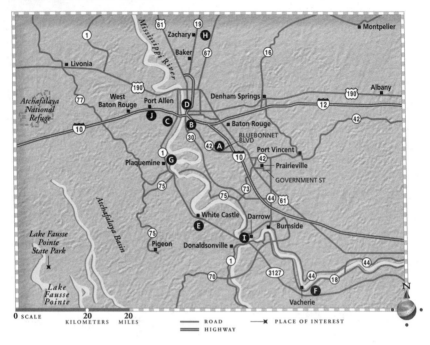

SIGHTS

Ⓐ Bluebonnet Swamp Nature Center
Ⓑ Magnolia Mound Plantation
Ⓒ Mississippi River Road
Ⓓ New State Capitol/Old Arsenal Museum
Ⓔ Nottoway Plantation
Ⓕ Oak Alley Plantation
Ⓓ Old State Capitol/Center of Political and Governmental History
Ⓖ Plaquemine Lock Museum
Ⓗ Port Hudson State Commemorative Area
Ⓑ Rural Life Museum and Windrush Gardens
Ⓘ Tezcuco Plantation
Ⓓ USS *Kidd* and Nautical History Center
Ⓙ West Baton Rouge Museum

Note: Items with the same letter are located in the same area.

A PERFECT DAY IN BATON ROUGE

To get oriented, take an overview guided tour, such as one provided by Lagniappe Tours. It will last an hour or so and may include admission to one or more attractions. If the tour does not include the Old State Capitol, Old Arsenal Museum, and New Capitol, visit them next.

Have an authentic Baton Rouge lunch of etouffee, a po' boy, or a muffuletta at Phil's Oyster Bar, then return to the waterfront and take a tour of the USS *Kidd* and the adjacent Nautical History Center. Take a step back in time at the Rural Life Museum and Windrush Gardens, where you can easily spend the rest of the afternoon.

Get dressed up for an out-of-this-world dinner at Lafitte's Landing. Depending on how many courses you order, this leisurely meal could take the rest of the evening and leave you so stuffed that you won't want to do anything else. If, however, you have energy to spare, the casinos offer wagering games and entertainment.

SIGHTSEEING HIGHLIGHTS

★★★★ MISSISSIPPI RIVER ROAD

Stretching along both sides of the Mississippi River from New Orleans to Baton Rouge, River Road is the site of some of the most magnificent plantations not just in Louisiana but in all of the South. Not only are several of them open for tours, but some also provide bed-and-breakfast accommodations and restaurants. The ones closest to Baton Rouge are **Nottoway**, **Tezcuco**, and **Oak Alley**, but you might want to venture a little farther to see **San Francisco** and **Destrahan**. The drive alone is well worth the trip.

Details: (2 hours for drive, 1 hour per plantation)

★★★★ NEW STATE CAPITOL/OLD ARSENAL MUSEUM
State Capitol Drive, 225/342-7317

Built in 1932 to replace the Old State Capitol, this state capitol is one of the only ones in the United States that is a skyscraper. You can tour the 34-story building, view the legislature when it is in session, see the bullet holes in the wall where Huey Long was assassinated, and ride the elevator to the top for a magnificent panorama of Baton Rouge and the Mississippi River. The Old Arsenal, which is on the capitol grounds, contains exhibits pertaining to Louisiana history, the Battle of Baton Rouge, and the development of the capitol.

Details: Daily 8–4:30; gift shop and observation tower close at 4.
Free; arsenal $1 adults, 50 cents children. (1 hour)

★★★★ NOTTOWAY PLANTATION
30765 Mississippi River Road, White Castle, 225/545-2730 or 225/545-2409

One of the most glorious plantation homes in the South, Nottoway
is the largest plantation mansion to survive the antebellum era and
the Civil War. Completed in the 1850s, it soon earned the nickname
White Castle—as well it should have with 65 rooms and 65,000
square feet of living space. It is an elegant combination of Greek
Revival and Italianate architecture. A restaurant and overnight accommodations are offered.

Details: Daily 9–5. $8 adults, $3 children. (1–2 hours)

★★★★ OAK ALLEY PLANTATION
3645 LA 18, Vacherie, 225/265-2151 or 800/44-ALLEY

The plantation is world famous for its quarter-mile alley of gigantic,
evenly spaced, 300-year-old live oaks leading up to the house. Built between 1837 and 1839, the house is a supreme example of Greek
Revival style and is furnished with period antiques and reproductions. A
restaurant and overnight accommodations are part of the plantation.

Details: Daily 9–5. $8 adults, $5 children 13–18, $3 6–12. (1 hour)

★★★★ OLD STATE CAPITOL/CENTER OF POLITICAL AND GOVERNMENTAL HISTORY
100 North Boulevard, 225/342-0500 (capitol) 225/342-0401 (arsenal)

This forbidding, gray, castlelike building facing the river was the state
capitol from 1850 until 1932, when Governor Huey Long decided it
wasn't big and impressive enough. Given the appearance outside,
you'll be pleasantly surprised by the cheerful interior. Black-and-white
checkerboard floors enhance the upstairs and downstairs areas in
the rotunda. A graceful, gleaming, brass and wood spiral staircase
connects both stories. Today the building contains the Office of the
Secretary of State and the Center for Political and Governmental
History, as well as many interactive exhibits.

Details: Old Capitol open Tue–Sat 10–4:30, Sun noon–4:30,
closed Mon. Old Capitol $4 adults, $3 seniors and veterans, $2 children.
(1 hour)

★★★★ PORT HUDSON STATE COMMEMORATIVE AREA
756 West Plains–Port Hudson Road, Zachary
225/654-3775

This attraction was the site of one of the most important campaigns of the Civil War. The 643-acre site was the last Confederate stronghold on the Mississippi River. Once Federal troops captured New Orleans, Vicksburg, and Port Hudson, the Confederacy was cut in half and its doom sealed. Original earthworks have been preserved, and a museum houses Civil War artifacts.

Details: Daily 9–5. $2 adults. (1 hour)

★★★★ RURAL LIFE MUSEUM AND WINDRUSH GARDENS
4600 Essen Lane, 225/765-2437

This outdoor museum is a project of Louisiana State University. It consists of 20 nineteenth-century plantation and rural buildings, moved to the site from other places in Louisiana. Enhancing the structures are hundreds of artifacts, including furnishings and equipment appropriate to the period. Adjacent to the museum is a 25-acre garden displaying classical statuary.

Details: Daily 8:30–5. $5 adults, $4 seniors, $3 children. (1–2 hours)

CYPRESS SWAMP

© Carol Thalimer

★★★★ TEZCUCO PLANTATION
3138 LA 44, Darrow, 225/562-3929

Built in 1855, the graceful Greek Revival raised cottage is framed by ancient live oaks and trimmed with wrought iron on the full-length front veranda. Other superb architectural details include ornate friezes and medallions; furnishings reflect French influence. The plantation features a restaurant and offers overnight accommodations.

Details: Daily 9–5. $7 adults; $6 seniors, AAA members, and teens; $3.25 children 12 and under. (1 hour)

★★★★ USS *KIDD* AND NAUTICAL HISTORY CENTER
305 South River Road, 225/342-1942

This World War II destroyer has been designated as a National Historic Landmark and is open for tours or just exploring. The Nautical History Center contains ship models, airplanes, a Hall of Honor, and a Vietnam War memorial.

Details: Daily 9–5. $6 adults, $5 seniors, $3.50 children. (1–2 hours)

★★★ MAGNOLIA MOUND PLANTATION
2161 Nicholson Drive, 225/343-4955

This restored French Creole home, which sits on 16 acres, dates to 1790 and is furnished suitably. Open-hearth cooking is demonstrated seasonally.

Details: Tue–Sat 10–4. $5 adults, $4 seniors, $2 students 13–22, $1 children 5–12. (1 hour)

★★★ WEST BATON ROUGE MUSEUM
845 North Jefferson Avenue, Port Allen

Located across the river in Port Allen, this open-air museum contains a working model of a 1904 sugar mill, an 1850 plantation cabin, and an 1830 French Creole cottage.

Details: Tue–Sat 10–4:30, Sun 2–5. Free. (1 hour)

★★ BLUEBONNET SWAMP NATURE CENTER
10503 North Oak Hills Parkway, 225/273-6405

Here you can hike on two miles of nature trails, winding through a magnolia and beech forest and into the heart of a 65–acre cypress swamp. The center houses Louisiana-based nature exhibits, including a large duck decoy display and more than 25 species of reptiles and amphibians, including live baby alligators. See what's really inhabiting that swamp.

Details: Tue–Sat 9–5, Sun 12–5. $3 adults, $2 children, $1 discount parish residents. (1 hour)

★★ PLAQUEMINE LOCK MUSEUM
57730 Main Street, Plaquemine, 225/687-7158 or 877/987-7158

The Plaquemine Lock on the Mississippi River was constructed in 1909. The adjacent museum features a working lock model, an observation deck overlooking the lock, and guided tours. It also serves as the Plaquemine Tourist Information Center.

Details: Daily 9–5. $2 adults, free seniors and children under 12. (^{1}/2 hour)

FITNESS AND RECREATION

One of the most popular walking/jogging paths in Baton Rouge is the level, paved levee, which stretches for miles along the waterfront. Fun-filled, family-oriented Blue Bayou Water Park (18142 Perkins Road, 225/753-3333) features 11 water slides, a wave pool, and lazy river, as well as snack bars. The campus of Louisiana State University offers many recreational activities, not only for students and faculty but also for the general public, who are welcome to use the running tracks, numerous fields, and gymnasium. The university has a golf course and several lakes.

FOOD

Begin with the best. World-famous Cajun/Creole/French chef John Folse presides over **Lafitte's Landing** (Bittersweet Plantation, Donaldsonville, 225/473-1232), an imposing house in a semi-rural setting with lovely grounds. Two bed-and-breakfast rooms are offered as well. Magnificent **Nottoway Plantation** (30765 Mississippi River Road, White Castle, 225/545-2730 or 225/545-2409), the largest plantation house in the South, has a restaurant in a building adjacent to the main house. The cuisine showcases progressive Cajun and traditional Southern dishes. The Culinary Arts Institute of Louisiana runs an elegant white-linen restaurant called **Caila's Fine Cuisine** (427 Lafayette Street, 225/343-6233 or 800/927-0839), operated by students at the institute. Demonstrations and tours of the institute are given to diners.

BATON ROUGE

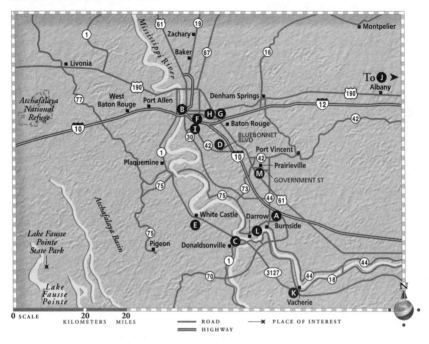

FOOD
- **Ⓐ** Cabin Restaurant
- **Ⓑ** Caila's Fine Cuisine
- **Ⓒ** Lafitte's Landing
- **Ⓓ** Mulate's
- **Ⓔ** Nottoway Plantation
- **Ⓕ** Phil's Oyster Bar

LODGING
- **Ⓑ** Allround Suites
- **Ⓖ** Best Western Chateau Louisianne
- **Ⓗ** Best Western Richmond Suites
- **Ⓘ** Embassy Suites

LODGING *(continued)*
- **Ⓙ** Garden Gate Manor Bed and Breakfast
- **Ⓔ** Nottoway Plantation
- **Ⓚ** Oak Alley Plantation
- **Ⓘ** Radisson Suite Hotel
- **Ⓛ** Tezcuco Plantation
- **Ⓜ** Treehouse in the Park

Note: Items with the same letter are located in the same area.

Get the flavor of rural Louisiana at the **Cabin Restaurant** (intersection of LA 22 and LA 44, Burnside, 225/473-3007). Located in a rustic log cottage, the restaurant is filled with farm memorabilia. Menu items include the restaurant's signature chicken and andouille gumbo. Also located on the property is an old country store and several slave cabins restored to their original condition. In addition to authentic Cajun cuisine, **Mulate's** (8322 Bluebonnet Road, 225/767-4794) is a popular place for traditional Cajun music, performed nightly. Although **Phil's Oyster Bar** (5162 Government Street, 225/924-3045), a favorite of locals, has a dated 1950s ambience, it has a fantastic menu of Cajun and Creole foods such as etouffee, andouille, boudin, muffulettas, po' boys, and other favorites.

LODGING

Historic townhouses, plantation houses, and even cabins in the swamp make perfect B&Bs, about a dozen of which are in the area. The premier B&B is **Nottoway Plantation** (30765 Mississippi River Road, White Castle, 225/545-2730 or 225/545-2409), which offers superior accommodations in the main house and in several historic outbuildings. First-class B&B accommodations are also offered at **Oak Alley Plantation** (3645 LA 18, Vacherie, 800/44-ALLEY) and at **Tezcuco Plantation** (3138 LA 44, Darrow, 225/562-3929).

Treehouse in the Park (16520 Airport Road, Prairieville, 225/622-3885 or 800/LE-CABIN) is actually a Cajun cabin in the swamp. However, the B&B offers modern amenities such as queen-size waterbeds, TVs, hot tubs, and a pool. Dinner can be arranged by appointment.

Thirty minutes northwest of Baton Rouge is New Roads, the oldest French settlement in the Old South. **Garden Gate Manor Bed and Breakfast**, 204 Poydras St., New Roads, 800/487-3890 or 225/638-3890, a Creole manor house, features five elegant guest rooms (non-smoking) with private baths. As guests arrive, they are offered a familiarity tour of the manor. English tea is offered each afternoon, and guests awaken in the morning to a sumptuous four-star breakfast. Garden Gate has been rated one of the "Top 10 Historic B&Bs in the South."

For whatever reason, Baton Rouge seems to have more all-suite hotels than most comparable cities. Perhaps it is because legislators and those with government or university business need to make long-term stays. Among these properties are **Best Western Chateau Louisianne** (710 North Lobdell Avenue, 225/927-6700 or 800/256-6263); **Best Western Richmond Suites** (5668 Hilton Avenue, 225/924-6500 or 800/332-2582), **Embassy Suites** (4914 Constitution Avenue, 225/924-6566 or 800/EM-BASSY), **Allround Suites** (2045 North Third Street, 225/344-6000), and **Radisson Suite Hotel** (4728 Constitution Avenue, 225/925-2244). Although each hotel has its own personality and amenities, in general, they offer a full breakfast and afternoon cocktails and hors d'oeuvres. Most feature a pool, and some have exercise facilities as well.

CAMPING

In addition to campsites, Baton Rouge KOA Campground (7628 Vincent Road, Denham Springs, 225/664-7281) offers a pool, kiddie pool, and hot tub. Cajun Country Campground (4667 Rebelle Lane, Port Allen, 225/264-8554) has full hookups, a pool, bathhouses, a laundry room, store, and free Cajun dinner on Saturday nights. Night's RV Park (14740 Florida Boulevard, 225/275-0679) is located in a quiet wooded area and offers cement pads, full hookups, and laundry facilities.

NIGHTLIFE

Like the other major river towns in Louisiana, the casino bug has bitten Baton Rouge. The Belle of Baton Rouge Casino at Catfish Town (103 France Avenue, 225/266-2692 or 800/378-LUCK) claims to be the largest land/riverboat casino complex in the United States. Casino Rouge (1717 River Road North, 225/381-7777 or 800/44-ROUGE), owned by Carnival Cruise Line, is open 24 hours a day and offers all the major wagering games, as well as a restaurant and bar.

A popular nightclub is Tabby Blues Box Heritage Hall (1314 North Boulevard, 225/387-9715). Or check to see if the Baton Rouge Little Theater (7155 Florida Boulevard, 225/924-6496) is doing a production.

In addition, with two universities in town, opportunities to watch college sports are numerous. Be sure to buy tickets in advance because many events—particularly football—sell out.

Scenic Route: Lake Charles to Thibodaux

National Geographic Traveler named this west-to-east route through Cajun country the best scenic route in Louisiana. The route parallels the Intracoastal Waterway.

Begin in Lake Charles. Located where I-10 and U.S. 171 cross in southwestern Louisiana, the city overlooks the lake from which it took its name and has the only white sand inland beach along the Gulf Coast. The city's Charpentier District has 20 blocks of Victorian architecture so unique it is called Lake Charles style.

Take LA 14 to Lake Arthur. In the historic district, sidewalks are paved with brick, and gaslights cast a romantic glow. Outside of town, the Lacassine National Wildlife Refuge (209 Nature Road, Lake Arthur, 318/774-5923) offers 30,000 acres of freshwater marsh.

Continue east on LA 14 to Gueydan, noted for the Gueydan Duck Festival—a four-day event that includes duck calling and duck carving. Just to the east is Kaplan, where you can tour a working farm. Continue east to Abbeville, which claims to be "the most Cajun place on earth." Nearby marshy land is inhabited by a multitude of waterfowl and marine life. Continue east to Erath and visit the Acadian History Museum (203 South Broadway).

Keep going east on LA 14 to U.S. 90, then turn south on the Old Spanish Trail to New Iberia, home of the Conrad Rice Mill (307 Ann Street, 318/364-7242 or

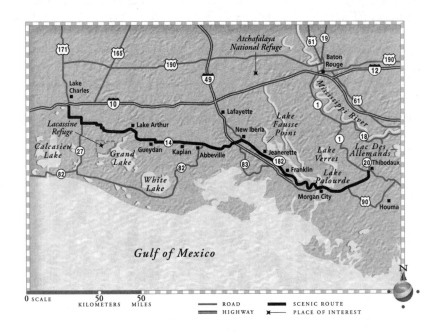

800/551-3245), the oldest operating rice mill in America. Reproductions and collectibles are on sale in the historic Oliver Plantation Store (6811 Weeks Island Road, 318/369-7696). Visit the authentically restored and interpreted 1834 house Shadows-on-the-Teche (317 East Main Street, 318/369-6446), one of the most famous homes in the South. An exciting way to explore the town's swamps, bayous, and sloughs is by airboat. Several companies offer tours.

Go northeast on LA 83 to LA 182, which is the LaFourche/Terrebonne Scenic Byway, and turn south to Jeanerette. The Jeanerette Museum (500 East Main Street, 318/276-4408) traces 200 years of sugarcane history. A Swamp Room displays taxidermied wildlife, and the Mardi Gras Room exhibits lavish costumes.

Continue south on LA 182 to Franklin, a city with more than 400 historic buildings. Among them are the Grevemberg House Museum (407 Sterling Road, 318/828-2092) and Oaklawn Manor Plantation (3296 East Oaklawn, 318/828-0434).

Stay on LA 182 until you get to Morgan City, site of a "black gold rush," where oil was stuck offshore. The International Petroleum Museum and Exposition (111 First Street, 225/384-3744, www.rigmuseum.com, e-mail: rigmuseum@petronet.net) features an authentic drilling rig that visitors can board. Stop at the Original Swamp Gardens (725 Myrtle Street, 225/384-3343) for a guided tour through 3.5 acres of natural swamp. The Brownell Memorial Nature Park and Carillon Tower and Bird Sanctuary (off U.S. 70, 225/384-2283) is a 9.5-acre park with one of the world's largest and finest cast-bell carillons. Scully's Swamp Tours (3141 LA 70, 225/385-2388) offers trips deep into the bayous. Cajun Houseboat Rentals (Stephensville, 225/385-2738) provides rentals on Bayou Long.

From Morgan City, leave the Old Spanish Trail and take LA 20 northeast to Thibodaux, where French is widely spoken. See the Edward Douglass White Historic Site (2295 St. Mary Street, 225/447-0915), an antebellum Creole plantation. Finally, visit the Wetlands Acadian Cultural Center at the Jean Lafitte National Historical Park and Preserve (314 St. Mary Street, 225/448-1375).

13
ST. FRANCISVILLE

This region is called Plantation Country, and when you see the rolling terrain dotted with Spanish-moss-draped live oaks, you'll understand why it was so attractive to eighteenth- and nineteenth-century planters. Many who built their magnificent homes here—often adding opulent gardens—were of French or French Creole descent.

Fortunately, most of the wonderful homes, gardens, and oak alleys survived the Civil War, natural disasters, and the ravages of time, and you can visit them today. Some are open for tours; others can be viewed only during annual pilgrimages. Still others operate as bed-and-breakfasts or restaurants.

Although visitors spend most of their time indoors touring the plantation houses, the area is ideal for outdoor activities such as hiking, bird-watching, and bicycling. A new resort boasts an Arnold Palmer golf course.

At night, not much goes on in the small, quiet town. In fact, when asked about nightlife, one local's advice was "bring a good book, there ain't none." For those who crave after-dark entertainment, the casinos and nightspots of Baton Rouge are only 40 minutes away.

A PERFECT DAY IN ST. FRANCISVILLE

Begin a leisurely day at the West Feliciana Historical Society Museum, which also serves as a visitors center. Pick up a *Walk Through History* brochure, which

183

ST. FRANCISVILLE

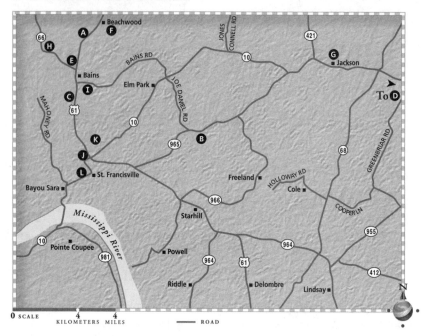

SIGHTS

- **A** Afton Villa Gardens
- **B** Audubon State Commemorative Area/Oakley House
- **C** Butler Greenwood
- **D** Casa de Sue Winery
- **E** Catalpa Plantation
- **F** Cottage Plantation
- **G** Feliciana Cellars Winery
- **H** Greenwood Plantation
- **I** Locust Grove State Commemorative Area
- **J** The Myrtles Plantation
- **K** Rosedown Plantation
- **L** Walk Through History Tour
- **L** West Feliciana Historical Society Museum

Note: Items with the same letter are located in the same area.

describes 140 significant buildings in and around St. Francisville. This tour, a feast for the eyes, can easily take all morning.

Enjoy both lunch and ghost stories at Myrtles Plantation. After lunch try to see two or more of the many plantations that surround the town. Begin with Greenwood Plantation and learn about its eventful past. Next, go to Rosedown Plantation, significant not only because the house and furnishings are so exceptional, but also because it has an impressive oak alley and one of the most important gardens in the South. Have dinner at the quaint St. Francisville Inn.

SIGHTSEEING HIGHLIGHTS

★★★★ GREENWOOD PLANTATION
6838 Highland, 225/655-4475
This famed Greek Revival mansion has had a dramatic past. Built in 1830, it is the centerpiece of a lovely plantation. Although it survived the Civil War, it was destroyed by fire in 1960, with only the stately columns surviving. Fortunately some of the furnishings and art were saved. The current owners rebuilt an exact replica of the house in 1980 and were able to obtain some of the original furnishings and art. The mansion is so representative of Southern plantation homes that it has appeared in several movies and the TV miniseries *North and South*. Bed-and-breakfast accommodations are offered in the main house and adjacent cottage.
Details: Daily Mar–Nov 9–5, 10–4 rest of the year. $6 adults, $5 groups and tours. (1 hour)

★★★★ THE MYRTLES PLANTATION
7747 U.S. 61, 225/635-6277 or 800/809-0565
Built in 1796, the plantation house has a rich history of elegance and intrigue. In fact, the Myrtles is reputed to be haunted by several ghosts and has even been called America's Most Haunted House. It has also been featured in several TV programs. The restored house is filled with art treasures and priceless antiques, many of them of French influence. Kean's Carriage House Restaurant (225/635-6276) is open for lunch and dinner Wed–Sat 11–9, Sun brunch 11–2. Bed-and-breakfast accommodations are offered in the main house and adjacent cottage.
Details: Tours daily 9–5. $8. (1 hour)

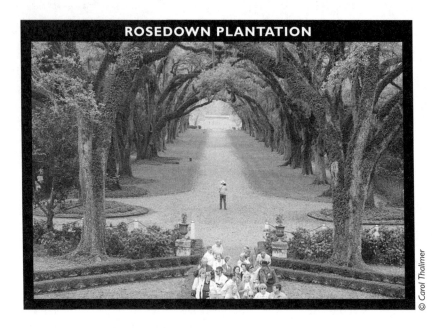

ROSEDOWN PLANTATION

© Carol Thalimer

★★★★ **ROSEDOWN PLANTATION**
12501 LA 10, 225/635-3332
The mansion is an exquisitely restored example of antebellum extravagance and is considered by many to be Louisiana's finest museum house. The majority of the furnishings are original to the house. The 28-acre garden is patterned on opulent gardens of eighteenth-century France. Bed-and-breakfast accommodations are offered in an adjacent house.

Details: Daily 9–5. $10 adults, $8.95 seniors and AAA members, free children under 10. (2 hours)

★★★ **CATALPA PLANTATION**
9508 U.S. 61, 225/635-3372
This late-Victorian home, filled with family treasures accumulated over five generations, sits in a serene, parklike setting.

Details: Daily Feb–Nov 10–noon and 2–4; closed Dec and Jan except by appointment. $6. (1 hour)

★★★ **COTTAGE PLANTATION**
10528 Cottage Lane, 225/635-3674

This early 1800s plantation, one of Louisiana's most complete plantation complexes, comprises 10 original dependency buildings as well as a big house from that period. One of the most striking features of the house is the 100-foot veranda. Overnight guests are welcome and a restaurant is on site.

Details: *Daily 9–5. $5 adults. (1 hour)*

★★★ LOCUST GROVE STATE COMMEMORATIVE AREA
Brains-Ristroph Road, 225/635-3739

The one-acre cemetery contains the graves of Sarah Knox Taylor, first wife of Confederate President Jefferson Davis, and General Eleazor W. Ripley, hero of the Battle of Lundy's Lane in the War of 1812.

Details: *Daily 9–5. Free. (1/2 hour)*

★★★ WALK THROUGH HISTORY TOUR
West Feliciana Historical Society Museum
11757 Ferdinand Street, 225/635-6330

Pick up a walking/driving tour brochure from the West Feliciana Historical Society Museum. The tour includes 140 historical structures, including Grace Episcopal Church, the state's second oldest Episcopal congregation, and Our Lady of Mount Carmel Catholic Church, designed by Confederate General P. G. T. Beauregard. The historic commercial buildings on Ferdinand Street house a dozen shops filled with gifts and antiques.

Details: *Mon–Sat 9–5, Sun 9:30–5. Free. (1–2 hours)*

★★★ WEST FELICIANA HISTORICAL SOCIETY MUSEUM
11757 Ferdinand Street, 225/635-6330

A former hardware store has been restored to house the museum, which contains memorabilia such as flags, wire sculptures of early residents, and charming miniature rooms. The museum has a gift shop and serves as the ticket office for the annual Audubon Pilgrimage.

Details: *Mon–Sat 9–5, Sun 9:30–5. Free. (1/2 hour)*

★★ AFTON VILLA GARDENS
9247 U.S. 61, 225/635-6773

Afton Villa was a Gothic-style mansion that was destroyed by a 1963 fire. However, the surrounding gardens, modeled after those of eighteenth-century France, survive and are open in season.

You'll approach them through a serpentine avenue lined with oaks and azaleas.

Details: *Daily Mar–May and Oct–Dec 1 9–4:30. $4. (1 hour)*

★★ AUDUBON STATE COMMEMORATIVE AREA/ OAKLEY HOUSE
11788 LA 965, 225/635-3739
Famed naturalist and painter John James Audubon lived and worked as a tutor at Oakley House while painting 32 of his famous *Birds of America* series. The house, built in 1799, has definite West Indian influences such as a raised brick basement, jalousied galleries, and exterior staircases. The furnishings are of the late-Federal style.

Details: *Daily 9–5. $2. (1 hour)*

★★ BUTLER GREENWOOD
8345 U.S. 61, 225/635-6312
Begun in 1795, the plantation amazingly remains in the same family. The tour includes the house, furnished in opulent Victorian style with many original antiques, and the gardens. The house offers bed-and-breakfast accommodations (see Lodging).

Details: *Daily 9–5, except Sun 1–5. $5. (1 hour)*

★★ CASA DE SUE WINERY
14316 Hatcher Road, Clinton, 225/683-5937
Louisiana's first licensed winery, Casa de Sue is an off-the-beaten-path attraction. It is open for tours and tastings.

Details: *Mon–Sat 10–6, Sun by appointment. Free. (1 hour)*

★★ FELICIANA CELLARS WINERY
1848 Charter Street, Jackson, 225/634-7982
Located in an elegant Spanish mission-style structure in the heart of the Feliciana, the winery specializes in wines made from the abundant muscadine grape. After a tour, there's a tasting, and a variety of wines are for sale.

Details: *Mon–Fri 10–5, Sat 9–5, Sun 1–5. Free. (1 hour)*

FITNESS AND RECREATION
The Bluffs on Thompson Creek (LA 965 at Freeland Road, 225/634-3410 or 888/634-3410) is a resort with an Arnold Palmer golf course, tennis courts, and

swimming. Steep loess bluffs and woodlands with winding trails characterize the 1,200-acre Clark Creek Preservation Area (182 Fort Adams Pond Road, Woodville, 601/888-4426). The preserve has five waterfalls of up to 50 feet in height and is a popular picnicking, hiking, and photography outing.

FOOD

Located in a historic dependency building on the famous, 200-year-old Myrtles Plantation, the upscale, bistrolike **Carriage House Restaurant** (7747 U.S. 61, 225/635-6276) serves lunch and dinner Wednesday through Saturday and brunch on Sunday. Afternoon tea is served by reservation only. Located in a unique country setting, **Mattie's House at the Cottage Plantation** (10528 Cottage Lane, 225/635-3674) offers candlelight dining Friday through Monday and features seafood and steak. **D'John's Restaurant** (5051 U.S. 61, 225/635-6982) specializes in seafood, steaks, and barbecue served in a comfortable family atmosphere. **Cotton's Seafood and Steaks** (U.S. 61, 225/635-4004) is known for its all-you-can-eat Friday night specials. All three meals are served daily. Local cuisine is served three meals a day, including a lunch buffet, at the **St. Francisville Hotel on the Lake** (LA 10 at U.S. 61, 225/635-3821). Louisiana and European cuisine are served three meals a day at **the Bluffs on Thompson Creek** (Sunrise Way off LA 965, 225/634-5088).

LODGING

This area, so rich in historical homes, offers almost two dozen B&Bs. One of the most outstanding is **Rosedown Plantation** (12501 LA 10, 225/635-3332), where elegant, antique-filled guest rooms feature canopied beds, private baths, and a full breakfast. The estate also offers a swimming pool and tennis courts.

The Audubon Pilgrimage, *held in March, is the only time many private homes are open for tours. Tickets, available from the West Feliciana Historical Museum, must be purchased in advance.*

The **St. Francisville Inn** (5720 North Commerce Street, 225/635-6502 or 800/488-6502) offers cozy, casual accommodations in the main house and dependency buildings. Guests are served a full buffet breakfast daily. The inn also offers breakfast to the public and serves prearranged meals to groups. **Butler Greenwood** (8345 U.S. 61, 225/635-6312) provides accommodations in cottages on the oak-shaded plantation grounds. Rates include a tour of the antebellum main house, use of the pool, and a continental breakfast. The

ST. FRANCISVILLE

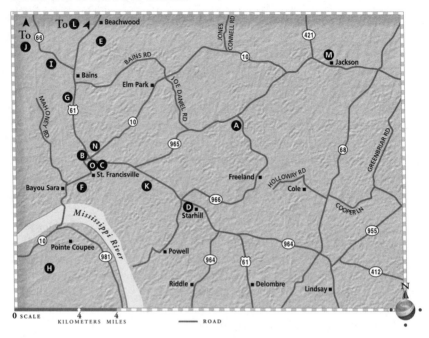

FOOD
- **A** The Bluffs on Thompson Creek
- **B** Carriage House Restaurant
- **C** Cotton's Seafood and Steaks
- **D** D'John's Restaurant
- **E** Mattie's House at the Cottage Plantation
- **B** St. Francisville Hotel on the Lake

LODGING
- **F** Barrow House Inn
- **G** Butler Greenwood
- **E** Cottage Inn
- **H** Garden Gate Manor
- **I** Green Springs Inn & Cottages
- **J** Greenwood Plantation Bed and Breakfast

LODGING (continued)
- **K** Hemingbough
- **H** Jubilee
- **L** Lake Rosemond Inn
- **A** The Lodge at the Bluff
- **M** Milbank Historic House
- **H** Mon Coeur
- **H** Mon Reve
- **B** The Myrtles
- **M** Old Centenary Inn
- **H** River Blossom Inn
- **N** Rosedown Plantation
- **G** Shadetree
- **B** St. Francis Hotel on the Lake
- **O** St. Francisville Inn
- **H** Sunrise on the River

Note: Items with the same letter are located in the same area.

Cottage Inn (10528 Cottage Lane, 225/635-3674) features a swimming pool and a restaurant. **Green Springs Inn & Cottages** (7463 Tunica Trace, 225/635-4232 or 800/457-4978, www.greensprings-inn.com), located in a quiet setting with lush gardens, wildlife, and a woodlands walk, offers spacious bedrooms, restored cottages with Jacuzzi tubs, and a plantation breakfast. The house was built by "Spinach" Madeline Nevill and features fine architectural details, antiques, and art.

Several plantations operate as B&Bs only. The **Barrow House Inn** (9779 Royal Street, 225/635-4791, wwwtopteninn.com) has earned rave reviews from *Southern Living* magazine and features among its attractions some original Audubon works, period antiques, and a teddy bear collection. Audubon works are also displayed at **Hemingbough** (10591 Beech Road, 225/635-6617). Other B&Bs in St. Francisville are **Lake Rosemond Inn** (10473 Lindsey Lane, 225/635-3176) and **Shadetree** (Royal at Ferdinand, 225/635-6116).

B&Bs can also be found in nearby small towns. In Jackson stay at **Milbank Historic House** (3045 Bank Street, 225/634-5901). New Roads has several B&Bs: **Garden Gate Manor** (204 Poydras Street, 225/638-3890 or 800/487-3890); **Jubilee** (11704 Pointe Coupee Road, 225/638-8333); **Mon Coeur** (7739 False River Drive, 225/638-9892); **Mon Reve** (9825 False River Road, 225/638-7848 or 800/324-2738, www.monreve-mydream.com, e-mail: monreve@eatel.net); **River Blossom Inn** (300 North Carolina Avenue, 225/638-8650, e-mail: ebarry@bellsouth.net); and **Sunrise on the River** (1825 False River Road, 225/638-3642 or 800/644-3642).

Although not a bed-and-breakfast, the **Old Centenary Inn** (1740 Charter, Jackson, 225/634-5151) is a charming, historic inn that offers modern amenities such as Jacuzzis. **St. Francis Hotel on the Lake** (U.S. 1 and LA 10, 225/635-3821) is perched on a wooded piece of property overlooking a small lake. **The Lodge at the Bluff** (Sunrise Way off LA 965, 225/634-3410 or 888/634-3410, www.thebluff.com) is a resort with all-suites accommodations and a restaurant.

The Myrtles, 7747 Hwy. 61, 225/635–6277, was built by David Bradford, a general in George Washington's army and the leader of the historic Whiskey Rebellion. And speaking of spirits, you might be visited by the resident ghost if you stay overnight in one of 10 antique-filled guest rooms. Incredible iron grillwork embellishes a front gallery stretching 107 feet, and double parlors boast chandeliers, gilded mirrors, and Carrera marble. Enjoy the continental breakfast in the morning and be sure to sample the homemade biscuits and preserves.

Rocking chairs on the front porch and balconies on the second floor provide wonderful spots to relax at the **Greenwood Plantation Bed and Breakfast**, 6838 Highland Rd., 225/655–3850. Twelve guest rooms include one that is handicapped accessible. Enjoy a full, hot breakfast before touring the main plantation house.

14
LAFAYETTE

It's called Acadiana, but you may not be able to find Acadiana on a map. It's also called Cajun Country. That's a state of mind, not a place, so that name may not be much help either. By any name, Lafayette is the heart and soul of French Louisiana. Now we're getting somewhere.

If you think of Louisiana as a boot, Lafayette is centrally located in the foot portion. French explorers, trappers, and traders settled this area of Louisiana. A major influx of Catholic French Canadians occurred after they were expelled from Acadia, Canada, because they refused to pledge allegiance to England and the Anglican Church. They took the name Acadia with them, and the descendants of these Acadians are today's Cajuns.

The region also shows evidence of an incredible blend of Native American, Spanish, English, and African American cultures. Other characteristics are spicy food, zydeco music and dance, and a distinctive regional dialect—almost a separate language.

Southern Louisiana has a more diverse terrain than other regions of the state. Part of the area is coastal, part is bayou and swamp, and part is prairie. Although Lafayette is the main city, it has a small-town feel. Small villages—often surrounded by plantations—characterize the remainder of the area. Breaux Bridge is known as the Crawfish Capital of the World, and St. Martinville is the third oldest town in Louisiana. It is no surprise that a region so rich in history has many historic homes to visit as well as museums and bed-and-breakfasts.

LAFAYETTE

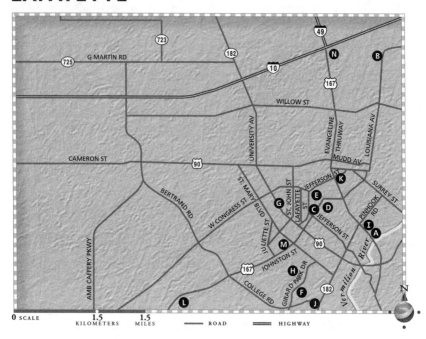

SIGHTS

Ⓐ Acadian Cultural Center/Jean Lafitte
   National Historical Park and Preserve
Ⓑ Acadian Park Nature Station and Trail
Ⓒ Alexandre Mouton House/Lafayette
   Museum
Ⓓ Cajun Country Store
Ⓔ Children's Museum of Acadiana
Ⓕ Lafayette Natural History Museum
Ⓖ St. John Cathedral, Cemetery,
   Museum, and Oak Tree
Ⓗ University Art Museum
Ⓘ Vermilionville

FOOD

Ⓙ Café Vermilionville
Ⓚ Dwyer's Café
Ⓛ La Fonda Restaurant
Ⓜ Prejean's

LODGING

Ⓝ Holiday Inn Central/
   Holidome

A PERFECT DAY IN LAFAYETTE

Spend the morning learning about Acadian history and culture at the living history villages at the Acadian Culture Center and Vermilionville. Have lunch at Dwyer's Café. Find out more about Lafayette at the Alexandre Mouton House/Lafayette Museum. To really understand what the Acadians encountered when they first came to Louisiana, take a swamp/bayou tour. Several are offered; we suggest Angelle's Atchafalaya Swamp Tours. Switch gears again to have dinner at Café Vermilionville. End the evening two-stepping at Randol's or watching horse races at Evangeline Downs.

SIGHTSEEING HIGHLIGHTS: LAFAYETTE

★★★★ ACADIAN CULTURAL CENTER/JEAN LAFITTE NATIONAL HISTORICAL PARK AND PRESERVE
501 Fisher Road, 318/232-0789
www.nps.gov/jela/acadianculturalcenter.htm

At the cultural center, a film chronicles the departure of the Acadians from Canada and their arrival in Louisiana. Exhibits and artifacts show their history, language, cuisine, music, architecture, and way of life—in early Louisiana as well as today.

Details: Daily 8–5, movie shown on the hour 9–4. Free. (1 hour)

★★★★ VERMILIONVILLE
1600 Surrey Street, 318/233-4077 or 800/99-BAYOU
www.vermilionville.org

Acadian/Creole folklife from the mid-1700s to the late 1800s is explored at the 23-acre park. Located on Bayou Vermilion, the park features carefully crafted period homes filled with artifacts and antiques. Craftspeople and living history interpreters give demonstrations of old-time skills and crafts. Other activities include music, Cajun/Creole cooking, and art. Also on the grounds are an art gallery, bakery, gift shop, and restaurant.

Details: Daily 10–5. $8 adults, $6.50 seniors, $5 children. (2 hours)

★★★ ALEXANDRE MOUTON HOUSE/LAFAYETTE MUSEUM
1122 Lafayette Street, 318/234-2208

The nineteenth-century house was the home of Lafayette's first mayor and Louisiana's first Democratic governor. The house is filled with Acadiana artifacts as well as one-of-a-kind antiques and Mardi Gras costumes.

Details: Tue–Sat 9–5, Sun 3–5. $3 adults, $2 seniors, $1 students. (1 hour)

★★★ CHILDREN'S MUSEUM OF ACADIANA
201 East Congress Street, 318/232-8500

In the hands-on educational facility, children have so much fun, they don't realize they are learning, too. The museum is dedicated to demystifying everyday puzzles for kids.

Details: Tue–Sat 10–5. $5 adults and members, free children under 1. (1 1/2 hours)

★★★ LAFAYETTE NATURAL HISTORY MUSEUM
637 Girard Park Drive, 318/291-5544, www.lnhm.org

Changing exhibits depict area culture and the natural world. In addition, the complex features a planetarium where you can see various sky shows.

Details: Mon, Wed, Thu, Fri 9–5, Tue 9–9, weekends 1–5; call for planetarium's schedule. Free. (1 1/2 hours)

★★ ACADIAN PARK NATURE STATION AND TRAIL
East Alexander, 318/291-8448 or 318/291-5544

Set in 50 acres of bottomland forest, the park offers 3 1/2 miles of trails. Nature studies and workshops are held at the center.

Details: Mon–Fri 9–5, weekends 11–3. Free, guided tours for school groups, weekend guided trail walk at 1. (1 hour)

★★ CAJUN COUNTRY STORE
401 East Cypress Street, 318/233-7977 or 800/252-9689, www.cajuncountrystore.com

Located in a 1930s warehouse, the authentic country store, affectionately known as the One-Stop Cajun Shop, features the work of local craftspeople, artists, and musicians, as well as regional books, cookbooks, T-shirts, and other items.

Details: Daily 10–6. Free. (1/2–1 hour)

★★ ST. JOHN CATHEDRAL, CEMETERY, MUSEUM, AND OAK TREE
914 St. John Street, 318/232-1322

Although churches have stood on this spot since 1821, this cathedral is the third structure and is of Dutch Romanesque architecture. The museum features church history. A gift shop is located on the premises. The oak is reputed to be 500 years old. Many founders of Lafayette are buried in the cemetery.

Details: Weekdays 9–noon and 1–4. Free. (1 hour)

★★ UNIVERSITY ART MUSEUM
Corner of East Lewis and Girard Park Circle
318/482-5326

The only fine arts museum in Acadiana, the facility features exhibitions of different artists. Nineteenth- and twentieth-century works make up the bulk of the permanent collection.

Details: Mon–Fri 9–4, Sat 10–4. Free. (^{1}/2 hour)

SIGHTSEEING HIGHLIGHTS: LAFAYETTE REGION

★★★★ ACADIAN VILLAGE
200 Greenleaf Drive, 318/981-2364 or 800/962-9133

This reconstructed, early-nineteenth–century village on a winding bayou provides an authentic glimpse into the early Acadian lifestyle.

Details: Daily 10–5. Admission is charged; group rates available. (1^1/2–2 hours)

★★★★ CHRETIEN POINT PLANTATION
665 Chretien Point Road, Sunset, 318/662-5876 or
800/880-7050

This authentic, antebellum brick house—the centerpiece of a 10,000-acre cotton plantation—was constructed in 1831. White columns support verandas on the first and second floors. The handsome interior stairway was copied for Tara in Gone With the Wind. If a tour of the mansion isn't sufficient, you can spend the night; B&B accommodations are offered.

Details: Daily 10–5. $5.50 adults, $2.75 children. (1 hour)

★★★ ZOO OF ACADIANA
116 Lakeview Drive, 318/837-4325

Emphasis is on natural habitats where 600 animals roam in a lush, shaded, 37-acre park. Humans stroll on boardwalks to view the animals. An aviary contains more than 500 birds.

Details: *Daily 9–5. $6.95 adults, $3.95 children. (2 hours)*

★★ CONRAD RICE MILL AND KONRIKO COMPANY STORE
307 Ann St., New Iberia, 800/551-3245 or 318/364-7242
The oldest rice mill in America is still in operation, using traditional methods and much of its original, turn-of-the-century belt-driven equipment. A slide presentation on Cajun culture begins the tour, led by local guides who explain how rice is grown and harvested. The tour includes a walk through the mill. The company store is a replica of an early plantation store, with hot Cajun coffee for sampling.

Details: *$2.75 adults, $1.25 children under 12. (1 hour)*

★★ PETIT PARIS MUSEUM
103 South Main Street, St. Martinville, 318/394-7334
Located on St. Martin de Tours Church Square, the museum features costumes from a Mardi Gras ball depicting the famous 1870 double wedding of Oak Alley plantation owner Louis Durand's two daughters. Also on the square are a 1765 church and rectory and a statue of Longfellow's Evangeline.

Details: *Daily 9:30–4:30. Tours of the square given daily 9:30–4:30. $1 adults, 75 cents others. Tours available; call for details. (1/2–1 1/2 hours)*

FITNESS AND RECREATION
You'll get plenty of exercise walking to Lafayette's Sightseeing Highlights. Among those sights, Acadiana Park Nature Station and Trail features a 3.5-mile nature trail. The site of a Civil War battle, Girard Park, which is adjacent to the University of Southern Louisiana campus, offers walking trails, picnic areas, and a playground.

Several companies offer guided tours aboard pontoon or airboats into the swamps and bayous. One of these is Angelle's Atchafalaya Swamp Tours (1175 Henderson Levee Road, Henderson, 318/228-8567). De la Houssaye's Swamp Tours (Breaux Bridge, 318/845-5332) offers personally guided tours from Lake Martin Landing into bird rookeries and alligator habitats.

Family-oriented fun awaits you at Kart Ranch, Inc. (508 Youngsville Highway, 318/837-5278), which has go-carts, bumper boats, a miniature golf course, kiddie karts, pool tables, and other games. You can play golf at Le Triomphe Golf and Country Club (100 Club Boulevard, Broussard, 318/856-9005) or at Vieux Chenes' de Lafayette Golf Course (LA 89, Broussard, 318/837-1159). If you're up to a real challenge, Rok Haus (109 Grand Avenue, Lafayette, 318/981-8116) is an indoor rock-climbing facility for all skill levels. Catfish Heaven Aqua Farm (1554 Cypress Island Highway, St. Martinville, 318/394-9087) features fishing, swimming, baseball, camping, volleyball, and a kiddie train ride. The 6,000-acre Lake Fausse Pointe State Park (5400 Levee Road, St. Martinville, 318/229-4764) offers boating, canoeing, hiking, a playground, and swamp tours.

FOOD

It's no surprise that the vast majority of restaurants in Acadiana specialize in hotly spiced Cajun dishes and feature fresh fish and shellfish caught in the bayous, rivers, and Gulf of Mexico. **Café Vermilionville** (1304 West Pinhook Road, 318/237-0100) is located in a beautiful building listed on the National Register of Historic Places. Built in 1800, it was Lafayette's first inn. Several award-winning chefs serve fine Cajun, Creole, and French cuisine at the casually elegant inn.

Catahoula's, located in an old general store near Grand Coteau (234 Martin Luther King Drive, Grand Coteau, 318/662-2275) is named for a breed of hound dogs with one blue eye and one brown eye. The floors are polished, the walls are a cheery yellow, and lots of sunlight streams in through a wall of windows. The menu includes traditional dishes and unusual recipes—all using local ingredients. Seafood is prominently featured. For those who get an early start (and for those who don't), **Dwyer's Café** (323 Jefferson Street, 318/235-9364) has been serving family-style home cooking (Cajun, of course) since 1927. Various egg dishes are served for breakfast, and more than 20 sandwiches are on the menu for lunch.

Enola Prudhomme's Cajun Café (4676 Northeast Evangeline Thruway, Carencro, 318/896-3646) is another restaurant of the famous Prudhomme culinary family. (Enola is Chef Paul's sister.) Located in an 1800 country home, the restaurant serves Cajun and Creole steaks and seafood. **La Place d'Evangeline** (220 Evangeline Boulevard, St. Martinville, 318/394-4010) is located in the Old Hotel Castillo Inn in the shade of the famous Evangeline Oak along Bayou Teche. The scenic and historic setting lends extra charm to the delicious French Cajun cuisine.

Prejean's (3480 U.S. 167N, 318/896-3247) serves traditional cuisine—seafood, steaks, and alligator are specialties—in a fun, casual atmosphere. Live music is offered nightly. **Randol's Restaurant and Cajun Dancehall** (2320

LAFAYETTE REGION

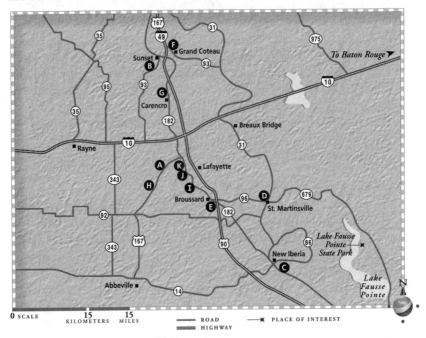

SIGHTS
- **A** Acadian Village
- **B** Chretien Point Plantation
- **C** Conrad Rice Mill and Konriko Company Store
- **D** Petit Paris Museum
- **E** Zoo of Acadiana

FOOD
- **F** Catahoula's
- **G** Enola Prudhomme's Cajun Café
- **H** La Fete de Lafayette
- **D** La Place d'Evangeline
- **I** Randol's Restaurant and Cajun Dancehall

LODGING
- **J** Best Western Hotel Acadiana
- **B** Chretien Point Plantation
- **E** La Grande Maison B&B
- **K** Lafayette Hilton and Towers
- **D** Old Hotel Castillo Inn

Note: Items with the same letter are located in the same area.

Kaliste Saloom Road at Ambassador Caffery Parkway, 318/981-7080) also offers Cajun and Creole food and music in a rustic atmosphere. The menu features alligator, crab, crawfish, and oysters. **La Fete de Lafayette**, 4401 Johnston St., 318/981-9979, is famous for its Cajun seafood buffet. The restaurant is closed on Monday.

For a change of pace, **La Fonda Restaurant** (3809 Johnston Street, 318/984-5630) serves Tex-Mex cuisine. The restaurant is noted for its warm atmosphere and margaritas.

LODGING

More than two dozen historic homes in Acadiana provide bed-and-breakfast accommodations. The most beautiful and luxurious is **Chretien Point Plantation** (665 Chretien Point Plantation, Sunset, 318/662-5876 or 800/880-7050), which offers five guest rooms, one with a Jacuzzi, as well as a swimming pool, tennis courts, complimentary wine, mint juleps, and hors d'oeuvres.

Another historic hostelry is the **Old Hotel Castillo Inn** (220 Evangeline Boulevard, St. Martinville, 318/394-4010 or 800/621-3017), which offers five guest rooms, a restaurant (see Food), a coffee shop, and a gift shop. **La Grande Maison Bed and Breakfast** (302 East Main Street, Broussard, 318/837-4428 or 800/829-5633) occupies one of the most beautiful Queen Anne Victorian houses in the South. Built in 1911, it is also the largest Victorian home in Lafayette Parish. Guest rooms, which all have private baths, are beautifully appointed. A fabulous veranda and attractive grounds bring guests outdoors.

The largest hotel in Lafayette, the **Lafayette Hilton and Towers** (1521 West Pinhook Road, 318/235-6111 or 800/33-CAJUN, www.hilton.com), offers every amenity you would expect in a large hotel including lounges, executive suites, a Jacuzzi, laundry service, restaurant, coffee shop, fitness center, and swimming pool. Other large Lafayette hotels with comparable services are the **Best Western Hotel Acadiana** (1801 West Pinhook Road, 318/233-8120) and the **Holiday Inn Central/Holidome** (2032 Northeast Evangeline, 318/233-6815 or 800/942-4868).

CAMPING

Bayou Wilderness RV Resort (201 St. Claire, Carencro, 318/896-0598) provides quiet camping on the bayous at 120 sites with full hookups. The Lafayette KOA Kampground (exit 97 off I-10, Scott, 318/235-2739) offers 175 concrete pads with full hookups. Fishing, swimming, mini-golf, paddleboats, and some cabins are available. Maxie's Mobile Valley and Overnite Park (4350 U.S. 90E, Broussard, 318/837-6200) offers 72 sites with full hookups. De la Houssaye's Swamp Tours (see Fitness and Recreation) also offers camping, as does Catfish Heaven Aqua Farm and Lake Fausse Pointe State Park (see Sightseeing Highlights).

NIGHTLIFE

Cajuns and Creoles are energetic, fun-loving people who need no excuse for a party or dance. To satiate this yen, several restaurants have live entertainment and dancing seven nights a week. In addition, Lafayette has no shortage of nightclubs. Among the favorites are Antler's (555 Jefferson Street, 318/234-8877) and Hamilton's Place (1808 Verot School Road, 318/984-5583).

Those interested in the performing arts should check into productions at the Artists' Alliance (121 West Vermilion, 318/233-7518) and the Performing Arts Society of Acadiana (Heymann Performing Arts Center, 318/237-2787).

If you don't mind driving a little, you'll find a full range of wagering games, including 2,000 slot machines, 55 table games, live poker, and Caribbean stud poker, at the Grand Casino Coushatta (777 Coushatta Drive off U.S. 165, Kinder, 800/58-GRAND) located between Lafayette and Lake Charles. Owned by the Coushatta Indian tribe, the casino has several dining options, lounges, and live entertainment.

Evangeline Downs (3620 Northwest Evangeline Thruway, 318/896-RACE) features thoroughbred horse racing from April through Labor Day and off-track betting on simulcast races year-round. Post times are Thursday through Monday at 6:45 p.m. The course offers indoor and outdoor seating and dining in the clubhouse.

15
SHREVEPORT
AND BOSSIER CITY

Shreveport had an interesting and unusual beginning. Caddo Indians first inhabited the area, and because the Red River was choked off by a tremendous, 165-mile-long log jam, whites did not settle the area until the mid-nineteenth century. In 1835 Captain Henry Miller Shreve and his crews cleared the jam and opened the area to white settlement. Shreveport soon became an important shipping port and trade center. It was also the beginning of the overland route to Texas.

Today Shreveport and Bossier City (across the Red River) are linked by the Texas Street Bridge, the nation's largest neon-lit bridge. A diverse community, Shreveport–Bossier City is a metropolis of contrasts. On the one hand, it is an outdoor paradise with the Red River, several lakes, 3,000 acres of landscaped parks, and many protected wilderness areas. On the other hand, it has succumbed to the casino craze of the nineties and already has four gambling emporiums. The city also seems to be more dedicated to art and the performing arts than most comparable communities.

A PERFECT DAY IN SHREVEPORT AND BOSSIER CITY

Begin at Shreveport's beautiful Riverfront Park and adjacent Barnwell Garden and Art Center. Spend the rest of the morning at Museum Mile, which includes

SHREVEPORT AND BOSSIER CITY

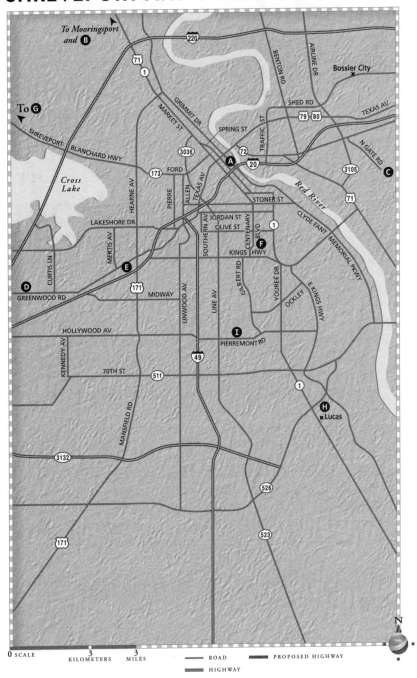

To Mooringsport and **B**

To **G**

220

71
1

BENTON RD

AIRLINE DR

Bossier City

SHED RD

GRIMMIT DR

MARKET ST

SPRING ST

TRAFFIC ST

79 80

TEXAS AV

SHREVEPORT-BLANCHARD HWY

N GATE RD

Cross Lake

3036

72

20

3105

C

173 FORD

A

Red River

71

HEARNE AV

PIERRE

ALLEN

TEXAS AV

STONER ST

SOUTHERN AV

JORDAN ST

OLIVE ST

CENTENARY BLVD

CLYDE FANT

1

LAKESHORE DR

MERTIS AV

KINGS HWY

F

MEMORIAL PKWY

CURTIS LN

E

GILBERT RD

YOUREE DR

E KINGS HWY

D

GREENWOOD RD

171

MIDWAY

LINWOOD AV

LINE AV

OCKLEY

HOLLYWOOD AV

KENNEDY AV

PIERREMONT RD

I

49

70TH ST

511

1

H
▪ Lucas

MANSFIELD RD

3132

526

171

523

N

0 SCALE
3 KILOMETERS   3 MILES
━━━ ROAD   ▬▬▬ PROPOSED HIGHWAY
═══ HIGHWAY

the Spring Street Museum, Ark-La-Tex Museum, and Sci-Port Discovery Center. Have a light English lunch at Glenwood Tearoom. More art is on tap for the afternoon: Meadows Museum of Art and the R. W. Norton Art Gallery. If you have time left over, stroll through Roseland, the American Rose Center. Have an elegant gourmet dinner at Monsieur Patou, then two-step the night away at Randol's Cajun Restaurant and Dance Hall or visit a casino or race track.

SIGHTSEEING HIGHLIGHTS

★★★★ **GARDENS OF THE AMERICAN ROSE**
8877 Jefferson–Paige Road, West Shreveport
318/938-5402, www.ars.org
Experience nature's best at America's largest rose garden. On its 118 acres, more than 20,000 vibrant roses are planted in 60 individual gardens. The garden also displays waterfalls, fountains, gazebos, babbling brooks, the stately Wind Sounds Carillon Tower, and the Little Log Chapel. You'll see miniature, antique, hand-painted, and celebrity roses. The newest hybrids are on display as well as experimental thornless and single-petal roses. At Christmas, one million lights bring the gardens to life. The gardens are home to the American Rose Society.
Details: Mon–Fri 9–5, weekends Apr–Oct 9–dusk. $4 adults, free children under 12. (1 hour)

★★★★ **LOUISIANA STATE EXHIBIT MUSEUM**
3015 Greenwood Road, Shreveport, 318/632-2020
The museum is noted for its gigantic murals and its 22 life-size dioramas depicting the history of Louisiana from Native American times to the space age. The murals, painted in 1938 by Conrad Albrizio,

---

SIGHTS

- ⓐ Ark-La-Tex Antique and Classic Vehicle and Firefighters Museum
- ⓐ Barnwell Garden and Art Center
- ⓑ Caddo Pine Island Oil and Historical Society Museum
- ⓒ Eighth Air Force Museum
- ⓓ Gardens of the American Rose

- ⓔ Louisiana State Exhibit Museum
- ⓕ Meadows Museum of Art
- ⓖ Mooringsport Mini Museum
- ⓗ Pioneer Heritage Center
- ⓘ R. W. Norton Art Gallery
- ⓐ Sci-Port Discovery Center
- ⓐ Spring Street Museum

Note: Items with the same letter are located in the same area.

---

are believed to be the first outdoor frescoes in the United States. The museum also hosts traveling exhibits.

Details: Mon–Fri 9–4, Sat and Sun noon–4. $2 adults, $1 children 6–18. (1 1/2 hours)

★★★★ R. W. NORTON ART GALLERY
4747 Creswell Avenue, Shreveport, 318/865-4201
www.softdisk.com/comp/norton

A contemporary version of a classic Greek temple, the museum is located in a 40-acre landscaped park, which in spring blooms with more than 10,000 azaleas. Inside, 20 galleries display American and European paintings, sculptures, and decorative arts spanning four centuries. The museum has earned national acclaim for its permanent collection of works by Frederic Remington and Charles M. Russell. Included in the Remington Collection are the artist's personal letters, many of which he illustrated. Among the other collections are Civil War art, rare books and folios, celestial and terrestrial globes, tapestries, Wedgwood, contemporary art, antique firearms, Steuben crystal, antique dolls, and research materials.

Details: Tue–Fri 10–5, weekends 1–5. Free. (2 hours)

★★★ ARK-LA-TEX ANTIQUE AND CLASSIC VEHICLE AND FIREFIGHTERS MUSEUM
601 Spring Street, Shreveport, 318/222-0227
www.softdisk.com/comp/classic

Located on Museum Mile on the riverfront, the museum is housed in the George T. Bishop building, a 1921 Graham truck/Dodge car showroom. Displays include classic and antique vehicles, vintage clothing, music boxes, tools, photos, and toys.

Details: Tue–Sat 9–4:30, Sun 1–5 for self-guided tours; guided tours by appointment. Hours extended in summer. $5 adults, $4 seniors and military, $3 children. (1 hour)

★★★ BARNWELL GARDEN AND ART CENTER
601 Clyde Fant Parkway, Shreveport, 318/673-7703

A combined art and garden center may be unusual, but it is successful. The south wing is a 7,850-square-foot glass-domed conservatory filled with tropical, seasonal, and regional plants. A fragrance garden provides enjoyment for the visually impaired.

Rotating art exhibits fill the halls of the main structure, which also contains a gift shop. Adjacent to the center is the Riverfront Park along the Red River.

Details: *Weekdays 9–4:30, weekends 1–5. Free. (1 hour)*

★★★ EIGHTH AIR FORCE MUSEUM
Barksdale Air Force Base, Bossier City
318/456-3067, or public affairs at 318/456-3065
www.aerowebb.brooklyn.cuny.edu/museums/la/eafm.html
More than a dozen historic aircraft are on display at this museum, which honors the Eighth Air Force and the Second Bomb Wing—the oldest aerial bombardment unit in the U.S. Air Force. Also on display are uniforms, dioramas, barracks, and battlefield exhibits. Air force films are shown in a replica World War I briefing room.

Details: *Daily 9:30–4. Free. (1 1/2 hours)*

★★★ MEADOWS MUSEUM OF ART
2911 Centenary Boulevard, Shreveport, 318/869-5169
Located on the campus of Centenary College, the museum contains an impressive collection of 360 southeast Asian works of Jean Despujois. Among the collection are paintings, Indochinese artifacts, golden Buddhas, baskets, a machete, and a chieftain's hat. In addition, the museum sponsors traveling exhibitions.

Details: *Tue–Fri noon–4, Sat 1–4. Free. (1 hour)*

★★★ SCI-PORT DISCOVERY CENTER
528 Commerce Street, Shreveport, 318/424-3466
www.softdisk.com/comp/sciport
Explore the world of science at this interactive museum for all ages. In addition to the hands-on exhibits, visitors can participate in fascinating demonstrations and watch movies in an IMAX theater. The museum is located on Museum Mile on the riverfront.

Details: *Mon–Fri 9–5, Sat 10–6, Sun 1–6. $6 adults, $4.50 children. IMAX theater $6 adults, $4 children. Combo tickets $10 for adults, $7 children. (1 hour)*

★★★ SPRING STREET MUSEUM
525 Spring Street, Shreveport, 318/424-0964
Located in Shreveport's oldest building on Museum Mile on the riverfront, this museum traces the city's rich history with rare antiques

and priceless artifacts. The customs of the early 1800s are brought to life with clothing, home furnishings, jewelry, books, and newspapers.
Details: Tue 10–1, Fri–Sun 1:30–5. $2 adults, $1 children. (1 hour)

★★ CADDO PINE ISLAND OIL AND HISTORICAL SOCIETY MUSEUM
200 South Land Avenue, Shreveport, 318/995-6845, www.sec.state.la.us
Dedicated to the boom times in the oil industry, the museum is located in a tiny former railroad depot of the Kansas City Southern Line. Turn-of-the-century oil field artifacts are displayed inside and outside. A large collection of boomtown and gusher photographs from the same period, early postcards, and railroad memorabilia are displayed. In addition, a Caddo Indian Room houses early relics and arrowheads.
Details: Mon–Fri 9–4. Free. (1 hour)

★★ MOORINGSPORT MINI MUSEUM
Croom at Gremen Streets, Mooringsport, 318/996-7490 or 318/996-7660
Among the displays are Caddo Indian relics and memorabilia depicting life in Mooringsport between 1837 and 1940.
Details: Tours by appointment only. (1 hour)

★★ PIONEER HERITAGE CENTER
Louisiana State University–Shreveport, 318/797-5332
Located on the campus of Louisiana State University–Shreveport, the center includes six authentic northwestern Louisiana pioneer buildings from the 1830s to the 1860s. Among the buildings are a dogtrot cabin, doctor's office, commissary, and blacksmith shop.
Details: Sun 1:30–4:30, during the week by appointment. $2 adults, $1 children. (1 hour)

FITNESS AND RECREATION
The Shreveport–Bossier City area is alive with participatory and spectator sports. The two cities offer more than 3,000 acres of landscaped parks with lakes, jogging paths, nature trails, and picnic areas. Riverfront Park along the Red River in Shreveport offers bicycling and walking trails, a Frisbee golf course, waterfall, extensive landscaping, and an amphitheater created from lawn terraces.

Explore nature at its best at the Walter B. Jacobs Memorial Nature Park (8012 Blanchard–Furrh Road, 318/929-2806), a 160-acre park with 5 miles of trails, a visitors center with hands-on and live animal displays, and guided tours. With an abundance of plant life, from bottomland species to wildflowers, the park is a favorite for bird-watching, nature studies, painting, and photography. Trails are well marked to help you identify natural features and animal habitats.

Cypress–Black River Bayou Recreation Area (135 Cypress Park Drive, Benton, 318/965-0007, www.cypressblackbayou.com) is a beautiful, 340-acre garden and recreational facility. It offers camping, swimming, fishing, a petting zoo, three large piers with covered shelters, a marina and boat launch, four miles of chip trails, a 1,400-foot paved trail, and a nature center.

For canoe enthusiasts, Norris Outfitter's (U.S. 80E, Princeton, 318/949-9522) provides adventures that range from moonlight lobster and steak dinners to 12-day journeys through the swamps. The company has a 23-person canoe that replicates an eighteenth-century trading canoe and another outfitted for the physically challenged. Rolling River Ranch (206 Buckshot Road, Plain Dealing off LA 2, 318/326-5844) on the Red River provides numerous outdoor adventures with a Native American theme.

Bodcau Wildlife Management Area (east of Plain Dealing off LA 2, 318/326-4198) and Loggy Bayou Wildlife Management Area (Loggy Bayou Road off U.S. 71, 318/752-5634) provide thousands of acres of river- and bayou-laced bottomland and upland forests for hiking, birding, canoeing, camping, boating, and fishing. Farther afield, the Kisatchie National Forest near Minden (324 Beardsley, Homer, 318/927-2061) offers the 7.6-mile Sugar Cane National Recreation Trail. Lake Bistineau State Park (LA 163, Doyline,

HISTORICAL FAIRFIELD-HIGHLAND TOUR
Pick up a walking/driving tour brochure from the Highland Restoration Association (520 Olive Street, 318/221-7629) or the Shreveport–Bossier Convention and Tourist Bureau. In the Fairfield–Highland neighborhood you will see styles ranging from neoclassical to Queen Anne, cottage, craftsman bungalow, Colonial Revival, and Mediterranean Revival—sometimes combined in one house. Several homes operate as bed-and-breakfasts.

SHREVEPORT AND BOSSIER CITY

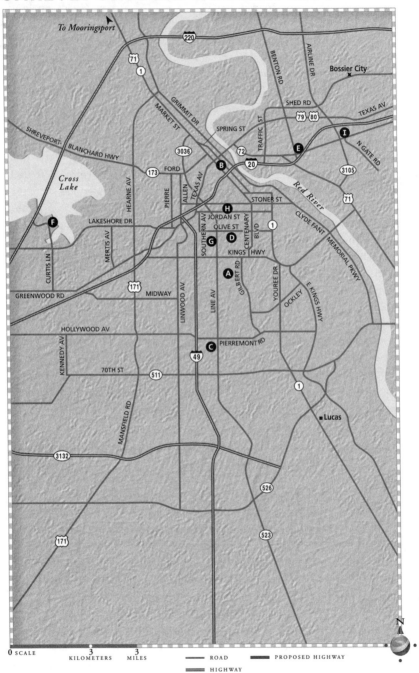

318/745-3503) is set in the heart of a pine forest and features fishing, swimming, picnicking, and hiking trails.

Hamel's Amusement Park (3232 East Seventieth Street, 318/869-3566) is the largest such park in Louisiana. Heart-pounding excitement is provided on roller coasters, flume rides, and other take-your-breath-away attractions. A carousel, mini-train, and kiddie rides provide fun for younger children. In addition, the park offers horseshoes, basketball, volleyball, a dunking tank, and arcade games. You can beat the summer heat at Water Town U.S.A. (7670 West Seventieth Street, 318/938-5475), which offers a wave pool, speed slide, tube slide, body slide, lazy river, flume, and adventure pool. The park also offers volleyball, horseshoes, softball, bingo, and snack shops.

When it comes to spectator sports, Shreveport doesn't sit on the sidelines. The city is the home of the Shreveport Captains (318/636-5555), an AA Texas-league championship team affiliated with the San Francisco Giants. The Shreveport Patriots, a Western Professional Hockey League team, plays at Hirsh Coliseum (318/222-1997). Two special annual events are the Poulan/Weedeater Independence Bowl and the Champion Lake Pro Classic, a national pro water ski tour.

FOOD

Monsieur Patou, Your French Restaurant (855 Pierremont Road, #135, 318/868-9822), guarantees a memorable dining experience. It has been voted the best elegant restaurant in northwestern Louisiana. The food, atmosphere, and service are impeccable. Established in 1934, **Don's Seafood and Steak House** (3100 Highland Avenue, 318/865-4291), an internationally renowned restaurant, specializes in Cajun and Creole cuisine. At **Smith's Cross Lake**

FOOD
- Ⓐ Don's Seafood and Steak House
- Ⓑ Glenwood Tearoom
- Ⓒ Monsieur Patou
- Ⓓ Olive Street Bistro
- Ⓔ Ralph and Kacoo's
- Ⓕ Smith's Cross Lake Inn

LODGING
- Ⓖ 2439 Fairfield
- Ⓔ Beauvais House Cottage
- Ⓑ Best Western Chateau Suite Hotel
- Ⓗ The Columns
- Ⓖ Fairfield Place
- Ⓘ Horseshoe Casino Hotel Towers
- Ⓔ Isle of Capri Hotel
- Ⓑ Remington Suite Hotel
- Ⓖ Slattery House

Note: Items with the same letter are located in the same area.

Inn (5301 South Lakeshore Drive, 318/631-0919), you'll get a beautiful view across the lake while you enjoy seafood or a charbroiled steak dinner.

Glenwood Tearoom (3310 Line Avenue, 318/868-3651) is the area's only authentic British tearoom. The restaurant features scones, tea, and British and American luncheon fare. In addition, the tearoom sells royally appointed British toiletries, tea fare, gilts, and gourmet items.

The chefs at the **Olive Street Bistro**, 1027 Olive St., 318/221-4517, make their own mozzarella and ricotta cheeses, as well as fresh pastas of all types. Their sauces are seasoned with herbs grown in their own garden in front of the restaurant. Finely prepared authentic Italian dishes are the forte here, although a popular pot roast and other all-American dishes are also available.

Ralph and Kacoo's (1700 Old Minden Road, #141, Bossier City, 318/747-6660) is a popular Louisiana chain known for its Gulf Coast seafood and crawfish platters.

LODGING

The historic Fairfield–Highland neighborhood offers four B&Bs in magnificent homes. The home that started this trend is **Fairfield Place** (2221 Fairfield Avenue, 318/222-0048), a turn-of-the century Victorian. Painstakingly restored, the mansion features high ceilings, spacious rooms, European and American antiques, European feather beds, clawfoot tubs, and upstairs and downstairs verandas. Guest rooms are also offered in the house next door, a restored, turn-of-the-century Greek Revival. A gourmet breakfast is included. Located in a 1905 Victorian, **2439 Fairfield** (2439 Fairfield Avenue, 318/424-2424) has four guest rooms and provides amenities such as whirlpool baths. Private balconies overlook English gardens, a gazebo, fountain, and swing. A full English breakfast is served. A beautifully restored, turn-of-the-century neoclassical mansion known as **The Columns** (615 Jordan, 318/222-5912 or 800/801-4950, www.bbonline.com/la/columns/, e-mail: BnB615@aol.com) offers three guest rooms, a pool, Jacuzzi, antiques, gardens, and Southern charm. The antique-filled **Slattery House** (2401 Fairfield Avenue, 318/222-6577) is one of the avenue's oldest homes. A Queen Anne Victorian, it offers four rooms, a pool, and Jacuzzi. The nightly rate includes a full country breakfast. Bossier City's first B&B is the **Beauvais House Cottage** (1289 Delhi Street, 318/221-3735), which offers four rooms.

Among Shreveport's hotels, the **Remington Suite Hotel** (220 Travis Street, 318/425-5000) is a gem. Twenty-two luxury suites, some of them multilevel, offer king-size beds, Jacuzzis, fully stocked wet bars and refrigerators, robes, and other amenities. Complimentary continental breakfast is included.

The hotel is within easy walking distance of the casinos. The downtown **Best Western Chateau Suite Hotel** (201 Lake Street, 318/222-7620 or 800/845-9334) offers a full complimentary breakfast, afternoon cocktails and hors d'oeuvres, and more.

Both the Horseshoe and the Isle of Capri Casinos have hotels. The **Horseshoe Casino Hotel Towers** (711 Horseshoe Boulevard, Bossier City, 318/747-0711 or 800/789-0711) offers 200 spacious rooms with free HBO, an outdoor pool, Jacuzzi, and free shuttle service to the casino. The **Isle of Capri Hotel** (3033 Hilton Drive, Bossier City, 318/747-2400, 800/221-4095, or 800/525-5143) offers a tropical island getaway, comfortable rooms, an intimate lounge, and a pool.

CAMPING

Cypress Black Bayou Recreation and RV Park (135 Cypress Park Drive, Benton, 318/965-0007) offers 73 wooded RV sites with full hookups and two large bathhouses. A large primitive camping area is also available with only a water spigot and a rest room closeby. The park has four rustic cabins and a triplex apartment as well. The KOA Shreveport–Bossier (6510 West Seventieth Street, Shreveport, 318/687-1010) has 60 RV sites, 14 tent sites, rest rooms, showers, a pool, laundry facilities, store, and spa. Maplewood Park in Bossier City (452 Maplewood Drive, 318/742-5497) offers 35 RV sites, 12 pull-throughs, tent sites, rest rooms, showers, and laundry facilities.

NIGHTLIFE

Shreveport–Bossier City, like most Louisiana riverfront cities, has joined the gaming bandwagon with riverboat casinos and horse racing. Harrah's Casino Shreveport (315 Clyde Fant Parkway, 318/424-7777 or 800/HARRAHS) provides gambling excitement on the west side of the river. The Horseshoe Casino (711 Horseshoe Boulevard off Traffic Street, Bossier City, 318/742-0711 or 800/895-0711), Isle of Capri Casino (711 Isle of Capri Boulevard, Bossier City, 318/747-2400 or 800/THE-ISLE), and Casino Magic (300 Riverside Drive, Bossier City, 318/746-0711) create the thrills on the Bossier City side. In addition to a wide selection of games, the casinos have restaurants, bars, and live entertainment. Admission and parking are free.

Louisiana Downs in Bossier City (8000 East U.S. 80, 318/742-5555 or 800/551-RACE) features thoroughbred races from late April through early October. Spectators can sit in the air-conditioned, glass-enclosed grandstand or enjoy up-close action at the rail. The track offers three dining options.

Whether you prefer the symphony, opera, a Broadway show, the ballet, or theater, Shreveport and Bossier City offer a wide array of cultural activities. The Shreveport Symphony (619 Louisiana Avenue, Suite 400, 318/227-8863) performs 125 concerts a year. Many shows are performed in the opulent, historic Strand Theater.

If you'd like to sample Shreveport's lively nightspots, three of them are located within a very small area downtown: Action Central (614 Commerce Street, 318/221-4177), Freddie Mack's (618 Commerce Street, 318/222-4350), and James Burton's Rock 'n' Roll Café (616 Commerce Street, 318/424-5000).

16
NATCHEZ

Natchez, founded in 1716, is the oldest settlement on the Mississippi. Settlers originally chose the 200-foot bluffs here because this position was strategic for observing the river to the north and south. In fact, French explorer Robert LaSalle declared Natchez "the most desirable site on the river."

Wealthy planters built magnificent townhomes in Natchez. In fact, in the mid-1800s, one-half of all American millionaires lived here. But the city had less refined citizens too. At the boat landing at the foot of the bluffs, in an area called Natchez-Under-the-Hill, a culture grew of rough river men, gamblers, and other rowdies, giving Natchez the nickname Barbary Coast of the Mississippi.

Natchez came through the Civil War relatively intact (more than 500 buildings from the antebellum period survive) because it was occupied by Federal troops early on. Those residents who were able to hold onto their houses, however, were too impoverished after the war to make the needed repairs, and the mansions deteriorated badly.

Eventually, some enterprising women turned their homes into boarding houses. Then someone got the idea of opening the houses for tours, and the pilgrimage was born. Three times a year—spring, fall, and Christmas—many private homes are open for tours.

An old-fashioned trolley takes visitors around the historic district, and

NATCHEZ

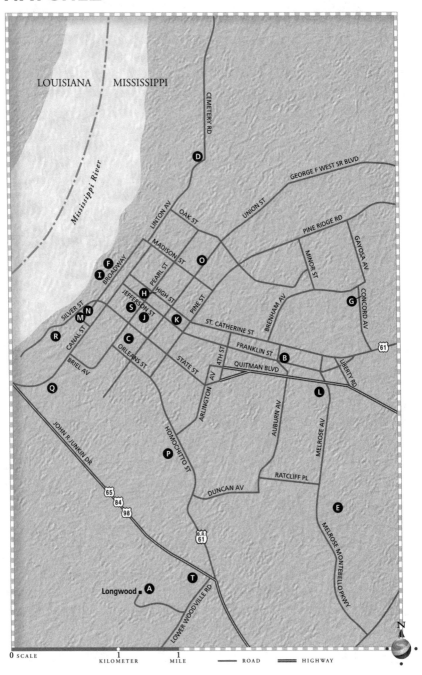

LOUISIANA | MISSISSIPPI

Mississippi River

CEMETERY RD

D

GEORGE F WEST SR BLVD

LINTON AV

OAK ST

UNION ST

PINE RIDGE RD

MADISON ST

GAYOSA AV

BROADWAY

F

I

PEARL ST

HIGH ST

O

MINOR ST

BRENHAM AV

CONCORD AV

SILVER ST

H

JEFFERSON ST

PINE ST

G

M **N**

S

K

ST. CATHERINE ST

CANAL ST

J

R

C

FRANKLIN ST

61

BRIEL AV

ORLEANS ST

STATE ST

4TH ST

B

QUITMAN BLVD

LIBERTY RD

Q

ARLINGTON AV

AUBURN AV

L

JOHN R JUNKIN DR

HOMOCHITTO ST

MELROSE AV

P

RATCLIFF PL

65

84

98

DUNCAN AV

B.R. 61

E

MELROSE MONTEBELLO PKWY

T

Longwood **A**

LOWER WOODVILLE RD

N

0 SCALE   1   1
   KILOMETER   MILE   ROAD   HIGHWAY

several companies offer romantic horse-drawn carriage rides as well. You can still find gamblers at Natchez-Under-the-Hill, but now they're on the Lady Luck riverboat casino.

A PERFECT DAY IN NATCHEZ

Spend the morning touring some historic homes. Longwood should be at the top of your list. Then have a casual lunch on the front porch at Natchez Landing on the waterfront. After lunch, poke around in the small shops at Natchez-Under-the-Hill. From there, visit Natchez National Cemetery and the Natchez National Historical Park. After dinner, spend the evening at the Lady Luck Casino, then turn in at one of the city's luxurious B&Bs.

SIGHTSEEING HIGHLIGHTS: NATCHEZ

★★★★ LONGWOOD
Lower Woodville Road, 601/446-6631 or 800/647-6742

This stunning, octagonal brick house with an onion-shaped cupola and intricate gingerbread trim was almost finished when the Civil War broke out. The family lived in nine rooms in the raised basement during the war and planned to complete the 21 rooms on the upper two floors when the war was over. Unfortunately, by that time, they were impoverished, and the house was never completed. Family members continued to live there until 1970, when it was donated to the

SIGHTS
- Ⓐ Longwood
- Ⓑ Mostly African Market
- Ⓒ Natchez Costume and Doll Museum
- Ⓓ Natchez National Cemetery
- Ⓔ Natchez National Historical Park
- Ⓕ Natchez Under-the-Hill
- Ⓖ Old South Winery
- Ⓗ Stanton Hall

FOOD
- Ⓗ Carriage House Restaurant and Lounge
- Ⓘ Cock-of-the-Walk
- Ⓙ Fare Café
- Ⓚ King's Tavern
- Ⓛ Monmouth Plantation
- Ⓜ Natchez Landing
- Ⓝ Wharf Master's House

LODGING
- Ⓞ The Burn
- Ⓟ Dunleith
- Ⓠ Lady Luck Casino Hotel
- Ⓡ Mark Twain Guest House
- Ⓛ Monmouth
- Ⓢ Natchez Eola
- Ⓣ Ramada Inn Hilltop

Note: Items with the same letter are located in the same area.

Pilgrimage Garden Club. The living quarters still contain their original furnishings and artwork.

Details: *Daily 9–4:30, tours every 20 minutes. $6. (1 hour)*

★★★★ NATCHEZ UNDER-THE-HILL
Silver Street

In the nineteenth century, this waterfront section of town was a bawdy area of saloons, gambling halls, and cheap hotels. Today, the remaining buildings have been converted into a bed-and-breakfast, restaurants, bar, and shops. A casino boat sits at the dock. All these features make the area extremely popular with cruise passengers off the Delta Steamboat Company's three steam-powered paddle wheelers, as well as with land-based visitors to Natchez.

Details: *(1–3 hours)*

★★★★ STANTON HALL
High and Pearl Streets, 601/446-6631 or 800/647-6742

One of the most palatial residences in Natchez, Stanton Hall was built in 1857. Reminiscent of New Orleans, the imposing Greek Revival design is embellished with ornate ironwork on the porches and balconies. Another preservation project of the Pilgrimage Garden Club, the exquisitely restored house is filled with some original Stanton family pieces and other antiques. The carriage house is occupied by a restaurant.

Details: *Daily 9–4:30, tours on the half hour. $6. (1 hour)*

★★★ NATCHEZ NATIONAL CEMETERY
41 Cemetery Road, 601/445-4981

Most of the country's national cemeteries hold only the remains of Union soldiers, but the Natchez cemetery is the final resting place of 3,000 soldiers from both sides of the Civil War.

Details: *Mon–Fri 8–4:30. Free. (1/2 hour)*

★★★ NATCHEZ NATIONAL HISTORICAL PARK
1 Melrose-Montebello Parkway, 601/442-7047

The park was established to preserve and interpret the history of Natchez. It includes the grand antebellum house museum **Melrose** and the **William Johnson House**, which is being restored. Johnson was a free black who was prominent in antebellum Natchez. Eventually, his home will be a museum dedicated to black history in Natchez.

Details: Daily 8:30–5 with tours 9–4. Tours $6 adults, discounts for seniors and children under 17; admission to grounds is free. (1 hour)

★★ MOSTLY AFRICAN MARKET
St. Catherine and McCabe Streets, 601/442-5448
prosocro@bkbank.com

As its name implies, this market presents African American art exhibits and regional arts and crafts, many of which are for sale.

Details: Sept–May Wed–Sat 1–5; closed summer. Free. (1 hour)

★★ NATCHEZ COSTUME AND DOLL MUSEUM
215 South Pearl Street, 601/442-6672

Located upstairs at Magnolia Hall, the museum not only contains antique and collectible dolls but also displays costumes from various pilgrimages and pageants.

Details: Daily 9–5; Spring and Fall Pilgrimage open every fourth day only. $6 for home and museum guided tour. (1 hour)

★★ OLD SOUTH WINERY
64 South Concord Avenue, 601/445-9924

Muscadine grapes have been grown in the region for centuries, and many residents turned them into homemade wines, although it was illegal to make wine in Mississippi until 1978. This winery opened that year. You can tour the winery and taste and purchase the wine.

Details: Mon–Sat 10–5, Sun 1–5. Free, $3 per person charge for groups of 20 or more. (1 hour)

SIGHTSEEING HIGHLIGHTS: NATCHEZ REGION

★★★★ ROSEMONT PLANTATION
Woodville, 601/888-6809

Built in 1810, this plantation was the boyhood home of Jefferson Davis, who later became a senator from Mississippi and then president of the Confederacy. On the property are plantation outbuildings and the family cemetery.

Details: Located one mile east of Woodville. Weekdays Mar–Dec 15 10–5. Weekends during Natchez spring and fall pilgrimages. $6. (1 hour)

PILGRIMAGE TIPS

Visiting Natchez during one of the pilgrimages has its pros and cons. The upside is that all the homes and gardens are at their best, especially at Christmas. On the negative side, crowds are large, and lines at restaurants can be long. If you are going to visit Natchez during a pilgrimage, book your accommodations and buy your tour tickets far in advance. Tickets are not sold at individual houses. For more information, contact **Natchez Pilgrimage Tours**, 800/647-6742.

If you are making your first visit to Natchez, we suggest a guided tour. Contact either **Natchez Pilgrimage Tours** (800/647-6742) or **Natchez Historic City Tours**, 508 Orleans Street, 601/445-9300. **Magnolia Carriage Tours** (601/442-4518), **Southern Carriage Tours** (601/442-2151), and **Trace City Tours** (601/445-5913) offer carriage rides.

★★★★ **SPRINGFIELD PLANTATION**
MS 553 at Natchez Trace Parkway, Fayette, 601/786-3802
Built between 1786 and 1791, this plantation is an excellent example of Old South architecture. It was one of the first homes in the Mississippi Valley and the first to add a full colonnade across the front. Inside, the architectural details are almost all original, and visitors should take note of the hand-carved woodwork and mantels. The house was the site of Andrew Jackson's wedding to Rachel Robards in 1791. In addition to appropriate period antiques, it showcases Civil War and railroad memorabilia.
Details: *Daily 9:30–dark. $6.50 adults, $3 children. (1 hour)*

★★★ **GRAND VILLAGE OF THE NATCHEZ INDIANS**
400 Jefferson Davis Boulevard, 601/446-6502
www.mdah.state.ms.us
This site was home of the Natchez Indians from the 1500s until they were driven out by the French in 1730. Visitors can see a reconstructed Natchez house, a corn granary, a ceremonial plaza, and several earthen mounds. Artifacts excavated on site are displayed in the museum.
Details: *Mon–Sat 9–5, Sun 1:30–5. Free. (1 hour)*

★★★ NATCHEZ TRACE PARKWAY/SUNKEN TRACE

Natchez Trace begins at Natchez and continues all the way to Nashville. Before European settlement, animals and Native Americans used the path. Alongside the paved parkway are sections of the original pathway, called the Sunken Trace. It was created by buffalo and humans who walked over it for hundreds of years. It is an excellent place for hiking or bicycling.

Details: *(1 hour–full day)*

★★ EMERALD MOUND
601/445-4211 or 800/300-PARK

The second-largest ceremonial mound in America, Emerald Mound was built by Native Americans of the Mississippian culture—ancestors of the Natchez and Choctaw Indians—about a.d. 1300. This mound, which covers eight acres, is different from all the other mounds in the South because it is topped by two smaller mounds.

Details: *Daily dawn–dusk. Free. (1 hour)*

★★ OLD COUNTRY STORE
U.S. 61, Lorman, 601/437-3661

Actually a museum, the store has been in continuous operation for more than 100 years. Today it showcases local memorabilia. Lunch and dinner are served.

Details: *Mon–Sat 8–6, Sun noon–6. Free. ($^1/_2$ hour)*

FITNESS AND RECREATION

Visitors can get plenty of exercise strolling through the historic districts of Natchez and around the grounds of some of the plantations. The Natchez Trace Parkway begins in Natchez and meanders to the northeast. Some hiking can be done beside the parkway, and bikers enjoy cycling it. Bicycle rentals are available at Natchez Bicycling Center, 334 Main Street, 601/446-7794.

Several parks offer activities. The 3,000-acre Natchez State Park (230-B Wickliff Road, 601/442-2658) offers places for hiking and biking and a large lake where two state-record bass have been landed. Duncan Park in the heart of the city (Duncan and Auburn Avenues, 601/442-5955) has a pool, tennis courts, nature trails, and an 18-hole golf course.

Places you can play golf are Belwood Club (Cargill Road, 601/442-5493) and Winding Creek Golf Course (U.S. 84, 601/442-6995). Popular places to fish are Sunnyside Plantation and St. Catherine Creek National Wildlife Refuge,

NATCHEZ REGION

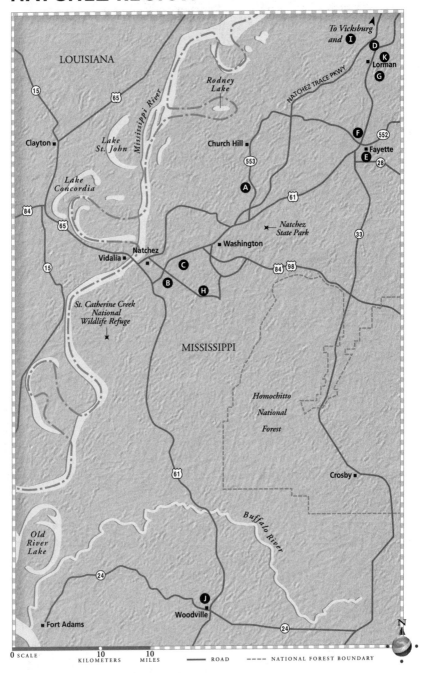

LOUISIANA

To Vicksburg
and **I**

D
K
Lorman
G

NATCHEZ TRACE PKWY

Rodney
Lake

15

65

Lake
St. John

Clayton

Church Hill

553

F
552

Fayette
E
28

Lake
Concordia

A

61

33

84

65

Natchez
State Park

15

Vidalia

Natchez

Washington

C

84 98

B

H

MISSISSIPPI

St. Catherine Creek
National
Wildlife Refuge

Homochitto

National

Forest

61

Crosby

Buffalo River

Old
River
Lake

24

J

Woodville

Fort Adams

24

N

0 SCALE   10   10
    KILOMETERS   MILES   ——— ROAD   - - - - NATIONAL FOREST BOUNDARY

which also has nature trails. Other places to hike are the Grand Village of the Natchez Indians and Jefferson College.

FOOD

Dine in antebellum style at gorgeous **Monmouth Plantation** (John A. Quitman Parkway, 601/442-5852), which serves Continental cuisine with a Southern flair. The restaurant is open nightly with seating at 7:30 p.m. During pilgrimages only, seatings at 6 and 8:30 p.m are also available. Located on the grounds of Stanton Hall, the **Carriage House Restaurant and Lounge** (401 High Street, 601/445-5151) occupies the mansion's carriage house. You can sit on the patio with a mint julep or some other frosty drink and imagine what life was like in the era of the millionaires. The specialty of the restaurant is fried chicken, but they have numerous other choices for lunch and dinner. Open for dinner only during spring and fall pilgrimages.

Cock-of-the-Walk (200 North Broadway, 601/446-8920) resembles an historic railroad station and is part of a southern chain. Specialties include catfish served fried or blackened, fried chicken, fried dill pickles, and hush puppies. Reservations are not accepted. The **Fare Café** (109 North Pearl, 601/442-5299) is a small, dinerlike restaurant known for its homemade soups, desserts, salads, and sandwiches. You can also order take-out box lunches. The decor is rustic and the ambience is casual at **Natchez Landing** (35 Silver Street, 601/442-6639) at Natchez-Under-the-Hill. Its menu includes barbecue, ribs, smoked chicken, gumbo, and steaks. Open for lunch only during pilgrimages. The **Wharf Master's House** at Natchez-Under-the-Hill (57 Silver Street, 601/445-6025) offers charbroiled steaks and regional cuisine. Menus are written in English, French, Spanish, and German.

Originally an eighteenth-century tavern and the first building in Natchez, **King's Tavern**, 619 Jefferson, 601/446-8845, serves up prime rib, beef, and seafood specialties. Other specialties are tales of ghosts—both Indian warriors and Madeline, the mistress of the original tavern builder.

SIGHTS

- Ⓐ Emerald Mound
- Ⓑ Grand Village of the Natchez Indians
- Ⓒ Natchez Trace Parkway/Sunken Trace
- Ⓓ Old Country Store
- Ⓔ Rosemont Plantation
- Ⓕ Springfield Plantation

LODGING

- Ⓖ Canemount Plantation
- Ⓗ Cedar Grove Plantation
- Ⓘ China Grove Plantation
- Ⓙ Desert Plantation
- Ⓚ Rosswood Plantation

LODGING

Natchez has an astounding 33 bed-and-breakfasts—all of them located in historic homes. In general, they cost more than $100 per night per couple. Among them, **The Burn** (712 North Union Street, 601/442-1344 or 800/654-8859), circa 1832 to 1836, is Natchez's first and best historically documented Greek Revival residence, with a majestic front portico supported by large Doric columns. Originally constructed on one hundred acres, the Burn was once the largest private estate in Natchez. Furnished with exquisite antiques and fine art, it is also one of the city's most visited homes. Sleeping accommodations are offered in the main house and guest house; several rooms boast gas-log fireplaces. Tours are available. The imposing **Dunleith** (84 Homochitto, 601/446-8500 or 800/433-2445) was built in 1856 and has full-length verandas on the first and second stories. The plantation house, which sits on 40 landscaped acres, is furnished with superb, French-inspired antiques. The estate has been used frequently as a backdrop in movies. Eleven guest rooms are offered, some of which feature wood-burning fireplaces. **Monmouth** (36 Melrose Avenue, 601/442-5852 or 800/828-4531), built in 1818, sits on 26 acres lush with formal gardens and moss-draped live oaks. Both *Glamour* and *USA Today* have called it "the Most Romantic Place in America." Twenty-five rooms and 13 suites are offered in the main house and outbuildings, and many boast fireplaces or whirlpools. In addition to breakfast served to overnight guests, a restaurant serves dinner to the public. For a B&B that's totally different, try the funky **Mark Twain Guest House** (25 Silver Street, 601/446-8023), located in an 1830 commercial building at Natchez-Under-the-Hill. Two rooms have a fantastic view of the Mississippi River. Guests have to share a bathroom, and you might want to stay elsewhere if you prefer to turn in early and want a quiet night. For information about other B&Bs, contact Bed and Breakfast–Natchez at 800/647-6742.

Both a plantation and a B&B, **Cedar Grove Plantation**, 617 Kingston Road, 601/445-0585, is situated on 150 acres of heavily wooded forest and farmland. Fronted by grand galleries and columns, the graceful Greek Revival plantation was built in the 1830s. Exquisite furnishings fill the seven guest rooms (two at poolside), and many rooms have Jacuzzis and fireplaces. Freshly mixed mint juleps with complimentary hors d'oeuvres add to the southern hospitality and pampering. Call ahead to reserve kennel space for your canine traveling companion.

Outside Natchez, several small towns also have B&B accommodations in historic homes. At **Canemount Plantation** (MS 552W, Lorman, 601/877-3784), accommodations are offered in private cottages scattered on the 6,000 acres. Wild animals, including turkey, deer, and boar, roam the property. In addition to touring the main house, you can go safari touring, fishing, nature trail hiking, swimming, and biking. The Greek Revival house at **Rosswood Plantation** (MS 552, Lorman, 601/437-4215 or 800/533-5889) was built in 1857, and the slave quarters are still standing behind the house. Guest rooms, which are in the main house, feature canopy beds and antiques. The property also offers a pool and whirlpool. Rosswood is also a working Christmas tree farm. Built in 1800, **China Grove Plantation** (106 West Jackson Street, Belzoni, 601/247-4466) is a story-and-a-half house with a full-length veranda. The two guest rooms share a bath. A pool and walking trails are available. Woodville has one historic bed-and-breakfast: **Desert Plantation** (Pinckneyville-Pond Road, 601/888-6889).

Originally built in the 1920s, the restored **Natchez Eola** (110 North Pearl Street, 601/445-6000 or 800/888-9140) offers upscale accommodations in 130 rooms and suites, including an executive level. Many rooms have superb views of the city and river. The facility features one restaurant and two bars. The **Lady Luck Casino Hotel** (645 South Canal Street, 601/446-6688 or 800/274-5532) is a mid-rise hotel with 145 rooms, a restaurant, bar with live entertainment, pool, and whirlpool. Guests at the **Ramada Inn Hilltop** (130 John R. Junkin Drive, 601/446-6311 or 800/256-6311) have spectacular views of the Mississippi River. The hotel offers 162 rooms and suites, a restaurant, bar with live entertainment, and a pool.

CAMPING

Natchez State Park (Hwy. 61 N., 230-B Wickliff Road, 601/442-2658) offers cabins, 21 improved campsites, and eight tent sites. Camping is also available at Plantation Park (U.S. 61, 601/442-5222) and at Traceway Campgrounds (1113 U.S. 61, 601/445-8278).

NIGHTLIFE

Just as it was in the bad-old-days, Natchez-Under-the-Hill is the place to be at night. The Under-the-Hill Saloon (Silver Street, 601/446-8023) is a hot spot, and the Wharf Master's House restaurant (Silver Street, 601/445-6025) has a lively lounge. The Lady Luck Casino (Silver Street, 800/722-LUCK) has entertainment on weekends in addition to wagering games every day.

Check with your concierge or the welcome center to see if Natchez Little Theater is giving any productions, or call the organization at 601/442-2233. During pilgrimages, additional activities include a pageant, gospel singing, and an old-fashioned medicine show.

Old Man River, the mighty Mississippi, is not only the lifeblood of the state that took its name but is also a scenic border on the state's western edge. Beginning in Helena, a town with numerous antebellum homes, you can drive along the river on MS 1, passing through dozens of small towns. This scenic route detours from MS 1 occasionally to permit visits to some important attractions.

Leave Helena going south and follow MS 1 to Sherard, then detour east on County Road (CR) 322 to Clarksdale. The town is identified with one of Mississippi's greatest gifts to the world—the blues. The area was home to blues pioneers W. C. Handy, Muddy Waters, Howlin' Wolf, and others. Learn more about the musical form at the Delta Blues Museum (Carnegie Library, upstairs, 114 Delta Avenue, 601/627-6820). Among the exhibits are B. B. King's guitar "Lucille" and Muddy Waters' guitar "Muddywood." The earliest human habitation in Mississippi is explored at the Archaeological Museum (Carnegie Library, downstairs, 114 Delta Avenue, 601/624-4461), where pottery and related artifacts are displayed.

Return to MS 1 and continue south to Rosedale, home of Great River Road State Park (601/759-6762). From Rosedale, take a detour east on MS 8 to Cleveland, home of Delta State University. There, visit the Roy E. Wiley Planetarium

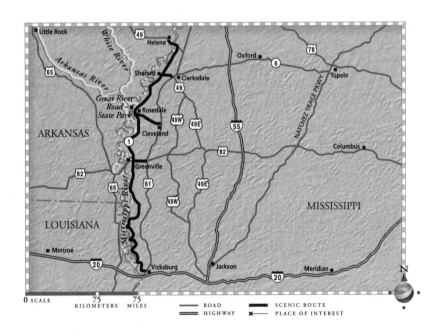

(601/846-4250), the Museum of Natural History (601/846-4240), and the Fielding Wright Art Center (601/846-4720), which includes works by Salvador Dali.

Return to MS 1 and continue south. At Scott, the Delta and Pine Land Company (1 Cotton Row, 601/742-4006) invites visitors to tour a cotton farm. Next go to Greenville, which was hit by a catastrophic flood in 1927. You can also see one of the largest Indian mounds in the Mississippi Valley at the Winterville Mounds Museum State Park (MS 1, 601/334-4684). Greenville has turned out some world-famous authors and journalists, such as Shelby Foote, Hodding Carter (father and son), and Walker Percy. Their works are displayed at the William Alexander Percy Library (341 Main Street, 601/378-3141). Vintage firefighting equipment, hands-on displays, and dress-up clothing for children make the Old Number One Firehouse Museum (230 Main Street, 601/335-2331) fun for the whole family. Don't leave Greenville without driving atop the Mississippi River levee along the Million Dollar Mile. There you'll see shipbuilding under way, as well as shipping, towing, and barge operations.

Detour east on U.S. 82 to Leland to see the Birthplace of the Frog (South Deer Creek Drive East, 601/686-2687). The frog in question is the Muppets' Kermit, and Leland is where creator Jim Henson grew up. Muppets characters are displayed as well as Henson's Christmas card designs and early videos.

Return to MS 1 and go south to Vicksburg, where at the very least you should see the film The Vanishing Glory and visit the Vicksburg National Military Park. (For more details about Vicksburg, see Chapter 17.)

17
VICKSBURG
AND PORT GIBSON

Vicksburg, which stands on a bluff overlooking the Mississippi, was once a stopping point for riverboats, a hotbed of gamblers and scoundrels, and home to refined aristocrats.

The city occupied a strategic point, coveted by both sides, during the Civil War. Federal troops under General Ulysses S. Grant were determined to take Vicksburg and tried to do so over an entire winter in 1862 and 1863. The Union armies finally began a siege, which lasted more than a month. While the city endured constant bombardment, many citizens fled, and the ones who remained were forced to take shelter in caves. Vicksburg eventually fell on July 4, 1863, giving the Union control of the entire Mississippi River, cutting the Confederacy in half and hampering Confederate efforts to supply its troops.

Fortunately, the city was not completely destroyed. The old courthouse still stands on the highest point in town, and many buildings and homes have been restored for use as shops, restaurants, and bed-and-breakfasts. Historic preservation is a way of life here.

The Civil War is still very much in evidence. For example, the present town is surrounded by the Vicksburg National Military Park. Port Gibson, near Vicksburg, also has significant Civil War history. General Grant reportedly said that the town was too beautiful to burn.

Two of the most exciting times of the year in Vicksburg are the spring

VICKSBURG

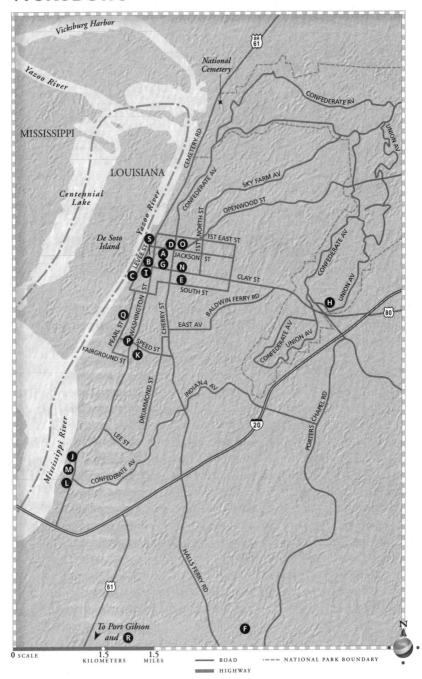

Vicksburg Harbor

Yazoo River

National Cemetery

BR 61

CONFEDERATE AV

UNION AV

MISSISSIPPI

LOUISIANA

CEMETERY RD

Yazoo River

Centennial Lake

CONFEDERATE AV

SKY FARM AV

OPENWOOD ST

De Soto Island

LEVEE ST

NORTH ST

1ST EAST ST

1ST

S

D **O**

A

JACKSON ST

CONFEDERATE AV

UNION AV

B **G**

N

CLAY ST

C **I**

E

SOUTH ST

WASHINGTON ST

CHERRY ST

BALDWIN FERRY RD

H

UNION AV

US 80

Q

EAST AV

PEARL ST

P

SPEED ST

K

CONFEDERATE AV

UNION AV

FAIRGROUND ST

DRUMMOND ST

INDIANA AV

PORTERS CHAPEL RD

LEE ST

US 20

Mississippi River

J

M

L

CONFEDERATE AV

61

HALLS FERRY RD

To Port Gibson and

R

F

N

0 SCALE

1.5 KILOMETERS

1.5 MILES

ROAD

NATIONAL PARK BOUNDARY

HIGHWAY

and fall pilgrimages to private homes and gardens. During pilgrimages, additional activities, such as an arts-and-crafts show and a river festival, are held.

A PERFECT DAY IN VICKSBURG

First see the film *The Vanishing Glory*, which describes the siege of Vicksburg. You'll then have the background you need to understand many other important sights. Stop next at the Old Court House Museum, which has one of the largest collections of Civil War artifacts in the country. Have lunch at Walnut Hills, located in a historic home, then spend some time at the Vicksburg National Military Park. There you can visit the USS Cairo Museum and the Vicksburg National Cemetery. If you have any time left, visit one or more of Vicksburg's historic house museums. Have an elegant dinner at Delta Point Restaurant on the waterfront. Later in the evening you can gamble or watch a show at a casino.

SIGHTSEEING HIGHLIGHTS: VICKSBURG

★★★★ OLD COURT HOUSE MUSEUM
1008 Cherry Street, 601/636-0741
www.vicksburg.org/cvb/museums.htm
Vicksburg's most historic and most revered building, the courthouse was constructed by slaves in 1858 in imposing Greek Revival style. It was only five years old when victorious Union troops lowered the

---

SIGHTS
- Ⓐ Biedenharn Coca-Cola Museum
- Ⓑ Gray and Blue Naval Museum
- Ⓒ Mississippi River Adventure Hydro-Jet Boat Cruise
- Ⓓ Old Court House Museum
- Ⓔ Southern Cultural Heritage Complex
- Ⓕ U.S. Army Engineers Waterways Experiment Station
- Ⓖ *The Vanishing Glory*
- Ⓗ Vicksburg National Military Park
- Ⓘ Yesterday's Children Antique Doll and Toy Museum and Shop

FOOD
- Ⓙ Calypso's
- Ⓚ Cedar Grove Mansion
- Ⓛ Delta Point River Restaurant
- Ⓜ Goldie's Trail Bar-B-Que
- Ⓝ Walnut Hills

LODGING
- Ⓞ Anchuca
- Ⓟ Annabelle
- Ⓚ Cedar Grove Mansion Inn
- Ⓠ The Corners
- Ⓡ Grey Oaks
- Ⓢ Harrah's Casino Hotel Vicksburg

Note: Items with the same letter are located in the same area.

Confederate flag and raised the Federal flag over it after the siege of Vicksburg. Now a National Landmark, the building serves as a museum of Vicksburg's history with emphasis on the Civil War.

Details: Mon–Sat 8:30–4:30, Sun 1:30–4:30. $3 adults, $2.50 seniors, $2 children. (1–2 hours)

★★★★ THE VANISHING GLORY
717 Clay Street, 601/634-1863
This poignant film is an account of the siege and fall of Vicksburg and features many local reenactors. Their story is told from the diaries and writings of citizens and soldiers.

Details: Daily 9–5 with presentations on the hour. $5 adults, $3 students. (¹/2 hour)

★★★★ VICKSBURG NATIONAL MILITARY PARK
3201 Clay Street, 601/636-2199, www.nps.gov/vick
Begin at the visitors center to see a film, exhibits, and artifacts about the campaign to take Vicksburg. You can hire a guide to take you on the 16-mile drive of the battlefield or buy a cassette tape and take the tour on your own. Portions of fortifications, artillery batteries, and stockades remain. Historical markers describe various stages of the battle. Many pieces of artillery are still in place, and monuments honor groups who fought on both sides. In the north section of the park, you can see the **USS Cairo Museum**. The gunboat was used by the Union in its bombardment of Vicksburg, but was sunk and remained under water for 100 years. Its pitiful remains were raised and displayed along with artifacts found on board. Adjacent to the park is

MISSISSIPPI RIVER CRUISES
Take a romantic cruise on the Mississippi aboard the ***American Queen***, ***Delta Queen***, or ***Mississippi Queen***, the only steamboats in the United States that offer overnight accommodations. The *Delta Queen* is an authentic steam-powered paddle wheeler built in 1927 and listed on the National Register of Historic Places. The other two boats are authentic but of new construction.

the **Vicksburg National Cemetery** where 17,000 Union soldiers are buried.

Details: Visitors center daily 8–5, USS Cairo Museum 8:30–5. $4 per car, step-on guide $20, audiotape $4.50. (2 hours)

★★★ **GRAY AND BLUE NAVAL MUSEUM**
1102 Washington Street, 601/638-6500
www.grayandbluenavalmuseum.usrc.net
This museum houses the world's largest collection of Civil War gunboat models. Visitors can examine a large diorama of the siege of Vicksburg, as well as Civil War paintings and artifacts. The museum has recently added a naval vessel display, as well as towboats and riverboats.

Details: Mon–Sat 9–5. $2 adults, $1 children under 12, maximum family admission $6. (1 hour)

★★★ **MISSISSIPPI RIVER ADVENTURE HYDRO-JET BOAT CRUISE**
City Waterfront at Foot of Clay Street, 601/638-5443 or 800/521-4363
Narrated cruises present history, scenery, and adventure on the Mississippi and Yazoo Rivers.

Details: One-hour cruises daily 10, 2, and 5. $16 adults, $8 children. (1 hour)

★★ **BIEDENHARN COCA-COLA MUSEUM**
1107 Washington Street, 601/638-6514
Although Coca-Cola was developed in Georgia, it was first bottled in this very building in Vicksburg in 1894. A reproduction of the bottling works shows how it was done. Lots of Coca-Cola memorabilia is displayed and sold. You can also satisfy your sweet tooth with fountain Cokes, ice cream floats, and homemade candy at the 1900s soda fountain and late-nineteenth–century candy store.

Details: Mon–Sat 9–5, Sun 1:30–4:30. $1.75 adults, $1.25 children. ($\frac{1}{2}$ hour)

★★ **SOUTHERN CULTURAL HERITAGE COMPLEX**
1021 Crawford Street, 601/631-2997
The four-story building, built in 1830, was originally the St. Francis Xavier Convent and Academy and was the first example of Gothic

VICKSBURG/PORT GIBSON REGION

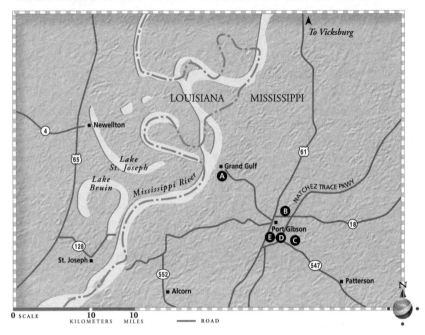

To Vicksburg

LOUISIANA   MISSISSIPPI

Newellton

Lake
St. Joseph

Grand Gulf

Lake
Bruin   Mississippi River

NATCHEZ TRACE PKWY

Port Gibson

St. Joseph

Patterson

Alcorn

N

0 SCALE   10   10
          KILOMETERS MILES   ———— ROAD

SIGHTS

Ⓐ Grand Gulf Military Monument
Park/Grand Gulf Cemetery
Ⓑ Port Gibson City Hall
Ⓒ Ruins of Windsor
Ⓓ Wintergreen Cemetery

LODGING

Ⓔ Oak Square Country Inn

Revival architecture in Mississippi. At different times during the Civil War, either Confederate or Union troops used the building for barracks. Tours show how the building looked in 1830 and 1868.

Details: *Mon–Fri 9–4 or by appointment. $2 adults, $1 children. (1 hour)*

★★ U.S. ARMY ENGINEERS WATERWAYS EXPERIMENT STATION

3909 Halls Ferry Road, 601/634-2502
Visitors can take self-guided walking and driving tours of the largest research, testing, and development facility within the Army Corps of Engineers. Examine scale models of many of the nations waterways including Niagara Falls. In addition, the facility has a nature trail and picnicking area.

Details: Mon–Fri 7:45–4:15, weekend tours are self-guided and do not cover the entire facility, special group tours by appointment. Free. (1 hour)

★★ **YESTERDAY'S CHILDREN ANTIQUE DOLL AND TOY MUSEUM AND SHOP**
1104 Washington Street, 601/638-0650
Housed in an 1836 building, the museum contains more than 1,000 dolls, toys, and accessories dating from the 1880s to the present. The gift shop sells antique and new dolls.

Details: Mon–Sat 10:30–4. $2 adults, $1 children under 12. (1 hour)

SIGHTSEEING HIGHLIGHTS: VICKSBURG/PORT GIBSON REGION

★★★ **GRAND GULF MILITARY MONUMENT PARK/GRAND GULF CEMETERY**
Grand Gulf Road, Port Gibson, 601/437-5911
www.grandgulfpark.state.ms.us
The park includes several historic buildings and the remains of Forts Coburn and Wade. What remains of Fort Coburn, which never fell to Union troops, are the earthworks. Remains of Fort Wade include the original parapet, ammunition magazine, earthworks, and fortifications. A museum displays hundreds of Civil War artifacts, including carriages, wagons, a Civil War ambulance, and a one-of-a-kind Civil War submarine. The cemetery is the final resting place of African Americans who fought for the Union.

Details: Park open during daylight hours, museum open Mon–Sat 8–5. Park and museum $1.50 adults, $1 seniors, 75 cents children; park only $1 adults and seniors, 50 cents children. (1 hour)

★★★ **PORT GIBSON CITY HALL**
1005 College Street, Port Gibson, 601/437-4234

Once the centerpiece of the Port Gibson Female College (the first girls' school in Mississippi), the elegant Greek Revival building was constructed in 1840 and recently restored. Today it serves as City Hall and houses the Allen Collection, Picturing Our Past, which includes vintage photographs of life in Port Gibson and Claiborne County between 1906 and 1915.

Details: Mon–Fri 8–noon and 1–4, other times by appointment. Free. (¹/₂ hour)

★★ RUINS OF WINDSOR
MS 552W, Port Gibson

Built around 1860 and once the largest and most opulent antebellum mansion in Mississippi, the estate house survived the Civil War intact but was destroyed by fire in 1890. All that is left are the 23 splendid fluted columns. They have appeared in several period movies.

Details: Free. (¹/₄ hour)

★★ WINTERGREEN CEMETERY
Greenwood Street, Port Gibson

Begun in 1807, this plot was originally the family cemetery of Samuel Gibson, the founder of Port Gibson. It evolved over time to include the graves of others and is now one of the most beautiful cemeteries in Mississippi.

Details: Daily dawn–dusk. Free. (¹/₂–1 hour)

FITNESS AND RECREATION

The Vicksburg area provides many opportunities for walking, jogging, hiking, and biking. A popular place for any of these activities is the Vicksburg National Military Park (see Sightseeing Highlights), where you can walk 16 miles of paved roads. Riverfront Park along the banks of the Mississippi (4100 Washington Street) provides picnic facilities, a playground, and walking trails. Funtricity Family Entertainment Park (1444 Warrenton Road, 601/631-0303) offers miniature golf, bumper boats, bumper cars, batting cages, kiddie rides, video and virtual reality games, a space shuttle simulator, and play areas in settings that range from western boomtowns to medieval castles. Clear Creek Golf Club (1566 Tiffentown Road, Bovina, 601/638-9395) is an 18-hole public course. The complex also has a driving range and tennis courts.

VICKSBURG'S HISTORIC HOMES

In the last 25 years, a strenuous preservation effort has restored many of Vicksburg's historic homes to their former grandeur. Tour fees provide some of the funds needed to keep the houses in tip-top shape. Some of them also operate as bed-and-breakfasts. Among homes to visit are **Anchuca**, a Greek Revival built in 1830 (1010 First East Street, 601/631-6800 or 800/469-2597); **Annabelle**, an Italianate circa 1868 (501 Speed Street, 601/661-0111 or 800/686-0111); **Balfour**, a Greek Revival built in 1835 (1002 Crawford Street, 601/638-7113 or 800/294-7113); **Belle of the Bends**, an Italianate circa 1876 (508 Klein Street, 601/634-0737 or 800/844-2308); **Cedar Grove Mansion**, a Greek Revival built between 1840 and 1858 (2200 Oak Street, 601/636-1000 or 800/862-1300); **The Corners**, a combination of Greek Revival and Victorian built in 1873 (601 Klein Street, 601/636-7421 or 800/444-7421); **Duff Green Mansion**, built in 1856 (1114 First East Street, 601/636-6968 or 800/992-0037); **McRaven**, begun as a frontier house in 1797 and adapted to Empire style in 1836 with Greek Revival embellishments added in 1849 (1445 Harrison Street, 601/636-1663); and the small brick **Martha Vick House**, circa 1830 (1300 Grove Street, 601/638-7036). Three other tour houses were built early in this century. They are the Greek Revival **The Columns** (2002 Cherry Street, 601/634-4751 or 800/971-1220); the Prairie-style **Shlenker House** (2212 Cherry Street, 601/636-7086 or 800/636-7086) and the Mission-style **Stained Glass Manor** (2430 Drummond Street, 601/638-8893, 800/771-8893, or 888/VICKBND).

FOOD

Cedar Grove Mansion (2200 Oak Street, 601/636-1000 or 800/862-1300), one of the most magnificent of Vicksburg's mansions, offers bed-and-breakfast accommodations and dining. Romantic candlelight dinners are served in the courtyard accompanied by piano music after 6 p.m. Reservations are a must. The highly acclaimed **Delta Point River Restaurant** (4144 Washington Street, 601/638-1000) is located next to the Ameristar Casino on the waterfront and is operated by the same company. Elegance, good food, and a spectacular view of the Mississippi River make the restaurant popular for special occasions. Steak, veal, and seafood lead the menu. A classical jazz pianist performs Wednesday through Saturday.

Walnut Hills (1214 Adams Street, 601/638-4910) offers down-home cooking in an 1880s house. Round tables seat diners—often strangers—who can help themselves to several entrees and heaping portions of vegetables and other side dishes. Reservations recommended. **Calypso's** at the Isle of Capri Casino (3990 Washington Street, 601/630-4477 or 800/WIN-ISLE), a casual restaurant with a Caribbean theme, serves three meals daily. Buffets are served at lunch and dinner, but you can also order a la carte. Among the menu favorites are peel-and-eat shrimp, crab, lobster, and fried oysters. The pit-cooked barbecue at **Goldie's Trail Bar-B-Que** (4127 South Washington Street, 601/636-9839) has been featured in regional magazines and a book about barbecue. The menu includes pork, beef, chicken, and sausage. The casual, down-home atmosphere is as popular as the food.

LODGING

Anchuca (1010 First East Street, 601/661-0111 or 800/686-0111), a Greek Revival home built in 1830, is listed on the National Register of Historic Places. The luxurious home, superbly furnished with antiques and gas-burning chandeliers, offers a pool, Jacuzzi, laundry facilities, honor bars, cable TV with HBO, and landscaped gardens and brick courtyards. The magnificent **Cedar Grove Mansion Inn** (2200 Oak Street, 601/636-1000 or 800/862-1300) is a Greek Revival mansion built in 1840. Listed on the National Register of Historic Places, it overlooks the Mississippi River and is surrounded by formal gardens, courtyards, fountains, and gazebos. Many of the antique furnishings are original to the house. Luxurious accommodations are offered in the main house, carriage house, and five cottages. Some rooms have canopy beds, mini-bars, terraces, fireplaces, and whirlpools. Afternoon tea and wine are served. **The Corners** (601 Klein Street, 601/636-7421 or 800/444-7421), an Italianate/Greek Revival house built in 1872, has a 70-foot veranda across the front. It overlooks the Mississippi and Yazoo Rivers and is surrounded by an original parterre garden. Beautifully decorated guest rooms in the main house and a newly constructed adjacent cottage feature either fireplaces or whirlpools.

The highly rated **Oak Square Country Inn** (1207 Church Street, Port Gibson, 601/437-4350 or 800/729-0240) is located in a fabulous, 1850 Greek Revival house with a full-length veranda supported by elegant columns. Gracefully decorated rooms offer heirlooms and cable TV; some have canopy beds and terraces. For a more complete list of B&Bs in the area, contact the Vicksburg Convention and Visitors Bureau: 601/636-9421 or 800/221-3536. Guests who stay at **Harrah's Casino Hotel Vicksburg** (1310 Mulberry Street, 601/636-3423 or 800/HARRAHS) are only steps away from all the games, restaurants, bars, and entertainment. Complimentary buffet breakfast is included in the nightly rate.

Grey Oaks, a fine southern plantation home, 4142 Rifle Range Rd., Vicksburg, 601/638-4424, was built in 1834. One hundred years later it was dismantled and moved to its present site, which includes six acres of gardens and nature trails. The facade is a replica of Tara from *Gone With the Wind*. Guests staying in one of the three poster-bed- and antique-filled rooms enjoy a tour of the mansion.

Annabelle, 501 Speed St., Vicksburg, 800/791-2000 or 601/638-2000, is a lovely, Victorian Italianate residence filled with family heirlooms. The six rooms and one suite are furnished with antiques, while offering all the modern conveniences of cable TV, air-conditioning, telephones, and private baths. Laze away your afternoons napping in the hammock, reading in the landscaped brick courtyard, or swimming in the pool. Enjoy a welcome beverage and hearty southern breakfasts.

CAMPING

Vicksburg Battlefield Campground (4407 I-20 Frontage Road, 601/636-2025) offers 80 campsites with pull-throughs and full hookups as well as a laundry room, rest rooms, a store, playground, and swimming pool. Magnolia RV Park (211 Miller Street, 601/631-0388) has 66 campsites with pull-throughs and hookups, laundry facilities, a game room, pool, playground, basketball court, and horseshoes. The Isle of Capri RV Park (Lucy Bryson Road, 601/631-0402 or 800/946-4753) provides 67 campsites, laundry facilities, showers, pool, hot tub, and free shuttle to the casino as well as special coupon offers.

Grand Gulf Military Monument Park (seven miles north of Port Gibson, 601/437-5911) has RV sites and hookups, a boat ramp, nature trails, showers, and picnic shelters, and a laundry is being added. The park, which is on the National Historic Register, also has remains of Civil War forts, a museum, and a cemetery.

NIGHTLIFE

For a variety of nighttime activities, including gambling and entertainment under one roof, you can't beat the casinos: Ameristar Casino (4146 South

Washington Street, 601/638-1000 or 800/700-7770); Harrah's Casino Vicksburg (1310 Mulberry Street, 601/636-3423 or 800/HARRAHS); Isle of Capri Casino (3990 Washington Street, 601/636-5700 or 800/WIN-ISLE); and Rainbow Casino at Vicksburg Landing (1380 Warrenton Road, 601/636-7575 or 800/503-3777).

Now in its 61st year, the old-time melodrama *Gold in the Hills* is performed from mid-March through mid-April and in July at the Parkside Playhouse (3101 Confederate Avenue, 601/636-0471). The production includes songs and dancing, and playgoers are encouraged to get into the spirit of things by cheering, booing, and throwing peanuts at the cast.

During football season you can watch games in the bar at the Beechwood Restaurant and Lounge (4449 MS 80E, 601/636-3761). Live entertainment is provided in the bar Tuesday through Sunday night. The larger hotels also offer live entertainment in their lounges.

18
JACKSON

Both the largest city in Mississippi and the state capital, Jackson sits on a bluff along the Pearl River. It began as a trading post called LeFleur's Bluff. Only later was the fledgling city named after Andrew Jackson. Jackson was burned three times during the Civil War until only five buildings and rows and rows of chimneys were left, earning the remains of the city the nickname Chimneyville.

In the early twentieth century, the city was home to blues musicians and played an instrumental role in the development of this distinctly American musical form. Today the city bustles with the affairs of government, commerce, and manufacturing. Sitting at the midpoint of the Natchez Trace Parkway (from Natchez to Nashville) and at the junction of I-20, I-55, and U.S. 49, Jackson now has a new nickname—Crossroads of the South.

June is an exciting time to visit Jackson because several major festivals are held that month: Hog Wild In June, Mississippi Championship Hot Air Balloon Race, and the International Crawfish Festival, to name just a few.

A PERFECT DAY IN JACKSON

Start at the Old Capitol Museum to learn more about Mississippi and to admire the beautiful old building. Then see the new capitol and the governor's mansion. Have a quick lunch at the Old Tyme Delicatessen and Bakery. In the afternoon tour two historic homes: the Oaks and Manship House. If the

DOWNTOWN JACKSON

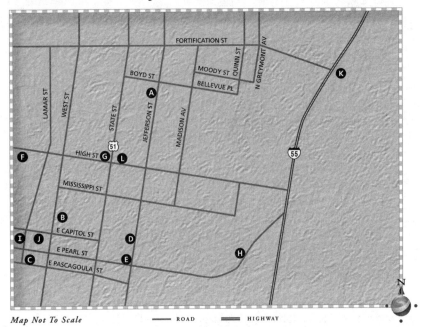

Map Not To Scale ━━━ ROAD ═══ HIGHWAY

SIGHTS

- **A** Boyd House (The Oaks)
- **B** Governor's Mansion
- **C** Mississippi Museum of Art
- **D** Mississippi Museum of Natural Science
- **E** Old Capitol/Mississippi State Historical Museum
- **F** Russell C. Davis Planetarium/Ronald McNair Space Theater
- **F** Smith Robertson Museum
- **G** State Capitol

FOOD

- **H** Dennery's
- **I** The Elite

LODGING

- **J** Edison Walthall Hotel
- **K** Marriott Residence Inn
- **L** Millsaps-Buie House

Note: Items with the same letter are located in the same area.

weather is nice, take a trip to Mynelle Gardens or Jackson Zoological Park. If the weather is inclement, try the Mississippi Museum of Art or the Jim Buck Ross Mississippi Agriculture and Forestry/National Agricultural Aviation Museum. Have an elegant, romantic dinner at the Elite. Afterward check to see whether any of the city's cultural organizations have a performance.

SIGHTSEEING HIGHLIGHTS: DOWNTOWN JACKSON

★★★★ GOVERNOR'S MANSION
300 East Capitol Street, 601/359-6421
The stately, classic, Greek Revival mansion was built in 1842 and is the second-oldest continuously occupied gubernatorial mansion in the country. It has been meticulously restored to its original design and is one of only two governors' mansions listed as a National Historic Landmark. The mansion is furnished with museum-quality antiques appropriate to the 1820s and 1830s, and the manicured grounds are beautifully landscaped.

Details: Tue–Fri 9:30–11 a.m. with guided tours every half hour. Free. ($^1/_2$ hour)

★★★★ MISSISSIPPI MUSEUM OF ART
201 East Pascagoula Street, 601/960-1515
www.msmuseumart.org
This art museum is the state's oldest and largest. It holds a varied collection of 5,000 pieces, including works by and relating to Mississippians, nineteenth- and twentieth-century American landscapes, eighteenth-century British paintings, Japanese prints, Southern photography, pre-Columbian ceramics, and oceanic art. The Impressions Gallery is a stimulating, high-tech, interactive learning experience for children.

Details: Tue–Sat 10–5, Sun noon–5. $3 adults, $2 seniors, students, and children. (1–2 hours)

★★★★ OLD CAPITOL/MISSISSIPPI STATE HISTORICAL MUSEUM
100 South State Street, 601/359-6920
Designed in Greek Revival style, the capitol was begun in 1833 and served as the statehouse until 1903. Today it houses 30,000 artifacts

chronicling Mississippi's past, including prehistory, the Civil War, Reconstruction, cotton culture, and the Civil Rights movement. Portraits of 84 prominent Mississippians are hung throughout the building.

Details: Weekdays 8–5, Sat 9:30–4:30, Sun 12:30–4:30. Free. (1 hour)

★★★★ STATE CAPITOL
400 High Street, 601/359-3114

At the turn of the century, the 1833 capitol building was no longer adequate to accommodate the state government, so this beautiful Beaux Arts structure, based on the U.S. Capitol, was erected. You can watch the legislature in session.

Details: Weekdays 8–5, guided tours 9, 10, 11, 1:30, 2:30, and 3:30. Free. (1 hour)

★★★ BOYD HOUSE (THE OAKS)
823 North Jefferson Street, 601/353-9339

Jackson's oldest house, the Greek Revival cottage was built between 1853 and 1858 by Mayor James Hervey Boyd. Union General William Tecumseh Sherman occupied the house and used it as his headquarters during the siege of Jackson in 1863. Perhaps it was because Sherman had used the house that he spared it when he burned the city. It is one of only five Jackson homes to survive the war. Now restored, the cottage is filled with antiques, including a sofa from Abraham Lincoln's law office in Springfield, Illinois.

Details: Tue–Sat 10–3, guided tours on hour and half hour. is $2 adults, $1 children. (1 hour)

★★★ MISSISSIPPI MUSEUM OF NATURAL SCIENCE
111 North Jefferson Street, 601/354-7303

Beginning with a few specimens in 1932, the collection has grown to a quarter million examples of Mississippi flora, fauna, and minerals.

Details: Weekdays 8–5, Sat 9:30–4:30. Free. (1 hour)

★★★ RUSSELL C. DAVIS PLANETARIUM/ RONALD MCNAIR SPACE THEATER
201 East Pascagoula Street, 601/960-1550

Adjoining the Mississippi Museum of Art, the planetarium is one of the largest in the Southeast, and the theater is one of the best equipped. Star shows, laser shows, and wide-screen films are shown. Starlight concerts and stage shows are performed periodically.

Details: Shows daily. Call for current schedule. $4 adults, $2.50 seniors and children; for laser shows $5 adults, $3.50 seniors and children under 12. (1 hour)

★★★ **SMITH ROBERTSON MUSEUM**
528 Bloom Street, 601/960-1457, www.city,jackson.ms.us/
Housed in the city's first school for African Americans, this museum is the first in the state entirely devoted to African American history and culture. Artifacts and exhibits begin with life in Africa and trace the journey to the present day. The emphasis is on the contributions of black Mississippians in the fields of history, education, business, politics, and the arts. Folk art demonstrations and workshops are given periodically.

Details: Weekdays 9–5, Sat 9–noon, Sun 2–5. $1 adults, 50 cents children. (1 hour)

SIGHTSEEING HIGHLIGHTS: JACKSON REGION

★★★★ **JIM BUCK ROSS MISSISSIPPI AGRICULTURE AND FORESTRY/ NATIONAL AGRICULTURAL AVIATION MUSEUM**
1150 Lakeland Drive, 601/354-6113
The history of two of Mississippi's most important industries are traced at the museum. The Fortenberry-Parkman Farm Restoration depicts life on a 1920s farm, and the crossroads town gives a glimpse of a rural town of the same period. Living history demonstrations are often given. In addition, the complex features a miniature train ride, the Chimneyville Crafts Gallery (see next entry), and an historic rose garden listed on the National Register of Historic Places.

Details: Mon–Sat 9–5, Sun 1–5. $4 adults, $2 children 6–18, $3 seniors, 50 cents children 3–5. (1–2 hours)

★★★ **CHIMNEYVILLE CRAFTS GALLERY**
1150 Lakeland Drive, 601/981-2499
Located at the Agriculture and Forestry Museum and operated by the Craftsmen's Guild of Mississippi, the gallery features original,

JACKSON REGION

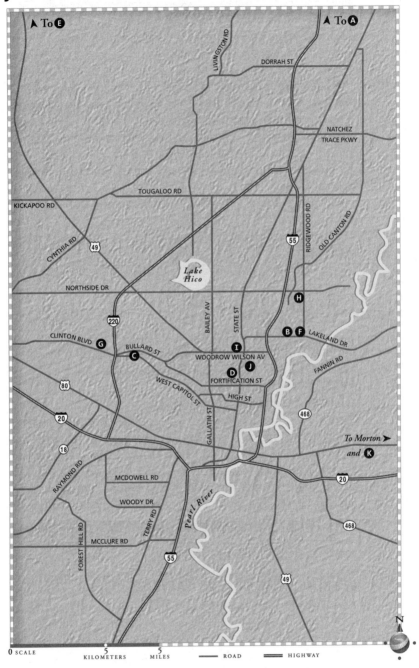

handmade, traditional, and contemporary crafts. During warm weather members demonstrate their crafts on Saturday.

Details: Mon–Sat 9–5, Sun 1–5. Free. (1 hour)

★★★ JACKSON ZOOLOGICAL PARK
2918 West Capitol Street, 601/352-2580

Founded in 1919, the zoo has one of the finest collections of wild animals in the world. More than 100 acres of re-created habitats are home to 500 animals. The children's Discovery Zoo has entertaining and imaginative hands-on exhibits.

Details: Daily 9–5; to 6 in summer. $4 adults, $2 seniors and children 3–12, free 2 and under. (1–2 hours)

★★★ MANSHIP HOUSE MUSEUM
420 East Fortification Street, 601/961-4724

This Greek Revival house was built in 1857. It was the home of the city's Civil War mayor, Charles Henry Manship, who was a craftsman known for his faux wood graining. Examples of his work are found throughout the house.

Details: Tue–Fri 9–4, Sat 10–4. Free. (1 hour)

★★★ MYNELLE GARDENS
4736 Clinton Boulevard, 601/960-1894

A botanical wonderland, the facility includes manicured grounds and several fragrant gardens of annuals and perennials covering seven acres.

SIGHTS
Ⓐ Casey Jones Museum
Ⓑ Chimneyville Crafts Gallery
Ⓒ Jackson Zoological Park
Ⓑ Jim Buck Ross Mississippi Agriculture and Forestry/National Agricultural Aviation Museum
Ⓓ Manship House Museum
Ⓔ Mississippi Petrified Forest
Ⓕ Mississippi Sports Hall of Fame
Ⓖ Mynelle Gardens

FOOD
Ⓗ Old Tyme Delicatessen and Bakery

LODGING
Ⓘ Cabot Lodge
Ⓙ Fairview
Ⓚ Roosevelt State Park

Note: Items with the same letter are located in the same area.

Details: Daily Mar–Oct 9–5:15; rest of the year Mon–Sat 8–4:15, Sun noon–4:15. $2 adults, 50 cents children under 12. (1 hour)

★★ CASEY JONES MUSEUM
10501 Vaughn Road #1, Vaughn, 601/673-9864
The museum honors Jonathan Luther "Casey" Jones, a railroad engineer and folk hero. Railroad history in Mississippi is interpreted as well. A 1923 oil-burning steam engine is on display.
Details: Mon–Sat 9–5, Sun 1–5. $1 adults, 50 cents children. (1 hour)

★★ MISSISSIPPI PETRIFIED FOREST
Petrified Forest Road, Flora, 601/879-8189
The only petrified forest in the eastern United States, it is 36 million years old and has been named a Registered National Natural Landmark. An easy walking trail meanders through the forest, past many giant trees transformed to stone. The trail ends at a museum where you can examine other examples of petrified wood, as well as fossils, minerals, and other unusual items.
Details: Daily 9–5; to 6 between Apr 1 and Labor Day. $5 adults, $4 children. (1 hour)

★★ MISSISSIPPI SPORTS HALL OF FAME
1152 Lakeland Drive, 601/982-8264 or 800/280-FAME
www.msfame.com
The interactive museum contains touch-screen TV kiosks where visitors can access archival footage, statistics, biographical information, and 500 interviews with famous Mississippi athletes such as Brett Favre and Dizzy Dean.
Details: Mon–Sat 10–4, Sun 1:30–4:30. $5 adults and $3.50 seniors and students 6–17. (1 hour)

FITNESS AND RECREATION
Bicycling, hiking, bird-watching, tennis, and golf are popular pastimes in and around Jackson. The city maintains more than 40 parks, and four golf courses are located in the vicinity. Ross Barnett Reservoir (exit 103 off I-55N, 601/354-3448) provides innumerable opportunities for water sports. Rapids on the Reservoir (1808 Spillway Road, 601/992-0500) is a water park. LeFleur's Bluff State Park (2140 Riverside Drive, 601/987-3923 and 601/987-3985), which in-

cludes Mayes Lake, features a boat ramp, playground, nature trail, pool, tennis courts, a driving range, and a nine-hole golf course. Roosevelt State Park (2149 MS 13S, Morton, 601/732-6316) has a 150-acre lake, lighted tennis courts, miniature golf, and a nature/wildlife observation center.

On the spectator sports front, the Jackson Generals, the Texas-League, AA farm team of the Houston Astros, play at Smith-Wills Stadium (1200 Lakeland Drive, 601/981-4664).

FOOD

To create a romantic ambience, **Dennery's** (330 Greymont Avenue, 601/354-2527) installed an interior fountain with the Greek goddess of love, Aphrodite, in the center. Greek specialties lead the menu, but you can also choose from steak and seafood entrees. Reservations are recommended.

The Elite (141 East Capitol Street, 601/352-5606) sounds like a formal restaurant, but it is actually a casual eatery with simple decor reminiscent of an old diner. The fare is humble as well, with southern-style vegetables and home-made dinner rolls accompanying entrees such as fried chicken. Reservations and credit cards are not accepted.

The only kosher deli in Jackson, the **Old Tyme Delicatessen and Bakery** (1305 East Northside Drive, 601/362-2565) offers soups, sandwiches, and salads. In addition to the bakery, a small shop sells gourmet items.

LODGING

One of the finest places to stay in Jackson is the elegant **Millsaps-Buie House** (628 North State Street, 601/352-0221 or 800/784-0221), a bed-and-breakfast. Located in the heart of the historic district with a commanding view of the capitol, the imposing, three-story Victorian house was built in 1888 and is on the National Register of Historic Places. It is filled with exquisite antiques and artwork. Amenities include hair dryers, cable TV, dataports, a guest lounge, and fresh fruit and flowers. Some guest rooms have terraces and some have refrigerators. Bed-and-breakfast accommodations can also be found at **Fairview** (73334 Fairview Street, 601/948-1203), located in the historic district and built in 1908. A stately colonial revival home with a two-story, white-columned portico, Fairview is listed on the National Register of Historic Places and was named the Top Inn of 1994 by *Country Inns* magazine. Six luxury suites and two luxury rooms are available.

The elegant **Edison Walthall Hotel** (225 East Capitol Street, 601/948-6161) offers 200 rooms and suites with coffee makers, hair dryers, and dataports. Some feature mini-bars and whirlpools. An executive level offers additional amenities. Other facilities include a restaurant, bar, and fitness room. Apartment-style accommodations make the **Marriott Residence Inn** (881 East River Place, 601/355-3599 or 800/331-3131) ideal for an extended stay. Suites feature kitchens, living/dining areas, and bedrooms. Amenities include coffeemakers, refrigerators, and fireplaces. Some units boast whirlpools. The hotel has a swimming pool, whirlpool, and laundry. **Cabot Lodge** (2375 North State Street, 601/948-8650 or 800/874-4737 and 120 Dyess Road, 601/957-0757 or 800 342-2268), a small chain, is not well known, but it should be. The hotels are classy, well decorated, and offer numerous amenities. The lobbies have fireplaces and cozy sitting areas. Guest get complimentary beverages, continental breakfast, and snacks. Nearby **Roosevelt State Park** (2149 MS 13S, Morton, 601/732-6316) has a lodge with 20 rooms with kitchenettes. Cabins are available as well.

CAMPING

LeFleur's Bluff State Park (2140 Riverside Drive, 601/987-3985) has 30 camping pads with water and electric hookups, as well as bathhouses, a nine-hole golf course, nature trail, clubhouse, pool, rest rooms, and a store. Ross Barnett Reservoir (exit 103 off I-55N, 601/354-3448) has camping facilities and recreational attractions. Private campgrounds include Cleveland's Trailer Town (Old Highway 49S, 601/939-4873); Cox's Cumrovin' Campground (135 Cox Avenue, 601/992-1582); and Timberlake Campground (Old Fannin Road, 601/992-9100). Although it is farther afield, Roosevelt State Park (2149 MS 13, Morton, 601/732-6316) has 109 campsites and numerous recreational facilities.

NIGHTLIFE

Jackson's performing arts organizations offer productions year-round. The city boasts two ballet companies, a chamber music society, choral society, opera company, and the Mississippi Symphony Orchestra (201E Pascagoula Street, 601/960-1565). Several theater groups, including the Repertory Theater of Mississippi (New Stage Theater, 301 North State Street, 601/948-6633) stage productions. Ask your concierge for a schedule of events.

In a city that gave birth to the blues, it isn't unexpected that the musical form is widely available. Red Hot and Blue (1625 East County Line Road, 601/956-3313) features live blues bands on weekends.

19
TUPELO AND OXFORD

Northern Mississippi boasts natural beauty unlike any other place in the state. In the extreme northeastern corner, you'll find the rocky outcroppings and tumbling streams of the foothills of the Appalachian Mountains, as well as clear lakes and deep woodlands. On its southwestern journey from Tennessee to Natchez, the scenic Natchez Trace Parkway passes through northern Mississippi. The parkway's headquarters and visitor centers are located in Tupelo.

This region saw major action during the Civil War, and reminders of that time are lovingly preserved. When the war broke out, the University of Mississippi in Oxford closed its doors, and a company of faculty and students formed the University Greys, a unit all but destroyed in 1864. Wounded soldiers from the battles of Shiloh, Tennessee, and Corinth were treated on the campus of the university, and a major battle near Tupelo ended in Confederate victory.

Above all else, the region is famous as the birthplace of the King of Rock and Roll, Elvis Presley. Even 22 years after Presley's death, the tiny, two-room house in which he was born and the adjacent museum and chapel draw thousands of visitors each year from around the world.

The region is also home of legendary blues men such as Robert Johnson, Muddy Waters, and B. B. King. Finally, Nobel Prize–winning author William Faulkner lived here. In his antebellum mansion called Rowan Oak, he created the fictional world of the residents of Yoknapatawpha County—drawn from the people and surroundings he knew so intimately.

TUPELO

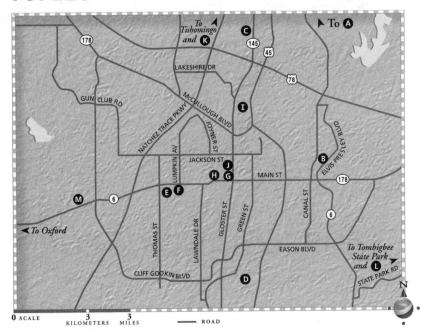

SIGHTS

- **A** Brice's Crossroads National Battlefield Site
- **B** Elvis Presley Birthplace and Museum
- **C** Natchez Trace Parkway Visitors Center
- **D** Private John Allen National Fish Hatchery
- **E** Tupelo Battlefield
- **F** Tupelo Museum

FOOD

- **G** Gloster 205 Restaurant
- **H** Rossens
- **I** Vanelli's

LODGING

- **J** Mockingbird Inn
- **K** Tishomingo State Park
- **L** Tombigbee State Park
- **M** Trace State Park

A PERFECT DAY IN TUPELO AND OXFORD

Spend the morning visiting the Elvis Presley Birthplace and Museum, the Natchez Trace Parkway Visitors Center, and the Brice's Cross Roads National Battlefield Site. Have a leisurely lunch at Jefferson Place, located in a lovely historic home, then make the short drive to Oxford, where you will spend the afternoon. Visit William Faulkner's home, Rowan Oak. Then spend the rest of the afternoon at the university's Center for the Study of Southern Culture and the other museums. Have an elegant, romantic dinner at the Downtown Grill. For your evening's entertainment, check to see whether any sports events, plays, or concerts are taking place on the Ole Miss campus.

SIGHTSEEING HIGHLIGHTS

★★★★ BRICE'S CROSSROADS NATIONAL BATTLEFIELD SITE
MS 370, Baldwin, 601/680-4025
This attraction was the site of an 1864 Civil War battle, which resulted in one of the few Confederate victories. Interpretive maps and markers tell the story of the battle. The adjacent cemetery holds the remains of 100 Confederate soldiers.
Details: *Daily sunrise–sunset. Free. (1 hour)*

★★★★ ELVIS PRESLEY BIRTHPLACE AND MUSEUM
306 Elvis Presley Drive, 601/841-1245
The King of Rock and Roll was born in this two-room shotgun house in 1935. The tiny house, furnished as it would have been when Presley lived there, was repossessed when Elvis was only three. The family lived in several other houses in Tupelo before they moved to Memphis when Elvis was 13. Adjacent to the house is the Elvis Presley Memorial Chapel, built with fans' donations, and the Elvis Presley Museum: Times and Things Remembered. Extensive Elvis memorabilia, including rare photographs and articles of clothing, are displayed.
Details: *May–Sept Mon–Sat 9–5:30, Sun 1–5; Oct–Apr complex closes at 5. House $1, museum tour $4. (1 hour)*

★★★★ NATCHEZ TRACE PARKWAY VISITORS CENTER
Milepost 266, 601/680-4025 or 800/305-7417
The Natchez Trace is an 8,000-year-old Indian trail that was originally traced out by buffalo. The Indians used it to get from the area that became Natchez, Mississippi, to what became Nashville, Tennessee. It was trampled into an actual road by traders, trappers, and missionaries. Today's two-lane, 450-mile scenic highway closely follows the original path through national forest. The visitors center has an orientation program about the trace, exhibits, and a nature trail.
Details: *Daily 8–5. Free. (1 hour)*

★★★ **TUPELO BATTLEFIELD**
West Main Street, 601/680-4025 or 800/305-7417
In addition to the battle at Brice's Cross Roads, several other skir-
mishes and battles took place around Tupelo. A miscommunication
of orders cost the Confederates the battle here, but Union troops
withdrew because they were exhausted and poorly supplied. The
small Tupelo National Battlefield Park contains cannon, monuments,
and displays commemorating both armies.
Details: Daily sunrise–sunset. Free. ($^1/_2$ hour)

★★★ **TUPELO MUSEUM**
West Main Street at James L. Ballard Park, 601/841-6438
or 800/533-0611
Near the Tupelo Battlefield, the museum contains artifacts from the
battle and a diorama that depicts the events. Other exhibits relate
to Native Americans, life in early Tupelo, and the Space Age. Among
the exhibits are an old-time country store, a sorghum mill, and a turn-
of-the-century Western Union office. Also on the grounds are a train
depot and a caboose.
Details: Mon–Fri 8–4, weekends 1–5. $1, free children under 5.
(1 hour)

★★ **PRIVATE JOHN ALLEN NATIONAL FISH HATCHERY**
111 Elizabeth Street, 601/842-1341
Millions of fish are hatched here each year, and you can see them in
various stages of development. The 1903 manager's house and
Grandmother's Garden are included in the tour. The Tupelo Garden
Club maintains the house.
Details: Mon–Fri 7–3:30. Free. (1 hour)

SIGHTSEEING HIGHLIGHTS: OXFORD

★★★★ **CENTER FOR THE STUDY OF SOUTHERN CULTURE**
Barnard Observatory, University of Mississippi
601/232-5993, www.cssc.olemiss.edu
Located in the antebellum Barnard Observatory on the University of
Mississippi campus, the center is a research facility devoted to the
preservation of Southern music, folklore, art, and literature.
Details: Mon–Fri 8–5. Free. (1 hour)

★★★★ ROWAN OAK
Old Taylor Road, Oxford, 601/234-4651
www.ci.oxford.ms.us/
Built in 1844, the gracious southern house was the home of William
Faulkner, Oxford's most famous native son, for the last 30 years of
his life. He wrote most of his works at Rowan Oak, and an outline
for a novel is even scribbled on the study wall. Faulkner's typewriter
remains on his desk.

Details: Tue–Sat 10–noon and 2–4, Sun 2–4. Free. (1 hour)

★★★★ UNIVERSITY OF MISSISSIPPI
Oxford
The university, affectionately known as Ole Miss, was founded in
1848. When Union General Ulysses S. Grant and his troops captured
Oxford, they occupied the college buildings for a time and then
torched them when they left. A few, however, survived. In addition
to the Center for the Study of Southern Culture, the university has
several museums. The **University of Mississippi Blues Archive**
has an extensive collection of blues recordings and other memorabilia, including B. B. King's personal record collection. The archive is
for the serious blues enthusiast or researcher. It is not a museum with
displays.

*Details: Walking tours of campus daily except Sun. University of
Mississippi Blues Archive (Farley Hall, Room 340, 601/232-7753) weekdays 7:30 a.m.–9 p.m., Sat 10–5, Sun 1–9. Free. (1 hour)*

★★★ BARKSDALE-ISOM HOUSE
1003 Jefferson Avenue, Oxford, 601/236-5600
The white-columned mansion, built in 1838, is a classic example of
planter-style architecture. It was constructed of native timber using
Indian and slave labor. It is open for tours and also operates as a bed-
and-breakfast.

Details: Tours Tue at 1 or by appointment. Free. (1 hour)

FITNESS AND RECREATION

Natchez Trace Parkway provides excellent, although challenging, riding conditions for bicyclists. The majority of the two-lane road is well paved, the
speed limit is 50 miles per hour, and no commercial traffic is allowed. The road
is gently graded, well drained, and merges evenly onto the grassy shoulder.

At places along the trace, cyclists can ride portions of the original trail, although it is rough and ungraded. For information call 601/680-4025 or 800/305-7417, www.npf.gov/natr.

Several state and national parks provide a wide variety of outdoor activities. Tishomingo State Park (Milepost 304 off Natchez Trace Parkway, Tishomingo, 601/438-6914) offers float trips, a 13-mile nature trail system, swinging bridge, pool, playing fields, and an 18-hole disc golf course. Tombigbee State Park (MS 6, 601/842-7669) features swimming, fishing, three nature trails, a tennis court, an archery range, and disc golf. Trace State Park (MS 6, Belden, 601/489-2958) has fishing, boating, and hiking, as well as off-road vehicle trails. Wall Doxey State Park (MS 7 South, Holly Springs, 601/252-4231) offers a boat ramp, canoeing, tubing, swimming, and a nature trail. John W. Kyle State Park (State Park Road off MS 315 South, Sardis, 601/487-1345) features bicycle rentals, a pool, tennis courts, a boat ramp, fishing, a nature trail, and water sports. Puskus Lake in the Holly Springs National Forest (10 miles east of Oxford, 601/252-2633) offers boating and fishing.

If your interest is in spectator sports, the University of Mississippi Rebels play basketball at the C. M. "Tad" Smith Coliseum in Oxford, and the football team plays at Vaught-Hemingway Stadium. For ticket information, call 601/232-7522, www.olemisssports.com.

FOOD

For a romantic dinner, try the simple yet elegant **Downtown Grill** (1115 Jackson Avenue, Oxford, 601/234-2659). The cuisine is billed as regional American; the menu includes beef, fish, seafood, and homemade desserts. Reservations are accepted. Live jazz is performed. **Gloster 205 Restaurant** (205 North Gloster, 601/842-7205) is an elegant and romantic restaurant where many diners celebrate special occasions. Each of the separate dining rooms has a different atmosphere. There's the Garden Room, State Room, Wicker Room, Gaslight Room, Upstairs Room, and Library. In addition, the restaurant has a pleasant bar/lounge. Menu items are led by steak and prime rib, but also include seafood and pasta. Reservations are recommended. Not only is **Jefferson Place** (823 Jefferson, Oxford, 601/844-8696) housed in an exquisitely restored nineteenth-century home, but it is also reputed to be haunted by a Dr. Nash. However, he won't keep you from having a scare-free dinner. Although the restaurant is known for its steaks, the menu includes items for health-conscious diners as well. Entertainment includes blues, jazz, and rock.

OXFORD

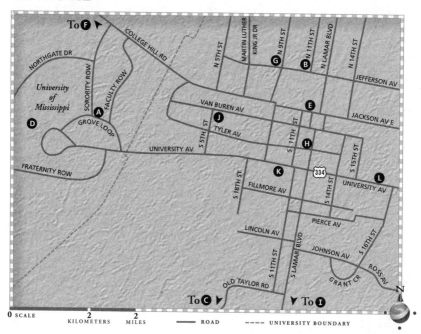

SIGHTS
Ⓐ Center for the Study of Southern Culture
Ⓑ Barksdale-Isom House
Ⓒ Rowan Oak
Ⓓ University of Mississippi

FOOD
Ⓔ Downtown Grill
Ⓕ El Charro
Ⓖ Jefferson Place
Ⓗ Smitty's

LODGING
Ⓑ Barksdale-Isom House
Ⓘ John W. Kyle State Park
Ⓙ Oliver Britt House
Ⓚ Puddin Place
Ⓛ Wall Doxey State Park

Note: Items with the same letter are located in the same area.

El Charro (1417 West Jackson Street, Oxford, 601/236-0058) is a fun Mexican restaurant known for its quesadillas, burritos, and other South-of-the-border specialties. The ambience is festive with ponchos and piñatas and other Mexican memorabilia. **Smitty's**, housed in a simple historic building just off the Oxford town square (208 South Lamar, Oxford, 601/234-

9111), is a particularly good bargain, as it has been for many years. William Faulkner used to frequent the place, and it's a local, family-oriented favorite for breakfast, lunch, and dinner. The menu is as modest as the decor. Specialties include catfish, homemade bread, and homemade desserts. Reservations are not accepted.

Vanelli's (1302 North Gloster Street, 601/844-4410) has been owned by the same Greek family for more than 20 years. The decor is eclectic and offbeat. The menu is more Italian than Greek and features pizzas and pastas. Reservations are not accepted.

Rossens, 124 West Main St., Tupelo, 662/840-1971, is located in the historic downtown district in a renovated building that looks and feels much like Bourbon Street in New Orleans. It's a favorite for Creole dishes, and guests frequently ask for take-home quantities of the crab–corn bisque. Crab cakes are also a great favorite. Evening selections are more classic, with beef, veal, lamb, and seafood entrees.

LODGING

Both Oxford and Tupelo have historic homes that operate as bed and breakfasts. In Oxford the **Barksdale-Isom House** (1003 Jefferson Avenue, 601/236-5600), which is open for public tours, was built in 1838. Among the five antique-furnished guest rooms, one features a fireplace and a Jacuzzi. Turndown service, wine in the evening, and a gourmet breakfast are offered. The **Oliver-Britt House** (512 Van Buren Avenue, Oxford, 601/234-8043), built in 1905, is a red-brick Greek Revival home with white columns. Guests during the week get breakfasts at Smitty's. On the weekend they partake of a full southern breakfast at the B&B. **Puddin Place** (1008 University Avenue, Oxford, 601/234-1250) is located in a charming Victorian cottage built in 1892. From there it's only a short walk to Ole Miss, Rowan Oak, and the town square. The **Mockingbird Inn** in Tupelo (305 North Gloster Street, 601/841-0286) is located in a large Prairie-style house. Each of the guest rooms is decorated to represent a different corner of the world.

At the other extreme, rustic accommodations are available in cabins at several state parks: **John W. Kyle State Park** (State Park Road off MS 315 South, Sardis, 601/487-1345), **Tishomingo State Park** (Milepost 304, Natchez Trace Parkway, Tishomingo, 601/438-6914), **Tombigbee State Park** (MS 6, Tupelo, 601/842-7669), **Trace State Park** (MS 6, Belden, 601/489-2958), and **Wall Doxey State Park** (MS 7 South, Holly Springs, 601/252-4231).

CAMPING

Several state and national parks near Tupelo offer camping. Puskus Lake in the Holly Springs National Forest (10 miles east of Oxford, 601/252-2633) allows primitive camping; John W. Kyle State Park (State Park Road off MS 315 South, Sardis, 601/487-1345) offers developed campsites, cabins, and group camp housing; Tishomingo State Park (Milepost 304, Natchez Trace Parkway, Tishomingo, 601/438-6914) has both developed and primitive campsites, as do Tombigbee State Park (MS 6, Tupelo, 601/842-7669), Trace State Park (MS 6 Belden, 601/489-2958), and Wall Doxey State Park (MS 7 South, Holly Springs, 601/252-4231).

NIGHTLIFE

Among nightspots in Oxford, Proud Larry's (211 South Lamar Boulevard, 601/236-0050) is popular with the college crowd. The establishment serves light dinners, pizza, and pasta and offers bands every night. Two restaurant/bars on the Oxford town square attract an older crowd. City Grocery (156 Courthouse Square, 601/232-8080) is known for its excellent chef and for live jazz and blues. The restaurant offers dining inside as well as outside on a balcony. The Downtown Grill (110 Courthouse Square, Oxford, 601/234-2659), which features an enclosed balcony overlooking the square, serves meals and offers a piano bar in the evening.

20
SELMA AND
TUSCALOOSA

Selma and Tuscaloosa, two cities often overlooked by travelers, have played important roles in the state's development. Both deserve a lingering visit. Hundreds of years before either of these cities existed, however, Native American Mound Builders lived south of present-day Tuscaloosa. Remnants of their civilization fascinate modern visitors.

Selma is a graceful city laid out in the early 1800s. The Battle of Selma was one of the last of the Civil War, so the city was spared from serious destruction. The first African Methodist Episcopal Church in Alabama was formed in Selma in 1867.

Events in Selma during the Civil Rights movement of the 1960s were among the most significant in the South. Today, Selma has several historic districts and enough attractions to keep you busy for days.

Established in 1816, Tuscaloosa, the second capital of Alabama, is home to the University of Alabama. Named for an Indian chief who opposed Spanish explorer Hernando deSoto, Tuscaloosa wasn't as fortunate as Selma during the Civil War. It suffered extensive destruction, but numerous historic structures survived, and the city preserves an Old South atmosphere.

Get a schedule of University of Alabama sporting events and try to avoid Tuscaloosa on game weekends—unless you're specifically going for a game. If you are, make reservations far in advance.

Both Selma and Tuscaloosa have spring pilgrimages to historic homes and

SELMA

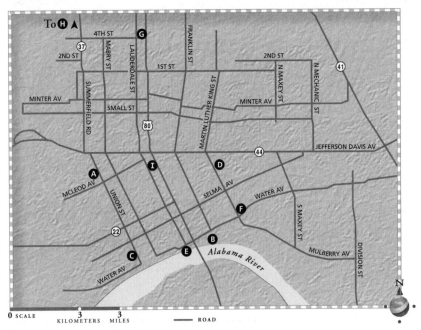

SIGHTS

- **A** Heritage Village/Old Town Historic District
- **B** Historic Water Street District
- **C** Joseph T. Smitherman Historic Building
- **D** Martin Luther King Jr. Street Historic District
- **E** National Voting Rights Museum
- **F** Old Depot Museum
- **A** Sturdivant Hall

FOOD

- **G** Faunsdale Bar and Grill
- **B** Major Grumbles
- **H** Tally Ho

LODGING

- **I** Grace Hall
- **B** St. James Hotel

Note: Items with the same letter are located in the same area.

gardens, and Selma's candlelight cemetery tours are very popular. Contact the convention and visitors bureau for more details.

A PERFECT DAY IN SELMA AND TUSCALOOSA

It would be a strenuous day to see the highlights of both Selma and Tuscaloosa, but it can be done. Do a driving rather than walking tour of the Martin Luther King Jr. Street Historic District in Selma, then drop in for a quick visit to both the Old Depot Museum and the National Voting Rights Museum. Spend some time touring the beautiful, antebellum Sturdivant Hall.

Have lunch at Major Grumbles overlooking the river and then drive to Tuscaloosa. The Old Tavern Museum and Capitol Park will give you a quick introduction to the city. Then tour the historic Gorgas House on the campus of the University of Alabama. Afterward, eat a relaxing dinner at the Cypress Inn on the shores of the Black Warrior River.

SIGHTSEEING HIGHLIGHT: SELMA

★★★★ MARTIN LUTHER KING JR. STREET HISTORIC DISTRICT

During the turbulent Civil Rights movement of the 1960s, several important events occurred in Selma. Two abortive attempts—one violent and one nonviolent—to march to Montgomery were made before a successful march was completed. A historic district along a street renamed for Dr. King includes several sights relating to the protests. Get a brochure for the walking tour from the Selma–Dallas County Chamber of Commerce (513 Lauderdale Street, 334/875-7241 or 800/45-SELMA). In addition, 20 historical markers with powerful photographs and commentary line the street. One important sight is the **Brown Chapel A.M.E. Church** (410 Martin Luther King Jr. Street, 334/874-7897), where rallies were held and marches began. A room there is dedicated to Dr. King, and a bust of the Civil Rights leader stands out front. Another rally site was the **First Baptist Church** (Martin Luther King Jr. Street and Jeff Davis Avenue, 334/874-7331), built in 1894. Designed by a black architect, it is one of the finest nineteenth-century black churches in the state. The most significant sight is the **Edmund Pettus Bridge** (off Water Street), where marchers

OLD DEPOT MUSEUM

© Carol Thalimer

were attacked by state troopers and dogs on Bloody Sunday, March 7, 1965.

Details: (1 hour)

★★★★ NATIONAL VOTING RIGHTS MUSEUM
1012 Water Avenue, Selma, 334/418-0800

Located in an old commercial building overlooking the Edmund Pettus Bridge, the museum is a touching tribute to those who gave their efforts and sometimes their lives during the Civil Rights struggle. Primarily run on a shoestring by volunteers, this museum is not glitzy but rather an expression of the heart. Among the outstanding exhibits is *Footprints to Freedom*—the footprints of marchers memorialized in plaster of Paris. Poignant, handwritten notes pinned to a wall describe their experiences. Names of the marchers are printed on the window so that you see them silhouetted against the Edmund Pettus Bridge in the background.

Details: *Mon–Fri 8:30–5, Sat and Sun by appointment. $4 adults, $2 students. (1 hour)*

★★★★ OLD DEPOT MUSEUM
4 Martin Luther King Jr. Street, Selma, 334/874-2197

Housed in the ornate, multistory, turn-of-the-century railroad depot are exhibits relating to more than 200 years of life in Selma and Dallas County. Of particular interest are displays relating to black history, the Civil War, medical and dental practices, and farm life.

Details: *Mon–Sat 10–4, Sun by appointment. $4 adults, $3 seniors, $2 students. (1–2 hours)*

★★★★ STURDIVANT HALL
713 Mabry Street, Selma, 334/872-5626

The crown jewel among Selma's many magnificent antebellum homes, Sturdivant Hall, built in 1853, is an outstanding example of neoclassical design. Its soaring white pillars enhance the lovely formal garden surrounding the mansion. Painstakingly restored, the mansion showcases fine examples of early craftsmanship: plaster moldings and medallions, elaborately carved woodwork, graceful mantelpieces, and cabinets. Ten high-ceilinged rooms are filled with appropriate antiques. A separate, two-story kitchen building houses an exceptional gift shop.

Details: *Tue–Sat 9–4, Sun 2–4. Admission is charged. (1 hour)*

★★★ HISTORIC WATER STREET DISTRICT
Selma

Running along the Alabama River in Selma, Water Street is a restored, nineteenth-century commercial district. The rejuvenated offices and warehouses house antiques stores, shops, and restaurants. Brick paving, three pocket parks, and a restored bridge tender's house enhance the district. The National Voting Rights Museum is at one end, the Old Depot Museum is at the other, and the Edmund Pettus Bridge crosses the river from there.

Details: *(1–2 hours)*

★★ HERITAGE VILLAGE/OLD TOWN HISTORIC DISTRICT
713 Mabry Street, Selma, 334/875-7241

Five historic structures from the mid-1800s have been relocated to property adjacent to Sturdivant Hall. Among the buildings are small offices, a cottage, servants' quarters, and a pigeon cote.

Details: *Tue–Sat 9–4, Sun 2–4. Free. (1/2–1 hour)*

★★ JOSEPH T. SMITHERMAN HISTORIC BUILDING
109 Union Street, Selma, 334/874-2174

TUSCALOOSA

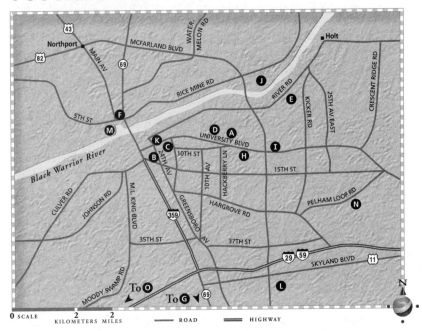

SIGHTS

- **A** Alabama Museum of Natural History
- **B** Battle-Friedman House
- **C** Children's Hands-On Museum of Tuscaloosa
- **D** Gorgas House
- **E** Gulf States Paper Corporation Art Collection
- **F** Kentuck Art Center and Museum
- **G** Moundville Archaeological Park
- **H** Paul "Bear" Bryant Museum

FOOD

- **I** Bob Baumhower's "Wings" Sports Grill
- **J** Cypress Inn
- **K** DePalma's
- **L** Dreamland Barbecue
- **M** The Globe
- **N** Kozy's Fine Dining

LODGING

- **H** Four Points Hotel by Sheraton
- **O** Myrtlewood
- **O** Willowbrook

Note: Items with the same letter are located in the same area.

Period furniture and historic relics from the mid-1800s, combined with loving attention, have helped restore this unique public building. It is still used for public functions and houses a small museum containing artifacts from the collection of Art Lewis, a Civil War expert. Indian artifacts, coins, stamps, and glass are also frequently exhibited.
Details: Tue–Fri 9–4, Sat 8–4. Free. ($^{1}/_{2}$ hour)

SIGHTSEEING HIGHLIGHTS: TUSCALOOSA

★★★ CHILDREN'S HANDS-ON MUSEUM OF TUSCALOOSA
2213 University Boulevard, Tuscaloosa, 205/349-4235
www.chom.org
Visitors enter the museum through the Cave of Subtracting Years and find themselves in a Choctaw Indian village. There, children can make shell jewelry and pottery, learn Choctaw games, and sit in an authentic dugout canoe. Then youngsters advance to nineteenth-century Tuscaloosa, where they can cash a check at the bank, shop in the general store, or print something at the print shop. An ample supply of vintage clothing in Grandmother's Attic allows children to dress themselves appropriately for the turn of the century. Modern Tuscaloosa features a miniature TV studio, hospital, tugboat, and city park. In addition, the museum features a planetarium and science department.
Details: Tue–Fri 9–5, Sat 1–5. $5, free children under 3. (1 hour)

★★★ GORGAS HOUSE
Capstone Drive, Tuscaloosa, 205/348-5906
The oldest structure on the University of Alabama campus, the building first served as a dormitory and dining hall. General Josiah Gorgas was the seventh president of the university, and he used the structure, which was recently updated, as a residence. The family treasures displayed include furniture and silver flatware and hollowware.
Details: Tue–Sat 10–4, closed Sun, Mon, and University of Alabama holidays. Donations suggested. (1 hour)

★★★ GULF STATES PAPER CORPORATION ART COLLECTION
Company headquarters: 1400 River Road, N.E., Tuscaloosa
205/562-5222
Industrialist Jack Warner, CEO of the company, has a passion for art.

SIDE TRIP: CAHAWBA

A short drive from Selma, Cahawba, Alabama's capital from 1820 to 1826 and a seat of black political power during Reconstruction, is little more than a ghost town today. A welcome center displays artifacts and photographs, and you can stroll around the town to see moss-covered ruins. Archaeologists are often at work.

Unlike some collectors who hoard their treasures, Warner shares his with his employees and the public. Reputed to be the largest private collection of American art, Warner's includes paintings, primitive artifacts, porcelains, and sculpture. A third of the works is in the North River Yacht Club and is not accessible to the public. Another third is on display at company headquarters. Another third is exhibited at the Mildred Warner House.

Details: *Mon–Fri for tours 5:30–6:30 p.m., Sat 10-5, Sun 1-5. Mildred Warner House: 1925 Eighth Street, 205/562-5222. Weekends 1–5. Free. (1 hour per exhibit)*

★★★ **MOUNDVILLE ARCHAEOLOGICAL PARK**
AL 69, Moundville, 205/371-2572
This 317-acre site was probably the largest community of Native Americans of the Mississippian culture, which lasted from a.d. 1000 to 1500. They were noted for their ceremonial temple and funeral mounds, and two dozen mounds have survived at this site. A museum interprets artifacts excavated from the various mounds. Several movies about the Mississippian culture can be viewed. A temple has been re-created atop a mound, as has a village near the Black Warrior River. Recreational facilities include a campground, gift shop, nature trail, and picnicking areas. The mounds make a dramatic backdrop for an annual Easter sunrise service.

Details: *Park daily 8–8, museum daily 9–5. Admission is charged. (1–2 hours)*

★★★ **PAUL W. "BEAR" BRYANT MUSEUM**
300 Paul W. Bryant Drive, Tuscaloosa, 205/348-4668

Located in a modern building on the university campus, the museum uses 100 years of memorabilia to honor the most-winning coach in Crimson Tide football history, as well as the entire football program.
Details: Daily 9–4. $2 adults, $1 seniors and children. (1 hour)

★★ **ALABAMA MUSEUM OF NATURAL HISTORY**
Smith Hall, University of Alabama, Tuscaloosa
205/348-2040
Among the exhibits in the stately neoclassical building constructed in 1909 are displays about natural history, geology, and mineralogy. Coal Age and Ice Age fossils are of particular interest.
Details: Mon–Fri 8–4:30, Sat 1–4. Free. (1 hour)

★★ **BATTLE-FRIEDMAN HOUSE**
1010 Greensboro Avenue, Tuscaloosa, 205/758-6138
Built in 1835 by a wealthy planter, the Greek Revival house has been restored, filled with antiques, and opened as a house museum and cultural center.
Details: Tue–Sat 10–noon and 1–4. $3 adults, $2.50 seniors, $2 students. (1/2–1 hour)

★★ **KENTUCK ART CENTER AND MUSEUM**
501 Main Street, Northport, 205/758-1257
Tuscaloosa bleeds across the Black Warrior River into a separate community called Northport, which has become a hub for artisans and a center for antique shops. At the art center you can watch potters, photographers, woodworkers, jewelry designers, glassblowers, a metalsmith, and even a harpsichord maker at work. The museum features the works of these artisans and others from around Alabama. The annual October Kentuck Arts Festival is one of the South's foremost arts fairs.
Details: Mon–Fri 9–5, Sat 10–4:30. Free. (1 hour)

FITNESS AND RECREATION
Touring the Martin Luther King Jr. Street Historic District, Old Town Historic District, and Water Street Historic District in Selma on foot offers plenty of exercise, as does touring the University of Alabama campus in Tuscaloosa and the Moundville Archaeological Park.

Lake Lurleen State Park (13226 Lake Lurleen Road, Coker, 205/339-1558), north of Tuscaloosa, offers more than 1,600 acres to explore, as well as fishing, swimming, boating, and hiking. Paul M. Grist State Park (1546 Grist Road, Selma, 334/872-5846) features more than 1,000 acres. North of Selma the Talladega National Forest provides endless hiking opportunities. The Dallas County Public Lake south of Selma is another good spot for fishing and other water sports.

In Tuscaloosa challenging golf can be played at the 18-hole Harry Pritchett Golf Course (University of Alabama, 205/348-7041) and the 18-hole Mimosa Golf and Country Club (5700 Eighteenth Avenue, 205/752-8112). In Selma nine holes are available at the Craig Golf Course (Craig Air Force Base, 334/872-4451).

FOOD

The wings at **Bob Baumhower's "Wings" Sports Grill** (500 Harper Lee Drive, Tuscaloosa, 205/556-5658) are Buffalo wings, and their degree of spiciness ranges from mild to "911." This casual eatery, owned by former pro football player Bob Baumhower, is popular with the college crowd and features Crimson Tide memorabilia. Reservations are not accepted. **Dreamland Barbecue** (5535 15th Avenue East, Tuscaloosa, 205/758-8135) is the place to go for ribs. Extremely casual, the restaurant serves only ribs, beer, and soft drinks. The decor is old license plates and autographed photos. Reservations are not accepted.

When you want to splurge for a romantic special occasion, **Kozy's Fine Dining** (3510 Pelham Loop Road, Tuscaloosa, 205/556-0665) is the place to go. The ambience is pure 1940s, with a jukebox playing oldies and photos of old actors and musicians decorating the walls. The menu ranges from pasta to duck. Reservations are recommended. The **Cypress Inn** (501 Rice Mine Road, Tuscaloosa, 205/345-6963), perched on a steep hillside overlooking the Black Warrior River, is a romantic, although rustic, restaurant. The menu, billed as Southern, is led by fish entrees, but steak and chicken are served as well. In good weather, it's pleasant to have a drink out on the patio. Reservations are accepted during the week.

If you're ready for great pasta then try **DePalma's**, 2300 University Boulevard, Tuscaloosa, 205/759-1879. The traditional Italian American dishes are all cooked to order, extremely fresh, and complemented by wine from an extensive list. All doughs for the pasta, pizza, and calzones are made from scratch daily, as are the sauces.

Located in a historic general store in Northport, **The Globe** (430 Main Avenue, 205/391-0949) strives to re-create the Globe Theater in England. A publike bar pours hearty ales, and scenes from Shakespeare's plays adorn the walls. The restaurant offers an extremely varied menu, influenced by the cuisine of several countries.

In Selma, **Major Grumbles** (1 Grumbles Alley, 334/872-2006) is located in an historic building on Water Street overlooking the river. Brick walls and exposed ceilings create a cozy atmosphere. The menu runs to items such as burgers and salads. You won't be hungry when you leave, despite the skeleton on the wall. Ask how the restaurant got its name. The story is amusing, but too long to relate here. The nucleus of **Tally Ho** restaurant (334 Magnum Avenue at Summerfield Road, Selma, 334/872-1390) is an authentic log cabin that has been built onto several times. Fish and steak entrees lead the menu. Reservations are recommended.

Located in the tiny, almost ghost town–like hamlet of Faunsdale near Selma, the **Faunsdale Bar and Grill** (U.S. 80, 334/628-3240) occupies an historic commercial building with exposed brick walls and ceilings. The dining style is casual, the food is especially good, and the portions are large. Steaks and seafood are the specialties. Live entertainment is offered on the weekends.

LODGING

Grace Hall (506 Lauderdale Street, Selma, 334/875-5744), a bed-and-breakfast, was built in 1857 and is furnished with exquisite antiques. Connected to the main house by a covered walkway is a two-story servants' quarters with full-length verandas on both floors. Lovely antique-filled guest rooms in the main house and servants' quarters provide amenities such as cable TV and air conditioning. Some rooms have fireplaces. A stay at Grace Hall includes a full Southern breakfast and afternoon wine. A formal Williamsburg garden enhances the front of the house, and a New Orleans–style courtyard provides a hidden oasis in the rear. The house is said to have a ghost, but that doesn't stop guests from flocking there. Also in Selma, the **St. James Hotel** (1200 Water Street, 334/872-3234), located in a restored historic riverfront property, is Selma's only full-service hotel.

In Tuscaloosa, the **Four Points Hotel by Sheraton** (320 Paul Bryant Drive, 205/752-3200), located on the university campus across from the Bear Bryant Museum, is a modern hotel with a restaurant, bar with live entertainment, and swimming pool. Guest rooms have coffee makers, dataports, and pay-per-view movies and Nintendo games. Nearby Aliceville boasts two bed-and-breakfasts. **Myrtlewood** (602 Broad Street, Aliceville, 205/373-8153 or 205/373-2916) offers four rooms with private baths in a 1909 Victorian with two wraparound porches. **Willowbrook** (501 Broad

Street, Aliceville, 205/373-6133) features three rooms with two baths in a 1911 Edwardian house.

CAMPING

Moundville Archaeological Park (AL 69S, Moundville, 205/371-2234) has several modern campgrounds, some administered by the U.S. Army Corps of Engineers. The main park location has 31 sites, Prairie Creek Access Area has 67, Six Mile Creek Park has 31, and Deerlick Creek Park has 46. Lake Lurleen State Park (13226 Lake Lurleen Road, Coker, 205/339-1558) offers 91 modern campsites as well as a camp store and comfort stations. Paul M. Grist State Park (1546 Grist Road, Selma, 334/872-5846) has six improved campsites as well as primitive campsites and comfort stations. The Lake Lanier Travel Park west of Selma (U.S. 80, 205/874-8638) offers a shaded setting, full hookups, laundry facilities, a bathhouse, and a six-acre lake.

NIGHTLIFE

In Tuscaloosa, Bob Baumhower's "Wings" Sports Grill (500 Harper Lee Drive, 205/556-5658) is the place to go to watch sports on big-screen TV. Barrett's Brewpub and Eatery (2325 University Boulevard, 205/366-0380) often has entertainment. The Globe restaurant (430 Main Avenue, Tuscaloosa, 205/391-0949) in Northport has a guitarist.

Scenic Route: Pickensville to Marion

West-central Alabama is often overlooked by tourists, much to their loss. This region, known as the Black Belt because the prairie is underlain with rich black soil, began to prosper from the growth of cotton in the early 1800s. Tuscaloosa and Selma were the last cities burned in Alabama as the Civil War came to an end, and the towns to the west were saved.

AL 14 runs through several of these historic towns. Begin in **Pickensville**, where the Tom Bevill Visitor Center (Government Access Road, 205/373-8705), recreates the 1830–1860 era with appropriate furnishings. Displays, exhibits, and audiovisual programs describe the Tombigbee River Valley from prehistory through the twentieth century. Climb up to the belvedere for a magnificent view of the river. Moored beside the center and open for tours is the U.S. Snagboat Montgomery, a steam-powered stern-wheeler that removed stumps and fallen trees from seven rivers between 1927 and 1982. Adjacent to the site is the Tom Bevill Lock and Dam.

From Pickensville, take AL 14 southeast to **Aliceville**. The Aliceville Museum and Cultural Arts Center (104 Broad Street Plaza, 205/373-2363) is devoted to a prisoner-of-war camp that operated in Aliceville during World War II. The more than 6,000 German prisoners spent their time printing books and making artwork.

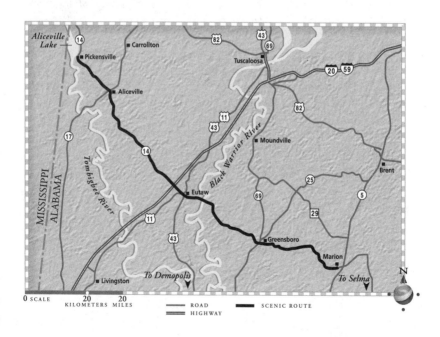

Although the camp is gone, memorabilia including books and artwork are displayed. Interestingly, former prisoners have held several reunions.

Continue southeast on AL 14 to **Eutaw**, a charming town with a large district of significant antebellum homes. Among these, Kirkwood (111 Kirkwood Drive, 205/372-9009) is a standout. Under new management, it now has private baths and central heat and air. Restored to its original grandeur, the house is open for tours and operates as a bed-and-breakfast. At the Greene County Visitor Center in the historic Vaughn-Morrow House (310 Main Street), you can pick up a brochure describing other antebellum and Victorian structures in and around town. Contact Eutaw City at 205/372-4212.

Staying on AL 14, continue southeast to **Greensboro**, where more than 150 antebellum structures survive. Recently restored, Magnolia Grove (1002 Hobson Street, 205/624-8618)—an 1840 Greek Revival home indeed surrounded by venerable magnolia trees—is open for tours.

Continue southeast on AL 14 to **Marion**. Of the five colleges that existed there before the Civil War, two remain active: Judson College, a women's college, and the Marion Military Institute (MMI), a coed preparatory school and junior college. Among the lovely buildings on the Judson campus is A. Howard Bean Hall, the repository of the Alabama Women's Hall of Fame (334/683-5242), which honors Helen Keller, Lurleen Wallace, Julia Strudwick Tutwiler, and others. The chapel on the campus of MMI (1101 South Washington Street, 334/683-2343) was used as a hospital during the Civil War, and can be seen by appointment. Also on the campus is the Alabama Military Hall of Fame. Luxurious accommodations can be found in Myrtle Hill (303 West Lafayette Street, Marion, 334/683-9095), an imposing Greek Revival–style home furnished with exquisite antiques and artwork.

21
BIRMINGHAM

Birmingham, the largest city in Alabama with 1 million residents, is big enough to have cosmopolitan panache but small enough to be user-friendly. Once the leading iron and steel center of the South, Birmingham was named for Birmingham, England—an Old World steel center.

Tumultuous Civil Rights battles took place here in the 1960s. Afterward, the people of Birmingham quietly went about the business of living together. The city is now the home of a Civil Rights District and an impressive Civil Rights Institute.

Modern Birmingham is also an important medical, educational, and technological center. The only remnants of the steel industry are a statue of Vulcan, god of the forge, and the Sloss Furnaces, which have been transformed into an activity center.

Located in the foothills of the mountains, Birmingham's natural beauty is further enhanced by antebellum, Victorian, and art deco structures, in addition to gleaming new skyscrapers. Sports and cultural activities share the entertainment spotlight.

A PERFECT DAY IN BIRMINGHAM

Begin downtown at Kelly Ingram Park, the nucleus of the Civil Rights District. From the park, stroll across the street to the Civil Rights Institute to learn

BIRMINGHAM

N

143

HOLLOW RD

78

20

159

OLD LEEDS RD

RUFFNER RD
L

MADRID AV

59

GEORGIA RD

BRIARCLIFF RD

To H W
W

77TH AV

N
MONTEVALLO RD

MOUNTAIN BROOK PKWY

E LAKE BLVD

CRESTWOOD BLVD

AIRPORT HWY

5TH AV S

79

PINSON VALLEY PKWY

59
20

M
3RD AV S

6TH AV S

D
F

CAHARA RD

ELTON B STEVENS EXPWY

FRED L SHUTTLESWORTH RD

1ST AV N

5TH AV N

P
20TH ST S

31

N 26TH ST

B
R
Q E

U
J
G T
S

Y
I

65

19TH ST

6TH AV N

65

GREEN SPRINGS HWY

N AV N

32ND AV N

COTTON AV

A

K
X
V

To

DANIEL PAYNE DR

77

G

MARTIN LUTHER KING JR DR

FORESTDALE BLVD

PEARSON AV

105

78

59
20

O

0 SCALE   2   KILOMETERS   MILES   2

ROAD   ———   HIGHWAY

more about that period of history. You can visit the Sixteenth Street Baptist Church, still an active congregation, where four little girls were killed in a bombing that galvanized the protesters.

Then browse through the Alabama Jazz Hall of Fame in the restored, art deco–style Carver Theater. Have a lunch of soul food at Hosie Barbecue and Fish. If Hosie himself is there, talk to him about his city and how he started his small business. After lunch spend some time at the Birmingham Museum of Art and take a stroll through its outdoor sculpture garden. Marvel at the heroic exploits of early aviators at the Southern Museum of Flight.

Have an elegant dinner at the Grill in the Tutwiler Hotel. Take in a play at the opulent Alabama Theater or a performance or sports event at the Birmingham-Jefferson Civic Center, or ride the glass elevator to the top of the Vulcan statue for a spectacular view of the lighted downtown skyline.

SIGHTSEEING HIGHLIGHTS

★★★★ **BIRMINGHAM MUSEUM OF ART**
2000 Eighth Avenue North, 205/254-2565
www.artsbma.org
The largest municipal art museum in the South, this outstanding

SIGHTS

- **A** Alabama Jazz Hall of Fame
- **B** Alabama Sports Hall of Fame
- **C** Arlington Antebellum Home and Gardens
- **D** Birmingham Botanical Gardens
- **E** Birmingham Museum of Art
- **F** Birmingham Zoo
- **G** Civil Rights District
- **H** Desoto Caverns
- **I** Five Points South
- **J** McWane Center
- **K** Oak Mountain State Park
- **L** Ruffner Mountain Nature Center
- **M** Sloss Furnaces
- **N** Southern Museum of Flight
- **O** Tannehill Historical State Park

FOOD

- **P** Bottega/Café Bottega
- **Q** Courthouse Cafeteria
- **R** The Grill
- **S** Hosie's
- **T** Julian's
- **U** La Paree
- **V** Meadowlark Restaurant
- **W** Ralph and Kacoo's

LODGING

- **X** Jemison Inn Bed and Breakfast
- **Y** Pickwick
- **T** The Redmont
- **Q** Tutwiler/Wyndham Hotel

Note: Items with the same letter are located in the same area.

© Carol Thalimer

facility houses a permanent collection of more than 17,000 works. Among the premier collections are European and American masters, art of the American West, and the largest collection of Wedgwood outside England. In addition, the museum often sponsors renowned traveling exhibitions. The multilevel sculpture garden is impressive as well.

Details: *Tue–Sat 10–5, Sun noon–5. Free except for some traveling exhibitions. (1–4 hours)*

★★★★ CIVIL RIGHTS DISTRICT
520 Sixteenth Street North, 205/328-9696
www.bham.net\bcri
Kelly Ingram Park sets the scene for the story of the Civil Rights struggle in Birmingham. Readers old enough to remember the frightening scenes on TV will see some of them re-created here. Paths lead toward the center of the park, where a statue of Martin Luther King Jr. stands in quiet contemplation. However, to reach this oasis, you must pass statues that re-create the horrors that were suffered by the protestors: the knife-sharp teeth of lunging, snarling dogs; fire hoses that plaster children against walls. This display is powerful and disturbing. If you have small children with you,

they may be upset by the sculptures. The **Birmingham Civil Rights Institute** (520 16th Street, 205/328-9696) isn't simply a museum. It is also an active organization working toward racial equality. Exhibits and audiovisual presentations tell the story of the Civil Rights struggle in Birmingham and throughout the world. The congregation of the **Sixteenth Street Baptist Church** (1530 Sixth Avenue North, 205/251-9402), site of the infamous Sunday School bombing, welcomes visitors to admire its sanctuary and beautiful stained-glass window, a gift of the people of Wales.
Details: (1–3 hours)

★★★ ALABAMA JAZZ HALL OF FAME
1631 Fourth Avenue North, 205/254-2731
www.jazzhall.com\jazz\jazz
Located in Birmingham's art deco–style Carver Theater, the museum displays Jazz Age memorabilia and commemorates the contributions of state and local jazz musicians.
Details: Tue–Sat 10–5, Sun 1–5. Free, but donations are appreciated. (1 hour)

★★★ ARLINGTON ANTEBELLUM HOME AND GARDENS
331 Cotton Avenue, S.W., 205/780-5656
This graceful Greek Revival home was built around 1850, and Union troops occupied it during the Civil War. Today it operates as a house museum and is filled with nineteenth-century furniture, textiles, silver, and works of art, as well as Civil War memorabilia.
Details: Tue–Sat 10–4, Sun 1–4. $3 adults, $2 children, discounts for AAA and AARP members. (1 hour)

★★★ BIRMINGHAM BOTANICAL GARDENS
2612 Lane Park Road, 205/879-1227, www.bbgardens.org
Rhododendrons, camellias, wildflowers, ferns, bonsai plants, roses, and desert flowers are among the many displays you'll see at the gardens. Escape modern life in the Japanese Garden with its lovely tea house. See the largest clear-span greenhouse in the Southeast. A bird sanctuary is home to more than 200 species of birds.
Details: Daily sunrise–sunset. Free. (1 hour)

★★★ McWANE CENTER
200 19th Street North, 205/714-8300, www.mcwane.org

Discovery 2000 and Red Mountain Museum have merged to form a unique state-of-the-art science center. An Adventure Hall for children features hands-on activities that examine the world around us, including health, science, communications, and energy. The museum has the only solar telescope in the country open to the public. Sports and other rotating exhibits plus an IMAX theater are offered.

Details: Mon–Fri 9–5, Sat 9–6, Sun noon–5. Call for IMAX show times. $7.50 adults, $6.50 children 6–12, $5.50 3–5, free 2 and under. Combo tickets also available. (1–2 hours)

★★★ OAK MOUNTAIN STATE PARK
AL 119 off I-65, 205/620-2524 or 620-2520
With almost 10,000 acres, this state park is the largest in the Alabama system. In addition to hiking and fishing, Oak Mountain offers golf, horseback riding, a petting zoo, and a BMX racetrack. Its most unusual feature is the Treetop Nature Trail, an elevated boardwalk that puts visitors up close and personal with hawks, owls, and vultures in their natural setting. From May through October, musicians perform at nearby Oak Mountain Amphitheater.

Details: Daily 7 a.m.–1 hour before sunset. $2 adults and children 12 and up, $1 6–11, free under 5; admissions to performances vary. (half–full day)

★★★ RUFFNER MOUNTAIN NATURE CENTER
1214 81st Street South, 205/833-8112
An urban wilderness of more than 500 acres, the center offers unusual geologic formations, free-flowing springs, conservation programs, 10 miles of hiking trails, and a fabulous view of the downtown skyline.

Details: Tue–Sat 9–5, Sun 1–5. Free, but donations are accepted. (1–2 hours)

★★★ SLOSS FURNACES
20 32nd Street North, 205/324-1911
The furnaces, a reminder of Birmingham's steel industry, have been designated as a National Historic Landmark. They now operate as an industrial museum and a gathering place for musical performances and festivals. A ghost also reputedly resides there.

Details: Tue–Sat 10–4, Sun noon–4. Free. (1 hour)

★★★ SOUTHERN MUSEUM OF FLIGHT
4343 73rd Street North, 205/833-8226
www.bham.net\flight\museum
At this museum, you can see everything from the lightbulb that lit the Wright Brothers' first night flights to an F-4 Phantom jet.

Details: Tue–Sat 9:30–4:30, Sun 1–4:30. $3 adults, $2 seniors and children, free 4 and under. (1–2 hours)

★★ ALABAMA SPORTS HALL OF FAME
22nd Street North at Civic Center Boulevard
205/323-6665
This high-tech facility inside the Birmingham-Jefferson Convention Complex honors Alabama's sports greats such as Bear Bryant, Jesse Owens, and Bart Starr. Several Heisman, World Series, and Super Bowl trophies are displayed.

Details: Mon–Sat 9–5, Sun 1–5. $5 adults, $4 seniors, $3 students, free 6 and under. (1 hour)

★★ BIRMINGHAM ZOO
2630 Cahaba Road, 205/879-0408,
www.birminghamzoo.com
With nearly 1,000 animals in residence, the zoo is a favorite with families. In fact, it is one of the most visited attractions in Alabama. Among the stars of the zoo are rare Siberian tigers and the world's only self-sustaining colony of golden spider monkeys in captivity. A miniature train circles the wooded, parklike setting.

Details: Daily 9–5. $5 adults, $2 seniors and children. (1–4 hours)

★★ DESOTO CAVERNS
5181 DeSoto Caverns Parkway, Childersburg
256/378-7252
These magnificent underground rock formations and caverns are just a short drive from Birmingham. After your tour of the caverns, the kids will have fun at 10 outdoor activities, such as panning for gems or playing wacky water golf.

Details: Mon–Sat 9–5:30, Sun 1–5:30. $10 adults, $7 children 4–11 for caverns only. $16–$19 for Mega-fun package that includes all attractions. (1 hour minimum)

★★ FIVE POINTS SOUTH
20th Street South at 11th Avenue South

Anchored by Frank Fleming's fountain sculpture, *The Storyteller,* this neighborhood is always hopping with live music and is noted for its fine dining and shopping. It features a rich collection of architectural styles—everything from Spanish Baroque to art deco.
Details: *(1–3 hours)*

★★ **TANNEHILL HISTORICAL STATE PARK**
12632 Confederate Parkway, McCalla, 205/477-5711
Self-guided tours of the restored ironworks blast furnace and a large collection of nineteenth-century cabins give visitors a view of the life lived by Alabamians during the 1800s. A train ride is fun for the kids, and a restaurant is on site.
Details: *Daily 7 a.m.–sunset. $2 adults, $1 children 6–11. (1–2 hours)*

FITNESS AND RECREATION

Birmingham offers a wide variety of participatory and spectator sports. The city's hilly terrain makes for challenging mountain biking and hiking. Canoeing, fishing, swimming, water-skiing, and boating are popular on area rivers and lakes. Oak Mountain State Park and the Ruffner Mountain Nature Center (see Sightseeing Highlights) provide golf, hiking, tennis, cycling, and water sports. Alabama Small Boats (Shelby County 52, 205/424-3634), offers five-hour canoe trips on the Cahaba River.

The Birmingham Park and Recreation Board (205/254-2391) and the Highland Park Racquet Club (205/251-1965) can tell you about tennis courts. The Birmingham area has 16 public golf courses, including a Robert Trent Jones Golf Trail course, Oxmoor Valley (167 Sunbelt Parkway, 205/942-1177).

Spectators can enjoy greyhound racing at the Birmingham Race Course (1000 John Rogers Drive, 800/998-UBET). The Birmingham Barons minor-league baseball team plays at Hoover Metropolitan Stadium. Call 205/988-3200 for a schedule and ticket prices. The Birmingham Bulls ice hockey team plays at the Birmingham-Jefferson Civic Center Coliseum. Call 205/458-8833 for schedule and ticket information.

FOOD

At the upper end of the dining scale, **The Grill**, in the historic Tutwiler/Wyndham Hotel (Park Place at 21st Street North, 205/439-9116), specializes in steaks and has an extensive wine list. Reservations are recommended for dinner. One of the most popular restaurants in the Birmingham area, **Meadowlark Restaurant** (534 Industrial Road, Alabaster, 205/663-3141) offers elegant European dining in a farm setting. **La Paree** (2013 Fifth Avenue North, 205/251-5936), the oldest restaurant downtown, has been serving Greek cuisine (surprise) for nearly 50 years.

Bottega (2240 Highland Avenue, 205/939-1000) is an upscale restaurant with cuisine built around pastas, scaloppinis, and other Italian dishes. **Café Bottega** next door is a more casual trattoria that serves gourmet pizza prepared in a wood-burning oven. Reservations are recommended. **Julian's** at the Redmont (2101 Fifth Avenue North, 205/324-2101) is an American bistro. **Ralph and Kacoo's** (3500 Grandview Parkway, 205/967-4087) is a popular southern chain that features Cajun seafood, pasta, and beef dishes. Its bar and appetizers are popular with the after-work crew, and Sunday brunch is crowded. Reservations are not accepted.

For economic, home-style cooking every day, try the **Courthouse Cafeteria** (716 21st Street North, 205/325-5752). Some of the best soul food, fish, and barbecue around can be found at **Hosie's** (321 17th Street North, 205/326-3495), a casual eatery in the Civil Rights District. Pigs' ears and croaker (a fish) are specialties. Hosie himself might share his upbeat philosophy with you.

LODGING

Birmingham is extremely fortunate to have preserved three historic hotels downtown. The **Redmont** (2101 Fifth Avenue North, 205/324-2101) was built in the 1920s and has been painstakingly restored to its original grandeur. More than 100 rooms and suites are offered, as well as an executive level, restaurant, and bar. The **Pickwick** (1023 20th Street South, 205/933-9555) is an art deco–style property in the popular Five Points South neighborhood, close to many restaurants, nightspots, theaters, and activities. More than 60 rooms and suites are offered. The **Tutwiler/Wyndham Hotel** (Park Place at 21st Street North, 205/322-2100 or 800/845-1787, www.wyndham.com) was built as a luxury apartment building in 1913. The hotel, listed in the National Trust for Historic Preservation's *Historic Hotels of America*, offers European elegance and Old World charm. The hotel has 147 rooms and suites and an executive level, all furnished with antiques and reproductions. Some rooms feature fireplaces. Amenities include fresh flowers, turndown service with chocolates, a restaurant, and a bar. Art on loan from the Birmingham Museum of Art is displayed in public spaces.

Stroll through the formal gardens, swim in the pool, and enjoy the antique-filled house at the **Jemison Inn Bed and Breakfast** in Jemison, 212 Hwy. 191, 205/688-2055. The inn is a 35-minute drive south of Birmingham, and you'll feel "40 miles and 100 years away from the big city." One of the three rooms, all with private baths, will be a haven, with turndown service, fresh flowers, and fruit and snacks. A full breakfast is served.

NIGHTLIFE

The arts are alive and well in Birmingham. The city has several theaters, a Broadway series, a children's theater, a ballet, the Metropolitan Orchestra, opera, and more. In nice weather, many performances are held outdoors.

As for nightspots, the 22nd Street Jazz Café & Brewery (710 South 22nd Street, 205/252-0407) and Zydeco (2001 South 15th Street, 205/933-1032) offer live entertainment, and they have cover charges. Cover is also charged at Louie Louie (2001 Highland Avenue, 205/933-2778), but no live music is performed. Two other popular nightspots are the Redmont Bar at the Redmont (2101 Fifth Avenue North, 205/324-2101) and Yesterday's at the Ramada Inn Airport (5216 Airport Highway, 205/591-7900). For comedy, try the Comedy Club at the Stardome (1818 Data Drive, 205/444-0008).

22
HUNTSVILLE

Huntsville, located in the northeastern corner of the state, was the first English-speaking settlement in Alabama, the birthplace of the state constitution, and the first state capital. With its position on the Tennessee River, the community quickly became a trade and transportation hub, where barges, stagecoaches, and, later, railroad lines converged. Huntsville was occupied by the Union early in the Civil War. But because its many historic buildings were used as housing and offices for Federal soldiers, the city was spared the torch.

Early in the twentieth century, the clear air above Monte Sano attracted people for health reasons, and a health resort opened on the mountain. The city remained primarily a textile town until German scientists, led by Dr. Werhner von Braun, arrived in the 1950s to develop rockets at Redstone Arsenal. Huntsville became part of the U.S. space program and is now called the Space Capital of America.

Huntsville is also known as the Silicon Valley of the South. In fact, Huntsville's high-tech workforce is the third largest in the nation. The city is also one of the fastest growing communities in United States. For visitors, Huntsville is two different destinations—the historic downtown and the ultramodern space center—rolled into one. The city also attracts music lovers from all over with its annual Big Spring Jam, where big names in music perform a host of outdoor concerts.

HUNTSVILLE

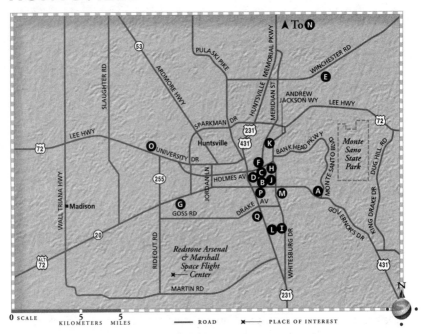

SIGHTS

- **A** Burritt Museum and Park
- **B** EarlyWorks
- **C** Harrison Brothers Hardware
- **D** Huntsville Museum of Art
- **E** North Alabama Railroad Museum
- **F** Twickenham and Old Town Historic Districts
- **G** U.S. Space and Rocket Center
- **H** Weeden House Museum

FOOD

- **I** Café Berlin
- **J** Clementine's Bountiful Basket
- **K** Eunice's Country Kitchen
- **L** Green Bottle Grill
- **M** Mill Bakery, Eatery, and Brewery

LODGING

- **N** Church House Inn Bed and Breakfast
- **O** Country Inn and Suites Hotel
- **P** Hilton Huntsville
- **Q** Huntsville Marriott
- **Q** Radisson Suites

Note: Items with the same letter are located in the same area.

A PERFECT DAY IN HUNTSVILLE

Start your day with breakfast at Eunice's Country Kitchen, where the in crowd meets. If you're lucky you can sit near the "liar's table" or even join in the fun. Then, to learn about local history, visit Early Works, a complex that brings Alabama's heritage to life.

Have lunch at the Mill Bakery, Eatery, and Brewery. Spend the entire afternoon at the U.S. Space and Rocket Center. Have dinner at Richard's on the Square, and if you have any energy left, see if a performance is playing at Huntsville Opera Theater or Von Braun Civic Center.

SIGHTSEEING HIGHLIGHTS

★★★★ EARLYWORKS
404 Madison Street, 256/564-8100

The best way to learn about history is to live it, which is exactly what children and adults get to do at this three-part history complex. Hands-on learning takes place at the **EarlyWorks Museum,** where visitors are urged to touch and explore as they learn about Alabama's history, from early territorial days until the cotton boom. You can sack crops in the general store, separate seed from boll as you gin cotton, and step onto a 46-foot keelboat in the riverboat section.

You can almost hear the cry of "All aboard!" at the **Historic Huntsville Depot**, where you'll tour train engines, passenger cars, and cabooses. Model-train exhibits depict the depot during the Civil War era.

In 1819, 44 men met in Walker Allen's cabinet shop to draft Alabama's constitution, making it the 22nd state. This store and surrounding buildings, such as a print shop, sheriff's residence, library, and post office, now form the reconstructed **Alabama Constitution Village**. Here you can experience crafts of the nineteenth century, such as pressing cider, spinning, and candle making.

Details: Mon–Sat 9–5. $6–$13 adults, $3.50–$10.50 children. (1 1/2 hours–full day)

★★★★ HUNTSVILLE MUSEUM OF ART
300 Church Street South, 256/535-4350
www.hsv.tis.net/hma

The museum is renowned for its permanent collections of nineteenth- and twentieth-century American paintings and graphics.

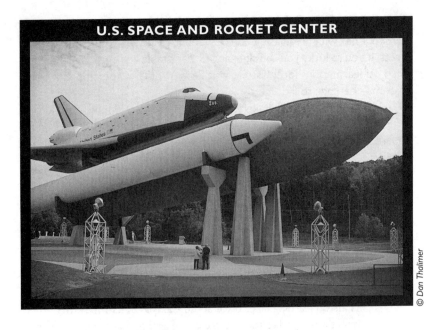

U.S. SPACE AND ROCKET CENTER

© Dan Thalimer

Details: Tue, Wed, Fri, Sat 10–5, Thu 9–9, Sun 1–5. Free, but donations are appreciated. (1 hour)

★★★★ U.S. SPACE AND ROCKET CENTER
1 Tranquility Base, 256/837-3400 or 800/447-6874

The largest space museum in the world, the center exhibits full-size rockets, lunar modules, a life-size replica of a lunar crater, early space suits, interactive displays, simulations, and more. The center also has an OMNIMAX theater and provides a bus tour of the adjacent **Marshall Space Flight Center**. Also on the property is the U.S. Space Camp, which welcomes 19,000 youngsters each year, and Space Academy, which offers similar experiences for adults.

Details: Daily 9–5; to 6 in summer. $14 adults, $10 children for museum and IMAX movie. Separate museum and IMAX tickets are available. (half–full day)

★★★ BURRITT MUSEUM AND PARK
3101 Burritt Drive, 256/536-2882, www.ci.huntsville.al.us

Located on 167 acres, the park is crisscrossed with trails, springs, and waterfalls and offers one of the best views of Huntsville. The museum is located in a large home built in 1935. Among the collections are antique furnishings, geological displays, Indian artifacts, antique medical and pharmaceutical instruments, nineteenth-century decorative arts, memorabilia from the Monte Sano Health Resort, and works by local artists. Explore the outbuildings, which include log cabins, a blacksmith shop, smokehouse, and church. Several special events take place during the year.

Details: Museum open Mar–mid-Dec Tue–Sat 10–4, Sun noon–4; grounds open daily 7 a.m. –sunset. Free. (1–2 hours)

★★★ HARRISON BROTHERS HARDWARE
125 Southside Square, 256/536-3631

Built in 1897 and in continuous use since then, Harrison Brothers is the oldest hardware store in Alabama. Occupying two storefronts, it serves as both a working store and a museum. On one side, the store looks much like it did at the turn of the century, with floor-to-ceiling shelves and drawers and long ladders on rollers. Also featured are an old cash register, an ancient safe, a coal-burning potbellied stove, a hand-operated rope elevator, old-fashioned tools, and logbooks that tell what various pieces of hardware cost over time. The other side of the store is dedicated to gifts, candy, modern gadgets, rocking chairs, gardening equipment, bird feeders, and more.

Details: Mon–Fri 9–5, Sat 10–4. Free. ($1/2$–1 hour)

★★★ TWICKENHAM AND OLD TOWN HISTORIC DISTRICTS
700 Monroe Street, 256/551-2230

These two neighborhoods are on the National Register of Historic Places. Twickenham has one of the largest concentrations of antebellum homes (65) in the country. Old Town is comprised of opulent Victorian homes built between 1870 and 1930. You can pick up a descriptive brochure for a walking/driving tour of the neighborhoods at the Huntsville–Madison County Convention and Visitors Bureau.

Details: (1–2 hours)

★★★ WEEDEN HOUSE MUSEUM
300 Gates Avenue, 256/536-7718

The Federal-style High House, built in 1819, was the birthplace of Maria Howard Weeden, a noted artist and poet. Although the family was originally well-to-do, they were impoverished by the Civil War, and Maria supported them by teaching, writing poetry, and painting.

Her paintings are much admired for portraying ex-slaves with sensitivity. She accompanied the paintings with poetry written in African American dialect. Many of her works are displayed in the museum.

Details: Tue–Sun 1–4. $2 adults, $1 children. (1 hour)

★★ **NORTH ALABAMA RAILROAD MUSEUM**
694 Chase Road, Chase, 256/881-3629 or 256/851-6276
www.suncompsvc.com/narm
Take a short jaunt north on U.S. 72 to the small town of Chase to visit the museum. Displays in the old depot depict railroad history in the area. Outside you can explore 25 passenger and freight cars and the two locomotives.

Details: Wed and Sat. Free. Tickets for train ride are $9 adults, $5 children under 12. (1 hour)

FITNESS AND RECREATION

The mountainous terrain and forested areas around Huntsville are ideal for outdoor pursuits such as hiking, jogging, and mountain biking. Monte Sano State Park, which towers 1,000 feet above the city, offers challenging hiking trails. Trails through Burritt Park often skirt streams and waterfalls. A nature trail on Green Mountain, part of which circles a lake, has woods, a covered bridge, a Braille trail, and a wildlife area. For those who prefer a more urban walk or run, Huntsville Cross Country Running Park near the old airport offers a two-mile and a three-mile loop. Ditto's Landing Marina (Hobbs Island Road off U.S. 231, Huntsville, 256/883-9420 or 800/552-8769) offers access to the Tennessee River and a BMX trail.

Redstone Arsenal is an active research facility working on the joint U.S.-Russian space station. Sometimes tours are not allowed because work is being kept secret.

FOOD

Begin at least one day with breakfast at the unassuming **Eunice's Country Kitchen** (1006 Andrew Jackson Way, 256/534-9550), where politicians often stop to press the flesh and plan strategy. Eunice jokes that people pay her not to reveal all the schemes she's overheard. In addition to booths and small tables, friends and acquaintances like to sit at a large communal table and swap stories and lies; hence the name Liar's Table. Eunice will obligingly give you a Liar's License if you want to join the fun. Breakfasts are gargantuan Southern meals with several kinds of meat, eggs, grits, pancakes, biscuits and gravy, and more. You certainly won't need lunch after eating breakfast there.

For casual lunches and dinners, plenty of choices are available. **Clementine's Bountiful Basket** (525 Madison Street, 256/533-4438) serves sandwiches and salads, and in the evenings, it's a "white tablecloth" restaurant. The **Mill Bakery, Eatery, and Brewery** (2003 Whiteburg Drive, 256/534-4455) is known for its extensive selection of freshly made baked goods, pastas, salads, and sandwiches. Live entertainment is often offered. Reservations are not accepted.

For a more upscale evening, elegant, European-style **Café Berlin** (Westbury Square at 975 Airport Road, 256/880-9920) not surprisingly specializes in German food. They serve traditional favorites, such as schnitzels and sauerbraten, as well as American choices. Even if you don't eat a meal here, drop by for one of the to-die-for desserts. The **Green Bottle Grill** (875 Airport Road, S.W. at Westbury Square, 256/882-0459) serves dinner in a formal but relaxed atmosphere. The cuisine is regional, and specialties include veal and lamb as well as steak, fish, and pasta. The wine list includes more than 100 choices. In nice weather, you'll probably opt for dining on the patio.

LODGING

Located conveniently near the space center, a mall, and many restaurants, the **Country Inn and Suites Hotel** (4880 University Drive, 256/837-4070 or 800/456-4000) is perfect for families. Rooms and suites have refrigerators, and a "continental plus" breakfast is provided. Amenities include a fitness center, pool, whirlpool, spa, and sauna. The sprawling **Hilton Huntsville** (401 Williams Avenue, 256/533-1400 or 800/228-9290) is located across the street from the Von Braun Center near the historic districts. The hotel offers close to 300 rooms and suites, an executive level, a pool, restaurant, and bar with live entertainment some nights. A comedy club has performances Thursday through Saturday nights. The **Huntsville Marriott** (5 Tranquility Base, 256/830-2222 or 800/228-9290) is located near the space center. It offers nearly 300 rooms and suites, an executive level, two restaurants, a bar with live entertainment, sauna, and whirlpool. Also close to the Redstone Arsenal and the space flight center, the **Radisson Suites** (6000 South Memorial Parkway, 256/882-9400 or 800/333-3333) offers 140 suites and efficiencies. Some units boast whirlpools.

Church House Inn Bed and Breakfast, 2017 Grimwood Road,

SIDE TRIP: LOOKOUT MOUNTAIN

*Northeast of Huntsville, you can take a spectacular scenic drive along Lookout Mountain Parkway. Natural attractions such as **Sequoyah Caverns**, **DeSoto Falls**, and **Little River Canyon** take center stage, but you can also visit appealing small towns such as **Mentone** and **Fort Payne**, as well as a dude ranch and a ski resort. For information, contact the Lookout Mountain Parkway Association (P.O. Box 288, Mentone) or call the Etowah Tourism Board at 256/549-0351.*

Toney, 256/828-5192, takes its name from the stately church entry tower and windows that grace this modern building less than 30 minutes from Huntsville. Guest rooms open to balconies overlooking a large great room with a spectacular fireplace. The owners provide binoculars for your bird-watching or star-gazing enjoyment.

CAMPING

Monte Sano State Park (5105 Nolen Road, 256/534-3757) offers rustic cabins and camping. Goose Pond Colony near Scottsboro (off AL 279, Scottsboro, 256/259-1808) provides rental cottages and campgrounds around a lake. The facilities include golf, a bait and tackle shop, pool, amphitheater, marina, and hiking trails.

NIGHTLIFE

Check out the schedule for the Von Braun Center (700 Monroe Street, 256/533-1953, www.vbcc.com, where a variety of shows and concerts are performed year-round. For a change of pace, the Huntsville Stars AA baseball team plays at Joe W. Davis Stadium. Call 256/882-2562 (www.huntsvillestars.com) for a schedule. The Huntsville Channel Cats of the Southern Hockey League play in the Von Braun Center from October through April. For a schedule or tickets, call 256/551-2383 (www.channelcats.net).

Hopper's at the Holiday Inn Research Park (5903 University Drive, 256/830-0600) offers live entertainment, including golden oldies.

23
MONTGOMERY

Montgomery is much more than just the capital of Alabama. It is known as the Cradle of the Confederacy because Jefferson Davis was sworn in here as president of the Confederate States of America. It also served as the temporary capital of the Confederacy for a few months before the seat of government was moved to Richmond.

Montgomery is also recognized as the birthplace of the Civil Rights movement. It was in Montgomery that seamstress Rosa Parks refused to give up her seat on a city bus to a white man. She was arrested, and the rest, as they say, is history. The Montgomery bus boycott lasted almost a year. It was ultimately successful and sparked other protests throughout the South.

Montgomery also has some significant musical, theatrical, and literary history. The city is honored to have the only Shakespeare festival in the United States allowed to fly the official flag of the Royal Shakespeare Company.

A PERFECT DAY IN MONTGOMERY

Located in historic Union Station, the Montgomery Visitor Center is the perfect place for first-timers to begin a visit to the city. Old Town Alabama, a collection of historic homes and stores that are open for tours, provides a glimpse into the past. The 1850 House is a restaurant, so have lunch there before moving on. Several other important attractions are grouped together:

MONTGOMERY

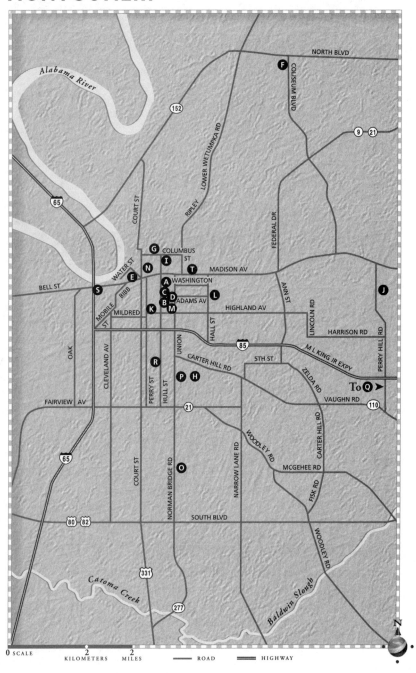

NORTH BLVD

Alabama River

152

COLISEUM BLVD

F

9 21

COURT ST

LOWER WETUMPKA RD

RIPLEY

FEDERAL DR

65

WATER ST

COLUMBUS ST

G

I

N

E

T

MADISON AV

ANN ST

J

BELL ST

S

WASHINGTON

A

C

D

ADAMS AV

L

LINCOLN RD

BIBB

B

M

HARRISON RD

MOBILE ST

MILDRED

K

HIGHLAND AV

HALL ST

PERRY HILL RD

OAK

CLEVELAND AV

85

M L KING JR EXPY

UNION

CARTER HILL RD

5TH ST

ZELDA RD

R

PERRY ST

HULL ST

P

H

To Q ▶

110

FAIRVIEW AV

21

VAUGHN RD

65

COURT ST

NORMAN BRIDGE RD

O

NARROW LANE RD

WOODLEY RD

CARTER HILL RD

MCGEHEE RD

FISK RD

331

SOUTH BLVD

80 82

WOODLEY RD

Catoma Creek

Baldwin Slough

277

N

0 SCALE   2   2
        KILOMETERS   MILES   —— ROAD   ▦▦▦ HIGHWAY

the State Capitol, First White House of the Confederacy, Civil Rights Memorial, and Dexter Avenue King Memorial Baptist Church. Go to the outskirts of town to visit the Montgomery Museum of Fine Art. End your day by enjoying an elegant dinner at Vintage Year and then attending a performance at the Alabama Shakespeare Festival.

SIGHTSEEING HIGHLIGHTS: MONTGOMERY

★★★★ ALABAMA STATE CAPITOL
Bainbridge Street and Dexter Avenue, 334/242-3935
Built in 1850, with wings added in 1885, 1905, and 1911, this gorgeous Greek Revival structure is one of the few state capitols designated as a National Historic Landmark. The capitol, the most visited tourist attraction in Alabama, sits regally on a hilltop overlooking downtown. A small bronze star imbedded in the floor of one of the porticos identifies the spot where Jefferson Davis took his oath of office in 1861. Inside, two gorgeous, self-supporting stairways spiral up three stories. Eight murals and a stained-glass skylight crown the dome of the rotunda. Restored to its pre–Civil War appearance, the senate chamber is where Alabama legislators voted to secede from the Union. The chambers of the house of representatives and supreme court, as well as the governor's ceremonial office, have been restored to their opulent Victorian-era appearance. Visitors can take self-guided tours or guided tours can be arranged in advance.
Details: Mon–Fri 9–5, Sat 9–4. Free. (1 hour)

SIGHTS
- Ⓐ Alabama State Capitol
- Ⓑ Civil Rights Memorial
- Ⓒ Dexter Avenue King Memorial Baptist Church
- Ⓓ First White House of the Confederacy
- Ⓔ Montgomery Visitor Center
- Ⓕ Montgomery Zoo
- Ⓖ Old Alabama Town
- Ⓗ Scott and Zelda Fitzgerald Museum

FOOD
- Ⓘ 1850 Young House
- Ⓙ Chappy's Deli
- Ⓚ Chris' Hot Dog Stand
- Ⓛ Commerce Center Cafeteria
- Ⓜ Farmer's Market Cafeteria
- Ⓝ Montgomery Brewery Co. and Cafe
- Ⓞ Sahara Restaurant
- Ⓟ Vintage Year

LODGING
- Ⓠ Comfort Suites
- Ⓡ Lattice Inn Bed and Breakfast
- Ⓢ Red Bluff Cottage
- Ⓣ Statehouse Inn

SIDE TRIP: TUSKEGEE

Tuskegee, only 38 miles east of Montgomery, is home of the famous **Tuskegee Institute**, *1212 Old Montgomery Road, 334/727-3200. Booker T. Washington founded this educational institution for blacks in 1881. George Washington Carver also carried out his experiments with Southern crops at the school. Tuskegee began with an allocation of only $2,500, with classes held in a dilapidated church. Today it has grown to 161 buildings on 268 acres and a population of 5,000 students, faculty, and staff. It has been designated a National Historic Site. The school is open to the public at all times.* **George Washington Carver Museum** *and* **The Oaks**, *Booker T. Washington's home, are open seven days a week, 9–5.*

★★★★ **CIVIL RIGHTS MEMORIAL**
Washington Avenue at Hull Street
Located on the grounds of the Southern Poverty Law Center, the starkly beautiful memorial was designed by Maya Lin, creator of the Vietnam Veterans Memorial in Washington, D.C. The centerpiece of the memorial is a large, black granite tabletop, carved around the edges with the major events of the Civil Rights movement and the names of 40 people who died in the struggle between 1954 and 1968. The plaza is backed by a wall engraved with the words of Dr. Martin Luther King Jr. Water, representing healing, constantly flows down the wall, across the tabletop, and into a shallow pool.
Details: *Open at all times. Free. ($^1/_2$ hour)*

★★★★ **DEXTER AVENUE KING MEMORIAL BAPTIST CHURCH**
454 Dexter Avenue, 334/263-3970
Dr. Martin Luther King Jr. accepted his first pulpit at this church in 1954, and he served as its pastor until 1960. After Rosa Parks' arrest, meetings and rallies were held at the church to make plans for the bus boycott and Civil Rights marches. Still an active church, the building is listed on the National Register of Historic Places. A pow-

erful mural depicts King's journey from Montgomery to Memphis, where he was assassinated in 1968. Both black and white people, those who were helpful and those who were obstructive, are portrayed in the mural.

Details: *Guided tours Mon–Thu 10 and 2, Fri 10, Sat 10:30, 11:15, noon, and 12:45. Advance notice required. Free, but donations are accepted. (1 hour)*

★★★★ FIRST WHITE HOUSE OF THE CONFEDERACY
644 Washington Avenue, 334/242-1861

After he was sworn in as president of the Confederacy, Jefferson Davis and his family moved into this attractive Italianate mansion, built in 1835. They lived here only from March to May, when the Confederate capital was moved to Richmond. Today the house is filled with Civil War memorabilia, period antiques, and family heirlooms donated by Mrs. Davis. The articles in the president's bedroom were the Davis' personal belongings and are placed according to a diagram Mrs. Davis made before her death in 1906.

Details: *Mon–Fri 8–4:30. Free. (1 hour)*

★★★★ OLD ALABAMA TOWN
301 Columbus Street, 334/240-4500

Thirty restored historic houses, some in their original locations and others moved here, make up a three-block village, which portrays Alabama life between 1800 and 1930. The village is conveniently located downtown, in the Old North Hull Street historic district. Tours begin at 301 Columbus Street, where pioneers stopped when they entered Alabama territory in 1817. Buildings include an 1820 log cabin and a Depression-era drugstore, which houses the **Alabama Pharmaceutical Association Drugstore Museum**. Another favorite on the tour is a fully stocked turn-of-the-century grocery store. The **Young House**, built in 1850, is a restaurant specializing in Southern cuisine. Costumed guides demonstrate old-fashioned skills and crafts.

Details: *Year-round Mon–Sat 9–3, Sun 1–3. $7 adults, $3 children 6–10. (1–2 hours)*

★★★ MONTGOMERY VISITOR CENTER
300 Water Street, 334/262-0013
www.montgomerychamber.com

MONTGOMERY REGION

Map legend:

ROAD ——— HIGHWAY ——— NATIONAL FOREST BOUNDARY -----

SCALE
0   20 MILES
0   20 KILOMETERS

Locations on map:
- Union City
- Tuskegee
- Dadeville — H
- Good Hope
- Tallahassee
- Shorter
- Wetumpka — C, B, A, D, E
- Montgomery — F
- Prattville — G
- Clanton
- Selma

Water features: Lake Martin, Lake Jordan, Mitchell Lake, Tallapoosa River, Alabama River

Talladega National Forest

Highways: 280, 29, 80, 49, 9, 14, 21, 231, 22, 37, 82, 190, 40, 183, 41, 80, 97, 21, 31, 65, 331, 153, 152, 110, 85

The center is located in the stately old Union Station. See the 8½-minute movie about Montgomery and get advice about your stay from the friendly staff.

Details: Mon–Fri 8:30–5, Sat 9–4, Sun noon–4. Free. (1 hour)

★★★ **MONTGOMERY ZOO**
North Boulevard, 334/240-4900
Updated in 1991 and enlarged to its current size of 40 acres, the zoo features barrier-free habitats for 800 animals from five continents. You can mosey around at your leisure or enjoy the narrated train ride. Exhibits include a walk-through aviary and a new reptile building.

Details: Daily 9–5. $4.50 adults, $2.50 children. (2–4 hours)

★★ **SCOTT AND ZELDA FITZGERALD MUSEUM**
919 Felder Avenue, Apartment B, 334/264-4222
Zelda Sayre was a Montgomery native and a highly talented artist and a writer. She met Scott when he was stationed at nearby Camp Sheridan before World War II. They lived in this apartment in Montgomery for two years and had one daughter. The museum, the only one in the country devoted to the two of them, contains the famous couple's personal effects such as books and some of Zelda's paintings. A video presentation teaches more about them.

Details: Wed–Fri 10–2, Sat and Sun 1–5. Free. (1 hour)

SIGHTSEEING HIGHLIGHTS: MONTGOMERY REGION

★★★★ **ALABAMA SHAKESPEARE FESTIVAL**
Carolyn Blount Theater, 1 Festival Drive, 334/271-5353 or 800/841-4ASF, www.asf.net

SIGHTS
Ⓐ Alabama Shakespeare Festival (ASF)
Ⓑ Fort Toulouse/Jackson Park
Ⓒ Jasmine Hill Gardens and Outdoor Museum
Ⓓ Montgomery Museum of Fine Art

FOOD
Ⓔ Green Lantern

LODGING
Ⓕ Holiday Inn Downtown and Suites
Ⓖ Plantation House
Ⓗ Still Waters Resort

Located in a modern, state-of-the-art facility with two theaters, the company presents top-quality performances year-round. The ASF is the fifth largest Shakespeare company in the world. In addition to the Bard's works, it presents other world-class classical and contemporary plays. Two different plays are given simultaneously and on a repertory basis, so you may be able to see several plays in a week's time. Tours of the building, including behind the scenes, are given as well. Be sure to order tickets far in advance. Buying tickets the day of a performance is often difficult or impossible.

Details: Box office open Mon–Sat 10–6, Sun noon–4, on performance days until 9 p.m. Admission to building is free; performance prices range from $15–$30. (1 hour for tour; 2¹/₂ hours for performances)

★★★★ MONTGOMERY MUSEUM OF FINE ART
1 Museum Drive in the Wynton M. Blount Cultural Park
334/244-5700, www.fineartsmuseum.com

Repository of the fabulous Blount Collection of American Art, which traces the evolution of art in the United States from the eighteenth century to the present, the museum has an outstanding permanent collection of more than 2,500 pieces, including American and European art. **ARTWORKS** is an interactive studio and art museum for young people. Even if you aren't visiting the museum with children, stop in this gallery for a treat. The delightful **Café M** overlooks a lake, an English-style park, outdoor art, and the Alabama Shakespeare Festival theater.

Alabamians have a pervasive interest in families. To use the local vernacular, they like to know "who are your people?" If you have any family from Alabama, be prepared to talk about them.

Details: Tue, Wed, Fri, and Sat 10–5, Thu 10–9, Sun noon–5. Free, but donations are accepted. (1–2 hours)

★★★ JASMINE HILL GARDENS AND OUTDOOR MUSEUM
3001 Jasmine Hill Road, Wetumpka, 334/567-6463
www.jasminehill.org

Located near the small town of Wetumpka, the gardens are often called Alabama's Little Corner of Greece. The couple who lived here were world travelers who decorated their extensive gardens with antiquities and reproductions of ancient pieces. Today the facility covers 20 acres. It showcases 41 pieces of Greek sculpture and a full-size replica of the Temple of Hera ruins, where the Olympic flame is ignited every four years.

Details: Year-round Tue–Sat 9–5. $5 adults, $3.50 children. (1½ hours)

★★ FORT TOULOUSE/JACKSON PARK
2521 Fort Toulouse Road off U.S. 231, Wetumpka, 334/567-3002

Located between Montgomery and Wetumpka, the fort was built by the French in 1717 at the confluence of the Coosa and Tallapoosa Rivers, where they meet to form the Alabama. However, evidence indicates that humans lived here as much as 5,000 years ago. Hernando deSoto visited the area in 1540. First named Fort Toulouse by the French, the stronghold was taken over by the British and later by the Americans. The fort was updated in 1814 under the direction of Andrew Jackson, and the name was changed to Fort Jackson. Today on the 165 acres you'll see archaeological excavations, partial reconstruction of the forts, historic buildings, a museum, and an Indian mound. In addition, you can stroll through the **William Bartram Arboretum** and walk on hiking trails. Living history programs are presented from spring through fall.

Details: Year-round sunup–sundown. $2 adults, $1 children 6–12. (1 hour)

FITNESS AND RECREATION

Good places for walking include the historic districts, Riverfront Park, Jasmine Hill Gardens, Wynton M. Blount Cultural Park, the Montgomery Zoo, and Fort Toulouse/Jackson Park. For water sports, most residents head for Lake Martin, a 40,000-acre lake northeast of the city. Real Island Marina, U.S. 231, Dadeville, 334/857-2741 or 334/857-3590, is a full-service marina with a public launching ramp and boat rentals. Still Waters Resort offers an 18-hole golf course, pools, tennis courts, a marina, and beaches.

Golf is available at Kolomi Golf Course's 18-hole facility (800 Dozier Road, 334/279-6686), two nine-hole courses and a driving range at the Montgomery Golf Center (4507 Mobile Highway, 334/288-9662), and another 18-hole course at Lagoon Park (2855 Lagoon Park Road, 334/271-7000). Funtasia (5761 Atlanta Highway, 334/277-4653) is a miniature golf course with a tropical setting.

Lagoon Park (334/271-7001) offers a 17-court tennis center, a fishing lake, a softball complex, and a 400-meter jogging trail with fitness stations. O'Connor Tennis Center (500 Anderson Street, 334/240-4884) offers 11 lighted tennis courts, handball courts, and other recreational facilities.

You can ice-skate at the Ice Palace in Eastdale Mall (Atlanta Highway, 334/277-2088)—lessons and rentals available—or practice marksmanship by reservation at Seven Bridges Sporting Clays (Woodly Road, Ramer, 334/288-5150). Sports fans who prefer being spectators will enjoy Montgomery Motor Speedway (480 Booth Road, 334/263-3267) and Victoryland Greyhound Racing Park (exit 22 off I-85, 800/688-2946).

FOOD

Montgomery boasts a great quantity and variety of eating establishments. **Green Lantern**, 5275 Troy Highway, 334/288-9345, has been a local favorite for dinner for more than 60 years. This off-the-beaten-track restaurant is worth searching out. The hearty menu consists of steak, fried chicken, and other traditional fare accompanied by the restaurant's famous cheese biscuits.

Sahara Restaurant, 511 East Edgemont Road, 334/262-1215, is where Montgomeryites go when they want to splurge. In business for more than 40 years, the romantic restaurant offers a varied lunch and dinner menu with seafood and char-grilled steaks among the most popular items. Another upscale and very romantic restaurant is **Vintage Year**, 405 Cloverdale Road, Montgomery, 334/264-8463, which specializes in seafood with an Italian flair. Visiting celebrities and politicians often frequent this fashionable restaurant.

Montgomery has no shortage of places to have lunch. Located in a restored home in Old Alabama Town, **1850 Young House**, 310 North Hull Street, 334/240-4500, is a perfect place to eat during your visit to the historic village. In fact, you can purchase a combination ticket that includes a tour and lunch. The cuisine is simple, Southern home cooking with generous portions. Another place for lunch is **Chappy's Deli**, 1611 Perry Hill Road, 334/279-7477, which serves three meals a day and is known for its hearty breakfasts of Belgian waffles, French toast, eggs, omelettes, pancakes, and more. Lunch and dinner choices include a wide variety of soups, sandwiches, and salads.

For a very casual lunch, **Chris' Hot Dog Stand**, 138 Dexter Avenue, 334/265-6850, has been a mainstay in Montgomery since 1917 and is now operated by the son of the original owner. One of the specialties is a secret sauce made from onions, peppers, and spices. The 1950s ambience is created with vinyl and chrome, and a game room and gift shop are attached. At the **Commerce Center Cafeteria**, Alabama Center for Commerce, 401 Adams Avenue, 334/834-9962, breakfast is served as well as lunch. **Farmer's Market Cafeteria**, 315 North McDonough Street, 334/262-9163, is frequented by many state and local legislators and their staffs. Rather Spartan, the cafeteria is decorated with photos of Alabama athletes. Breakfast includes Southern favorites such as ham, sausage, and biscuits and gravy. Lunch fare includes vegetables and such entrees as baby back ribs, fried chicken, and catfish.

Adhering to local laws stating that a brewpub must be housed in a building that predates Prohibition, the **Montgomery Brewery Co. and Cafe,** 12 W. Jefferson, 334/834-2739, is located in an historic 1913 structure. Entrées include hamburgers, pizza, and fine seafood, served with five different beers. The sauteed crab claws and Parmesan-crusted trout are excellent.

LODGING

Montgomery has a full complement of chain motels and hotels in every price range. **Red Bluff Cottage**, 551 Clay Street, 334/264-0056, is a newly constructed bed-and-breakfast located in an unusual raised cottage in Montgomery's Cottage Hill district of pre– and post–Civil War homes. Poised high above the Alabama River, the cottage offers exceptional views of the river and the capitol from its porch and gazebo. Other bed-and-breakfasts include the **Lattice Inn Bed and Breakfast**, 1414 South Hull Street, 334/832-9931, which occupies a 1906 Victorian cottage, and the **Plantation House**, 752 Loder Street, Prattville, 334/361-0442, located in a 165-year-old home.

Among hotels, **Comfort Suites**, 5924 Monticello Drive, 334/272-1013, www.hostsmart.com, has 49 suites and is an extremely good value. Rooms contain coffee makers, and some sport whirlpools. Near the capitol, the **Holiday Inn Downtown and Suites** (120 Madison Avenue, 334/264-2231) offers hair dryers in rooms as well as dataports for business travelers. It also has a swimming pool, restaurant, bar, and laundry facilities. Children under 18 stay free in a room with their parents, and children under 12 eat free in the restaurant. The **Statehouse Inn**, 924 Madison Avenue, 334/265-0741 or 800/552-7099, a block from the capitol, is frequented by legislators and visiting government workers and dignitaries. Amenities include a restaurant, bar, and laundry facilities.

On nearby Lake Martin, **Still Waters Resort**, 1000 Still Waters Drive, Dadeville, 800/825-7021, offers accommodations in two- and three-bedroom condominiums. Amenities and facilities include two restaurants, a general store, a beach, golfing, tennis courts, a sauna, exercise room, and boating.

CAMPING

Toulouse/Jackson Park (see Sightseeing Highlights) offers 39 campsites. At Woodruff Lake near Haynesville, Gunter Hill Campground (Booth Road off U.S. 80, Montgomery, 334/269-1053) offers 146 sites. On Lake Martin, Real Island Marina (2700 Real Island Road, Equality, 334/857-2741) has 52 sites as well as a full-service marina and public boat launch. Camping is also available at Montgomery KOA (250 Fisher Road, Hope Hull, 334/288-0728).

NIGHTLIFE

The height of any trip to Montgomery should be a performance, or several, at the Alabama Shakespeare Festival (see Sightseeing Highlights). With two theaters in the facility, two plays performed nightly, and rotating performances, a visitor in town for a week should be able to see several plays. The Montgomery Symphony Orchestra, Alabama Dance Theater, Montgomery Ballet, and other groups perform in the restored 1929 Davis Theater (251 Montgomery Street, 334/241-9567). Family-oriented shows can be seen at the Faulkner University Dinner Theater (5345 Atlanta Highway, 334/260-6190).

Victoryland Greyhound Racing Track, exit 22 off I-85, Montgomery, 800/688-2946, offers wagering on 13 races Monday through Saturday. The facility seats 1,400 and sports restaurants, cocktail lounges, and a glass-enclosed, climate-controlled clubhouse.

24
COLUMBUS

Bustling Columbus, Georgia, is a city of nicknames. Located at the northern-most navigable point on the Chattahoochee River, it is sometimes called the Port City. Because the river forms the boundary between Georgia and Alabama, Columbus is sometimes called (with tongue in cheek) Georgia's Other Coast or Georgia's West Coast. Coca-Cola was developed here, as well as several other soft drinks, giving Columbus another nickname: the Soft Drink Capital. Numerous fountains inspired the sobriquet Fountain City.

Columbus got international attention during the 1996 Summer Olympic Games when women's softball was played here. Visitors will be captivated by the city's riverfront, which is a National Historic Landmark, and several signif-icant districts of historic homes.

More sights are a short drive away. World-famous Callaway Gardens is located in nearby Pine Mountain. It is not only a world-class garden but also a popular resort that offers overnight accommodations, numerous recreational activities, golf, and many special events during the year.

Franklin D. Roosevelt's Little White House National Historic Site and his-toric Warm Springs Village are close by as well. Warm Springs Village, built in the late 1880s, came into prominence because of the curative powers of its min-eral waters. Franklin D. Roosevelt went there for treatment of his polio. He built a house there in 1932 and died there in 1945. The quaint village itself has been revitalized and includes shops, boutiques, restaurants, and a bed-and-breakfast.

COLUMBUS

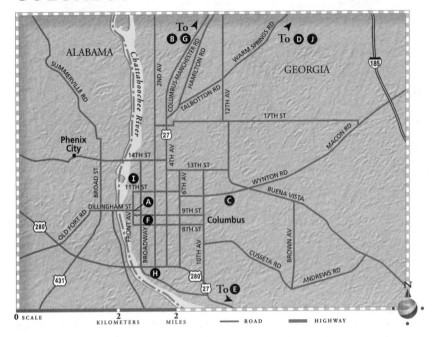

SIGHTS

- **A** Black Heritage Tour
- **B** Callaway Gardens
- **C** Columbus Museum
- **D** FDR's Little White House Historic Site
- **E** Fort Benning/National Infantry Museum
- **F** Heritage Corner
- **G** Pine Mountain Wild Animal Safari
- **H** Port Columbus Civil War Naval Center
- **I** Riverwalk
- **J** Warm Springs Village

A PERFECT DAY IN COLUMBUS

Begin with a visit to Callaway Gardens in Pine Mountain. An extra-special attraction is a huge butterfly center there. Have lunch at the Gardens Restaurant overlooking a lake and golf course. After lunch, drive to Warm Springs. Tour FDR's Little White House Historic Site, then browse in the village shops. Drive to Columbus and visit Heritage Corner—a collection of historic houses. Have dinner at the elegant Goetchius House. Finally, enjoy a performance at the historic Springer Opera House or take a horse-and-carriage ride along Riverwalk and through one of the city's historic districts.

SIGHTSEEING HIGHLIGHTS

★★★★ **CALLAWAY GARDENS**
U.S. 27, Pine Mountain, 706/663-2281 or 800/CALLAWAY
Covering 25,000 acres, this woodsy park includes thousands of azaleas, bulbs, and other plantings. It contains the five-acre **John A. Sibley Horticultural Center**, an indoor/outdoor garden, and the seven-acre **Mr. Cason's Vegetable Garden**. Other attractions include a 160-year-old pioneer cabin, the charming **Ida Cason Callaway Memorial Chapel**, and the **Cecil B. Day Butterfly Center**. New in 1999–2000 are the **Virginia Hand Callaway Discovery Center** and the **Callaway Brothers Azalea Bowl**—the world's largest azalea garden. Recreational opportunities include a miniature train ride, bicycling, golfing, tennis, and fishing and swimming on a lake with the world's largest artificial inland beach.
Details: Daily 9–5. $10 adults, $5 children, includes the listed attractions. (4 hours)

★★★★ **FDR'S LITTLE WHITE HOUSE HISTORIC SITE**
GA 85, Warm Springs, 706/655-3511
In 1926 FDR bought the mineral springs that gave the town its name and created the Georgia Warm Springs Foundation, dedicated to helping paralytic patients from all over the world. Roosevelt built a house for himself, later nicknamed the Little White House. He was sitting for a portrait here in April 1945 when he died. The house is almost exactly as he left it that day. Next door, the **Little White House Museum** displays more memorabilia from FDR's life and presidency. The completely restored Pools and Springs Complex, 1 1/2 miles away, is included in the admission price.
Details: Daily 9–5. $5 adults, $4 seniors, $2 children. (1 1/2 hours)

★★★★ **FORT BENNING/NATIONAL INFANTRY MUSEUM**
Building 396 on Baltzell Avenue, Fort Benning
706/545-2958
Fort Benning, southeast of Columbus, is home of the U.S. Army's Infantry School, the largest and most modern infantry school in the

world. The museum traces the history of the American foot soldier from the Revolution to the present, displaying uniforms, weapons, equipment, and memorabilia from each of America's wars. Captured enemy equipment is displayed, as well as art interpreting military conflicts.

Details: *Mon–Fri 8–4:30, weekends 12:30–4:30. Free. (1 hour)*

★★★★ HERITAGE CORNER
700 Broadway, 706/322-0756

These five historic homes, constructed between the 1820s and 1870s, provide a survey of architectural styles and are appropriately furnished. Begin by buying tickets at the large, brick, two-story Italianate structure that houses the Historic Columbus Foundation, then tour the tastefully furnished house.

The Victorian cottage around the corner belonged to John Stith Pemberton, who developed a concoction called French Wine of Coca, the forerunner of Coca-Cola. (He made only $1,500 from his formula.) In the rear of the cottage are a separate kitchen house and Pemberton's apothecary shop.

The Federal-style house was built in 1828 and is the oldest structure built in Columbus. Also on its grounds are an 1800s log cabin and an 1840 double-pen farmhouse. Both structures were moved to the site from outlying areas.

Details: *Guided tours Mon–Fri 11 and 2, weekends at 2. $5. (1 hour)*

★★★★ RIVERWALK

The industrial district along the bluffs of the Chattahoochee River was built in the late 1800s and is today designated as a National Historical Landmark. Many of the brick, one- and two-story former warehouses and industrial plants have been rejuvenated and now house modern businesses. Along the river's edge, a lovely brick walkway, benches, statuary, ironwork, historical markers, and overlooks combine to create a park called Riverwalk. From Riverwalk you can see the waterfall that marks the end of navigation on the Chattahoochee River. Depending on the time of year, carriage tours are often available from Riverwalk.

Details: *Park accessible 24 hours a day. Free. Visitors Center, 706/322-1613 or 800/999-1613. (1 hour)*

★★★★ WARM SPRINGS VILLAGE

Imagine the tiny village when FDR lived there. He would often come

SIDE TRIP: SOUTHWESTERN GEORGIA

Visiting Columbus, Pine Mountain, and Warm Springs will probably only whet your appetite to see more of southwestern Georgia. Be forewarned, there's so much to see, you might have to come back again and again. The town of **Americus** *boasts the magnificent Windsor Hotel, one of only five hotels in Georgia listed in the National Trust for Historic Preservation's Historic Hotels of America. Several of the town's other stately homes operate as bed-and-breakfasts.*

Plains is the home of former U.S. President Jimmy Carter, and his original election headquarters is a National Historical Site. **Andersonville** *was the site of an infamous Civil War prison, which is now a national cemetery. The quaint village has a museum and several other historic sights.* **Newnan** *and* **LaGrange** *are charming towns with extensive historic districts and several gorgeous bed-and-breakfasts. Cross the Chattahoochee River to visit lovely* **Eufaula, Alabama,** *another small town with historic districts and bed-and-breakfasts.*

into town and chat with the residents, drawing a big crowd. Secret Service men, reporters, and important visitors all stayed at the Hotel Warm Springs, ate in the town's restaurants, and spent money in its shops. From 1932 to 1945 the town was bustling. But prosperity ended when the train carrying FDR's body pulled out of town in April 1945, and Warm Springs almost became a ghost town. However, the story has a happy ending. FDR's home was made into a National Historic Site, and once again visitors poured into town. In the last few years, the village has been revitalized and now does a brisk tourism business with 65 shops that carry souvenirs, crafts, antiques, and furniture. The hotel has reopened as a bed-and-breakfast, and the town has a half-dozen restaurants.

Details: *(half–full day)*

★★★ COLUMBUS MUSEUM
1251 Wynnton Road, 706/649-0713

In addition to a significant permanent collection of art of the nineteenth and twentieth centuries, the museum displays Native

American relics and regional artifacts of historic significance. In addition, a movie called *The Chattahoochee Legacy* is shown and an interactive children's gallery entertains the kids.

Details: *Tue–Sat 10–5, Sun 1–5. Free. (1–2 hours*

★★★ PORT COLUMBUS CIVIL WAR NAVAL CENTER
202 Fourth Street, 706/327-9798

The museum contains Confederate artifacts, weapons, and model ships, as well as prototypes of experimental vessels that were never built. The scant remains of the ironclad *Jackson* and the gunboat *Chattahoochee* are on display. A new complex is scheduled for 2000, which will house interactive exhibits and living histories.

Details: *Tue–Fri 10–5, Sat–Sun 1–5. Free, but donations are requested. (1 hour)*

★★★ PINE MOUNTAIN WILD ANIMAL SAFARI
1300 Oak Grove Road, Pine Mountain, 706/663-8744 or 800/367-2751, www.animalsafari.com

Occupying 500 acres, the park provides naturalistic habitats for 300 exotic animals that are able to wander freely. You can take a self-guided tour or a bus tour. Other attractions include a farm, serpentarium, monkey house, and petting zoo.

Details: *Daily in summer 10–7:30; to 5:30 in winter. $11.95 adults, $7.95 children. One dollar off admission in winter. (2 hours)*

★★ BLACK HERITAGE TOUR

Prominent native-born Columbus African Americans include the jazz singer Gertrude "Ma" Rainey and Eugene Bullard, the first black combat pilot. Get a brochure from the Convention and Visitors Bureau and then take a self-guided walking and driving tour of 24 sights, including African American churches, cemeteries, a theater, and homes.

Details: *Visit or call Columbus Convention and Visitors Bureau, 1000 Bay Avenue, 706/322-1613. (1–2 hours)*

FITNESS AND RECREATION

With a few exceptions, the terrain in this area is fairly flat, which makes outdoor exercise easy and pleasant. Within Columbus itself, Riverwalk provides a level and attractive place to walk or jog. Strolling around the historic districts is good exercise as well, and bicycling and in-line skating are alternative ways to

HISTORIC TOURS

Columbus actually has three historic districts. The **Uptown District** is a commercial area that includes the Springer Opera House. The residential **High Uptown District** contains the Rankin House, which boasts the finest ironwork in Columbus. The **Historic District** is a mixture of commercial and residential. It includes the Folly, the nation's only antebellum double-octagon house. Using a brochure called *Down by the Riverside,* available from the Convention and Visitors Bureau, you can take a self-guided tour of these areas.

get around. Golden Park stadium in Columbus is the home of the Columbus RedStixx, a minor-league baseball team. For a schedule of games and ticket information, call 706/571-8866.

Miles and miles of paved roads and hiking trails are situated within Callaway Gardens. These byways are ideal for walking, jogging, bicycling, and in-line skating. You can enjoy the lake in a rental canoe or paddleboat. Fishing, tennis, and golf are available as well.

Walking the Pine Mountain Trail isn't quite as ambitious as hiking the Appalachian Trail, but the 27-mile, uphill and downhill jaunt between Pine Mountain and Warm Springs is still a challenge. Within Franklin D. Roosevelt State Park, 706/663-4858, you can walk another 30 miles of hiking trails. One of FDR's favorite picnic spots is here. The Civilian Conservation Corps, one of Roosevelt's New Deal programs, constructed most of the park's facilities and buildings. Visitors can also enjoy fishing, boating, swimming, and horseback riding. From the FDR Stables, 706/628-4533, you can take a horseback trip that lasts anywhere from one hour to five days.

Located not too far away in Lumpkin is one of the Seven Wonders of Georgia—Providence Canyon, 706/838-6202, also known as the Little Grand Canyon. Hiking trails take you down into the canyon.

FOOD

Columbus has earned a reputation for some unusual dishes. One is the Country Captain—a tomato and chicken dish. Another is the Scramble Dog,

COLUMBUS

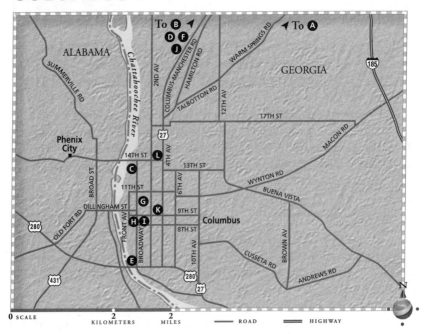

FOOD

- **A** Bulloch House
- **B** Callaway Gardens Resort
- **C** Country's Restaurant
- **D** Cricket's
- **E** Goetchius House
- **F** Oak Tree Victorian Restaurant
- **G** Olive Branch

LODGING

- **B** Callaway Gardens Resort
- **H** Columbus Hilton
- **D** Davis Inn
- **I** Gates House
- **D** Hotel Warm Springs Bed & Breakfast Inn
- **F** Magnolia Hall Bed and Breakfast

LODGING (continued)

- **D** Mountain Top Inn and Resort
- **J** Raintree Farms of Waverly Hall Bed and Breakfast
- **K** Rothschild-Pound House
- **D** White Columns Motel
- **L** Woodruff House Bed and Breakfast Inn

Note: Items with the same letter are located in the same area.

which you'd think includes scrambled eggs but instead includes everything but the kitchen sink. Then they have the famous tradition of peanuts in "Co-Cola"—yes, you put peanuts in your Coke and let them get soft and soak up the flavor. When you've finished your drink, you eat the peanuts. Columbus also claims to have the highest concentration of barbecue restaurants anywhere.

You should have at least one formal dinner while you're in Columbus. We recommend the elegant **Goetchius House,** 405 Broadway, 706/324-4863. Built in 1839, the stately mansion has exterior ornamental ironwork that will remind you of New Orleans. The interior is furnished with Victorian and Empire antiques. Reservations are recommended. You should also try some of that famous barbecue. **Country's Restaurant,** which has three locations, serves barbecue that has been slow cooked over a hickory and oak fire, plus other "country cooking" favorites. The locations are Mercury Drive (near Exit 4 off I-185), 706/563-7604; 1329 Broadway, 706/596-8910; and Veterans Parkway, 706/660-1415. The **Olive Branch,** 1032 Broadway, 706/322-7410, offers a variety of American dishes such as steaks, seafood, and smoked pork chops. The barbecued shrimp and grilled portabello mushrooms are popular choices.

Callaway Gardens Resort, 706/633-2281 or 800/CALLAWAY, has six restaurants that range from ice-cream-parlor casual to jacket-and-tie formal. Many vegetables are served fresh from the garden. People drive from miles around to eat a hearty Southern breakfast at the **Country Kitchen,** located outside the gardens in the Callaway Country Store. Even if don't think you like grits, try the speckled-heart grits, a Callaway delicacy. The restaurant is also open for lunch and dinner, and the view of the valley alone is worth a stop. Also outside the gardens, the main inn houses two restaurants: the **Plantation Room,** which serves breakfast, lunch, and dinner buffets, and the very formal and romantic **Georgia Room,** where the menu is Continental. A dress code is required, and reservations are suggested. Inside the gardens, an old barnlike building overlooking the lake houses the casual **Gardens Restaurant** and the formal **Veranda Restaurant,** which serves southern Italian cuisine for dinner. Reservations are suggested. Callaway is also renowned for its Georgia-cured hams and jams and jellies made from garden-grown muscadine grapes. You can purchase all these specialties to take home with you.

The town of Pine Mountain offers a casual eatery called **Cricket's** (GA 18, 706/663-8136), which specializes in informality and Cajun and Creole cuisine.

Located in a charming 1892 Victorian cottage, the **Bulloch House,** U.S. 27 ALT, 706/655-9068, is the most upscale place to eat in Warm Springs, but it isn't formal. The owners bill their cuisine as "country with class," and the menu consists of Southern home-cookin' such as fried green tomatoes, special tomato sauce, and homemade preserves. You can grab a bite to eat in Warm Springs at numerous other places that are a step above fast food. Drive over to the nearby small town of Hamilton to eat at the **Oak Tree Victorian Restaurant**, U.S. 27, 706/628-4218, appropriately located in an imposing Victorian house. It's been a longtime favorite with locals for cocktails and dinner. Menu selections include veal, beef, lamb, chicken, seafood, and hot appetizers.

LODGING

With as many historic districts as are located in Columbus, it was always surprising and disappointing that no bed-and-breakfasts could be found. In the last year or so, however, that lack has been greatly remedied. At last count, five outstanding B&Bs have opened—all in painstakingly restored historic homes and all filled with antiques and collectibles. Each also offers comfortable porches on which to relax and watch the world go by, as well as compact gardens to please the eyes and nose.

The first and foremost of these B&Bs is the magnificently restored, Second Empire-style **Rothschild-Pound House**, 201 Seventh Street, 706/322-4075 or 800/585-4075. This painted lady offers antique- and art-filled (one of the owners is a noted artist) guest rooms and suites, some of which have fireplaces and kitchens. Accommodations are offered in the main house and in a restored cottage, known as the Painter's Cottage, next door. The owners will pamper and feed you so much that you'll never want to leave. Ask them to tell you how the house ended up where it is and how they came to own it.

Nearby Broadway has an exquisite B&B. The **Gates House**, 737 Broadway, 706/324-6464 or 800/891-3187, is deceptively small from the outside, but it has generously proportioned rooms that seem to go on and on. All rooms are filled with magnificent antiques and artwork. **Woodruff House Bed and Breakfast Inn**, 1414 Second Ave., 706/320-9300, is located in the High Uptown Historic District. Built in 1885, the mansion has modern conveniences like private phones and cable TV. A deluxe continental breakfast is served.

Those who are traveling with children or who prefer the conveniences of a large hotel can try the **Columbus Hilton**, 800 Front Street, 706/324-1800 or 800/445-8667. Part of the building is the remains of a 125-year-old textile mill; the remainder is new construction. Many of the rooms and suites overlook the river. The hotel's Pemberton's Café is decorated with Coca-Cola memorabilia in honor of the drink's creator, and Hunter's Lounge has a sports-man motif.

Callaway Gardens Resort, U.S. 27, Pine Mountain, 706/663-2281 or 800/CALLAWAY, offers much more than just gardens—spectacular though they are. The complex also includes two-story motels; two-bed-room cabins with kitchen facilities, living/dining rooms with fireplaces, and screened-in porches; and magnificent villas with a variety of floor plans and bedrooms. In addition to recreational facilities and restaurants, the resort offers a sauna and steam room, swimming pools, whirlpools, and a laundry. Florida State University's Flying High Circus performs in summer. Meal plans are available.

Other accommodations in Pine Mountain are limited to several motels and cabins that date from about the 1950s. These include the **Davis Inn** (State Park Road, 706/663-2522), the **White Columns Motel** (U.S. 27, 800/722-5083), and the **Mountain Top Inn and Resort** (State 190 at Hines Gap Road, 706/663-4719 or 800/NIGHT-NIGHT).

Just as it did in FDR's day, the **Hotel Warm Springs Bed & Breakfast Inn**, 17 Broad Street, Pine Mountain, 706/655-2114 or 800/366-7616, receives visitors from all over the world. Once you step in-side the square, three-story cream-colored building, you'll feel as though you've been transported back to the 1940s. Everything in the lobby, from the black-and-white-tiled floor to the Stromberg-Carlson switchboard, is original. Spacious, high-ceilinged guest rooms are simply furnished with orig-inal or reproduction mission-style furniture from Eleanor Roosevelt's New Deal Val-Kill carpentry plant in Hyde Park, New York. FDR memorabilia, as well as antiques, crafts, and collectibles, add personality to each room. Clawfoot tubs enhance some of the bathrooms, and queen-size beds and TVs provide modern comforts and amenities. Given the hotel's understated decor, it comes as a complete surprise that the Honeymoon Suite contains a large, red, heart-shaped Jacuzzi. In nearby Hamilton, **Magnolia Hall Bed and Breakfast**, 127 Barnes Mill Road, 706/628-4566, is a delightfully or-nate 1890 Victorian cottage. Intricate gingerbread trim embellishes its wrap-around porch. Three spacious rooms and suites are furnished with antiques and reproductions.

Breakfasts are lavish at the **Raintree Farms of Waverly Hall Bed and Breakfast**, 8060 Georgia Hwy. 208, Waverly Hall, 800/433-0627 or 706/582-3227. The four guest rooms all have private baths and are furnished tastefully with period furniture and luxurious four-poster beds. The rear ve-randah opens onto wildflower gardens, a small lake, and three acres of an-cient pecan trees.

CAMPING

Franklin D. Roosevelt State Park in Warm Springs, 2970 GA 190E, 706/663-4858, offers several campgrounds. The park is open daily from 7 a.m.–10 p.m. The Pine Mountain Campground, 8804 Hamilton Road, Pine Mountain, 706/663-4329, offers pull-through and tent sites, a pool, hot tub, playground, pond, laundry, and TV lounge.

25
MACON

White columns and cherry blossoms characterize this beautiful, small city, located south of Atlanta in central Georgia. Spared during the Civil War, Macon retains several historic districts of lovingly preserved antebellum homes and commercial buildings, as well as others constructed in the late 1800s.

The city is rich in history. In fact, Macon has more acreage listed on the National Register of Historic Places than almost any other city in the South. A project called Lights On Macon shows off one historic neighborhood by night. The Antebellum Trail, a tour of historic Georgia, begins in Macon and meanders through several small towns before ending in Athens. The Tubman African-American Museum was named in honor of Harriet Tubman, a black woman who helped free hundreds of slaves via the Underground Railroad. It also showcases the achievements of other notable African Americans.

Macon has produced a large number of well-known musicians, among them Lena Horne, Little Richard, Otis Redding, and the Allman Brothers. Visitors to Macon can tour the Georgia Music Hall of Fame, which honors these musicians and others.

Visitors will also enjoy Macon's highly acclaimed Cherry Blossom Festival. The backdrop for this annual celebration is 180,000 Yoshino cherry trees (outnumbering those in Washington, D.C.).

MACON

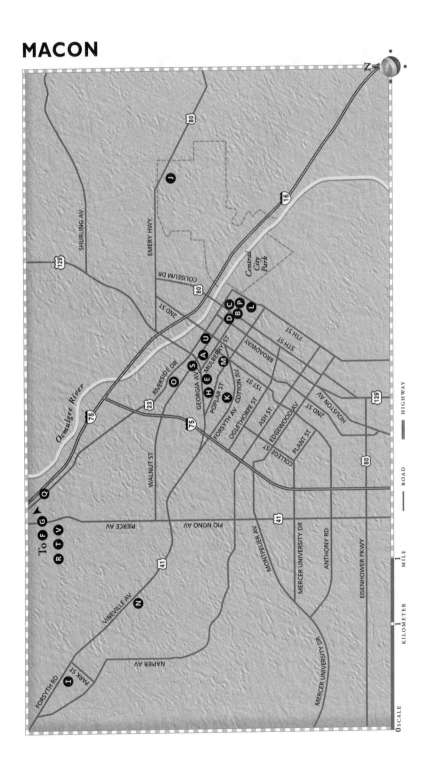

A PERFECT DAY IN MACON

Visit Terminal Station, home of the Macon Welcome Center and the pickup point for Sidney's Historic Tours. We'd suggest a half-day van tour, which includes an overview of the city and stops at the Hay House, Cannonball House and Confederate Museum, and Sidney Lanier Cottage.

When you return, go next door to the Georgia Music Hall of Fame, housed in a brand-new complex. Then stop by H&H Restaurant for a hearty, home-cooked southern lunch. From there, go to the Tubman African-American Museum, then on to the Ocmulgee National Monument, which contains several preserved Native American temples and burial mounds.

Have an elegant dinner at Jim Shaw's, noted for great seafood. Take a stroll, drive, or carriage ride to see Lights on Macon, a special project that illuminates historic homes. Finally, attend a performance at the City Auditorium, the Opera House, or the newly restored Douglass Theater.

SIGHTSEEING HIGHLIGHTS

★★★★ CANNONBALL HOUSE AND CONFEDERATE MUSEUM
856 Mulberry Street, 912/745-5982

This lovely Greek Revival structure was the only house in Macon to be struck during a halfhearted Union attack from across the river in 1864. A cannonball tore through one of the veranda pillars and a front wall, landed in the front parlor, and rolled into the entry hall, where it remains today. The Cannonball House is furnished to replicate the

SIGHTS
- Ⓐ Cannonball House and Confederate Museum
- Ⓑ Douglass Theatre
- Ⓒ Georgia Music Hall of Fame
- Ⓓ Tubman African-American Museum
- Ⓔ Hay House
- Ⓕ Jarrell Plantation State Historic Site
- Ⓖ Juliette
- Ⓗ Lights On Macon
- Ⓘ Museum of Arts and Sciences
- Ⓙ Ocmulgee National Monument
- Ⓚ Sidney Lanier Cottage
- Ⓛ Terminal Station

FOOD
- Ⓜ H&H Restaurant
- Ⓝ Jim Shaw's
- Ⓞ Jocks and Jills
- Ⓟ Len Berg's
- Ⓠ Music City Ale House and Grill
- Ⓡ Whistle Stop Café

LODGING
- Ⓢ 1842 Inn
- Ⓣ Carmichael House
- Ⓤ Crowne Plaza Macon Hotel (Holiday Inn)
- Ⓥ Jarrell Plantation Bed and Breakfast

chambers of Macon's old Wesleyan College, the first women's college in the country and home of the first national sororities. Many pieces of historic sorority memorabilia are on display. Civil War artifacts are displayed in the adjacent brick kitchen house and servants' quarters.

Details: Mon–Sat 10–4. $4 adults, $1 children (1 hour)

★★★★ **GEORGIA MUSIC HALL OF FAME**
200 Martin Luther King Jr. Boulevard, 912/750-8555 or 888/427-6257, www.gamusichall.com
This stunning new center, featuring displays, memorabilia, videos, and soundtracks, focuses on the state's diverse musical heritage. Visitors enter a "village" that showcases different periods and types of music—rock and roll in a café, gospel in a church, blues in a nightclub, and so forth. In addition to Macon's honorees, other Georgia artists, including R.E.M., the B-52s, James Brown, Gladys Knight, Johnny Mercer, Gertrude "Ma" Rainey, Travis Tritt, and Trisha Yearwood, are recognized.

Details: Mon–Sat 9–5, Sun 1–5. $7.50 adults, $5.50 seniors and college students, $3.50 children 6–16, free under 5. (1 hour)

★★★★ **HAY HOUSE**
934 Georgia Avenue, 912/742-8155, www.georgiatrust.org
This extravagant Italianate Renaissance Revival mansion, located high on a hill overlooking the city, is the most historically significant home in Macon. The 18,000-square-foot, 24-room house was built in the 1850s by William Butler Johnston, who later served as keeper of the Confederate treasury. A fabulously wealthy man, Johnston spared no expense to create spectacular interiors reminiscent of European palaces. In addition, he outfitted his home with the latest technology, such as indoor plumbing, an attic water tank, walk-in closets, an elevator, intercom, and advanced ventilation system. Among the outstanding architectural details are 12-foot-high, 500-pound front doors; 16- and 30-foot ceilings; elaborately carved marble and wood mantels; embossed cornices, medallions, and moldings; and trompe l'oeil wall and ceiling paintings. Rooms are filled with elegant Victorian furnishings and museum-quality objets d'art.

Details: Mon–Sat 10–5, Sun 1–5. $6 adults, $5 seniors and AAA members, $2 children over 12 and students, $1 under 12. (1 hour)

★★★★ JARRELL PLANTATION STATE HISTORIC SITE
Follow signs from I-75 or U.S. 23, Juliette, 912/986-5172
www.gastateparks.org
One family's working farm for more than 100 years (1840s to 1940s), the plantation is now a living history museum. The property holds two rustic homes, a sawmill, carpenter shop, blacksmith shop, cane furnace, cotton gin, gristmill, shingle mill, and wheat houses. Home and farming equipment, and some farm animals are on display. The staff demonstrates old-time skills and crafts.
Details: Tue–Sat 9–5 p.m., Sun 2–5:30. $3 adults, $1.50 children 6–18. (2 hours)

★★★★ JULIETTE
A tiny crossroads village north of Macon, Juliette earned international interest when it was chosen as the filming site for the movie *Fried Green Tomatoes*, starring Jessica Tandy and Kathy Bates. Since then, visitors have flocked here from all over the world to eat at the Whistle Stop Café and shop in the tiny antique shops and boutiques. Up the road from Juliette is the Jarrell Plantation Sate Historic Site (see above).
Details: (2 hours)

★★★★ LIGHTS ON MACON
912/743-3401 or 800/768-3401, www.maconga.org
In this ambitious project, the first of its kind in the country, homeowners in a huge, one-block square allow their historic homes to be specially lighted at night. Pick up a tour booklet from the welcome center or your hotel. Each house is identified and described in detail. In pleasant weather, the route is easily walkable. In inclement weather, you can see the neighborhood by car or engage one of Colonel Bond's horse-and-carriage tours.
Details: Houses are lighted from dusk–11 p.m. (1 hour)

★★★★ OCMULGEE NATIONAL MONUMENT
1207 Emory Highway, 912/752-8257
At this 683-acre site, you can see remnants of 12,000 years of human habitation in North America. Although the monument chronicles several Native American cultures, the Mississippian civilization of A.D. 900 to 1100 is highlighted. Begin by watching a movie about area history. Then examine the displays in the museum before venturing out to the temple and funeral mounds, a re-created earth lodge, prehistoric

trenches, and the site of a colonial British trading post. Numerous nature trails provide as much exercise as you want.

Details: *Daily 9–5. Free. (1–2 hours)*

★★★★ **SIDNEY LANIER COTTAGE**
935 High Street, 912/743-3851

This charming Victorian cottage was the birthplace of Georgia's revered poet Sidney Lanier, author of "The Marshes of Glynn" and "Song of the Chattahoochee." Although Lanier is best remembered as a poet, he was also a linguist, mathematician, musician, and lawyer. Memorabilia from his life is displayed at the house, which is also the home of the Middle Georgia Historical Society.

Details: *Weekdays 9–1 and 2–4, Sat 9:30–12:30. $3 adults, $1 children over 12, 50 cents under 12. (1 hour)*

★★★★ **TERMINAL STATION**
200 Cherry Street, 912/743-3401 or 800/768-3401
www.maconga.org

Now housing the Macon Welcome Center, this station was once one of the busiest in the South, receiving more than 100 passenger trains a day. The imposing, 520-foot-long Roman classical building was built in 1916 and is a reminder of the glory days of the railroads. Stop in to pick up brochures about local attractions, take one of Sydney's Old South tours, or ask for advice about Macon.

Details: *Mon–Sat 9–5. Free. (1/2 hour)*

★★★ **TUBMAN AFRICAN-AMERICAN MUSEUM**
340 Walnut Street, 912/743-8544

During the Civil War, Harriet Tubman was one of the forces behind the Underground Railroad, which spirited slaves to safety in the North. Although this museum is named in her honor, its subject matter is neither her life nor the Underground Railroad, but rather the artistic and technological achievements of many African Americans. The centerpiece of the museum is a huge mural that depicts 400 years of African American life. A new exhibit honors African Americans in the military.

Details: *Mon–Sat 9–5, Sun 2–5. $3 adults, $2 children. (1 hour)*

★★ **DOUGLASS THEATRE**
335 M. L King Jr. Boulevard, 912/742-2000

Take a visual tour of Macon and all it has to offer in this renovated theater, which was once a showcase for African American talents such as Cab Calloway, Otis Redding, and Little Richard. Restored after decades of neglect, the Douglass has exhibits on African American traditions in music, drama, and film. Evening and weekend events include classic film festivals and concerts with laser shows.

Details: Tue–Fri 9–5. $5. (1–2 hours)

★★ MUSEUM OF ARTS AND SCIENCES
4182 Forsyth Road, 912/477-3232

Just for starters, the museum boasts a 40-million-year-old whale fossil discovered nearby. Interactive science and art exhibits keep visitors of all ages coming back for more, as do planetarium shows and nature trails.

Details: Mon–Sat 9–5, Fri 9–9, Sun 1–5. Planetarium shows daily at 4 and Fri at 7. $5 adults, $4 seniors, $3 students 12 and older, $2 children under 12. Free all day Mon and after 5 on Fri. (1–2 hours)

FITNESS AND RECREATION

Macon is an easily walkable, although hilly, city. You can get plenty of exercise walking around its various historic districts, and you can walk to most of the attractions listed above, as well as to the restaurants and entertainment venues. The trails to and around the Ocmulgee National Monument provide exercise opportunities as well.

Not far from town is the Dauset Trails Nature Center (Mt. Vernon Road off GA 42, Jackson, 770/775-6798), where you can hike. You can indulge in water sports at nearby Lakes Jackson, Juliette, and Tobesofkee.

Macon is home to the Macon Braves, a minor-league baseball team that plays at Luther Williams Stadium. For a schedule or other information, call 912/745-8943. Hickory Hill Golf Course (Biles Road, Jackson, 770/775-2433) offers 27 holes of golf and a driving range.

FOOD

Len Berg's, Old Post Office Alley, 912/742-9255, has been a Macon institution for the last 30 years. Named one of *Georgia Trend's* Top 50 Georgia Restaurants, it's noted for its lunches of soul food and Southern home cookin'. Among the old standbys are fresh vegetables, homemade rolls, fried oysters, macaroon pie, and—during June and July—fresh peach ice cream.

Open for lunch only. No credit cards accepted. **Jim Shaw's**, 3040 Vineville Avenue, 912/746-3697, is known for the finest seafood in Macon. However you like your fish—broiled, blackened, grilled, or fried—it's on the menu here.

In honor of Macon's musical prominence, the **Music City Ale House and Grill** (2440 Riverside Drive, 912/741-1144) has a fun atmosphere created with Macon music Memorabilia. Open seven days a week, it is known for pasta, pizza, and salads.

H&H Restaurant, 807 Forsyth Street, 912/742-9810, is a simple and casual café. It's a favorite of such musical groups as the Allman Brothers, and you'll see many autographed pictures of artists on the walls. To give you an idea of the gargantuan size of the portions, when the Allman Brothers band was new, members could afford only one meal to share, but they didn't go away hungry.

The sports bar crowd can be found at **Jocks and Jills**, 4680 Sheraton Drive, 912/405-9232, on the north side of town. Settle down in front of one of the TVs and enjoy buffalo shrimp or pecan-crusted pork chops. One side of the restaurant is aimed at the quieter, more family-oriented crowd.

Just a few miles from Macon is the minuscule hamlet of Juliette. Step into the familiar-looking **Whistle Stop Café** (McCrackin Street, 912/994-3670), made famous by the movie *Fried Green Tomatoes*, and you'll feel you've stepped right into the movie. Once shooting was complete, all the accessories were left at the restaurant. Folks come from miles around to sign their name on the list on the screen door, then rock on the front porch while they wait for their tables. Of course, fried green tomatoes are prominently featured on the menu, but dozens of other southern favorites are served as well.

LODGING

When it comes to accommodations, what Macon lacks in quantity it makes up for in quality. Located in a gorgeous, white-columned Greek Revival mansion in the historic College Street district, the **1842 Inn** (353 College Street, 912/741-1842 or 800/336-1842) is *the* place to stay in Macon. Sumptuous rooms, many with fireplaces and some with Jacuzzis, are offered in the main house and in an adjacent Victorian cottage. The wide, wicker-filled veranda and lushly landscaped rear courtyard entice lodgers outside in nice weather. Late afternoon refreshments are served in one of the formal parlors. Continental breakfast is brought to your room on a silver tray, unless you prefer to eat in the parlor or outside in the courtyard.

If you prefer the amenities of a big hotel, try the **Crowne Plaza Macon**

Hotel (Holiday Inn) (108 First Street, 912/746-1461 or 800/2-CROWNE), located in the downtown historic district. The hotel features luxuriously furnished guest rooms, and an executive level is available. Some units offer minibars and terraces with nice views of the skyline. The hotel has two restaurants, one of which is the highly acclaimed **First Street Cafe**, as well as two bars and a fitness center.

When the Jarrell Plantation was given to the state for the historic site, the Jarrell family retained one house, and family members still live there. Recently they have opened up the home as the **Jarrell Plantation Bed and Breakfast** (Jarrell Plantation Road, Juliette, 912/986-3972). A stately white farmhouse with a full-length front veranda, the home is furnished in simple pieces—all original to the family.

A little farther north is the small town of Jackson, which has probably the most outstanding example of Queen Anne Victorian architecture in Georgia. It is the **Carmichael House** (149 McDonough Road, 770/775-0578), which operates as a bed-and-breakfast.

APPENDIX

Consider this appendix your travel tool box. Use it along with the material in the Planning Your Trip chapter to craft the trip you want. Here are the tools you'll find inside:

1. **Planning Map.** Make copies of this map and plot out various trip possibilities. Once you've decided on your route, you can write it on the original map and refer to it as you're traveling.

2. **Mileage Chart.** This chart shows the driving distances (in miles) between various destinations throughout the region. Use it in conjunction with the Planning Map.

3. **Special Interest Tours.** If you'd like to plan a trip around a certain theme— such as nature, sports, or art—one of these tours may work for you.

4. **Resources.** This guide lists various regional chambers of commerce and visitors bureaus, state offices, bed-and-breakfast registries, and other useful sources of information.

PLANNING MAP: Deep South

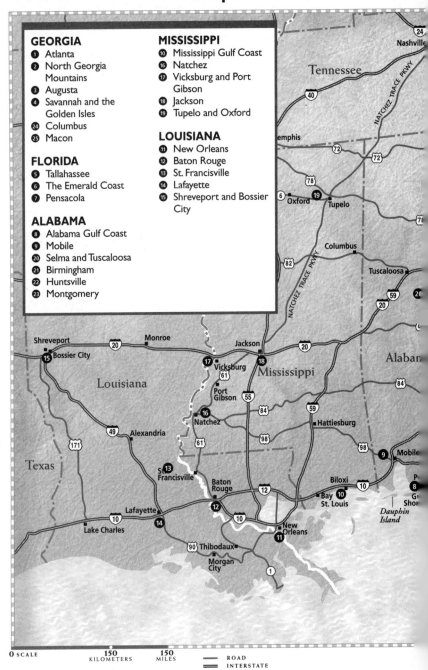

GEORGIA
1. Atlanta
2. North Georgia Mountains
3. Augusta
4. Savannah and the Golden Isles
24. Columbus
25. Macon

FLORIDA
5. Tallahassee
6. The Emerald Coast
7. Pensacola

ALABAMA
8. Alabama Gulf Coast
9. Mobile
20. Selma and Tuscaloosa
21. Birmingham
22. Huntsville
23. Montgomery

MISSISSIPPI
10. Mississippi Gulf Coast
16. Natchez
17. Vicksburg and Port Gibson
18. Jackson
19. Tupelo and Oxford

LOUISIANA
11. New Orleans
12. Baton Rouge
13. St. Francisville
14. Lafayette
15. Shreveport and Bossier City

Nashville

Tennessee

emphis

Oxford   Tupelo

Columbus

Tuscaloosa

Shreveport   Monroe   Jackson   Alaban
Bossier City

Louisiana   Vicksburg   Mississippi
Port Gibson

Alexandria   Natchez   Hattiesburg

Texas   St. Francisville   Mobile

Baton Rouge   Biloxi

Lafayette   Bay St. Louis   Dauphin Island

Lake Charles   New Orleans

Thibodaux

Morgan City

O SCALE   150 KILOMETERS   150 MILES   ROAD   INTERSTATE

You have permission to photocopy this map.

DEEP SOUTH MILEAGE CHART

	Atlanta	Augusta	Savannah	Tallahassee	Pensacola	Mobile	New Orleans	Baton Rouge	Lafayette	Shreveport	Natchez	Vicksburg	Jackson	Tupelo	Tuscaloosa	Birmingham	Huntsville	Montgomery	Columbus
Augusta	155																		
Savannah	252	143																	
Tallahassee	270	293	299																
Pensacola	342	463	437	194															
Mobile	330	533	539	240	59														
New Orleans	473	681	682	388	212	153													
Baton Rouge	550	688	739	440	259	200	79												
Lafayette	606	929	795	636	455	396	135	56											
Shreveport	605	763	830	680	507	448	333	253	213										
Natchez	495	650	708	472	292	232	176	94	150	175									
Vicksburg	429	584	642	485	304	226	232	196	216	193	66								
Jackson	584	541	635	458	262	184	190	202	256	213	108	42							
Tupelo	282	437	535	436	334	287	349	353	409	404	277	211	169						
Tuscaloosa	123	358	443	310	278	209	295	365	421	419	292	226	184	126					
Birmingham	148	304	409	307	260	262	342	397	453	461	349	283	239	144	57				
Huntsville	192	374	479	409	396	359	442	499	555	561	450	384	339	183	158	99			
Montgomery	160	318	364	214	175	170	318	370	426	466	358	292	244	229	103	92	189		
Columbus	105	226	258	174	237	251	405	451	507	567	450	384	332	288	185	141	242	82	
Macon	84	137	169	193	326	340	494	540	596	656	529	463	421	366	274	230	265	171	89

SPECIAL INTEREST TOURS

With *Deep South Travel•Smart* you can plan a trip of any length—a one-day excursion, a getaway weekend, or a three-week vacation—around any special interest. To get you started, the following pages contain five special interest itineraries geared toward a variety of interests. For more information, refer to the chapters listed—chapter names are in boldface, and chapter numbers appear inside black bullets. You can follow a suggested itinerary in its entirety, or shorten, length, or combine parts of each, depending on your starting and ending points.

Discuss alternative routes and schedules with your travel companions—it's a great way to have fun even before you leave home. And remember: Don't hesitate to change your itinerary once you're on the road. Careful study and planning ahead will help you make informed decisions as you go, but spontaneity is the extra ingredient that will make your trip memorable.

NATURE LOVER'S TOUR

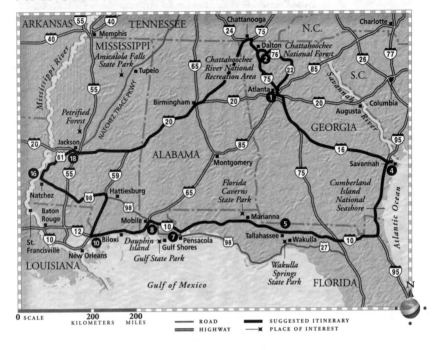

On this tour you'll explore bayous, mountains, islands, and more.

❶ Atlanta (Chattahoochee River National Recreation Area)
❷ North Georgia Mountains (Amicalola Falls, Chattahoochee National Forest, Appalachian Trail)
❹ Savannah and the Golden Isles (Cumberland Island National Seashore, Golden Isles)
❺ Tallahassee (Wakulla Springs, Florida Caverns State Park)
❼ Pensacola (Gulf Islands National Seashore, state parks)
❽ Alabama Gulf Coast (Dauphin Island, Gulf State Park)
❿ Mississippi Gulf Coast (Gulf Islands National Seashore)
⓰ Natchez (Natchez Trace Parkway to Tupelo)
⓲ Jackson (Mississippi Petrified Forest)

Time needed: 2 weeks

ART AND CULTURE LOVER'S TOUR

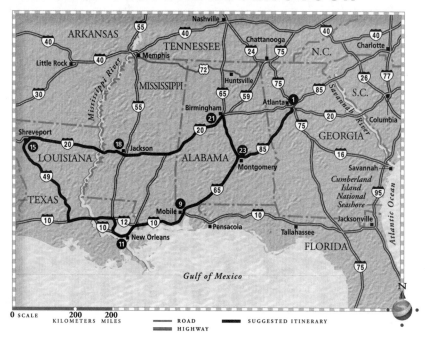

On this tour you'll see a play at America's foremost Shakespeare theater, explore the haunts of some of the South's best-known literary figures, visit outstanding museums, listen to a world-class symphony, and much more.

❶ **Atlanta** (state capitol, Atlanta Symphony Orchestra, High Museum)
❾ **Mobile** (Mobile Museum of Art, Museum of the City of Mobile, Bellingrath Gardens and Home)
⓫ **New Orleans** (Cabildo, French Quarter, New Orleans Museum of Art)
⓯ **Shreveport and Bossier City** (Louisiana State Exhibit Museum, Meadows Museum of Art, R. W. Norton Art Gallery)
⓲ **Jackson** (Mississippi Museum of Art, Chimneyville Crafts Gallery)
㉑ **Birmingham** (Alabama Jazz Hall of Fame, Birmingham Museum of Art)
㉓ **Montgomery** (Montgomery Museum of Fine Art, Scott and Zelda Fitzgerald Museum, Alabama Shakespeare Festival)

Time needed: 2 weeks

FAMILY FUN TOUR

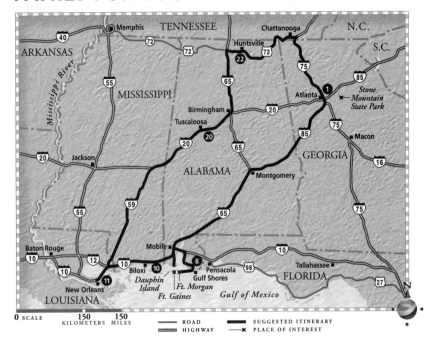

This tour takes you to space ships, race cars, outdoor activities galore, and more.

❶ Atlanta (Stone Mountain Park, SciTrek, Center for Puppetry Arts)

❽ Alabama Gulf Coast (beaches, Pirates Island, Waterville, USA, The Track, Zooland, Fort Gaines, Fort Morgan)

❿ Mississippi Gulf Coast (J. L. Scott Marine Education Center, Marine Life Oceanarium, Maritime and Seafood Industry Museum, Scanton Floating Museum, John Stennis Space Center, Biloxi Shrimping Trip)

⓫ New Orleans (Aquarium of the Americas, Audubon Zoo, Louisiana Children's Museum)

⓴ Selma and Tuscaloosa (Children's Hands-On Museum, Paul W. "Bear" Bryant Museum)

㉒ Huntsville (U.S. Space and Rocket Center, EarlyWorks)

Time needed: 2 weeks

CIVIL WAR BUFF'S TOUR

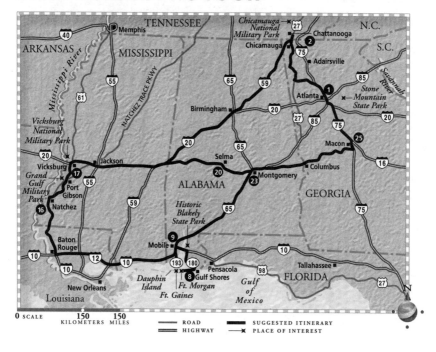

The vast majority of the Civil War was fought in the South, so it is here that you'll see monuments, battlefields, cemeteries, and much more.

❶ **Atlanta** (Cyclorama, Stone Mountain Park, Atlanta History Center, Kennesaw Mountain National Battlefield Park)

❷ **North Georgia Mountains** (Chickamauga, Barnsley Gardens)

❽ **Alabama Gulf Coast** (Fort Gaines, Fort Morgan)

❾ **Mobile** (Bragg-Mitchell Mansion, Historic Blakely State Park)

⓰ **Natchez** (plantations, cemeteries, historic homes)

⓱ **Vicksburg and Port Gibson** (Gray and Blue Naval Museum, Old Court House Museum, *Vanishing Glory*, Vicksburg National Park)

⓴ **Selma and Tuscaloosa** (Old Depot Museum)

㉓ **Montgomery** (capitol, First White House of the Confederacy)

㉕ **Macon** (Old Cannonball House)

Time needed: 2 weeks

MISSISSIPPI RIVER TOUR

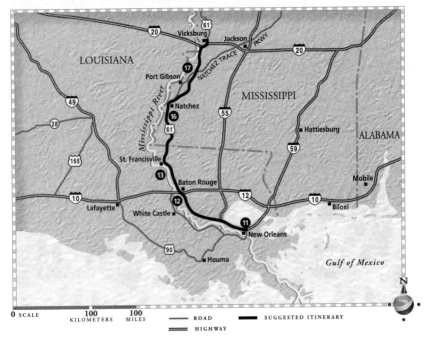

Cruising the Mississippi aboard the *Delta*, *Mississippi*, or *American Queen* steamboats is a dream trip. Step aboard to the sounds of Dixieland Jazz, settle back, and glide from town to town along the Big Muddy at a leisurely five miles per hour. Sightseeing excursions are available at each stop. Great food and entertainment are yours onboard.

- ⓫ **New Orleans** (French Quarter, Blaine Kern's Mardi Gras World, aquarium, zoo, museums)
- ⓬ **Baton Rouge** (Old and New Capitols, Rural Life Museum, plantations)
- ⓭ **St. Francisville** (plantations)
- ⓰ **Natchez** (historic homes, Natchez-Under-the-Hill)
- ⓱ **Vicksburg and Port Gibson** (historic homes)

Time needed: I week

RESOURCES

Alabama
Alabama Bureau of Tourism and Travel: 800/ALABAMA
Alabama Gulf Coast Area Chamber of Commerce: 334/968-6904
Alabama Gulf Coast Convention and Visitors Bureau (CVB): 800/745-SAND
or 334/968-7511
Greater Birmingham CVB: 800/458-8085
Huntsville CVB: 800/SPACE-4-U
Mobile Convention and Visitors Corporation: 800/5-MOBILE
Montgomery Convention and Visitors Division: 334/261-1100
Selma–Dallas County Chamber of Commerce: 800/45-SELMA
Tuscaloosa CVB: 800/538-8696

Florida
Emerald Coast CVB (Destin/Fort Walton): 800/322-3319
Pensacola Area Chamber of Commerce: 800/874-1234
Tallahassee Area CVB: 850/413-9200

Georgia
Atlanta CVB: 404/521-6600
Augusta–Richmond County CVB: 800/726-0243
Brunswick and the Golden Isles Visitors Bureau: 912/265-0620
Georgia Visitors' Center (Columbus): 706/649-7455
Georgia Department of Industry, Trade and Tourism: 404/656-3590
Georgia Visitor Information Center–Ringgold (Northwest Georgia Mountains):
706/937-4211
Macon–Bibb County CVB: 800/768-3401
Savannah Area CVB: 912/944-0456

Louisiana
Baton Rouge Area CVB: 225/383-1825
Lafayette Convention and Visitors Commission: 800/346-1958
New Orleans Metropolitan CVB: 504/566-5011
Shreveport–Bossier CVB: 800/551-8682

Mississippi
Metro Jackson CVB: 800/354-7695
Mississippi Gulf Coast CVB: 800/237-9493

Natchez CVB: 800/647-6724
Oxford Tourism Council: 800/758-9177
Tupelo CVB: 800/533-0611
Vicksburg CVB: 800/221-3536

INDEX

MAP INDEX

Guidebooks that really *guide*

City•Smart™ Guidebooks

Pick one for your favorite city: *Albuquerque, Anchorage, Austin, Calgary, Charlotte, Chicago, Cincinnati, Cleveland, Denver, Indianapolis, Kansas City, Memphis, Milwaukee, Minneapolis/St. Paul, Nashville, Pittsburgh, Portland, Richmond, Salt Lake City, San Antonio, San Francisco, St. Louis, Tampa/St. Petersburg, Tucson.* US $12.95 to 15.95

Retirement & Relocation Guidebooks

The World's Top Retirement Havens, Live Well in Honduras, Live Well in Ireland, Live Well in Mexico. US $15.95 to $16.95

Travel•Smart® Guidebooks

Trip planners with select recommendations to *Alaska, American Southwest, Arizona, Carolinas, Colorado, Deep South, Eastern Canada, Florida, Florida Gulf Coast, Hawaii, Illinois/Indiana, Kentucky/Tennessee, Maryland/Delaware, Michigan, Minnesota/Wisconsin, Montana/Wyoming/Idaho, New England, New Mexico, New York State, Northern California, Ohio, Pacific Northwest, Pennsylvania/New Jersey, South Florida and the Keys, Southern California, Texas, Utah, Virginias, Western Canada.* US $14.95 to $17.95

Rick Steves' Guides

See *Europe Through the Back Door* and take along guides to *France, Belgium & the Netherlands; Germany, Austria & Switzerland; Great Britain & Ireland; Italy; Scandinavia; Spain & Portugal; London; Paris;* or *Best of Europe.* US $12.95 to $21.95

Adventures in Nature

Plan your next adventure in *Alaska, Belize, Caribbean, Costa Rica, Guatemala, Hawaii, Honduras, Mexico.* US $17.95 to $18.95

Into the Heart of Jerusalem

A traveler's guide to visits, celebrations, and sojourns. US $17.95

The People's Guide to Mexico

This is so much more than a guidebook—it's a trip to Mexico in and of itself, complete with the flavor of the country and its sights, sounds, and people. US $22.95

JOHN MUIR PUBLICATIONS
P.O. Box 613 ◆ Santa Fe, NM 87504

Available at your favorite bookstore.
For a catalog or to place an order call 800-888-7504.

DAN & CAROL THALIMER

ABOUT THE AUTHORS

Freelance authors, photojournalists, and photographers Carol and Dan Thalimer have lived near Atlanta for more than 20 years. They have written many travel guides about the Southeast, have contributed to several national and international guides, and have written more than 500 articles for magazines and newspapers. Several of their travel guides and all of their articles are illustrated with their own photographs.

Former travel agency owners, the Thalimers are certified travel counselors, and they travel extensively. Carol is a member of the American Society of Media Photographers.

The Thalimers have four grown children and two grandchildren. They also have three cats and three dogs—one of whom traveled with them so they could write about traveling with pets.